To say Italians—and the world at large—love traditional Italian food is an understatement. An entire industry of gastronomic nostalgia has grown up around it, catering to tourists and natives alike. In its wake, this behemoth of commercial culinary lore has glossed over the less marketable—but nonetheless fascinating—aspects of the past, the very springboard from which "Italian cuisine" propelled itself onto the international stage.

Inglorious and uncelebrated though they may be, these foodways would be in danger of vanishing into the shadows of time, as if they had never existed—and the stories of endurance and inventiveness of an era of women along with it—were it not for the efforts of food historian Karima Moyer-Nocchi.

Chewing the Fat is a compendium of eighteen oral historical narratives from women who lived through the sparse and dangerous years of Italian fascism. Daily life, family, culture, and recipes blend into a fascinating accounting of these women's early lives. Each narrative is separated by a brief intermezzo, illuminating points of cultural, historical, and culinary interest to round out the overall mosaic effect.

Gently debunking much-loved myths of classic Italian fare, Moyer-Nocchi offers a fresh, realistic portrayal of traditional Italian food—not as we think of it but as it really existed.

Chewing the Fat

Chewing the Fat

AN ORAL HISTORY OF ITALIAN FOODWAYS
FROM FASCISM TO DOLCE VITA

Karima Moyer-Nocchi

ISBN: 099654660X
ISBN 13: 9780996546607
Library of Congress Control Number: 2015910898
Medea, Perrysburg, OH

Cover art: Giampaolo Tomassetti
giampoalot@yahoo.com

Interior Art: Jennifer Carlisle
http://www.studiojennifercarlisle.com

To my dearest Simone

Contents

Acknowledgments

A book like this would not have been possible without the many kind liaisons who helped me connect with the interviewees: Dino Agostini, Valentina Andreoli, Sandro Antonucci, Marco Baldicchi, Laura Cardellini, Pompeia De Corso, Yhara Formisano, Maria Grazia Guacci, Giuseppe La Rocca, Carlotta Lizzini, Daniele Manera, Lilianna Marchettini, Gianna Provezza, Luisa Oerker, Elisa Palombi, Chiara Terrosi, Maria Teresa Tirosi, Nicola Trois, Enrico Turotti.

Mille grazie to the many participants whose narratives were not selected for the final manuscript; they regardless broadened the vision of the project and deepened my perspective.

Two of the participants, whose narratives appear in the book, preferred that I not use their surname, for which I did not include anyone's, although I realize that for others this was a disappointment. Getting to know you and hearing your stories has enriched my life beyond measure. I thank you wholeheartedly for your generosity of spirit in contributing to this project. *Un caro abbraccio a tutte.*

Steady copy editor: Diane Martin.

Patient pre-readers: Lois Bouchard, Valerie Zanotto.

Research consultants: Ines Agostinucci, Bonizella Biagioli, Lorenzo Boriosi, Francesco Bulfaro, Roberto Burdese, Vincenzo and Lorenzo Chini, Yhara Formisano, Valeria Landucci, Simone Nocchi, Venanzio Nocchi, Gianna Provezza, Jennnifer Rockwood, Miriam Serni Casalini, Alvaro Tacchini, Rosaria Valenza.

Egregi professori who took a moment from their overburdened schedules to offer guidance: Paul Corner, Franco La Cecla, Christopher Duggan, John Dickie, Ernesto Di Renzo.

Generous Backers: Prof. Elisabetta Montanaro, Claudia Alexandria Scala-Schottman, Cindy Bunch, David O'Brien, Dwight Jacobson, Jennifer Carlisle, Dorothy Siegel.

Overture

There is a fantasy about Italy, a wonderful fantasy, which sells countless tour packages and millions of delectable meals in the myriad "rustic" restaurants peppered throughout Italy, eateries that beckon with historically come-hither names like *Vecchia Trattoria* or *Antica Osteria*. It is a well-loved fantasy that has not only foreigners swooning, but also unwitting Italians under fifty, who eagerly devour it wholesale. It is the pastoral delusion of the idyllic simple abundance of yesteryear, of country folk whiling away the days in lush fertile fields under the Tuscan sun, chalices brimming with ruby red wine and plates piled high with sauce-laden pasta.

If only it were true.

At the present writing, I have lived half of my life, twenty-five years, in Italy. Arguably, that would nestle me somewhere between the foreigners and the post-boomer Italians. Over the years, I have witnessed a curious concomitance: a bewildering decline in the quality and craftsmanship of Italian food, together with a skyrocketing deification of it, and an unabashed invention of gastronomic traditions. In a vicious circle, the post war migration from the countryside to the city brought on the decline. As generations distanced further and further in time and space from past foodways, the memory of hardship dulled, and a misty longing set in. The rumblings of the gastronomic nostalgia industry grew ever louder, keeping apace with expectations. Emboldened by credulous consumers, merchants flooded the marketplaces with bucolic offerings from neverland, in turn, hastening the very process they claimed to quell. A parallel fundamentalist food crusade was roused in retaliation. Their mission was to rescue the endangered culinary heritage from the ravages of modernity by championing (and packaging) the supposed foodways of bygone days, even if they had to do it one bean at a time. And so, for a price, the disposable income class would be able to bypass the trend of industrialization and partake in the wholesome goodness of the poor.

Well into the 1960s, the life of adversity led by farmers and landless laborers could still accurately be referred to as peasantry, with all of the connotations the word implies. After WWII and the fall of fascism, the desire to escape the unrelenting destitution of near serfdom spurred on a mass exodus to urban areas, tipping the balance of feeders to food producers. Industrialized farming and food production stepped in to respond to the growing demand. It not only fed the burgeoning urban population, but also created jobs. As living to eat supplanted eating to live, enterprising moguls deftly sniffed out marketing opportunities, satisfying the demand for staple items and the new concept of labor-saving leisure foods. Factories sprung up like mushrooms, churning out manufactured foodstuffs that would slowly recondition the public palate to ever-paling flavors, textures, and aromas.

With the passing generations, the nostalgia industry floodgates opened full force. It is a rare product whose label does not seductively peddle its contents as "authentic," "genuine," "homemade," "traditional," "rustic," "original," "old-fashioned," "country-style," "Mamma's," or "Grandma's," often tossing in the name of an enticing locale to bump up the salivation factor. Marketing language and packaging lured customers with the promise of authenticity, fostering the belief that we could eat our way back to a wistful time when all was inherently good, pure and nurturing, cajoling us to atone for the sins of modern life by way of the stomach.

The tourist industry sought to satisfy every possible desire for the romantic rustic past just as consumers imagined it to be, titillating them with "time-honored" *terroir* tales. Restaurants tripped over one another in the race to serve "typical foods" (the now ubiquitous translation in lieu of "traditional fare"), each attempting to dig deeper and deeper into the pockets of the past. But as they were catering to expectations and fantasy, authenticating an ancestry of their own invention sold just as well.

Human credulity rushes in where scholars fear to tread. Indeed, the annals of Italian food history say nothing of this glorious yesteryear of Italian food, at least not one enjoyed by any more than a tiny fortunate minority belonging either to society's upper crust or the high-end clergy, the original disposable income classes. But even then, with the exception of a few signature dishes, what was once considered standard fare is only vaguely similar to the culinary wonders that are daily plated up and touted, even in Italy, as "traditional" Italian cuisine. Italian cookery is now considered to be one of the few *classless* cuisines. Rich and poor alike indulge in the same sorts of foods (albeit not of the same quality), the stereotypical table groaning with delectable offerings. But while modern legends encourage us to believe that things have been that way since time immemorial, they stand in stark contrast to documented history.

The unprecedented focus on Italian cuisine that set the nostalgia industry in motion after the 1960s was initially looked upon with bemusement, a harmless enterprise that did much to bolster the Italian economy, to say nothing of much needed international pride and recognition. Through collective consensus, it slowly morphed into a reality that goes unquestioned by younger generation Italians whose parents were born post WWII. Whether willful or unwitting, they perceived the Photoshop retouch of their culinary past to be a mirror image of history, an unbroken continuum of feasting on the world's finest cuisine.

But what has become of the travails of the Italian "Greatest Generation?" There are still many who are alive and well whose experiences and recollections speak of an altogether different reality. Thus the question arose: What resemblance does the modern commercial packaging of Italian culinary lore bear to the actual experiences of those who lived that history before it was Born Again?

I decided to go to the authorities for some answers.

Although the pool of experts was ever dwindling, there were still a handful of women in Italy who had lived through the *Ventennio fascista*, the 20-year reign of fascism. Surely they would be able to shed some light on the evolution of Italian food from their own experiences. I accordingly set out on a two-year quest to capture their stories and bring this question into the public forum.

A comprehensive exploration of the Italian culinary landscape needed to cover, as far as possible, the length of the peninsula and include the islands, colonies, and territories once under Italian dominion. A broad-spectrum collection of histories also required that participants come from a variety of socio-economic backgrounds, specifically, the rural hierarchy strata, as well as a range of classes from large cities, small towns, and villages. In order to recruit participants, I relied on a network of trusted friends. The only requirements were that the subjects be women, well into their 80s, preferably 90s, lucid, and up for a chat.

To illustrate the delicacy of my request, this is a generation of Italians who had been inculcated from the time they were born to live and die for the state, or more specifically, for the *fascio*. After twenty years of a totalitarian regime, not only was the fascist's fall from power in 1943 profoundly disorienting for them, welcomed or not as it may have been, but the purging of fascism that followed and the baffling cascade of short-lived governments, many tinged with scandal, corruption and incompetence, fostered a general sense of mistrust in the decades to come. The weighty and oft repeated adage, *"fidarsi è bene, ma non fidarsi è meglio,"* "Trusting is good, but not trusting is better," sums up the cynicism of those who lived out their formative years under Mussolini's dictatorship. Furthermore, a constitutional law, dating back to 1952, expressly prohibits public discussion of fascism in positive terms, thereby reinforcing the wariness of potential interviewees. A trusted go-between to pave the way between the signora and myself was, therefore, a must. Some of the women were intimidated because of their lack of schooling, fearing they would disappoint me, or embarrass themselves or their family with their ignorance. Once they were reassured that I did not expect a history lesson with names and dates, that I "just" wanted to talk about food (even the lack thereof), the doors opened, and the interviews were underway.

Like most people my age, I do not travel in the same circles as 90 year olds. On the contrary, I had always been wary of traversing the abyss between my generation and people who had lived out their youth between the wars. Particularly in Italy, they seemed like so many flounder catapulted onto the dry beach of modernity. My interactions with the elderly had heretofore been limited to cordial smiles and brief superficial exchanges. The euphemism "elderly," *anziano* in Italian, had always struck me as a double-edged sword: masquerading as a term of respect while simultaneously driving a wedge between the generations, thereby creating an "otherness" that incites gerontophobia. Thus, I armed myself with a researcher's hat and a list of questions to shield me. I felt ready for the task: well versed in food history, fluent in Italian, fully integrated into the Italian community, university professor. Check. After the first two interviews I ditched the hat... and the list. With all due respect to haste and presumption, little did I realize that the story that was about to unfold before me would transport me on a journey through time far beyond my expectations, following an itinerary of its own devising.

Having been granted safe passage through a personal contact, what started as an interview became a dialogue, a heartfelt connection and collaboration between two women, one keen to listen and learn, and the other eager to have her voice heard, her experience valued and her story remembered. There was a tangible yet tacit awareness that at each interviewee was entrusting me with the urn of her youth, the spent embers of what were once ardent flames. I was humbled and awed by the weighty sense of responsibility that carried. It brought to mind a renaissance English song I had learned in high school:

> The silver swan, who living had no note,
> when death approached unlocked her silent throat.
> Leaning her breast against the reedy shore,
> thus sung her first and last and sung no more.

In order to establish myself as a credible conversation partner and put the interviewees at ease, proficiency in the language and a background in gastronomy were not sufficient. I needed to be fluent in their points of reference, conversant in their values, and to move confidently in the framework and jargon of their youth. Furthermore, I had to be knowledgeable about how these varied in each context from north to south, from rich to poor, from city to town to village to farm.

As my research continued, it was evident that any examination of foodways was inextricably embedded in both personal experience and the larger context of the daily life of the era. Consequently, the discussion of food was not something I wanted to flush out of the entanglement of details; rather, I came to value it as a vehicle to flesh out a fuller, richer history, one that included both the diamond and the rough. The intrinsic largesse of food offers an ideal vantage point from which to explore the broader question of social history, unveiling a unique perspective onto the past. By loosening the confines of the interview and allowing the process to unfold more organically, the curtains pulled back and I was bidden to enter family homes, private lives and intimate confidences, revealing life as it was lived day-by-day during the Ventennio fascista.

And I thought we were just going to talk about food.

Chewing the Fat is a testament to daily life under Mussolini, divulged not by scholars or celebrities, but through the first hand accounts of unassuming yet courageous women. Their stories are neither flashy exposés of the bizarre or macabre nor leaden history lessons. They are engaging personal disclosures that unfold within the easy flow of narration, with many unexpected turns and twists. They are true-to-life accounts arising from the vivid and lucid memories of the last living witnesses to one of the most devastating transitional periods in modern history. As a collection, these oral histories represent an endangered chapter in Italian social and culinary history, as the voices of these witnesses are silently slipping away, unnoticed.

The architects of culinary evolution profited greatly by romanticizing the past, whitewashing over the experiences of generations and elaborating traditions. Lovers everywhere are wont to drape the object of their desire the full metal jacket of their fantasy, and Italian food lovers are no less vulnerable to the enchantment of gastronomic tall tales. But that obscured, uncelebrated past plays a vital and integral role in the glory of Italian culinary history. Indeed, it was during the fascist reign that the behemoth that would become "Italian cuisine" was conceived and insisted upon as a foundation of national pride. The oppression, dearth and want that characterized the fascist era were the mother of invention and the springboard that moved the population to vow, like Scarlet O'Hara, that they would never be hungry again. It was through the determination of this generation to forge onwards and explore the potential of the bounty the country had to offer that Italian cooking spread its wings to become the most loved cuisine in the world.

A lucid examination of the past is not only intriguing in its own right, but essential to understanding the present state of affairs and our options for the future so that we are not mere puppets strung along by the wiles of the nostalgia industry. Suppressing and fictionalizing the past sullies this vision and denies us the opportunity to tip our hat to the unsung history makers, and to make our own informed choices. The oral histories presented here stand fully stripped of any such manipulative armament. They have no tour packages to sell, no products to hawk, no menu suggestions or taste-testing offers. They merely extend their hand to guide you on a rare journey through time and into the shadowy kitchens of the fascist era.

Translation note: The variations in expressions, dialects, accents, and even languages in Italy are incalculable. Fluctuations are noticeable within a space of even five kilometers, varying not only from place to place, but also among age groups and social classes. Though much is lost in the very act of translating, my aim was to faithfully reproduce not only the words, but also the voice and animus of each woman, drawing from the aural resources of the linguistic palette that is most familiar to me, American English. I also relied on my background in theatre to craft and hone each narration, so as to bring the reader as close as possible to the stream of the original experience. Given the international nature of the English language, I recognize that my choices may at times prove inaccessible or inappropriate to speakers of other varieties. All textual translations are mine unless otherwise indicated. A glossary of words left in the original Italian is located at the back of the book.

A note on the recipes: Before going to the interview, I requested that each interviewee contribute a recipe that, for her, represented the era in question. Whenever possible, I asked if we could prepare the selected dish together. I ate many things that I had never eaten in my twenty-five years in Italy. While we prepared the dishes, I took ample photographs. For many of them, it was the next best thing to being on a television food show, and I was happy to oblige. Although some of the recipes may seem like a ploy, an attempt to shock or disgust, they were all passed on to me with sincere pride and shared with joy.

Preambolo –

Before Their Time: 1861-1922

Setting the stage

In 2011, Italy celebrated its 150th year of nationhood. The year 1861 witnessed an end to the disparate network of feudal duchies and micro-kingdoms that kept Italian city-states locked in an erratic cycle of vulnerability to outside powers and perpetual internal turmoil. After a lengthy and agonizing labor, unification forces eventually succeeded in giving birth to the Kingdom of Italy. When statesman Massimo d'Azeglio recorded in his memoires, "We have made Italy. We must now make Italians," he realized that the forging of citizenry was going to be far more daunting than minting the new national currency. At the time of unification, there were precious few commonalities that united the people of the towns, villages and burgs besides religion and hunger. But two world wars and twenty years of a totalitarian regime (1922-1943) did much to hack away at the thicket of local customs, traditions and dialects. At the outset a mere 2.5% of the population spoke Italian as a first language. Homogeneity, or at least a semblance of it, would have to be largely pummeled into place.

By the mid-1800s, the words "calorie" and "nutrients" (carbohydrates, fats, proteins) had become political buzzwords throughout Europe. Experts of the day calculated the coefficients defining adequate intake, and western nations busied themselves with the task of ascertaining whether or not their populace was getting enough to eat. The vitamin would not have its heyday in the public sphere until after WWII; therefore, field research ultimately did not distinguish between filling one's stomach with digestible mass to stave off hunger and satisfying nutritional needs. To no one's surprise, the nations whose citizens were better fed were in turn more physically predisposed to producing larger supplies of food. Likewise, citizens who were routinely underfed were of little more use in the field than scarecrows, unable, as they were, to endure the rigorous demands of a day's toil. Comparative studies revealed that Italians consumed less than half the meat that the French and Germans did. The infamously gluttonous Americans were not tucking away quite as much as the British, the European frontrunner, but the top position by a long shot went to the Australians.

In turn of the century surveys, social scientists described the vacuous stare and half-opened mouths of Italian agricultural workers, their stunted stature, sluggishness and intellectual poverty. Some even correlated gradations of skin pigmentation, darker as one ventured southward, with increments of physiological and psychological inferiority, speculating that prolonged economic deprivation had an inverse effect on another hotly disputed theory: the evolutionary process. The Panic of 1873, referred to as the Great Depression until supplanted in 1930, plunged caloric intake down 20% below the absolute minimum, casting a long shadow of doubt as to the buoyancy of the new nation. The dearth would drag on well into the 1890s.

While a modicum of sharecroppers and small landholders in certain areas, where the soil was rich and fertile and the climate mild, consumed a moderate assortment of foodstuffs, most others, particularly in the southern and mountainous regions, subsisted on a diet that was glaringly poor in variety, quality, and quantity. In 1861, three quarters of Italy's 25 million inhabitants were peasant farmers, most of whom were landless field hands, socially marginalized and illiterate (up to 90% in the south). Field hands labored 12-14 hour days for miserable wages, subsisting with their families in abject poverty. Most people on farms and in villages shared their living quarters with farm animals, often depending on them as a source of warmth. Malaria, tuberculosis, and pellagra, were endemic due to wasting, as well as lack of sanitation and health care. Pellagra, called the illness of the three D's: dermatitis, diarrhea and dementia, scourged areas whose mainstay sustenance was cornmeal, hence, the northern regions in particular. It struck the poor almost exclusively and was consequently attributed to the hazards of working outdoors: too much sun, air, wind, or damp.

For many, cornmeal gruel, or polenta, was the only food, eaten at every meal. Although some agricultural workers took in a share of salt pork or wheat from the overlord, or *padrone,* at the season's end, they would often trade it for low quality cornmeal just to have enough food to get the family through the year. By inaccurate association, the idea spread that the cereal itself carried the disease. Another curious aspect was that women fell victim to pellagra twice as frequently as men. Women tended to eat lesser quality foods than men owing to the rigid agricultural hierarchy, which dictated the order in which household members ate. The head of the household had first choice, followed by the ranks of other male family members. Women then tended to leave choicer morsels of food to the children, in the end partaking of whatever remained.

In 1881, there were 104,000 documented cases of pellagra. In 1902, the government rushed to the rescue, boldly declaring a ban on the sale of rotten and unripe field corn. In all fairness, it wasn't until the late 1930s that pellagra was recognized as a dietary deficiency, although it had not escaped notice that those whose tables were graced by a generous spread avoided the blight.

Poor nutrition and general vitamin and mineral deficiency also contributed to the high infant mortality rate. Nursing mothers were physically fatigued and produced nutritionally deficient milk. Relentless poverty left many undernourished mothers unable to lactate, and infants to suckle on watery flour concoctions. For added sustenance these homemade formulas were enriched with fat or integrated with sheep or goat's milk, although proper sanitary precautions for handling or dispensing it were not always observed. In order to allow mothers to work longer hours, babies were sometimes given watered down wine to lull them into a cooperative stupor. Indeed, until recently bread soaked in wine and sprinkled with sugar was a commonplace afterschool snack that took the edge off a frenetic day at school.

Wine was long believed to have exceptional nutritive as well as medicinal qualities. The scientific world shied away from this claim towards the end of the nineteenth century, but as a folkway it persisted. *Bevi il vino che ti fa sangue,* "Drink some wine, it'll build up your blood," is still commonly said to someone feeling under the weather, though with the wink of an eye. Wine added to total caloric intake and so was also conveniently construed as a viable source of energy. At harvest time, in particular, a liter or two per day was the standard, meant to fortify peasant workers against the crushing fatigue. Some economists even encouraged wine consumption in place of food to lessen the burden on the family budget.

The countryside was not the exclusive haunt of the specter of poverty. Cities were teeming with have-nots, though Italian industrialization lagged far behind other European nations. While industrial production in 1880 registered at 30% in England, 18% in Germany, and 15% in France, Italy trailed far behind at 2.4%. During those years, nearly a third of Italian newborns would not make it through their first year of life, and adults on average did not live through their thirties. A massive national study entitled *Survey of Poverty in Italy,* published in 1951, revealed that even at that late date, 869,000 families were residing in "improper housing", such as makeshift shacks, rock shelters, cellars, and caverns. In the description of the town of Comacchio, located in the central north, the survey reported: "95% of the habitations are without a toilet. The wastewaters run off into the courtyards and pool nearby. Refuse is thrown into the canals, which are in essence, open cesspits in the city. Rare is the family of a field hand whose lodgings consist of more than one room, and consequently their domestic life is led in the most sordid filth and scandalous promiscuity."

For nearly all families of moderate to low income, both in the country and in urban centers, meat was a luxury item that exalted the table but a few times a year, generally only at Christmas, Easter, and festivals or when someone had fallen ill. Only in the twentieth century did meat begin to appear more than occasionally on the table, particularly in light of the growing white collar, or *piccolo borghese,* classes. Whereas a middleclass family could afford to spend two liras per day on meat, a peasant family spent one or two liras on their entire family meal, a day's income for a field hand. The bread eaten by the town poor was made with any combination of corn flour, legume flour, sorghum, or acorns, not to mention various mysterious extenders like ground corn stalks or even ashes, and paired with a repetitive selection of vegetables. White bread, obligatory on the modern Italian table, was again the reserve of the well heeled or the sick. City dwellers often battled the same nagging pang of hunger as their country cousins. Townsfolk were subject to additional food taxes that peasant farmers, *contadini,* were in part able to avoid. The distribution of food taxes was so excessive and arbitrary that they were familiarly nicknamed the "duty on hunger," much in the spirit of the English window tax, which had been dubbed the "tax on light and air."

The monotonous, almost monophagous diet consumed in this period makes speaking about a "popular cuisine", *la cucina popolare,* not only erroneous but also disrespectful, as it would refer to the meager daily fare of almost the entirety of the Italian population, who, day after day, struggled to obtain the minimum of food necessary to survive. The few who were fortunate enough to eat abundantly and regularly supped their way along the continuum between French haute cuisine, which looked to Paris as its epicenter and had dominated the tables of the Italian upper classes for centuries, and high Italian local gastronomy, whose specialties and delectable ingredients purposefully distinguished the privileged from the masses like a tacit sumptuary law.

Between 1876 and 1910, eleven million Italians expatriated. The turn of the century also witnessed an upturn in the economy, both conditions offering a welcome respite to the nation's perpetually empty stomach. With a little extra pocket money, common folks not only acquired a taste for luxury items, like coffee, liquor, and tobacco, but also became accustomed to them, although 60-80% of the family income was still being spent on household staples. The state of the nation progressed from "who could afford to eat," to "who could afford to eat what."

The Politics of White Bread
Wheat was slowly replacing other grains and starches as Italy's dietary backbone, while World War I loomed ever closer on the horizon. But there was simply not enough arable land to produce the amount of

wheat needed to meet the nation's newfound expectation for white bread. The government had no choice but to set about procuring substantial imports and commence stockpiling what reserves it could for its citizens and the military in preparation for war. Some statesmen warned that Italy was ill equipped to supply adequate food to troops while attempting to assuage the population's demand for bread. Government strategies to conserve and ration wheat met with nationwide riots and looting. Efforts to fix bread prices brought about work stoppages and strikes among bakers.

In order to stretch the wheat supply to its limits, the production of white bread was illegalized and only coarse whole wheat bread was allowed, though the funding and conviction to enforce the law were lacking. Disgruntled bakers, who made less profit from this *pane unico,* protested that whole grain bread was unhealthy, and this rippled into widespread belief. Bread had become a right of the people, and white bread a status symbol to which all aspired; dark breads henceforth bore the stigma of indigence. The slightest alteration in the purity or availability of the refined white loaf met with public outcry. By 1917, efforts to curtail depleting wheat stocks led to the construction of an official, government approved loaf that was described by the American Consul in Florence as being "dark, sour, unattractive and having a bad taste, provoking intestinal irritation above the limits of toleration" (Helskowsy, 2004).

As the war dragged on, importation became onerous, creating shortages that further aggravated civil discontent. Rioting intensified, incurring numerous casualties, while demonstrators forcibly took what they felt was their due, not only from bakeries but all other manner of shops. Meanwhile, on the military front, Italian soldiers gazed hungrily at the provisions of their European counterparts, themselves falling short, in terms of protein and total calories, of the minimum required for the rigors of combat and maneuvering. All in all, however, their rations were often more than had been available to them on the home front and included the comfort trio of coffee, liquor and tobacco. The government rebuffed the troops' cowardly complaints saying that the provisions should suffice, given that they were not used to having such a full plate at home. Both officials and enlisted men were accused of simply lacking the mettle necessary for military duty. But when ensuing catastrophic defeats were attributed to hunger, the government made an effort to step up consignments.

In the summer of 1918, Italy was granted "most favored nation" status and with it a double shipment of wheat from Allied nations mercifully arrived. By the time the war ended in November of that year, Italians had already readjusted their eating standards as a result of the artificial maintenance of wheat prices. Although food was still central to Italy's woes, subsidies had allowed more people across the board to increase their consumption of flour products, and the manageable bread prices had given them the purchasing power to enjoy a wider variety of higher quality foodstuffs and non-nutritive consumables. Surely, in peacetime it was only natural to expect even greater abundance than in a time of crisis. Universal male suffrage, granted in 1912, had upset the elite political balance by allowing peasants to have their say, and now they were out in droves, determined to be heard.

Untenable as they were, expectations promoted a sense of righteous entitlement, which soon clashed head on with spiraling inflation and devastating unemployment, as men returned from the war expecting to find the jobs the government had promised in exchange for serving their country. Not only was there no work, the government simply could not sustain wartime bread subsidies any longer without the economy capsizing. At the same time, industrialists were unwilling to raise workers' wages to cover the outrageous price hike on unsubsidized bread, and no reasonable amount of taxation could restore the subsidies. Looting and rioting once again became commonplace, and the prime minister, unable to cater to the public's clamor for its daily bread, stepped down in 1920.

The ruling party had proved both inefficacious and unwilling to rescind its highbrow style of governance, and the younger generation was fed up with their gradualist tactics. This primed the way for the more decisive approach of the newly formed National Fascist Party. They promised to fill the void and answer the call for the firm hand of law and order, albeit in their own unorthodox manner. By lucky coincidence, the next year the price of wheat fell on the international market, and within Italy itself there was a bumper crop exceeding all expectations. Deregulation could finally be set in motion, hand in hand with propaganda, for self-sacrifice. After systematically infiltrating the government, Mussolini, in his infamous March on Rome, finally succeeded in usurping power and eventually establishing himself as dictator. With the blessing of the king, Mussolini neatly commandeered popular consensus and approval, dispensing with the need for electoral process.

> *I don't drink, I don't smoke, and I am not interested in cards … As for the love of the table, it holds no interest for me whatsoever. In the last few years in particular, my meals have been as frugal as those of the indigent. My only interests are those that deal with the sublime purposes of life and … the Patria.*
>
> *Mussolini*

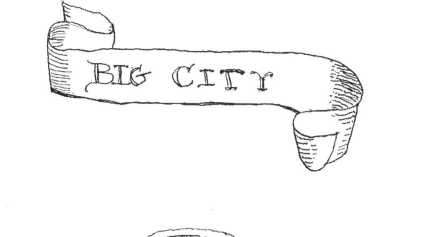

BIG CITY

Giulia

Born 1914 – Milan

I went to my interview with Giulia with reverence and awe, as she was the oldest person I had ever met. She lives in her own apartment in the heart of Milan with her caregiver. The week before, she had decided that she did not want to participate, not knowing what she could possibly have to say; then at the last minute, she let herself be persuaded. She chose to lie on her bed for our talk and, in spite of tiring after an hour, she was spirited throughout. Although she rarely feels up to leaving her house these days, she is a strong-willed and determined woman who makes no bones about her opinions. Giulia's experience typifies that of the inner-city poor of the great northern city of Milan. They had been completely dependent upon the infrastructure of food consignment from countryside to city, which was appallingly inadequate, particularly for the hordes of have-nots. In spite of their doggedly impoverished condition, the poor had believed overwhelmingly in the beneficence of the state and that Mussolini had had their welfare at heart. Indeed, even as the state of affairs worsened, blame was increasingly pinned on corrupt advisors, and rarely attributed to Mussolini himself. At the close of our conversation, before Giulia adjourned to the lunch her caregiver had prepared, she pulled out a right-wing newspaper from her bedside stand and waved it at me avowing that she reads the paper every day and that she is on top of what's what and who's who. "Let no one speak badly to me about Berlusconi!" she said, "He raised my pension three times! Three times, mind you!"

I am a pureblood Milanese, born, raised and lived here in the heart of the city all my life. I am now 99 years old. My father was in the First World War, but he got wounded, so he came home and set to work scratching out whatever living he could. He worked for a florist who had a stand in the city center; mostly he was a delivery boy. Took flowers round to the well-to-do folks.

I went to a big city school and finished all five years of elementary school. I started middle school too, but we were too poor for me to go on. After elementary school, it cost you to keep your kids learning. Why, already we were just barely making ends meet, so any more schooling was like playing at being rich.

We grew up under the Duce, so the school done taught us the fascist ideas, like being punctual, acting with good manners, and respecting other folks. Our Duce wanted everyone to go to school, not like before when most kids like me never learned reading and writing. In times before that, there wasn't no order nowhere. Fascism, well now, there was some good to it and some bad. Discipline was strict as could be; wasn't too much was tolerated back then. But the Duce really tried to help the poor folks in need because, you see, he came from a Socialist family and those were people who had to work. They knew about working and the strife the working people went through. You can't be lily-livered in this life! That's why he wanted us all to have a straight and narrow upbringing, to make us strong workers and respectful people.

I didn't start school until 1922, when our Duce reformed the school [*Giulia was unable to discuss her actual schooling in any detail as it rekindled something highly traumatic in her and set off a panic reaction*]. We were all of us poor at my school. The better-off families sent their children away to private schools so's not to mix with the likes of us. In Milan, of course, there were lots of your upper-crust families and a lot of very, very poor people. Boys and girls were together in the classroom and each grade had its own teacher because there was lots of us city kids. My parents let me start the first year at the Porta Garibaldi middle school, but like I said, things was hard for us so I had to quit. School started at 8 o'clock, and then we had an hour lunch break at noon. After lunch we did another two hours in the afternoon; then we did our homework at school, so all in all, it took up the whole day. That way parents could keep working at their jobs without the youngsters wandering around the streets and getting into trouble. Wasn't to be none of that under the Duce!

The district saw to getting us fed at school. It was a dish of plain pasta, polenta or rice. I say dish just as an expression, 'cause the portions were puny, just enough to hush up your growling belly. It's not like they were serving up a heaping plate of steaming pasta, eh, no! And that, sirs, was your school meal. We had to bring something from home if we wanted to have a decent lunch, but a lot of kids had to make do with what was dished up because wasn't nothing sent with them from home. It was hard for lots of the kids on account of the ones who weren't packing something extra for lunch were the same ones sent off without any breakfast in the morning. Plenty of parents counted on the school lunches to get their children fed.

At my house, for breakfast we weren't exactly living it up either. It was usually canned milk and surrogate coffee, then off you git.

Canned evaporated milk was developed for commercial use in the mid-1800s. The 60% dehydration process increased both shelf life and creaminess making it practical, cheap, and appealing. It was also considered safer because it circumvented the so-called "milk sick" that resulted from bacterially unsound raw milk. The process of concentrating the milk reputedly destroyed nutrients, resulting in rickets, but its widespread use in the military in WWI brought about a revival of trust, much like the Space Food fad of the 1970s. The market nosedived as soon as refrigerators were mass marketed and pasteurization and homogenization became standard practices.

After school, dinner was pretty much always soup or polenta. Sometimes we had rice, but never pasta. In my family, we couldn't afford it. In the city we had ration cards for the whole time even between the wars, and we could only buy what was allowed us on the card, and that's if we had the money. Bread back then was all coarse whole wheat bread. White bread was only for rich people who could splurge on the black market. That white bread was a real dangerous business.

My mother didn't want me to take no part in Fascist Saturday, and the authorities didn't make children from the really poor neighborhoods do it. Truth was, they didn't want kids like me because my folks didn't have the money to shell out on the *piccola italiana* uniform, and it wouldn't look too good having the raggedy kids marching with the clean, pressed ones outfitted proper like. There was a lot of us in the quarter who weren't about to spend good money on something like that. I know that in other places the parents were punished if children didn't take part, and that there was some explaining to do when the Blackshirts came a knockin', but not here. If children were disobedient, then yes sir, you bet, the fascio came to the house and gave the parents what for! That kept children doubly afraid to be naughty. So, yeah, Saturday I didn't go to school because the others were all out doing their marching.

A lot of folks in the poor quarters were in a state because we were only just scraping by, eh, but just the same, you held your tongue about it. Complaining was dangerous business even though some people didn't eat near nothing else but polenta and were ready to give you an earful 'bout it. There was a lot of trading between us poor folks, "I'll give you this if you give me that" sort of thing. If we happened on something of "value" to trade, we would buy things on the black market, even knowing you could end up in jail that way. They threw you in jail over nothing back then, not like today where you would get a fine, eh, no, no sir! It was jail for you, friend! So us poor folks tried to get along with each other because there was always the danger that some snitch might go sour on you and turn you in.

Some lucky people had kinfolk who lived in the country and they'd sometimes manage to get food from them, so they divvied it up to keep in good in the quarter. You always had to pretend to have less than what you really had, of course, but the handout served to hush up your neighbors. If they came to find out you were holding back on them, well, they didn't let you forget it. My father's earnings were all we had to live on because we didn't have a vegetable garden or relations in the country. He made his deliveries and when he wasn't doing that, he minded the flower stand in Via Torino selling to passersby, but it wasn't his business. I mean he just worked for another fella, a *padrone*. The padrone came every evening to collect the day's take and my father got his wages once a week. All of the shops kept a running credit list, so you didn't have to pay up till the end of the month. But, oh! Wasn't nobody working miracles for you! Shop owners weren't saints. They had to get by too.

I was one of two children. Well, I had a brother, but he died. My sister was sent out to a wet-nurse, *in balia*, and because that family took a liking to her, and my parents really couldn't afford to keep her, so the other family raised her.

Before the advent of infant formula, children were commonly sent to a wet nurse. Upper-class women customarily did not nurse their own children, but in the lower classes, the practice was often necessary due to poor nutrition and the consequent lack of maternal milk. Once the baby had been weaned, it was not uncommon for infants from poor families to remain with the wet nurse's family if they were better off and had bonded with the child. Wealthier families could opt for a live-in wet nurse. The high pay compensated for the traumatic separation from one's own family.

It's like with clothes, you know. They were handed around to the other poor people in the quarter once you grew out of them or they were used to patch other clothes. After a while, times being as hard as they were, my sister just became part of that other family. My mother wasn't awful put out about it, not at all. She was glad that Clara was in better conditions. My sister knew who her real parents were and I saw her sometimes. That's just the way it was. My parents brought me up and she was brought up by those other folks.

We lived in the housing blocks of the *quartiere popolare*, large tenements where each single housing set had three courtyards. Each courtyard had its own water pump because none of the flats had running water. Some of the houses were pretty crowded, either with more than one family or one real big family. Most of them were set-ups like ours, with a kitchen and a general room where you set out your cots for bed at night, not much more than a bedsit. We lived near the building where Garibaldi's aunt lived. She held me in her arms once. I can't remember her first name, but her surname was Garibaldi too. But that's just to tell you that the buildings where we lived were not new, even in 1914 when I was born.

Garibaldi is the central military hero associated with the Italian Unification of 1861 and, to this day, remains one of Italy's most admired patriots. As he was born in 1807, it is unlikely that an aunt of his would have been around to coo over the young Giulia. Perhaps it was some other descendant.

Inside the courtyard, each floor, and there were four floors, had a walkway and railing that looked into that courtyard. So then each floor also had its own communal lavatory with a sink and a toilet, which was used by all of the families on that floor. If we wanted to have a shower, we went to Cobianchi in the center of town. It was a public service place for bathing and showering. You went and waited your turn. Sometimes the wait was pretty darn long because there was lots of poor folks in Milan and there was a lot of wretches who did dirty, stinking jobs. Well, what do you expect? If you're down and out, you take what you can get and by God, you're gonna need a shower once a week! You could wash off a bit of crust at home in a basin during the week, but if you live on the fourth floor, well, you weren't exactly going to be hauling a tub of water up the steps. Already we had to bring up buckets upon buckets of water for everyday use. We had a wood-burning stove, and on one side of that was a sort of square pot that you put water in. So long as the oven was hot, it heated the water too, so there was always hot water when you needed it. Everyone had to buy their own stove because there weren't fireplaces in the flats, and the landlords sure weren't about to step up and buy one for you.

Back then, we didn't reason in the same way we do now. Our first thought was about filling our stomach. The fascio didn't bring poverty. Poverty had a stranglehold on Milan a good piece before they came along. If anything, the early 1930s was the first time that we were able to get our heads above water, for what it was. I got my first toothbrush in 1930 when I was 16. I didn't need one before because I was young and my teeth were still healthy. In the city, the First World War rang in our ears for a good long while, so it was quite a spell before anyone could think about extras like toothbrushes.

Here in Milan, we had the ration book from one war straight into the next without a break. But even though we were penniless, there weren't any thieves among us. They only stole from the gentlefolk, the *signori,* all those high and mighty people living on their estates and in their fine houses. They robbed from the rich and gave to the poor, in a noble kind of way. When you got your hands on something, first, of course, you took care of things at home, but then you passed on what you could. If someone in a bad way came around looking for a hand-out from a different someone who had happened onto a little good fortune, the answer was "yes."

Even though we lived by the ration card, there was more to eat in general. What changed under the fascio is that if you were caught out, or even if you were just suspected of something underhanded, the Duce's heavies threw you straight in jail. There was no mercy. He did what he could to give poor folks a hand, but if you disobeyed, they took no pity on you. There started to be a different class of people who were better off, neither rich nor poor, but they pretended to be poor! They were afraid of being put on the list with rich people because the rich people paid higher taxes. They knew that the Duce was a defender of the poor, and so they wanted to cash in on the rewards too. You know who I'm talking about, them middle-rich people.

But there were spies and meddlers everywhere. The patrols busted in on people in their homes at mealtimes to see what they were eating! If you were eating things you couldn't afford, it was trouble for you! They asked, "Where did you get the money for this? How did you come by these things?" The *squadristi* were on the lookout for hoarders too, folks with their secret supplies. It wasn't easy living then, always looking over your shoulder. You know what the crafty ones did? They changed their mealtime! They ate later or earlier. All of us did it that way when we got hold of something extra to eat. We snuck around and ate when no one suspected you'd be eating. There were snoops lurking around all the time, but they were just trying to get something extra for themselves and then after that they would leave you alone. We did whatever we had to just to get through another day, and that means we would do just about anything. I mean within reason, of course. No one got killed or anything. Any killing and you'd get locked up for the rest of your days! We all understood that folks did desperate things if it was the difference between eating or not eating that day. It wasn't about being a criminal.

Where we lived, there was a young woman who was a spy for the fascio. She blew the whistle on communists, and they got their heads shaved, so everyone would know well and good who they were. You had to steer clear of the reds; otherwise the fascio would keep their eye on you too.

In order to make money, lots of girls turned to working in brothels, but it was legal then.

Prostitution had enjoyed a long history of both tolerance and state regulation. Those laws were expanded upon in 1861 after Italian unification. Taxes were levied from operators and the government established price lists and service delineations. Quality brothels, for example, were permitted to uphold a 20-minute maximum for transactions. Popular consensus cheered on the reduction of prices in 1891, with a special discount allotted to soldiers and non-commissioned officers. Under fascism, restrictive measures were passed obliging prostitutes to be registered with the public security office and subjected to medical examinations, in spite of which, life expectancy for these women was low. After the Second World War, advocates argued that in the interest of public health, hygiene, and civility, continued legalization was necessary. It distinguished and safeguarded "decent" women destined to be wives and mothers, while allowing men an outlet for their sexual instincts. In 1948, a campaign began in earnest to make prostitution illegal. After considerable debate, the law was passed in 1958.

Milan was stuffed to the gills with brothels. There were never any streetwalkers. No one gave much of a thought to it; it was normal. It was better to have them in houses than on the streets. Better for everyone. If I could have my say about it, I would have them legalize brothels again. If nothing else, at least the situation was orderly. Milan has changed so much, too much. I have seen such changes in my life! With this Leftist government there is too much freedom and that has created disorder. I was raised with order and seeing all of this disorder this way, well, I don't like it, not one little bit. We were used to having law and it being obeyed. We knew what the consequences were for someone who just went and did whatever they pleased. Now it is a free-for-all.

When I finished my schooling, I went to be a *piccinina* [*child apprentice, literally: "little thing"*] for a tailor. I was there for a good many years and then I went to work for larger companies. In 1933, I married my husband. I was 18 and he was 21. He was the delivery boy for the bakery that made our bread. We started talking about this, that, and the other, and well, you know how that ends. We were engaged for three months and then we got married.

We rented a bedsit of our own at Porta Genova, and we stayed there ten years. I had two daughters, one in '39 and the other in '40. I had a son too but he passed on after three months, just like what happened to my mother. My husband did military service but he didn't never have to go abroad. He worked in the military hospital. Meantime, I went to work at Pirelli [*the tire factory*] and then I went to work in the Alfa Romeo factory after the war. I always worked, *always* worked. I sent my daughters to a baby sitter, a *balia asciutta* because I was always at work.

> *As opposed to the "wet" nurse, the* balia asciutta *was a "dry" nurse, essentially a babysitter or daycare provider.*

We had the ration card all the way through until 1949. The only bread we had was black bread, *pane nero,* that was practically uneatable, but we made a good soup with it called *pancottino:* leave your black bread for a half a day in water, boil it, and add Liebig.

> *Baron Justus Von Liebig, a German chemist, and George Christian Giebert, a Belgian engineer, came up with the idea of utilizing the bovine carcasses in Uruguay (discarded after use for their hides only) to make a cheap and nutritious meat extract for the underprivileged in Europe who could not afford the real thing. Initially, the product was the consistency of molasses, but later an even cheaper version was marketed in the form of a bouillon cube, at which point the name changed*

from Liebig to Oxo, as it is still known in the UK. It allowed less fortunate families to prepare meaty tasting dishes, without the expense of actual meat. The Italian advertisement in 1935 reads: "At the base of thrifty and healthy eating is a good soup, and at the base of a good soup are Liebig Cubes, the only ones that contain Pure Extract of Liebig Meat." Baron Liebig was also the propagator of the erroneous yet die-hard idea that searing meat seals in its juices.

We hardly ever had real meat, and even for us to come by a bit of Liebig we had to make a pretty decent trade with someone. It was good for everything you wanted to make. All you had to have was boiling water and if you had some oil or butter or lard, you threw that in as well. During wartime we used mostly lard for our cooking fat. Then we would try to get some *grana padano* cheese crusts so's we could grate a touch of that into the soup. *Grana padano* was too rich for our table, but sometimes we got hold of some leftover crusts.

Grana Padano is a northern Italian hard cheese similar to Parmigiano Reggiano. It is milder and less complex due to a shorter aging period.

People who had kin in the country would sometimes have crusts to trade. Eh, those people in the country! They lived the good life, they did! They always had white bread because they made it themselves! They had their own corn to make polenta. They cheated and held back on the ration what they were supposed to give to the city. So that's why city people always had to go to the country begging for food. We sure ate our share of polenta in my house, either with a spoonful of tomato *conserva* or milk. That's how children liked polenta best, with milk.

We didn't have meat more than once or twice a year. The only time we got meat was at Christmas when the district authorities passed out the holiday pack. They threw a lot of things in the pack, including a slab of meat. At Christmastide, rich people too brought things to the schools of the poor kids. The Church gave money to the city to make more packs for us, so we made out all right at Christmas. We tried to make what we got last as long as we could.

At Christmas in Milan, lots of us ate *cassoeula* because the country people slaughtered pigs when the weather turned cold, and cassoeula was made with the parts that had to be et up right away: the head, the tail, ribs, and rind. That was cooked up with cabbage, carrots and celery.

La Cassoeula Milanese – Winter stew

Serves 6
500 g savoy cabbage, cut into chunks
300 g pork ribs
100 g raw pork rind
2 small sausages per person
2 ham hocks with skin, cut in half
1 pig ear, shaved and cleaned
1 pig face (includes jowls and snout)
1 pig tail
100 g carrots
100 g celery
100 g onion
50 g butter
1 glass dry white wine
1 liter meat broth
pepper

Boil the feet, rind ears and face for an hour to render some of the fat. Skim off some fat for another use. In a large Dutch oven or cast iron pot, melt the butter over low heat. Cut the ear, face and rind into strips and cut the slab of ribs into singles. Brown them all plus the tail in the butter for a few minutes and add the carrot, celery and onion. Pour in the glass of wine and bring to a boil. Just barely cover with broth and simmer covered for an hour making sure it does not stick to the bottom. Salt and pepper to taste. After half an hour, add the cabbage and the sausages. Cook for another 30-45 minutes skimming any scum that may rise to the surface.

Weren't too many other times that we managed to get meat but at Christmas it was a free gift. There were too many hungry people that needed to be looked after, so we weren't expecting nothing more than what we got. From the Christmas pack we could whip up a holiday cake, and the church and the city would also give us a *panettone*. The Motta Company made panettone then. We ate it slowly, bit by bit, to make it last until San Biagio.

> Panettone *was originally the traditional Christmas cake of Milan. The cult of San Biagio celebrated the saint's day (February 3) by eating the last remains of panettone from the holiday season. Shops offered the last of their supply of panettone on that day at reduced prices. In the early 1920s, Angelo Motta altered the size, shape and texture of panettone, transforming it into the cake that is eaten today in every Italian household after Christmas dinner. Although it never caught on as a year-round cake as he had advertised it in the magazine* La Cucina Italiana, *by the early 1930s, Motta had already set up an industrial-sized bakery to meet increasing demand.*

We all made do with what we had and tried to stretch it as long as we could. In Milan we really and truly suffered from hunger, but wasn't a one of us dropped dead from poverty or starvation. Those country folks, though, they lived much better than we did, food hoarders the lot of them! In the country they had *tagliatelle* and all of those things. To make pasta in the city you had to be able to afford flour. No, no, no. We couldn't swing that, not in the Duce's time.

I remember when Mussolini was killed and he was brought back to Milan and hung upside-down in Piazza Loreto. There were lots of people celebrating, but not everyone, no, signore, not everyone. Other political parties came in then and...well, all right, Mussolini may have made his mistakes, but they made even more! Folks wanted to do anything that might help dig us out of our rut because we were so poor, and we didn't know what else we could do. After Mussolini gone and failed us, we hoped maybe the Left might be the answer. More than anything, we wanted to be free of rationing. After the fascio fell, the market was opened up and we could get fruit and vegetables. Before, they wouldn't let you get nothing but what was written on your ration card, and everyone was running scared about getting caught with extras they couldn't explain. Was only rich people had the cash for fresh fruit and vegetables before. They were just too pricy for us. We were in a frightful state. You couldn't just hand over a month's wages to the vegetable man! We're free now, yes, but the price we done paid for it is public morality. It is shameful. Simply shameful!

Giulia separated from her husband early on in their marriage, working long hours to keep her daughters in boarding school. In 1970, divorce was legalized in Italy but from its inception political factions relentlessly attacked it until it was finally put up for public referendum. In 1974, the matter was put to rest as the majority of voters approved of maintaining the law. After filing for divorce, however, a couple must still undergo a mandatory three-year separation before proceeding with the actual dissolution of the marriage, to rule out reconciliation. Giulia was, in a sense, a social pioneer, being one of the first women in Italy to obtain a divorce. At the time of this writing, a bill has been presented into Parliament proposing to reduce the period of purgatory to one year, or two in cases involving of children under eighteen.

Intermezzo

Minestra, minestrone, minestrina, zuppa, zuppetta, pappa – Soup

Proverb: She who wields the ladle
decides how the soup is made.

Water, the common denominator of soup, its most fundamental ingredient. Too much and you upset the balance
of comfort and nutrition, too little and you move out of
the realm of the spoon and into that of the fork. The tightrope act
of making water pass for food was a central part of the daily culinary
routine for many humble families during the Ventennio. On the thin
end of the *minestra* spectrum were the salt, water, and bread soups,
consisting of no more than a warm bowl of light brine poured over
chunks of heavy dark bread, drizzled sparingly with oil, pragmatically
called *acqua-sale*. A denser version added an egg, one per pot, or a few
grated sprinkles from a crust of cheese. Just as the Eskimos have many
words to describe snow, there is a variety of colorful derogatory terms
disdaining soup whose water content has overstepped its bounds,
like *brodaglia, acquiccia, sbroscia, sbromba* and the charming Neapolitan
sciaquapall' – ball wash.

Actual broth was one rung up, and in a society whose mantra was
"never throw anything away," gradations began with the by-product

water left after boiling pasta or vegetables. They progressed upwards to broths intentionally made with selected ingredients to obtain a foundation medium from which to build a soup. These broths were revered as tonics, vital liquid extracts of healthful properties that had been carefully coaxed from solids. Children were duly warned to eat their soup, and stories were told about the unhappy ends of naughty children who didn't. These elixirs formed the base of pasta soup, a pillar of the evening meal in many households. Usually the pasta was homemade *quadretti* or *quadrucci,* any way you say it – little squares. When dried pasta was used it was often to make use of an accumulation of broken chips of pasta that had been prudently set aside. Although the cooking times differed, the pieces were all tossed into the broth together and thus called "married soup" making for a sense experience of both mushy and crunchy moments.

Zuppe, gruel-like soups, ventured a step further into the creamy dominion though remaining strictly on the liquid side of the fence. At their most basic, they were no more than coarsely ground cereals, chestnuts, or legumes slowly simmered in water until they disintegrated, enriched perhaps with a bit of lard or made into a more substantive meal with the addition of pasta. Thicker yet were the *pappe,* another category on the bread-soup continuum, that veered towards fork territory. They essentially consisted of a semi-liquid mush made from hardened bread left to soften in some sort of soup or broth. The saturated bread would increase in volume creating the enticing appearance of heartier servings, thus the proverb: "When there's not much bread on the table, put it in the soup bowl." Favorites in this genre were *pappa coll'olio*: bread softened in broth and drizzled lightly with olive oil, and the now well-known *pappa al pomodoro,* with crushed tomatoes, onions, and garlic.

Soup went beyond being a mere sum of its parts. It was a veritable ritual akin to the sacredness of bread itself. Not only was it the essence of goodness, but the very act of amalgamating disparate, even unappealing scraps into a harmonious appetizing meal, was an economic godsend that filled the stomach while it pleased the palate. Virtuous exercises of extreme thrift led to concoctions that defy codification, but not mythological mystique.

"See you in the *buglione!*" said the fly to the hair. *Buglione* was a Tuscan soup of the throw-whatever-you-have-into-the-pot variety. By its very nature, it could never be exactly the same, as it was created anew with whatever was available on the spur of the moment. The ingredients derived from the salvaged comestible discards collected from the butcher, the kitchens of the wealthy – some of whom reputedly left food to waste for the very purpose of passing it on – and the marketplace at the close of the workday. If it was edible, it was good to go. Anthropologically speaking, this is a soup that required some contact with an urban context, though it also included a mince of whatever seasonal vegetables and aromatics were up for grabs from the garden and woods. The meaty parts were simmered first until they could be boned. Then the boned morsels and the other recovered ingredients gurgled long and slow in the cauldron suspended from a chain in the hearth. Everything disintegrated and, under a skillful hand and experienced eye, melded into a heartwarming fusion that was ladled over slices of dried out bread. Comfort food par excellence.

Ribollita, a reigning *trattoria* favorite both in Italy and abroad, is the vegetarian country cousin of *buglione*. Ribollita literally means reboiled. The contents of the soup pot in agrarian homes was a seasonal catch-as-catch-can affair, an endless cycle of being filled, boiled, partially-consumed, added to, and re-boiled, all in accordance with what was available. As was the case with most bread-soups, it made use of dried bread leftover from the weekly baking that would otherwise have been impervious to teeth. Like *buglione*, it was a folkway more than a recipe. However, *ribollita* lacked the haphazard junkyard dog aura of *buglione;* it was more limited in scope and easier to systemize from the limited number of classic Tuscan crops. Therefore, in the 1800s, when the population began to trickle from the country into the city, ribollita was gentrified and standardized in order to satisfy the longing for a taste of home. Despite the soup's deep meanderings into the agrarian past, the word ribollita itself would not come into being until after World War II; practices are wont to take on names as they transform into traditions. Sadly, souvenir food boutiques, that would bottle their grandmother if they could, now sell ready-mixed bags of dried ribollita. Just add water.

Renata

Born 1931 – Rome

Renata is an indomitable Roman woman whose savvy and talents lifted her out of the dire straits of abject destitution. Her neighborhood, San Lorenzo, was once a quintessential slum, and the life of hardship she describes was common to masses crowded into the tenements of the nation's new capital city. Renata's husband Franco, an amiable bombastic Roman caricature, was eager to participate in the interview as well. To set the tone, he showed me the sizeable gold pendant he wore around his neck, not of a saint or a crucifix, but of a hammer and sickle. His grandson Flavio, age 30, was covered in tattoos with a good portion of his left shoulder allocated to the face of Ché Guevara. The Italian Communist Party formed in 1921, shortly after the birth of the National Fascist party, but was forced underground during the course of events, reemerging full-throttle in the backlash following the fall of fascism. After a wink, Franco scurried off to get his hearing aid, while Renata adjusted the tubes leashing her to an oxygen machine. Once she caught her breath, her account unfolded.

I was born in 1931 in San Lorenzo, the derelict quarter of Rome's poorest poor. It was such a rough neighborhood that neither the Black Shirts nor the Germans dared stray too close to it. When I was eight, my parents split up, so I didn't see much of my mother after that. Neither one of my folks could really be bothered with us kids, my mother because she just wasn't made that way, and my father because his anti-fascist dealings forced him to live an underground life. One or the other of them turned up every so often to check in on us though.

As the war came nearer, my father was more and more involved with the communist resistance as a go-between, pamphlet writer, and undercover operator and so it wasn't safe for him to keep a permanent address. He paid for us children to room in a communal apartment in the Apia neighborhood. Me and my younger sister and baby brother lived in one of the three rooms of a tenement we shared with twenty other people. We were lucky 'cause the three of us had a room to ourselves, and them others were packed tight into the other two rooms. Even though it was all one flat, each room had its own rental contract, and then there was a common kitchen and toilet. Mind you now, I'm not talking about a bathroom, just a toilet, and one for the lot of us.

This was how Rome's poor lived. I'm not painting a picture of anything unusual or extraordinary for the time. Not that we didn't know full well and good that we were poor and others were rich, and not to say that we didn't suffer the hardship of it, because there was plenty of that! It's just that there was so many of us all living in that same way, bottom-of-the-barrel like. When my father had some spare change, which wasn't often, he would leave us what he could, but mostly us two older kids had to scrounge odd jobs where we could in order to make it, cleaning the stone stairways in buildings, washing dishes in an osteria, or clearing away garbage at the outdoor market. Even though I was just a kid myself, it was left to me to bring up my younger brother and sister. But the way life worked in San Lorenzo is that everybody looked after the strays. With that many people in a single flat, there were lots of other children and so someone was usually on hand to see to us too, make sure that we got fed, tend to us when we weren't well, and get us off to school. Yes, I did get some schooling, though not much.

There wasn't no choice about going to Fascist Saturday, so I went, but... we were far too poor to pay for the uniform. One of the activity leaders got me a *piccola italiana* uniform and she said that I could pay for it a little bit at a time. Well, I tell you, when my father saw that fascist outfit in our room, he took it outside and burned it like nothing doing! He was not having any daughter of his training to be a little fascist! The next week when I went to Fascist Saturday I had to make up some excuse for what happened. I couldn't tell the truth because I was afraid the fascist squads would come and kill my father. So I said that I lost it.

After that I just fell in with the other raggedy kids who didn't have the right outfit. We were put into corners, out of the way, so that we didn't wreck the sameness of the other kids. To a child's eyes, they looked so beautiful, everyone dressed up the same way, and the leaders made it fun. There were activities and singing, and sometimes there were sweets or snacks. It made you feel good, like things made sense, like for a little while there was order and things meant something, something wonderful and important. You could forget about being poor for a while. When I watched from the corner, I wished I could have the little pleated skirt with the crisp white shirt and neck scarf.

Franco and I were there when they took the Roman Jews out of our schools. One day we went to school and all of the Jewish kids were gone.

The Racial Laws of 1938 were a sign of Hitler's influence on Italian policy. The Jewish ghetto was established in 1555 and it wasn't until 1870, after Unification, that the ghetto was finally abolished and reno-vated. Reconstruction was completed in 1900. The Jews were granted full citizenship and for the first time in 300 years, scholars and all manner of professionals were allowed to enter into the fabric of Roman society. Their assimilation was so successful that in 1920 there were nineteen Jews serving in the Italian senate. They had a high inter-marriage rate (43.7% in 1938) and had served their country in WWI. In 1938, when Italy was recovering from international sanctions and needed an ally, they adopted the Racial Laws which repealed the law of 1870 and, after only seven decades, Jews were once again forced to return to the ghetto, stripped of their citizenship and denied the pos-sibility of continuing their professions. Ironically, in 1938, 10,000 Jews were fascist party members. Margherita Sarfatti, Mussolini's lover until 1933, was a Jewish intellectual who had written his biography in 1925. It was such a stunning success that it was translated into eighteen languages and proved instrumental in bolstering his image throughout the world. She had helped form fascist ideology only to find herself escaping from it to Argentina in 1938 as a Jewish refugee.

We remember the Jews walking through the streets with their wooden carts calling out for used clothes and rags that they used to make fabric and other things. They lived in the Jewish ghetto, and their kids could only go to Jewish schools. A lot of them got deported. Most of them never came back. All those centuries of isolation had made them a strong community. Food is a mighty force in their culture, but also because they are Italians. The *cucina romana*, Roman cooking, *is* Jewish. Roman food doesn't exist without Roman-Jewish cooking traditions.

Everybody in the world knows about *pasta alla carbonara,* in America and China and everywhere, and it comes from Italian-Jewish cooking. Have you ever had pig's liver *alla Romana?* Pig's liver is a dish that has been passed down to us from the time of the Roman Empire! And it is Jewish. What about the *pajata?* The intestines of lambs that have only ever had their mother's milk? Jewish, all of it.

Sephardic Jewish cooking originated in the Mediterranean basin and plays a strong role in the Roman culinary tradition. In spite of Renata's enthusiasm to support the Jewish contribution, the specific foods mentioned run directly contrary to Jewish dietary laws in that they include pork, in the case of the first two, and the combination of milk and meat in the case of the latter. The internationally renowned pasta alla carbonara, *widely believed to belong to age-old traditions, was first recorded in 1954. One of the legends of its origins claims that the dearth of foodstuffs in Rome was so dire at the end of the war that the population had to rely for a time on the military rations of the Allies, which included powdered eggs and bacon. The addition of pasta bulked it out and rendered a dish destined to make its mark around the world (Capatti, 2014).*

No matter what you might think, that Rome is a warm place, the winters *feel* cold, especially when there is no heat and you don't have warm clothes or bedding. The only warm place was the kitchen hearth, where I also learned to cook the food of Rome's poor people, what they call the *cucina povera*. There was no sort of choice to speak of, so I guess what you might say is that there was a range of foods *in arm's reach*, depending on the season, and how long your arm was! You ate what was there. You ate what you could scrape together. You ate what you could steal. You made whatever you could get your hands on into something eatable if at all possible.

> *Poor transport systems, lack of organization and limited means of storage made distributing food to a city the size of Rome an arduous and costly enterprise. Farmers tended to peddle their wares locally, or to make better money, they sold their products abroad making availability even more tenuous.*

Even though there isn't a whole lotta good to say about an overburdened, overcrowded kitchen, one bright spot was that I got to see a lot of clever tricks people came up with to make something out of nothing, in the way of the Roman poor. We were alone, me and my brother and sister, and so everyone tried to give me tips about what to do with what I managed to get hold of. The families didn't take turns cooking in the kitchen; there wasn't nothing organized or orderly about it. Sure, everyone was looking out for her own family first, but after that they lent a hand to others if they could.

There weren't any recipes, no one wrote anything down, and I'd say most of them couldn't read or write anyway, let alone shell out extra cash on paper and pencil. The idea of writing a recipe, well, it is like something for rich people, and that had nothing to do with us. We were just hand-to-mouth. With us poor people, cooking was handed down one to another, practical like. I did the same with my children and grandchildren. You can't do that with a book. It has to be done hands on at home, and only if the children give a hoot about learning it. You can't force it on anyone; it has to come natural. I tried following a recipe once. Disaster. Never again.

With our ration card we could go to the local bakery and get 200 grams of bread a day. 200 grams of dough was measured out to make small loaves like that, and everyone was allowed to buy one a day, so we'd go every day to the bakery in front of our building to pick up our piece of bread. It was brown government bread called *pane unico*, because that was the only bread you could get, well, legally anyway. You picked up your subsidy bread and managed your hunger the whole day with that one piece of bread and whatever else you could get hold of that day. There was a ration card for all foods, but the government didn't subsidize anything but bread so if you didn't have the money, card or no, you didn't get your ration. Simple as that. In the city, whatever supplies came in had to feed everyone, and so there was a limit on most everything. People who had the money could find whatever they wanted on the black market, but that was only for rich people. Rationing was different everywhere, but it was impossible in Rome because there you are talking about a huge city of hungry people who didn't produce any food and all of them needing to eat.

Franco: The black market was run by country peasants. They brought flour, vegetables, chickens, rabbits... because there was serious money to be had. They had to be fast and furtive and know their customers because it was a serious crime. Even so, the authorities knew what was going on and would only make an example of someone now and then just to keep it from getting out of hand. They were probably on the take and so turned a blind eye. Even bakers made bread for the black market.

> *Instead of gauging food production on the caloric and nutritional needs of the populace, Mussolini sought to curb the Italian appetite in correspondence with the availability of food, telling his people that they simply did not require the same amount of food as those puffy indolent Northern Europeans. Shortages increased, and at their height, 70% of food was procured on the black market. The Duce's propagandistic projections of himself as fatherly provider backfired in later years, as the most overpowering experience of fascism became hunger.*

Subsidized bread was whole wheat and who knows whatever else they put in it. White flour was set aside to make bread for people who could pay the price. Ah, but real Roman bread is good bread. Big crusty loaves. Oh! Not like this sickly Umbrian bread! They don't cook their bread! I say, THEY DON'T COOK THEIR BREAD!

Renata: She is not interested in what you think about Umbrian bread! She wants to hear about Rome! Poor people got the idea to gang up and steal the food brought in by black market sellers because what were they going to do? Call the police? We were hungry. And I mean, we were *hungry*. Franco's father worked as a tram operator and was able to buy a decent apartment for his family. He was a signore in comparison to us! Families like his could pick up a few things on the black market and could put out for the small meat ration the government let you have. Where I lived we didn't even know what meat was! The poor children in my neighborhood stole from market stalls. You walk by, put your hand out and snatch something. If they saw you they shooed you away, but for the most part they'd let you run off with an apple or an onion; after all it wasn't like you were going to take off with a crate of food. So they put up with it as far as they could. If you didn't steal, there just wasn't going to be enough to eat.

Franco: When my father and uncle were about eighteen years old they secretly stowed away on ship to America. Neither of them could read nor write; they were just a couple of country bumpkins. My father was born in 1891 before the '15-'18 War. Ok, so they managed to get to America and they stayed there a while and then, *they came back here to fight in the war for Italy!* Can you imagine!? They had made it all the way there and then THEY CAME BACK HERE with the American volunteer army! I can't hardly bear even thinking about it! During the war he was captured and sent to an Austrian camp. His brother, this is a different brother than that other guy, so this other brother was in that same camp and when he saw my father he said, "Christ almighty, man! I thought you were in America!" When my father explained that he had returned to Italy to fight in the war, his brother said, "Who in hell *escapes* to America and then *comes back!* And even worse COMES BACK FOR A WAR!*" Unbelievable!

One good thing that happened is that while he was in the states, he got a driver's license. No one but no one here had a driver's license and it paved the way to his getting a job with the public transport system in Rome in 1921. You see, in comparison to Renata we did seem rich because we had a two-bedroom apartment with a living room, bathroom and kitchen, and it was just me and my sister and our parents. My mother died when I was eight though. It was in an apartment building constructed by the public transport cooperative, the first 11-story apartment building in Rome. They like to say that Mussolini built it, but Mussolini did *not* build it, no sir!

Renata: You can't really talk about cooking well, or even good food until you get pretty well into the 1950s. You can only talk about making do with little there was. Some people were better at it than others. If you found something eatable you cooked it and ate it. End of story. The dish I am making for you today was a dish of the poor but from when times were fat.

Pomodori ripieni con patate – Stuffed Tomatoes with rice (A recipe for times of plenty)

10 good round medium tomatoes
1 ½ cups Italian white rice (like carnaroli)
1 small bunch of basil and parsley
olive oil
salt and pepper
1 or 2 garlic cloves
8 med potatoes

Remove the tops from the tomatoes by cutting into them diagonally and with your fingers, scoop out the insides of the tomato into a medium bowl. This does not need to be a clean, thorough job, as you want to maintain the structure of the tomato. Recap each tomato as you go. Put one heaping tablespoon of rice into the tomato mush for every tomato in the tray, plus two more. Add about a ¼ cup of olive oil and salt and pepper to taste. Salt the insides of the tomatoes. Chop the herbs and garlic finely and add to the rice mixture. Leave sit 20 min and prepare the potatoes in the meantime.

Peel and slice the potatoes in wedges and place them in a bowl. Toss with salt, pepper, and a generous amount of olive oil. Fill the tomatoes by spooning the rice in and pushing the rice down so that they are full and compact, replacing the caps on each and setting them in a large tray that will hold twice the capacity. Position the potatoes around so as to provide support to the tomatoes. Be sure to pour off any extra oil onto the potatoes. Cover with foil and place in the oven for 45 min. Remove the foil and put them back in the oven another 20-min until the rice and potatoes are cooked.

In general, we cooked over an open fire in the kitchen fireplace, but if you wanted something baked, you waited until 12:30 when the bakeries had finished their baking for the day and you took your tray of food so's to use whatever there was left of the heat from the wood burning ovens to roast or bake whatever you had managed to throw together. You see, we would have done the tomatoes that way. Most people in the city didn't have a home oven until the late 1950s, and even then it was more often than not your wood burning sort.

The only thing you could always find was pasta, bread and milk. Everything else was get-it-while-you-can. Generally, we would get a finger of oil [*1/4 cup*], a few cents worth of tomato paste, some pasta and if you could find something else, or steal it, we'd have that too. That way you got through one more day a little less hungry. The pasta was sold in bulk out of drawers. You told them what you wanted and they scooped it out. You didn't have your brand names until way later. Brand names started popping up around this time on account of all the messing around with food. They were putting anything and everything they could in to stretch foods as far as they could. Brands gave you a name you could trust for quality, so you could be sure you weren't going to be sick, or be disgusted. Poor people like me bought the broken pasta that cost less. We cooked it up in a broth made of the throw away part of vegetables: potato peels, legume pods, cabbage and cauliflower cores, broccoli stems, cardoon leaves. A lot of dishes grew out of what we *didn't* have, and a lot of things that folks think of today as garbage, we made good use of.

Minestra di buccia di Piselli - Pea pod soup

Wash emptied pea pods and bring them to a boil in enough water to cover them. Once they have started boiling, reduce the flame to low and cover. Simmer until soft. Press them through a sieve to get as much of the flavor as possible. Here are two serving suggestions for the broth:

1) *Add carrot slices or grated potato and reduce the broth. Finish with a bit of oil and grated cheese crust.*
2) *Sauté a handful of parsley or other herbs in oil or lard and then add the pea pod broth. Serve with cubes of toasted bread.*

What happened then was, in fatter times, you took one of those "make do" dishes that you used to *have to* eat because there wasn't anything else, like the Roman "pasta and potatoes", and made it into a "specialty" by adding a couple other finer ingredients. And there you have it! Tradition!

Lots of what are well known dishes, like eggplant Parmesan, I can hardly recognize now from how we made it in the old times. Our eggplant Parmesan was sweated, fried in oil, layered in a tomato basil sauce right in the same pan with the oil and given a couple gratings of Parmesan cheese. Then you finished cooking the eggplant slowly over the fire until thickened up. It was not a breaded casserole that baked in the oven oozing with cheese, also because hardly anyone had an oven. Ours was much better than the way people eat it today, and we only ate it in season. But I could say the same about my grandmother's time. Everything was stewed to mush in a cauldron, and that was pretty much it, and she probably thought her way was better. Take *ossobuco*. What is that stuff they serve in the restaurants? The names are the same, but now the recipes are heavier, more complicated or worse, "healthier". If I go to a restaurant, and I hardly ever do, I don't recognize the food. Everything is so sophisticated and elaborate even though they are all tripping over themselves to be "rustic".

There was no meat on our table while I was growing up. I make it for my family, but I hardly ever eat it. Sure, I can afford it now, but I never got used to it. When I do eat meat, I prefer the lowly parts that I had had every once in a blue moon, like nerves, organ meats, trotters, ears... I 'd rather have all those bits around the meat to the actual meat itself! Meat never really grew on me. I eat it but I don't go raving about it. I follow my instincts about cooking it, because there sure wasn't anyone in my San Lorenzo tenement fixing up a roast beef dinner! I don't mind fish, especially the fish you get in Rome. We sometimes managed to get those small fish like anchovies and sardines when I was growing up. And we made the famous Jewish fish soup with bones and scraps.

One of the culinary triumphs of Jewish cooking, and a dish with a story to tell, is fish soup. The Jewish ghetto was situated next to one of Rome's filthiest and most downtrodden areas where the open fish market was located. After the market closed for the day, the scraps and discards were piled up and Jewish women would collect them and put them to good use creating a soup that remains one of the most popular dishes in Rome.

I remember the end of the war when the Americans came. How we celebrated! The German army did not pull out until they had no other choice. We could see, literally see, the Germans on one side and the Americans on the other sweeping through our neighborhood. We had no idea of whose side we were supposed to be on, so you heard people yelling, "Run! It's the Americans," and then "Run! It's the Germans!" It was total chaos, pure insanity. That is something I remember very well. Then I remember the Americans handing out chocolate and cookies to everyone. Most of us had never had chocolate before. Wow. When we took care of them, doing their washing and ironing and things, they gave us food in exchange. Everything was so confusing then because the price controls on bread suddenly disappeared and from one moment to the next food prices soared to the stars! They passed out this temporary money so that at least we could all keep eating. Funny thing, well not so funny, is that when the Americans came there was more food, but the lira had bottomed out and so we couldn't buy anything! Before there was no food even if you had money, then there was food but no money. So for a while we used this money called the Am Lira, and that way we could get on with it while things settled. We got paid in Am Lira and were given change back in Am Lira, and that went on at least up to 1950.

The AM-lira (Allied Military Lira) was a provisional currency that was preconceived for distribution when the allies landed in Southern Italy in 1943. Its purpose was to buffer the sudden destabilization of the lira as the war drew to an end. Rampant counterfeiting quickly ensued due to unfamiliarity with the currency. The interim banknotes were used alongside regular lira notes until 1950 when the AM-lira was withdrawn from circulation.

Sometimes I say to my grandchildren, "You don't know what hunger is and I don't have the words to tell you what it is, but I'm glad you will never know what it is to be hungry like we were hungry." What am I supposed to say? That there were days when I was doubled over because there was nothing to eat, and then when there was something it was just as painful trying to get it down, because when you're not used to eating, nothing goes down well. If there was food to be had, you didn't just eat it, you devoured it, and then you paid the consequences.

A diet consisting of less than 1,200 calories per day is considered starvation for women. When it is experienced over a prolonged period, autophagy sets in and the body begins to consume itself. Increasing calorie intake suddenly can set off refeeding syndrome, wherein due to the depletion of minerals over a protracted period of time, the body is unable to process food, and the results can even be fatal.

I was determined not to suffer from hunger ever again.

Franco: Renata and I met in 1947 just after the war and married in 1955. There was a dance party at a friend of mine's house. There weren't enough girls so I asked my friend Rosa, who lived near Renata, to bring some of her girlfriends. Well, they weren't very good hoofers. Anyway, what can you do? My friend Ugo and I looked over at Renata and said, "heads or tails." And from there one thing led to another, you know? She too had an uncle that had escaped to America, but he at least had the good sense not to come back! Before we could marry I had to do two years of military service. I started my service in Rome. You can't imagine the revolting crap they fed us. It was served out of gasoline drums, like they were slopping pigs! Everything cooked beyond recognition. When I was transferred to Verona, ah, what finery! We ate off of plates, I mean *real* plates, not outta metal cups. Fresh pasta every day, wine from a bottle, a smidgen of meat every day. It was 1951 and meat and I were not so well acquainted then! On Sundays, we even got dessert! But, you want to know why the difference? I'll tell you. Because there were Americans stationed with us. They had their own cooks, and for them it was steak, steak, steak every day! But they checked out what our cook was serving up too and wanted to try what we were having. And, oh! Did they like it? You bet they did!

Renata: After the war I started learning tailoring with a well-known seamstress in Rome. I apprenticed during the day and washed dishes at night in a trattoria. I made fast progress and I had a talent for the work, so after not too long, I started working in the clothing industry. I wasn't just going to be a dressmaker, holed up stitching for someone else for the rest of my days. I wanted to know the business end of it and be my own boss. After I was married, I worked hard to save as much as I could and in short order I started up my own business making costumes. Wasn't long before my clientele were all from the top theaters and the new booming Italian film industry.

Franco: Tell her who you are! Tell her who you are!

Renata: I made costumes for the best actors of the day. Anna Magnani and Gina Lollobrigida, for example, were two of the finest actresses in Italian film history. But my *capo lavoro,* my masterpiece, was the ball gown worn by Claudia Cardinale in Visconti's *Il Gattopardo* [*The Leopard* (1963)]. I made a good living working in the entertainment business and I was the breadwinner of the family, but the work started coming in between me and my family life. They wanted me on the set at such and such an hour and that was it, no two ways about it. I saw my children less and less. After the life I had endured without my parents, how could I do that to them? If you decide to have children they come first. They did not ask to be born. I kept up the clothing end of the business, but stopped working for the entertainment industry. I didn't want my children to feel unloved and unwanted like I had felt growing up.

I don't know what can be done about food itself today. There is so much tasteless pre-cooked and packaged food they are pushing on you. Actually, there's not much else. Sure, people are buying it up, but it is like everyone having the same painting in their house. I think people are going to get tired of that and return to traditions. I really believe that there are plenty of people who are just going to up and refuse to eat that way anymore. My own grandchildren will call now and again and say, "Grandma, how is it you make such and such a dish?" They cook my dishes for their friends and would rather get together for a home cooked supper instead of going out.

Only way you're going to keep Italian traditions alive is to sit together at the table for a meal and talk. Lots of families eat together but they got the television on so's they don't have to talk to each other. Family meals have to come first. I know it doesn't work anymore for the family to come together at lunchtime like we always done in the past, so, all right, make it suppertime then. A piece of life is missing, I mean, parents aren't doing their job if sitting down together at the table once a day is not kept sacred. When things are important you make them work. I always held down a job and I *always* fixed meals for my family. I had my own business but I was up in the early morning to make lunch before I went to work, and then we would all be home at lunchtime when the kids finished school and my husband was on his break from the warehouse where he worked as a stock boy.

If young people don't keep the foodways alive, then it is over. It is the end of Italian culture because food is the center of who we are. It keeps us together as a family and as a country. If Italian food dies then there is no Italy. You can't have a tradition based on industrialized food, and more and more, that is all there is. You wouldn't catch me eating canned pasta sauce even if I was dying of hunger, *and I know what that means.*

Intermezzo

Sabato Fascista - Fascist Saturday

The fascist youth organization *Opera Nazionale Balilla* was established in 1926 as a Saturday addition to the school curriculum. "Balilla" was the nickname of the legendary Genoese boy whose David and Goliath gesture of throwing stones at the occupying Hapsburg armed forces in 1746 made him a symbol of Italian forthrightness and an example of patriotism for Italian youth.

The ONB was modeled after the British Boy Scout association founded in 1907, a separate section of which was set up in 1910 for girls, with the Brownies instituted later in 1915. The Scout philosophy, however, dates back to the ancient Greek and Roman credo of *mens sana in corpore sano,* a healthy mind in a healthy body.

> You should pray for a healthy mind in a healthy body.
> Ask for a stout heart that has no fear of death,
> and deems length of days the least of Nature's gifts,
> that can endure any kind of toil,
> that knows neither wrath nor desire and thinks
> the woes and hard labors of Hercules better than
> the loves and banquets and downy cushions of Sardanapalus.
> What I commend to you, you can give to yourself;
> for assuredly, the only road to a life of peace is virtue.
>
> *-Roman poet Juvenal, 1st century AD*

Scout groups emphasized the importance of physical education, a topic much in vogue in the 19th and early 20th century, and fostered a sense of civic duty, as well as a love for the great outdoors. Uniforms were employed to mask the differences in social status, thereby promoting equality, comradeship and single-minded purpose.

Under Catholic tutelage, the scout initiative spread throughout Italy in the first decade of the 1900s, but the Fascist regime was keenly aware that the keystone to achieving an airtight totalitarian state was to have complete control over the ideologies instilled in a child's formative years. Therefore in 1927, adherence to the ONB and attendance at Fascist Saturday became compulsory. All other youth groups were ordered to disband posthaste.

Fascist youth groups were delineated by age. For the girls these were:

- *Figlie della Lupa* – Daughters of the She-wolf, ages 6-8 (after 1936, membership was conferred at birth).
- *Piccole italiane* – Little Italian Girls, ages 8-14
- *Giovani italiane* – Young Italian Girls, ages 14-18
- *Giovani fasciste* – Young Fascist Women, ages 18-21, after which there were various fascist women's groups one could choose from such as Rural Housewives.

The Decalogue that all children learned by rote on Fascist Saturdays inculcated the following commandments:

1. Obey the Duce.
2. Hate, to your very last breath, the enemies of the Duce, that is, of the Patria.
3. Unmask traitors of the Revolution no matter how powerful they might seem.
4. Don't be afraid to be courageous.
5. Never make compromises about your fascist duties, even if it means losing your wages, your position, or your life.
6. Better to die proud and beloved than live gluttonous and despondent.

7. Despise usurpers.
8. Refuse ill begotten gains.
9. Favor war over peace, death over surrender.
10. Never give up.

Part of the day was dedicated to simplistic ideological indoctrination. The following is an excerpt from a children's reader for Fascist Saturdays:

> Mussolini, whom everyone calls "Duce", and whom you can call Papa, is a child of the people, who grew up in poverty. He is the greatest and kindest man in the world. In just ten years he has made Italy the leading nation in the world. With his March on Rome the government was removed from fearsome men and The Fascist Regime was inaugurated and will last more than a century. (Meletti, 1934)

Physical preparedness took precedence in the Saturday meets. In spite of his diminutive stature, the Duce took advantage of photo-ops to exhibit his strapping physique— here, working the fields or there, engaging in sports—making himself an example of manliness for his country's youth. Physical education for girls was considered a key factor in fulfilling the regime's population goals. The ideal fascist woman was strong and sturdy, with broad birthing hips and generous breasts. Sobriety, simplicity and submission were pinnacles of a pragmatic woman's ambitions. Frivolities like make-up and hair-dos were best left to the French.

As of June 1935, by government decree, all able citizens were expected to participate in *Sabato fascista*. A 40-hour workweek was instated allowing workplaces to close at one o'clock, leaving people free in the afternoon to participate. The government's ability to organize, fund and enforce their initiatives varied enormously from one area to another. Some towns never had any activities organized locally, while in others, residents found the fascist heavies interrogating them if they or their children had missed even a single rally.

The new decree put a cramp in the style of many parents, for whom Fascist Saturday had become *sabato dell'amore*, with no worries about the kids barging in. After all, weren't they still carrying out their duty to the regime by attempting to procreate, sanctioned, furthermore, by Pious XI's 1930 papal encyclical *Casti connubii* (Chaste Wedlock), wherein reproduction was to be the sole purpose of such undertakings?

Betta

Born 1922 – Bologna

Elizabetta was born into a noble family. Her father was a count and her mother a marquise. She herself is a countess, elegant and cultured, but not inaccessible. She was able to move seamlessly from the Ventennio to present without noticing significant culinary changes, because with the exception of a few errands during the war, Betta herself had never engaged directly in food procurement or preparation, neither did she experience the phenomenal economic change that transformed the eating habits of a nation. In the decades following the war, much of what had been traditional fare on the tables of the aristocracy was plated up in trattorias as standard Italian cooking, particularly dishes from the hearty Bolognese cuisine like tortellini and lasagna. Therefore, from Betta's perspective, Italian gastronomy has remained relatively static. I met up with her in Bologna where she has a room in a convent that she calls her prison cell. Although she is agile and lucid, she wasn't quite sure how long she had been lodging with the sisters, whether it had been weeks or months. She would like to live in her own home, but has been unable to find a suitable caretaker. As she has dismissed everyone her family has found for her, they now insist she stay at the convent where she can receive proper care.

I am grateful because I had always prayed the good Lord to be of sound mind when I got old. I have some friends who are not nearly as old as I am who are just not right in the head anymore. My saving grace is that I can still read; otherwise I really don't know where I'd be. Television today has become simply obscene. There's rarely anything interesting on these days that is worth the bother of turning the thing on.

I was born here in Bologna. You might find it strange, but we never owned our own house in Bologna because we are a noble family of Modena, and that is where our family palace was. I had a great aunt, married to my grandmother's brother, who was a Russian princess. She lived in the palace in Modena with one of my father's sisters. My father chose to live in Bologna when he got married because my mother was a marquise of Bolognese descent. My parents met at a party held by one of my mother's aunts who was fabulously wealthy and didn't have children, so she very much liked to have parties to bring the young people of aristocratic families together. She was an incorrigible matchmaker! After they had made each other's acquaintance, my aunt invited my mother to accompany her to Venice because she knew that my father's family was sojourning in Venice. She liked indulging in caprices like that. So, that is how their love blossomed, and after they were married they came to live in Bologna.

My maternal grandmother had had eight children, and my father's parents died when he was young. My grandmother, my mother's mother, lived alone, well, with a household of servants, of course, but what I mean is none of her children went to live with her when they married. When I was two, we went to live in a rented villa in Via Masaccio in Florence because my father, like many nobles, was in the military and he was stationed there for a time, but by the time I started school we had moved to Bologna. My father wanted to stay on in Florence, but my mother had nagged him to the point that he gave in, and we came back here because she wanted to be in her hometown with her family and friends and all of the things that were familiar to her.

So, once we had moved to Bologna we went to live in Via Belle Arte 8, at one of the homes of mother's childhood friend Giovannina Bentivoglio, one of the last descendants of an immensely important Bolognese family. The villa is still standing. I lived there until I was an adult, for some time after the war. We continued on as renters because my father was utterly obsessed with the idea that one day we were going to go back to take up our proper place in our palace in Modena. Families at that time were numerous and everything went to the males. Women were given a dowry, but the important properties were given to the men. My mother was given some land as her dowry, but my father didn't want to have to look after an estate so they sold it. It was a horrific error in retrospect because then they ended up without any property at all. In the end, the house in Modena was divided amongst my father, his brother and his sister, much to my father's chagrin. My father tried to buy them out but he didn't have enough money because they asked a ludicrously high price. The palace in Modena has since been turned into a hotel. Life passes and sometimes it stabs us in the back or between the eyes; I don't know which. I drove by our palace after it had become a hotel. I was crushed and said, "Let's get out of here, right now!" I just couldn't look at it. I was simply aghast.

Our house in Bologna had electric lighting in all of the rooms, two full bathrooms and a third one for the servants. For hot water, there was a tall copper tank that was heated by a small fire at the base of it. It was next to the bathtub and when the water was hot it was emptied out into the tub. The house had radiators that were heated centrally by a charcoal-burning furnace in the basement. I remember our man used to go down and stoke the fire of the furnace every now and again. As soon as it was possible, we also got a telephone. In the kitchen we had a refrigerator, as I recall, not too different from the ones we have today. I mean, it wasn't made of wood or anything. The "icebox" idea was something they used in the country. I remember in the country house there was one of those large open hearths like they had in the olden days with the copper pot that hung over the fire, those antique things that they used to cook in, like polenta and such, but we had a gas stove at my house. Goodness! No! We certainly didn't cook in a fireplace! But we loved going to my grandmother's manor in the country. It was an enormous house with an immense park filled with fruit trees. It has remained in the family to this day, through the male lineage that is.

I had a twin brother, but we went to different schools. He left me behind more than thirty years ago, may he rest in peace. I went to the St. Vincent de Paul Boarding School for Girls here in Bologna but I wasn't a boarder because we lived right here in town. It was an exclusive school where aristocratic and wealthier families sent their daughters for proper scholastic preparation. It was a comprehensive school; that is, it started with nursery school and one attended straight through to the last year of high school, so you could enroll as a child and stay until you were a debutant. The high school at St.Vincent's was magisterial because it was an all girls' school and teaching was considered the appropriate path for us.

> *The "magisterial" high school was essentially a teacher training high school. After elementary school there were three years of middle school (Magistero Inferiore) and four years of high school (Magistero Superiore), after which one was qualified to be a schoolteacher.*

Although it was by no means encouraged, girls were allowed by law to go to the classical or scientific high schools, though not many did. If you wanted to go on to college you had to have graduated from one of those schools. The magisterial was not college preparatory unless you wanted to major in pedagogy, which I had no interest in. I wanted to study medicine. So, although I had finished the magisterial school, after the war I started in right away preparing for the scientific high school equivalency test with a private teacher. But sadly, I never did go to university because I was already engaged to be married by then, and my husband said, "Once you're a married woman you'll have more than enough to occupy your time just looking after the family. Your ambitions need go no further." I will never forget that. The real reason he didn't want me to go was because he was a bit old school and didn't want his wife to have a profession. He needed to be the man. But I had received a good education because the teachers at my school were not all nuns; most of them were laical and many of them men, and all very good teachers. Nuns were allowed to teach in private schools even if they weren't qualified and that brought down the reputation of a school.

Every morning I was awakened by a servant, dressed and accompanied to breakfast. I had my breakfast alone because my mother was not so keen on getting up at that hour. The serving girl brought me *caffè latte* with fresh bread, butter and jam. There was always real coffee at our house, but until I was a little older mine was *caffè d'orzo* and milk, made with toasted barley. I breakfasted in the company of my Swiss *istruttrice*. An *istruttrice* is someone who comes from a good background, and is well educated and cultured, but whose family has perhaps fallen on difficult times. These families sought to place their daughters in homes that were suitable to their social station.

Marie had studied in Geneva and had received an optimal education. We found her because my father had asked my French teacher at school if she knew of anyone looking for a situation. The teacher wrote to the school in Geneva and they proposed Marie. She lived at our house as my tutor and companion, and we spoke only French together. She didn't know a word of Italian when she first came to Italy! My father was well aware that language lessons at school were not up to snuff and he wanted me to be proficient in French because my parents adored France and French culture, and we sojourned there quite frequently. It simply wouldn't do to have me speaking clumsy school French. France was considered the center of culture at the time and accomplished young women needed to be fluent in French. Indeed, I am bilingual to this day and still do a good deal of my reading *en français.*

The *istruttrice* took me to school and then picked me up in the afternoon. At school when we entered the classroom, we were taught to do the Roman salute to the portraits of Mussolini and the king, but of course, what do you expect? The girls at my school didn't do Fascist Saturday, all of that marching around nonsense, singing songs and what have you, but we did have to meet once a month wearing our fascist uniforms, dreadful things that they were, to prepare for the gymnastics performance held at the end of every school year. Participation in that was mandatory. At some schools they used the fascist uniform as the school uniform, but not in my school, I guess because it was a private Catholic school. Nonetheless, we felt the presence of fascism everywhere in everything. Buildings all over Bologna were covered in fascist slogans, and at other schools the doctrine was strongly emphasized in the curriculum. But at our school it wasn't placed at the forefront of the teaching. Of course, we did not escape it entirely, but we weren't subjected to a total brainwashing.

In the afternoon, I went home for lunch and, well, more or less, I guess we ate the same things everyone else did. The first course was a soup or pasta. There was all manner of pasta, all shapes and sizes, with and without egg, everything, just everything, because as you know, the important part of the dish was our famous Bolognese meat sauce. Absolutely everyone here and abroad knows the *sugo alla bolognese*. We in Bologna have the finest culinary tradition in Italy. We also had lasagna and all of the other kinds of baked pasta that Bologna is famous for, and of course, tortellini too. For the second course, there was always a meat dish; our cook was very good with meats, but nothing very fancy, veal cutlets, roast lamb, pork braised in milk, nothing elaborate, times being what they were. Then of course there were a couple of vegetable side dishes like buttered asparagus with lemon or eggplant Parmigiano, salads with balsamic vinegar... Our region of Emilia Romagna had the best of everything, everything! At the end of the meal we always had fruit, but again, prepared simply, cut up fresh with whipped cream, or stewed in sweet wine, something like that. But desserts we had only on Sunday or when there was company. Ours was not a family to indulge in ostentatious display.

Naturally, if there were guests everything was more elaborate. The heirloom silver was brought out and polished, the table set with fine china and cut crystal glassware, and many more courses were served. But truth be told, our family Sundays were not huge feasting days because on that day the servants were off duty, so food was prepared in advance and left for us in the kitchen, and we did our best to fend for ourselves. My mother, who wouldn't have been able to fry an egg to save her life, was kind to the servants and always had the cook prepare quick, simple dishes on Sunday morning so that she could be on her way to enjoy her free day.

We had one cook, a serving girl and a governess who looked after the house and the staff. My father was a career army officer, so he required his own manservant, a personal attendant to see to his needs. The manservant attended my father when he was home from his military assignments. He also took care of the heavy work in the house and acted as a butler on occasion, answering the door, presenting guests and so on and so forth. So you see, we weren't one of those families

with a house full of servants. We managed with the minimum necessary to keep the household running. Goodness! My father didn't even
have a car until I was ten, in 1932! Up till then, we travelled by horse-
drawn coach, or for longer trips, by train.

By the time of my father's death in 1944, he had been promoted to
General. Up until fifteen days before he died, he had been stationed
in Istria. It used to be part of Italy, but is now Croatia. He had managed
a narrow escape from Istria and miraculously made it home, just in
time to assist in our exodus to the countryside estate. With the war on
in full force, everything had to be purchased with a ration card. Well-
to-do families could forego that and find most everything on the black
market, but at monstrously inflated prices. That's one reason why we
wanted to retreat to the villa in the country, so that we'd be in direct
contact with food sources.

My grandmother employed many peasant families and they had all
sorts of things! It was scandalous to see how they hoarded all of that
food while the people in the city were starving! I remember before we
left town, going here and there on my bike to get food, and one time
I had to go so far just to get a bag of sugar, why, I nearly lost my way!
All of our servants, everyone's servants, had already fled back to their
homes in the country because they were all country folks, of course.
That's another reason we couldn't stay in the city; we had no idea how
to cook anything! Some of my grandmother's servants stayed on at the
country villa and they were on hand to prepare our food.

Bologna was in total chaos. The Second World War was fought
largely within cities, so regardless of the servants, we had no choice but
to flee to safety from our city home in Bologna to my grandmother's
country villa. You see, the Germans had invaded the south of Italy and
were working their way north so we thought that the best idea was
to hide out in the country, but when they caught sight of our splendid villa they moved right in and set up shop, leaving our family with
just three rooms and a bathroom to ourselves. So, while the villa itself was full to the brim with officers, the regulars set up tents in the
extensive parkland that was part of my grandmother's manor. But I
have to admit in all honesty that they were quite civil, perhaps because
they understood that they were not dealing with riff-raff. Although the

Germans gutted many homes on their sweep though Italy, oft times just for sport, destroying any food and property that they couldn't take with them, they stole nothing from us, and there were certainly many choice items they could have toted away with them.

At a certain point, when Italy had just changed sides in the war, both the Germans and the Americans were bombing us. Actually, the Americans arrived a bit later but the *partigiani*, ah, yes, the *partigiani*, had already organized and were indiscriminately killing whomsoever they suspected of collaborating with the Germans.

> *Emilia-Romagna has a long tradition as a leftist region and was fertile ground for the growth of a notable body of Italian resistance fighters who called themselves the Partisans or "Partigiani." Although their ideological bases varied in the extreme from monarchists to Catholics, to anarchists, to socialists, to republicans, their aversion to the fascist regime was sufficiently overriding to allay their mutual hostilities and unite them in a common goal. While they were little more than a loose network of gangs, bands and brigades, their formidable militancy and determination set the stage for a quasi-civil war within the Second World War. Towards the end, they took it upon themselves to execute Mussolini, after which Partisan activist and anti-fascist journalist Feruccio Parri became Prime Minister for a brief interregnum.*

There was a doctor we knew who was shot point blank on the street for alleged affiliation with the Germans. The carnage seemed so haphazard that it was difficult to distinguish who was killing whom and why. In a situation like that, well, you can understand that everyone was afraid of everyone else. There were even areas where groups of people were massacred wholesale and the gunmen would say, "Ah, you could just tell that they were siding with this or that other faction." But now that they are dead, who's to say? The mistake people make today is thinking that the *partigiani* saved us. When they surfaced, we too thought they were a force for good but no, they made everything worse. They positioned themselves in the hills and just fired shots at random. They had no training or central organization. Because of them, the Germans came down even harder on us and it was an out and out bloodbath. Plenty of the dead were Italians, slain at the hand of hair-trigger *partigiani*.

Every evening there was a reconnaissance plane everyone called "Pippo" that flew overhead.

> *"Pippo" is the name given to the Disney character "Goofy" in Italian dubbed cartoons. These flights were part of the Allied powers' "Operation Night Intruder." They flew at high altitude using the newly developed radar system to pinpoint targets. Flights began routinely in 1943 and continued for the duration of the war in a dual effort to bully the Italian populace into feeling abandoned by their own military and to cajole them into thinking the Allies were capable of looking after their interests. The fact that they flew at night heightened the sense of anxiety and drama, stoking the legend that waxed poetic around the mysterious "Pippo". In the popular mind, he was a solitary bomber, a dark knight flying the nocturnal skies over the shadowy peninsula. Whether seen as an arch villain or a superhero, he was someone to be reckoned with. The perverse irony is that in spite of his menacing aura and the lethal reality of his assignment, the name "Pippo" has an affectionate ring to the Italian ear. An inestimable number of Italian dogs go by that name.*

The Allies knew full well that our property was overrun with Germans. We had set up a refuge in the cellar of the villa, and when the bombing began, I would call to my father, "Papa! Come down with us!" But you know how men are. He was used to being the commander and calling the shots. One fateful night I called again and again, but he paid no heed. The end of that story is that a bomb came directly down on the villa and he was killed on May 19, 1944. After years at war, he gets killed at home. People who witnessed that part of the war, when the Germans came through and the Allies were in position, always said that after such ghastly horror they could not imagine that there would ever be another war. They could hardly believe it was happening, let alone imagine that anything so terrible could ever be repeated.

My mother, who had lived through the Great War of '15-'18, said that they had fretted endlessly about the young men sent to the front, but this was a war that was lived in the city, by everyone. It was more dangerous to be in the city than at the front! During the '15-'18 war, most people had not witnessed the use of planes. It was not a part of their daily lives. Airplanes themselves were a very new concept for us even in the 40s, those flying machines. Who had ever been on a plane?! And here there were planes flying overhead every day raining bombs on us from above. It was really too much to conceive of all at once. I mean, we hadn't even gotten used to the idea of air travel yet and here there were explosives cascading down on us from the sky! What I want to say is that this is how war is now, and everyone has become accustomed to the concept. Planes fly above targets and drop bombs, fine, but it was *beyond belief* then. It was terror beyond terror. What's worse is that Bologna had been declared a *città aperta*, an Open City, meaning that it was a military-free zone where people were supposed to be safe.

The declaration of "Open City" often comes when a war is arriving at its conclusion in an effort to safeguard cities of particular historical and/or cultural importance, or because of a markedly high concentration of civilians. Owing to the tenacity of German resistance, the Allied forces largely ignored Open City declarations.

But bombs and bullets showered down on marketplaces, on homes and on public buildings. Bologna was not very well known abroad, not like Rome or Venice, but it is one of Italy's most important centers of art and architecture. Many precious objects were hidden away and saved, but so many more buildings, churches, and artworks were destroyed. So much beauty lost to the hideousness of war.

Mussolini. Yes. At the beginning of his reign he had done good things for the country. For example, the "Battle for Wheat", just to name a famous one, and school reform. He made school obligatory for everyone, even girls. He placed a good deal of importance on education. But his ruin, his ruin was his friendship with Hitler. When Mussolini and Hitler first met, Hitler said, "I feel a deep friendship," while Mussolini was supposed to have said, "I don't like really him." Indeed, my mother always said, "Hitler is a monster."

More or less, Mussolini seemed like an intelligent man, and you can see that at the time, he hoped that the friendship with Hitler would have a positive effect on Italy. He did it for the betterment of Italy, but, you see, Hitler was clever and crafty because he already knew that he was going to go to war with France and England, so he knew well in advance that having Italy as an ally was going to be a feather in his cap. And, one has to confess that after the invasion of Ethiopia and the threat of sanctions, we were no longer able to stand on our own. The other European countries had become hostile to us and we had no one to lean on but Germany.

> *In 1935, Italy decided to act on its imperialistic manifest destiny to ex-pand its colonies in North Africa, and invaded Ethiopia. Approximately 650,000 troops were dispatched against the local army of 300,000 men. Word of international sanctions rippled down the peninsula, providing a much-needed unifying cause within Italy: tightening the belt was thenceforth a question of national pride. Propaganda implored housewives to "buy Italian" as the country moved toward stringent self-sufficiency.*

But Hitler was indeed a monster and he was only out for his own per-sonal ambitions. It's true, our Duce seemed like a well-intentioned man at the beginning, but as my mother said, his ruin was joining forces with Hitler. Even when he invaded Ethiopia, we were behind him. The colonies in North Africa were supposed to save Italy, and we all fervently prayed for it to be so. Then we would become a great nation again and usher in, as they said, a New Roman Era. At that point the words on everyone's lips were, "Thank goodness we've got a strong leader we can count on like Mussolini. He has our best welfare in mind." Italy simply didn't have enough resources to be self-suffi-cient. The "Battle for Wheat" was a noble effort, but it didn't work. We needed those colonies.

But, mind you, the upper classes, who were often those in offi-ciating positions in the army and government, were not necessarily Mussolini enthusiasts. We went along with the monarchy, according to tradition. Many of the nobility were astonished that the King of Savoy was so closely tied to the fascists, but it was lived moment by moment. Even Prince Humbert got fed up and left Italy for a while.

The Savoy-Carignano branch ruled united Italy from 1861 to the end of WWII, that is, until they were overthrown by a constitutional referendum proclaiming the Republic of Italy. The historic region of Savoy occupied parts of both Italy and France. In a let-them-eat-cake sort of uprising at the turn of the century over the price of bread, the reigning king Humbert I gave the command to open fire on a crowd of mostly women and elderly people, later decorating his general with a medal to commend him for the slaughter. This thoroughly and irrevocably marred public opinion of the House of Savoy.

The king had the power to unseat Mussolini, but turned a blind eye to one abuse after another, even after the pretense of democracy had been dropped. Theirs was a mutually fruitful relationship. Fascist colonial pursuits resulted in King Victor Emmanuel being crowned King of Ethiopia and later of Albania.

The association of the House of Savoy with Mussolini had destroyed any hope of maintaining an Italian monarchy after WWII. A last ditch attempt was made to save the family when Victor Emmanuel abdicated the throne to his son Humbert, but by then it was too late. The 1946 constitution referendum, won by a mere 54% of the vote, included a passage that forbade male descendants of the House of Savoy from entering Italy. Victor Emmanuel fled to Egypt, where he died in exile, and Humbert went into exile in Portugal where he died in 1983. In 2002, a provision was passed allowing the last claimant to the throne to return to Italy on the condition that he renounce all entitlements to kingship, which he did. He and his cousin are respectively the Prince of Naples and the Duke of Savoy. Upon return to Italy the family sought damages for their time in exile, requesting the restitution of property that was once part of their patrimony. But the constitution foresaw this event and states clearly that the Savoy family, upon exile, would be unalterably stripped of their wealth and holdings.

There was no agreement across the board. Some aristocratic families were in favor, others weren't. But really, the change in power had little effect on the noble families. We were unscathed by the dictatorship. In 1940 when I had my coming-into-society party, certainly, there was talk of war, and people went on about "that Hitler person," but our affairs and lifestyle glided along much as they had always done. We never dreamed of what was to come. I think even Mussolini realized, well certainly he must have done, that he had made a dire and grave mistake. But Mussolini had duped us. He was two-faced. First he was with this one and then with the other. Later, when the *partigiani* were about to kill him, he said, "Hey! Are you going to kill me just like that?!" Because they shoved him up against the wall and shot him quite unceremoniously. They had already shot his lover, Clara Petacci, in the car. In his town, Predappio, there is a monument dedicated to him. Rather distasteful, I'd say.

I had a very sheltered life. My parents didn't let me go about too much with other girls. I was naturally bookish. I liked books and studying and never paid too much attention to fashion. Naturally, I liked nice things but I was never the sort who had to have the latest shoes or handbag. Anyway, I had little opportunity to meet boys. I met my husband because he was my best girlfriend's boyfriend. I noticed that he always gave me too much attention, always saying to my friend Clara, "You should do this or that the way Betta does." Really, it became annoying. He did it too often.

Now, this friend was two years younger than I, and it's true that she had a somewhat lackadaisical character, but he always used me as an example to her and I thought she would start to dislike me because of it. That's how I understood that he had a certain, oh, I don't know, uh, let's say *interest* in me, yes, that's it. Anyway, Clara fell ill suddenly and was ill for quite some time. I went to see her every day, but medicine wasn't a very well developed science then, and they didn't know what was wrong with her. It must have been some sort of leukemia or something like that. So in the end, I saw *him* every day too. After a month, she died, and he began calling me, "Say, you know, I'd like to talk to you." This and that and what have you, you know, those excuses one invents. He wasn't from a wealthy family, though. His father was employed at the state railway and his mother was a teacher. So they were a normal middle class family, or not even that. We continued to see each other at Clara's house because she had a brother and sister and we would all get together, with them and other friends, in their beautiful garden. Then one fine day, he declared himself. What I mean is, he sort of let me know his intentions. One fine day he said, "If it would be alright with you, I'd marry you."

We were married in 1948, when I was already 26 years old. It was after the war, when my preparation to go to university was already underway and he put a stop to it. We had known each other for years by then. I had other suitors, one that my father had already earmarked for me from an aristocratic family. I've always said, "If my father had still been in this world he would never have permitted me to marry out of our class." Not only that, but I never would have dared even to dream of mentioning it to him. My husband was not from our circles. But he found the courage to go to my mother to ask her for my hand. She was a widow then and she saw that he seemed genuinely fond of me. And he really did love me. There was a time when I was gravely ill and a friend of his said, "What will happen to you if Betta dies?" and he answered, "Ah, if she dies, I will die the very next day."

We were married in our local church and the reception was held at home, as they all were in those days. The tradition back then was to have a large reception at the house where everyone mingled, with an assortment of hors d'oeuvres on a table and champagne. But after the wedding itself, there was a sit-down meal, mostly with members of the immediate family. His relatives come mainly from Piedmont and they could hardly believe that anyone would get married in September. "In September?! During the grape harvest!?" So, I didn't meet them until later.

He became a doctor of internal medicine, set up a family practice, and we lived a good life. He didn't want me to work, but I did have my interests outside the home, like the theater. I went to the theater as often as possible. Then, we went to the seaside every summer, particularly Forte dei Marmi. We travelled a good deal in France as well. I know France better than I do Italy! His father had bought a small villa many years previously where we went to live, and where we had a cook and a maid. They were country people, like most domestic help. They had to be taught certain things about keeping house, but the care of the silver I saw to myself; the help was not to be trusted with the silver. But that aside, all went well.

After his father died, my mother-in-law moved in with us and the worst part of my life began. She was terribly jealous. They say that the worst cases are when a widow has an only son. She was abominable, but when she was on her deathbed, after I had taken care of her, she said, "I beg your forgiveness for what I made you suffer." I said, "Oh, no, what are you saying?" and she said, "No, no. I know full well what I did." She recognized it and so we were both at peace. Soon I'll be going to join them in the family tomb. My husband and son are already there in Asti. My husband died either in 2002 or 2004; I can't remember. I lost a son just five years ago. It is the worst thing that can happen to a mother.

I think that where food is concerned, very little has changed in Bologna. The cuisine here has overall remained the same as it was 80 years ago. I can't say that I miss anything in particular because it is all the same as before. But I've never been much for the table. Men can't live without their pasta course, but if I don't have pasta for a couple days, I am not going to fall to pieces. I'd say our most important dish is lasagna. It was always served at holidays, and accompanied special days, special events. Tortellini too. We had always had meat every day, but on holidays, the dishes were quite extravagant. And of course, like everyone, we had lamb at Easter. As my husband was a doctor, we always had a house full of holiday cakes sent from his patients and often Emilian specialty liquor that the country people made, called Nocino:

Nocino: Digestive Liquor made from unripe green walnuts
The nuts must be picked at dawn on June 24, St James the Baptist feast day.
29 walnuts cut in quarters with the green peel still attached
1 liter of 95% proof spirit alcohol
599 g sugar
1 liter water
3 cloves
3 cm cinnamon stick
1 star anise
zest of one lemon

Put all of the ingredients except the water and sugar in a bottle for 40 days, shaking it now and again. Filter though a piece of muslin. Make syrup with the sugar and water by boiling it until it thickens. Add it to the filtered ingredients. Put all into a bottle and cork or cap it.

Do not consume until two winter solstices have passed.

Note: *Superstition dictates that the ingredients must be odd numbers. The 40 days refers to the number of days in Lent and other Old Testament events.*

This comes from the tradition of paying in kind for visits and treatment, as most people did not used to have cash to pay for a doctor's services. It was also a way of greasing the wheels just in case one should need the doctor in future. They say it is also connected with the idea of making a sacrifice to the gods as a harbinger of good health.

Many people are amazed to hear that I am as old as I am. I've always looked younger than my age. Until recently I never really stopped to think about aging. Time has passed so quickly. Now that I am alone, I've begun thinking about it, whereas before, with so many things to do and the family and so forth, getting old just didn't cross my mind. Now I find myself thinking about how much time I might have left and those sorts of things. I've had these thoughts since I have been put in this place with the nuns, but you know, I can't even remember how long I've been here. I couldn't say if it has been months or weeks. I'll have to ask my daughter. I want to go home to my own house. I feel as though I am in a prison here.

Intermezzo

Contadini e padroni – Peasants and Overlords

R igid systems of dependence, in which human resources were a disposable commodity, characterized the agrarian landscape from the far north to deep south. In 1930, large estate owners made up .005% of Italy's landowners, but possessed 47% of the total landmass, with an average of 565 hectares per property. To the south were the *latifondi,* immense landholdings, many dating back to Ancient Rome and consolidated in the Middle Ages. They were manned by throngs of farmhands, who practiced extensive farming: a single crop, predominantly wheat, produced for the landowner's profit. The overwhelming glut of available manual labor meant there was little impetus to upgrade antiquated agricultural practices. For the most part, the work was carried out not only without benefit of machinery, but even without beasts of burden. Minimum financial input for maximum gain. The laborers lived clumped together in agro-towns, clusters of houses aggregated near the fields, frequently rented out by the same wealthy nobleman or ecclesiastical institution that employed them. These absentee proprietors were uninterested in utilizing the land to its fullest, and often times left vast stretches of arable land untilled instead of going to the bother of leasing them to contadini, thus exacerbating the destitution of the southern regions and widening the abyss between social classes.

Fascist reclamation projects managed, in part, to chip away at the stranglehold of powerful overlords and encourage the creation of small family owned farmsteads. After World War II, the government dismantled many of the *latifondi*, but the plots were so miniscule that it was impossible to turn a profit in the broader context of modern farming. Lack of social assistance to help insolvent farmers get their farms up and running forced families to abandon the south and try their luck in the industrial north, whose flourishing factories promised an end to the backbreaking fatigue and unremitting hunger of the countryside.

The great agricultural landholdings of the north were set up as comprehensive farmstead complexes called *cascine,* including animal stalls, haylofts, dairy works, storage rooms, and lodgings. Some *cascine* accommodated large numbers of contracted farmhands and their families, each crowded into their room allotment. Large landowners of the north tended to have a more enterprising and capitalistic bent, sometimes directly overseeing the management of their estate and workforce.

Sharecropping, *mezzadria,* was the dominant agrarian system in central Italy, though it did exist to a lesser extent in both the north and south. In theory, sharecroppers lived on the land of an overlord, whose property was divided up into a patchwork of farms called *podere.* The head of the *contadino* household, the *capoccia,* supplied the workforce, consisting of his own and perhaps another family, while the padrone supplied the land, house, and farm implements. At the end of the growing season, the harvest was to be split up 50/50. Theoretically, this arrangement had an air of fairness about it; in actuality, however, it fell somewhat short of its utopic potential. The fascists championed the sharecropping system as one that leveled out class differences: two equal partners engaged in a stalwart pact. In practice, it merely reinforced the feudal roots from whence it came, dragging the concept of serf and lord from the Middle Ages into the modern age.

Just as the padrone was absolute ruler over his estate, the capoccia, was the absolute ruler over those residing under his roof. He oversaw the distribution of work, had the final word over family matters, and held the purse strings for each member of his podere. The female counterpart was the *massaia,* a domineering figure who managed the women and children's duties with a firm hand. Each sharecropper family lived isolated in a farmhouse on their plot of land in a rural micro-world, with limited outside contact. Schooling was rigorously discouraged as it empowered the contadino beyond the bounds of his station, enabling him to express educated opinions or worse, carry out accurate calculations. And it is here that the pastoral portrait runs amuck.

Large landowning padrone often presided over their affairs in absentia, delegating the practical responsibility of managing the estate to an overseer, a *fattore*, the most fearsome character on the agricultural landscape. He did the dirty work of settling accounts with the capoccia, systematically cheating him at the close of each harvest. Year after year, in an endless cycle, the contadino amassed a debt that kept him impoverished and shackled to the land. The fattore, notoriously duplicitous, skimmed the cream off the top from both the contadino and the padrone. At the end of the war, when the sharecropping system fell apart, it was the wily fattore who most often emerged from the ruins economically unscathed. The Italian sharecropping system was illegalized in 1964, although the practice continued covertly. In 1982, further measures had to be taken to suppress the scheme of abuse by requiring that farmers living under sharecropping conditions be given formal rental contracts, thereby offering standards of protection offered nationally to renters.

Landless wage earning field hands or *braccianti*, of various descriptions from fully-contracted to under-the-table day laborers, made up the bulk of the agricultural workforce throughout Italy. They were the bottom rung of the ladder, living a hand-to-mouth existence. Although there were laws regulating their pay and hours, landowners took advantage of the economic crisis of the early 1930s to lower the established wage for farmhands, in some cases substituting it wholly or in part with food. This placed the workers in a position of having to sell the food in order to obtain cash, or trade it for larger quantities of lower quality food, depending on the number of mouths to feed at home. Given the cyclical nature of agriculture, landowners were permitted by law to overstep the law that established the number of hours farmhands could be expected to put in per day. During the harvest, a workday could drag out to fourteen hours. These extra hours supposedly balanced the low periods, though employers were not required to keep a running tally. To make up for shortcomings, women took to working their husband's contracted hours while the husbands hired out to another farm. The fascist regime paid lip service to eliminating the slave labor forces of landless *braccianti*, dangling the carrot of landownership, knowing full well that they were the key players in achieving the regime's goal of self-sufficiency. Without the multitudes who toiled for low or even no wages, the dream of a New Rome would remain just that.

The great aspiration of both sharecroppers and farmhands was to own their own small plot of land, in effect, to become self-sufficient homesteaders. Of Italy's landowners, 49% possessed plots that were smaller than five hectares, amounting to only 11% of the total land mass. According to a law dating back to Roman times, land was partitioned and repartitioned amongst the male heirs to the point that the acreage gradually became meaningless as subsistence farms, forcing many to sell up. Economic crises and the war saw the ruin of many existing homesteaders and made the hope of becoming a landowner a pipe dream. While the state pursued self-sufficiency as its own ideal, the self-sufficient farm was counter-productive to their goals. Various taxes were created for smallholders, and they were required to contribute a share of their wheat to the state, putting them in the curious position of having to buy back some of that very same wheat in order to get through to the next harvest.

While fewer people died of starvation during the ventennio in comparison to the previous period, protracted under-nutrition was rampant. To keep the influx of foodstuffs flowing into urban areas, the regime worked shrewdly and intently on fabricating a myth that the peasants could believe, featuring them as heroic protagonists of a grandiose plan. Their desire to buy into the myth and play their part in the grander scheme of things cajoled them into willful self-abnegation: earning less, eating less, and working harder. Peasant women's groups like the Rural Housewives (inevitably run by upper and middleclass women), whose goal was to discourage the rural-urban shift, boasted an astounding three million members at the fall of fascism. For those who could not be lulled into collective suspended disbelief, laws were instated prohibiting movement from country to town, thereby establishing a schism between legal and illegal residents in urban centers.

AGRICULTURAL
LADDER

Aida

Born 1919 – Camporeggiano

While the exotic name Aida evokes the elegant ambient of lyrical opera, it is perhaps more appropriate in this case to recall that the heroine in Verdi's eponymous work was a slave girl. Signora Aida had grown up as a sharecropper, or mezzadra. *She was not "freed" until the 1960s, when political and economic conditions allowed families like hers to break the bonds of servitude. For our interview she sat next to a blazing fire wrapped in copious woolen clothes and covered with a blanket, in spite of the sweltering heat. I had a distinct feeling she was wary of me at first, sizing me up, but then a sense of urgency to tell her story, to have it down for the record, took over and we entered into symbiosis. Although I live in Umbria and am familiar with the various accents and expressions of the region, Aida's speech was so deeply mired in the country speak of Gubbio (Umbria) that it posed a considerable challenge to me. Fortunately, some of her family members were on hand to help me through the rough spots. In order to replicate the texture of that experience, I have attempted to situate her manner of speaking in an analogous stratum of American English.*

My papa was a sharecropper. We was a tenant farm family. I's the youngest of six. That'd be four brothers and a sister. We was all of us close in age, come out one right after th'other.

Our padrone wasn't such a bad sort, if you line him up with some of them other fellas. Mean and crafty bunch they were. No, our padrone he weren't one of them high mighty sorts. Only had four other families working under him 'sides us. All of us in different houses, though, each working our own separate plot of his land. So, see, our padrone wasn't nothin' like them big powerful overlords, like barons and what have you. Didn't hardly never come round, but we knew who he was. Him and his family lived some ways away in a big ol' manor house. The overseer, now, he was a right fearsome character, and that's bein' kindly. The watchman, his guard dog, well, them two lived on the manor farm near the padrone.

When you's a sharecropper, you live in the house on the padrone's land, but ain't nothin' yours. Everything was his, the house, the land… but the tools we had to pay half fer 'cause it was us used 'em and if he'd just give 'em to us, well, he's afraid we might not be so careful as we shoulda been 'bout 'em. Instead, if we broke 'em or wore 'em out too fast, we had already paid our part and didn't nobody owe nothing for it. You follow me here? I ain't talking 'bout machines, now. Weren't no machines on our farm. Every last thing done by hand. Hoeing, sowing, planting, picking, the lot of it. We planted wheat. That's what the Duce wanted. But we had millet and barley too. We had to grow everything we needed, and there's a lotta mouths in my family, so near wore us to the bone jus' getting by. This is a terrible story. It is a terrible story that folks don't know. I want to be the one who finally tells this story.

You see, with sharecroppin', half your yield went to the padrone, or so they said. Ain't never really worked out that way though. We was always on the losin' end of that stick come time to settle up. We kept a few animals too. Had a sow and took in some money from her litters, 'course the padrone always came sniffin' round for his share. Weren't possible to raise too many beasts on account of them havin' to eat too. They wasn't gonna just grow up outta the dirt like an onion, that's for sure! We give the chickens the hulls and bran left after threshing the wheat, but weren't much eatin' there, so weren't never more than a few bites on them scrawny little buzzards. What I'm sayin' is, you ain't raisin' no fine plump birds on that there feed. There was already so little for us, we could only toss 'em what we couldn't get down ourselves.

Weren't a scrap of it went to waste when we slaughtered a chicken though. Even used the head.

Collo di pollo ripieno – Stuffed chicken neck
1 chicken neck, head attached
vegetable scraps for broth (or prepared broth)
chicken offal - liver, gizzards, and/or heart
½ onion chopped
1 egg
1 slice old white bread soaked in water and squeezed dry
1 clove garlic, chopped
1 tbsp chopped parsley
salt, pepper, nutmeg

Take a chicken neck cut off close to the body, head intact. Pull the skin up to the head and cut the neck bones off. Boil the neck with whatever vegetable scraps you might have that are good for broth, celery, onion and the like. Remove the neck and pick off what meat there is. Chop it up fine with the onion and chicken offal and sauté it lightly in a skillet. Mix the egg, bread, garlic, parsley, a pinch of nutmeg, salt and pepper in a bowl and add the sautéed mixture. Fill the neck skin with the stuffing and tie it tight at the bottom with string. Tie the beak closed. Put the stuffed neck into the broth, salt and simmer for about a half hour. Remove and cool. When cool, slice and serve. Be sure to reserve the broth for the dinner soup.

We kept a few rabbits, a few sheep, a couple cows. All of 'em slept in the house with us, like they done everywhere in the country folk's houses in Umbria. Sheep, pigs, cows, chickens, even the mule, all of 'em on the ground floor, and us Christians on the floor above. You could see them and smell them through the slats in the wood planks of the floor. Whole night long it was squeal, cluck and moo! Not that we paid much mind. Weren't no different anywheres else. All the peasants in Umbria done it this way. For the padrone, folks like us were no better than the beasts anyway. We was the beasts under him like the animals were under us, we was *his* animals.

That's why he wasn't much likin' for us to go to school like the Duce said we could. If the padrone got wind that the children was goin' to school, well, all right, he'd let it slide for a year or two but then he'd say, "Get your boy out in the field!" Our school met at the parish church like most country schools. Didn't have a proper school and only one teacher for the lot of us.

I was in the very first ever class of our school, so, you see, the idea of schoolin' hadn't really taken a hold with the country folks yet. All us kids was supposed go, so I started, but my folks pulled me out after the 2nd grade. I started the third but weren't no sense wastin' workin' hands in school. And for what? Jus' to get your head full of learning that weren't no use to you on the farm. There's only four grades so what'd it matter anyhow if you missed them other two. That's how they thought. Even my brothers only did one year more than me. Weren't no one said nothing when they took us outta school, not the teacher, not the priest. The Duce said that we had to go to school to our fourteenth year, but weren't a lick of truth to it. When a boy turned fourteen, the padrone had to start paying a tax, like a health tax, for the state to help workers. That is why it was important to get the little ones and the girls working. Didn't cost 'em nothin'. Only if you had something rattling round in your head, some smarts I mean, and you done good at school, then *maybe* you finished elementary school. The law said one thing, but the peasants had their own ways. The padrone and his man saw to it that we minded the custom, lest we start gettin' uppity. Ain't none of the folks like us went to middle school. Closest one was 20-30 kilometers away. How you figure to do that on foot every day? Christ almighty!

We didn't do Fascist Saturday neither 'cause who in hell had ready cash for that uniform? We was in the fields since when we could pick a weed so then what? You gonna go asking young 'uns to labor all day every day and then go off and do all that there marchin' and jumpin' around? No, they didn't bother with us. That sort of thing was for folks lived closer to town. People like us was there to work, nothin' more. I reckon somebody had to look after the farm and see to the animals, didn't they?

The priests were in cahoots with the padroni. You maybe figured out already that when the crop was divvied up come harvest time, everyone was trying to pull a fast one. Your peasant's trying to tuck some away on the sly, more than he might've really had coming to him, you know, more than his share. Problem was, we was honest church goin' people, and some of them darned pious wives, well, they jus' couldn't keep their lip buttoned about what been done. They's sure they was lookin' in the face of eternal damnation. And so, come time to go to confession, the priest asked them straight if they done pinched a bit more for themselves. Well, some of them God fearin' women, they just had to confess it. Course, the priest went straight away to the padrone. Priests were spies because they weren't so well off neither, and the padrone give 'em rewards for keepin' an eye out on his interests. Already we had to hand over what they called "devotional wheat" the share the church took from us every year. It was a kind of a church tax called *la decima*, a tenth of our take of the wheat.

> The English translation "tithe" also derives from the number ten, indicating the 10% tax that had woven its tendrils into the fabric of society since ancient times. It is sanctioned in the Old Testament, but references to it in the New Testament are at best ambiguous, and could easily be interpreted as running contrary to the practice. Jesus's command to renounce worldly possessions was construed as an endorsement to relieve believers of a portion of their earnings, agricultural products and domestic animals. In exchange, the clergy could continue to provide spiritual guidance and administer the sacraments. History is rife with attempts both to withhold tributes and claim them illicitly. The most recent version of official Church canon, the 1983 Codex iuris canonici, discontinued the tradition, as it had been modernized by the optional check-box of 8‰, on the yearly state income tax form.

Not only that, but the priest had his land too. It was the Vatican's land really, but he had his own tenant farmers working the land and sharing crops. It sure did make us angry, but you daren't make a fuss, 'cause more than anything else we was powerful afraid of losin' our situation on the land. If you got up their nose, well, where you gonna go then? What you gonna do? Situations weren't growing on trees. See, it wasn't just *you* that got the boot; it was good riddance to your whole entire family. Weren't like leaving a factory job. And before you found another farm that could take on the lot of you, your whole darn family could starve. So we was trapped and they knew it. I ain't never talked to nobody about these things. Pains me.

Then there was "the book," the book of accounts. Every year the padrone settled the accounts with the capoccia: you got your animals raised and sold, crops grown and harvested, tools bought, and the like. But you see, the peasant, who didn't have no schoolin', was taken for a fool. Let's say the padrone sold one of the cows, or sheep, or pigs. Come time for countin' at the end of the year, he'd say that the market changed, that the animal weren't worth no more what it was when he gone and sold it, and so even though he sold it for a hundred liras, he'd say, "Wouldn't fetch more than sixty liras on the market today," so he'd pocket seventy and toss thirty to the poor wretch contadino. They worked them books over so that the peasant was always in debt to the padrone at the end of the year, and this kept him chained to that situation. He couldn't rightly leave 'cause he had that debt to work off. And so it went, year in and year out. So put that together with the priest, who was in charge of your soul, and you have a kind of slavery that you ain't never gonna shake off.

Then there was what's called the "obligations." Let's say some grains of wheat spilled out of a sack onto the ground, so the padrone says you gotta give him three or four chickens to make up for the loss. Then on holidays, it was your duty to rustle together the food for his table, a capon at Christmas, a lamb at Easter. See, that was your gift of gratitude to the padrone and his slave drivers for all they done for you. You know them of the castles that you see around these parts? All of 'em once belonged to the great landowners and their overseers. The overseers lived right there with them in a separate part of the house. He was the real boss man and kept a close eye on every last thing what happened on the farm, and his assistant, the groundskeeper, checked for slip-ups and cheating.

Just for example, your peasant had to have wood for heatin' and cookin', but he couldn't just go cuttin' down a tree anywhere he pleased. Had to pick up fallen branches and brambles and things like that. Anything he took that was against the rules got written up in the book of accounts. Other times they'd jus' out and out lie and say,

"Ah, you took two quintals of bran, or you took an extra quintal of semolina. Don't you remember?" The contadino would just shrug and scratch his head. Couldn't do nothin' else.

Overseers stuffed their pockets 'cause they were working it both ways. They took bribes and "payment" from the peasants and, working together with the groundskeeper, they did their own holdin' back from the padrone. There was one book of accounts for us, and another he showed to the padrone. That was why they didn't want the peasants' to get no learnin'. They needed to keep 'em running in circles. So then, after the priest, the padrone, and the overseer, the state come in wanting their share too! Couldn't win for losin'! Anyhow, once they all got through with us, we were left with enough to get by, but wasn't nobody livin' it up 'cause they had to keep us scared. Scared but alive.

A lot of the padroni sided with the fascists, and there was always the shadow of the squadristi lurkin' around. We peasants were a bit mixed, some fascist, others against, but you didn't really know because if you were against you'd best keep your trap shut about it. Lots of folks got it in their heads they was really something by goin' in with the fascists. They was throwing their weight around like they was some sort of big deal, goin' round and roughin' other folks up whenever they pleased. Weren't even really Mussolini's people. Just gangs throwed together under some local fella, just folk from these parts usin' fascism to get their way. All's you had to do was say you was a Black Shirt and then you went and did whatever you wanted. But let me tell you, after the war, the tables turned and those big mouths got their comeuppance.

Folks like to say, they like to think, that us country people were livin' high off the hog. Ain't a word of truth to it. May have been so for the homesteader, but not for the sharecropper. We just barely had enough to make it through. But there was one kind of slavery in the country and another kind in the town. Towns were plenty full of low-down wretches. If you was a down-and-out in the city, then your life wasn't worth crap 'cause you didn't even have the land to go scrounging for things from the ground or even tree bark. Just like us, them folks had a padrone, who at the end of the workday said, "This here's what I am gonna pay you. Take it or leave it." And so you took it or you starved.

Keeping the contadini on farms was an imperative for the regime.
Propaganda abounded decrying the wholesomeness of rural life. A law
was passed in 1931 restricting migration followed by a second more
stringent anti-urbanization law in 1939. Those who defied the law
and found clandestine work in the city were vulnerable to the whims
and will of their employer. After the war the laws were neither obeyed nor
enforced, but nevertheless, they were not officially abolished until 1961
when the so-called "economic miracle" was underway.

They had to buy things to eat, and we had our own. But even though some of them ne'er-do-wells was worse off than us, they looked down on us contadini like we was dirt. Even if you was clever, for them you was still a lowlife peasant. When the war come, most of the soldiers was rustled up from the countryside. And when the fighting hit in the towns, them townsfolk come pouring into the country, and we shared our food with them. We said, "Whatever we can spare for you, we will give," end of story. But didn't make no difference. After the war when they went back to town, they went right back to saying, "Eh, those stupid peasants."

Granted, what we had to give them wasn't much. It was lots of beans and cabbage. I had my fill of cabbage and beans, cabbage and turnip greens. Even for breakfast. We didn't have milk, even though we had cows. Like I said, weren't enough to feed them. We could only give the poor beasts straw, didn't have no hay for 'em, so their milk didn't come. In the summer we could take 'em out to pasture, but in the winter they stayed in the stall. Poor miserable creatures.

We had our own wheat, and so we had bread every day, but it was just ground as it was, and it made for some pretty coarse bread. Every share-cropper's home had a brick oven outside, and the womenfolk made their family's bread once a week. For the rest, we cooked everything in a cauldron hanging in the fireplace. Lunchtime was always homemade pasta and dinner again was field greens, cabbage, beans, or soup. The soup was a vegetable bean soup, more or less liquidy, depending on how many folks you were feedin' and how far you had to stretch it.

Our country pigs was raised to be more fatty than meaty. The fat was the most important part to the contadini, so when you killed the pig, there wasn't so much meat on it to make salami or prosciutto.

You minced your lardo good and fine with a knife and that dressed the pasta, and everything else too, like you would today with oil or butter, but then it was all *lardo*. Pasta was always tagliatelle. You cut 'em wider or thinner, depending, but the idea was always the same. We never had bought pasta, never. No spaghetti, none of that. If there was eggs we had egg noodles, but if not, just flour and water. Eggs was pretty scarce too, because if there wasn't much for us to eat, then for the chickens there was even less! And so they didn't give us a whole lotta eggs.

The few sheep we had got on a mite better because they was put out to pasture. We used them for the wool, cheese, and every now and then, like at Easter, we slaughtered a lamb. If you put a ram in with the ewes, they'da all had lambs in short order. So then, for a spell, we had enough sheep's milk for pecorino cheese. But like everything we had, the padrone come took his share, so half of the cheese went to him. The overseer and watchman was lookin' over you like a hawk, so you had to be quick and clever if you wanted to hold something back. It was a risky business 'cause if you were caught out, well, you might get the boot. Anyway, they knew full well how many sheep there were giving milk, and how much milk came, and how much cheese it made, and anyhow, they always worked their numbers high in their own favor. Cheese makin' is a lot of work, specially when you're milkin' by hand, but when the time came, the padrone breezed in like nothin' doin' and took his share. When the cows was up to it, we mixed the two milks together and they made a mighty fine cheese. If you're animals didn't up and die on you, well, then, on Sunday sometimes you could have yourself a real Sunday dinner. Weren't no small tragedy, an animal dying before the slaughter 'cause that was meat done gone to waste. You couldn't go eatin' the stuff that died or got sick but you couldn't help not looking at it with hungry eyes.

Some of our animals were just for work and not to eat. They helped plough and thresh the wheat. Threshing days was like a holiday season for us. Folk all gathered together and helpin' one another out to bring in the crop and thresh. It was a celebration because we knew that for another year there'd be food on the table. Breakfast for the threshing days was a simple rustic ring-cake we dipped into vin santo, a sweet wine.

Vin Santo affumicato Umbro, *is facing extinction, because in its origin, true vin santo is a homemade liqueur. The grapes used were harvested late in the season and late in the day, so that the morning dew had evaporated; the bunches had to be sparse but healthy, and clipped with extreme delicacy so as not to damage the fruit. The next phase was the most important for flavor development. The grapes were hung from the beams inside the house. In the wide-open hearth of a contadino's house, a fire was kept going constantly throughout the day, every day while the evenings were cold. The smoke and cooking residue collected on the outside of the grapes during the day as they slowly withered and turned brown, while the alternating cold nights kept them from rotting, all of which worked together to confer the incomparable, distinctly smoky taste of Umbrian vin santo. The juice was then put into small kegs with a "mother," the sticky sediment leftover from past batches, which set off the fermentation process and developed the unique aroma of each vin santo.*

Lunch was tagliatelle with chicken or goose. Weren't hardly any desserts because you didn't always have all the right ingredients all at the same time. You had to have milk and eggs at the same time, and then the money for sugar. Just didn't happen very often.

If people had all the illnesses back then that are around today, it would have wiped us all out because there wasn't no health service, no medicines. Folks didn't call on the doctor so much in those days. One, 'cause them charlatans didn't know too much more than anyone else and two, 'cause people were healthier even though there wasn't much food to go around. When I was little, I fell and broke the bridge of my nose. You can see it's smashed in here. So, my father takes off to fetch the doctor and says, "This girl of mine's got blood coming out of her nose! We can't stop it!" The doctor says, "So, uh, what you got to take me to her?" "I come with my donkey." "Well, I sure ain't going nowheres on no donkey! You get a horse, I'll come; otherwise I'm staying put." My mother, poor thing, tried to set it for me, but it come out this way. Lots of folks died because the doctor wouldn't come, probably some of 'em could've been saved. But what did they know anyway?

They were jack-of-all-trades from birthing to appendix, fumbling in the dark most of the time.

I met my husband because he lived on a neighboring farm owned by my same padrone. He was a tall, handsome man. In the evening, folks from neighboring families would meet up at someone's house to talk or play music on the squeeze-box, and dance, so that is how we made other folk's acquaintance. When Carnival was over and Lent started, weren't so much socializing goin' on. Lent was taken serious then, but they couldn't rightly ask us to eat less than we already did.

Lent is the 40-day period of reflection upon Jesus's sacrifice and retreat into the desert. From Ash Wednesday onwards, the faithful were obliged to abstain from luxury and entertainment, and intensify prayer and penance. Historically, one not only became a 40-day vegan, eliminating meat, fish, dairy and eggs, but meals were limited to one per day. Over the centuries, the church became more lenient about Lenten food laws, particularly as monks began to complain that after a hard day's labor, they felt somewhat peckish. Thus, the permitted meal was taken earlier, and a modicum of nibbles could be consumed in the evening with a restorative cup of wine, provided one exercised restraint. The dietary laws have been chipped away at or simply ignored to the point that today, the practice has all but disappeared, even among the faithful, though it is still traditional to eat fish on Good Friday before the Easter feasting.

After I knew my husband for a spell, he asked me one day if I might take kindly to the idea of marrying him. We was married on 26 November 1938. Mussolini promised everyone money if you married, but I ain't never seen mine! Them sorts of things didn't reach back into our parts. Then there was s'posed to be prize money if you give birth to a boy. Had me one of them too, but I still never got nothin'! Ha! I'm *still* waitin' for my money to show up, for the love of God!

Back then, all babies was born at home. My son, the one who's livin', was born without the local midwife. I am a touch embarrassed to tell about it though. See, I'd been in the family way before with another son. I was wracked with pains, and I was very, very big. So my sister-in-law says, "You oughta get over to the midwife to see what she says 'cause we all had our share of children and ain't nobody's had pain like that." My first born, he was called Carlo. Now, you see, this midwife, well, she liked her wine, and when we met up with her she was already drunk. So, my sister-in-law says, "Have a look at this here woman; she's really swole up. She's so big it just can't be right." "Eh, you girls these days! You'd think the lot of you with your first baby was giving birth to the Lord Jesus Christ! You's just lookin' to get attention for yourselfs, all of you!"

I done gone there to her in the night. When I got home my poor little baby was swimming around in so much water, that he just fell out of me. He just slipped right out and that child done gone and died right then and there. Back then, you didn't know what to do. Everyone runnin' round like they's in charge, but truth is, no one knew what the hell they was doin'. You took what you got. Later, that old drunk hag spread it around that she hadna seen that I was in trouble. Well, she sure enough hadna seen it 'cause she was blind drunk! We women mostly counted on each other when it was our time. The elder women come around to help for my second child. That's how it was usually done. I wouldn't have that midwife bitch! My father-in-law went on a horse to get a midwife from another town, and that son come out big and strong.

My husband went to war when my baby boy was only five months. When he left, he said, "You do as you see fit. I just ask that you look after our boy." I already lost that one son, and so he was frettin' for this one. He was twenty-two when he left. I lived with his folks. They loved me plenty and made sure that no harm ever come to the child. Mario got himself captured by the Americans in Sicily and taken to a prison camp in Tunisia. Was lots of our men taken there, and some of the boats were sunk goin' to Africa. He managed to get to land and was put in a concentration camp. He says commanders asked the boys a few questions and then they said, "Ok, you go here, you go there," depending on their answer. They asked, "You ever been a card hold-ing member of the Fascist Party? If you got back to Italy, would you fight for Mussolini again?" So that way they was separated into camps.

My husband ain't never signed up as a member, but he said, "If commanded, I go where I am told, but if I have a choice I wouldn't fight for nobody."

The folks in my husband's group had to pick oranges. So they was out in the morning and they come back in a truck in the evening. They had plenty to eat. But, his friend who got put in the next prison over didn't work and didn't have near nothin' to eat. They were forced to stay awake all night long and sing songs about Mussolini. My husband dug a hole under the fence and passed food to him when he could.

Meantime, the German cavalry came barrelin' through these parts. They tried to bomb the bridges so that the English couldn't follow them, but their aim weren't too good, and weren't one of them bridges fell. So then they took to putting mines under 'em to blow 'em up, but we didn't know nothin' 'bout that. The bridges was part of the railroad, see? One day, I was fixin' to set lunch on the table. My father-in-law had the boy in his arms, as he always did, sitting on the front stoop, and I called them in saying, "You're gonna catch a chill outside, come on in or you're eatin' your food cold!" We heard a terrible noise, and just then a huge chunk of bridge come plunk down right where they'd been sittin'. If hadna been for me callin' 'em in then and there, they'da both been laid flat by that stone. Both of 'em would be dead. We was half a kilometer from the bridge!

The Germans came into our house when they passed through and, well, I had this little creature to protect. I raised up the knife I used for cuttin' pasta and with the force of God in me I said, "You all be getting along out of here!" Well, I tell you, they turned right around and ran straight out. It done scared the hell outta them, but I wasn't gonna have no Germans breaking my balls! My brother-in-law went down to the English campsite tryin' to track those Germans, to see if he could find 'em, but when the English brought him down to where the Germans were camped, he saw there was a whole damned regiment of 'em.

Sometime later the Germans come into the house in the night. A Corporal peeked into each of our rooms lookin' to see how many adults there were, and he made 'em get up outta bed. When they got to my room, they done seen that I was with my boy, and he said, "No, leave this one, she's got a child." More of 'em showed up though, and they had the devil about 'em. I couldn't stay in bed no more, and I left the boy there to sleep. They said that they wanted bread, and I said that I had some on the rise but weren't none cooked. So they filled a pan with oil, fixin' to fry the bread dough. Them two took our demijohn of oil and spilt half of it on the floor trying to get an inch into a pan. There was more oil on the floor than in the pan! We was lucky enough to have some olive trees so we had a bit of oil. Good God in heaven. Oil was like gold! So one of them fellas who spoke Italian good says, "Gosh, look at what a mess we made." [*Many Italian fascists retreated with the Germans, fearing the Partisans and the backlash of public rage.*] And I says, "Of course, and you ain't got no idea of the work that went into gettin' that little bit of oil!" And I thought, now what the hell am I going to do with all this oil soaking into the floor!? So this same fella here who spoke Italian says, "What a sight. Such a waste." The floor ate more of it than they did! So he says, to me, he says, "I'll help you hide the other demijohn that's left so they don't take that." So he and I went to stow it away outta sight. That's when I saw that outside on the land there were 200 mules. During the war they was used to move around supplies, but now that the men was retreatin', they rode 'em.

Donkeys and mules were requisitioned from farms during the war. These were the main means of transportation for the contadino and a significant source of power for carrying out the more burdensome tasks on the farm.

Them Germans was crazy for eggs, I tell you. They tried to suck on them but weren't nothin' comin', and they wanted to know why. "'Cause there's chicks in them eggs, crazy fools!" They done broke all of them trying to find one with egg inside. They took shots at our kegs of wine, just to watch it pour out. We tried much as we could to stop 'em up so's it wouldn't run out all over. They done it outta pure spite. Whatever they couldn't eat or steal, they tried to destroy, so's we couldn't have it neither. They knew we weren't fascist so they tried to ruin whatever they could. The padrone headed off to the mountains for safety three months before, and hadn't taken his part of the cheese. We didn't eat it neither 'cause it weren't ours to eat. I tell you, those Germans they took that cheese out the yard and smashed it, just to waste it.

> *One of the most tragic civilian incidents of the German retreat from Italy occurred a short distance from Aida's home in an area called Penetola. At one o'clock in the morning a group of drunken soldiers entered into a sharecropper's farmhouse, stole what there was to steal and locked the twenty-four family members in a single room. On the ground floor, the animals were let out and fire was set to the hay and straw. All perished.*

When it was all over, they left and the war ended, and life went on just as before. The padrone returned and he said not to worry 'bout the wine and the cheese, and so we went back to our work just like nothing had happened. In town, things was a bit different. There were three days without law. A lot of folks were out to get their revenge on fascists that done mistreated 'em. Them were some dark days for sure. Then when the English arrived, there was a lotta black men among the troops. They was like hungry wolves looking for women. We had to carry scythes; Well, they was afraid of those, I'll tell you! Those were days you had to stay close to your husband.

Mario made it back home when my boy was five years old. Dino hadn't never seen his father, and in all that time we never heard a single word from him. I done cried my eyes out year in year out. Who was to say he wasn't on one of them boats at the bottom of the sea? I never lost hope that he would come back, but there was no word, ever. When he come back, he didn't want to shock us by just showing up, so he got himself dropped off at my brother-in-law's house and sent word that he was there. I cried with joy when I heard. I didn't think my eyes had anymore tears left, what with this poor boy being raised with no father and all the rest, and him leaving saying, "Take care of my boy, take care of my boy." But it weren't all smooth sailin' 'cause my boy didn't understand why I was letting this stranger sleep in my bedroom! He didn't like it one bit! All this while he been his granddad's little angel and was a touch spoiled, not having no father and all.

Mario didn't hold no grudge whatever against the Americans. Just the opposite: in 1948 he got a check from the United States government for his work pickin' oranges! In the end, them fellas who said they would fight again for the fascio were the ones up a singin' the whole night.

After the war, round 'bout the 1960s when there started to be factories, it all changed. Slavery don't work if you got choices. Folks packed up and moved to towns where there was plenty of work to be had. Price of crops bottomed out and lots of padrone had to sell up. To keep folks workin' the land, they had to pay a decent wage or weren't no way to keep 'em on there. They had to start buyin' machines to do the work too 'cause weren't no more children round. They was all goin' to school.

We was slaves, but no one wants to talk about it now. We's too ashamed. We jus' wanna forget. The more land a padrone had, the worse you got treated 'cause you had more henchmen to kowtow to, and all of them were on the take. That is why I said our padrone wasn't such a bad sort. He wasn't no baron or nothin', and we knew him personally. Some people only ever saw the henchmen.

Them overseers, now they done good for themselves. All the while they was cheatin' us and thinkin', "Ah, this numbskull can't do his numbers. He can't read." Meantime, they was tuckin' it away. Ended up with a pot of money, they did. I may not remember what I had for lunch today, but I sure remember these things.

We went on just like before for about fifteen years, just as we had always done. Then things started to change. New laws helped farm people earn more money, get treated decent. Everyone was packing up so the laws had to protect us. Weren't no one gonna live that way no more. There was lots of new factories and a better life in the towns, clean, modern houses, and more food than we ever known, different foods that we ain't never heard of before. My son decided he wanted that life. He got a job in a factory and I never looked back. He has a soft spot for the country life, but not me. It was a hard life and I ain't got no sentimental ideas about it. If you got money, you can live a good life in the country, but not if your life is workin' the land. I feel tied to it only because I put my life into it. I want to forget it, but I need to remember it. My son's gone and bought him a piece of land in the country 'cause he's still got a piece of his heart in the country. When I see the old house where we lived, it was bought up by some rich folks from Pavia, I'm glad I am not there anymore. It was just hard work, back breakin' hard work.

When I look at young people today, ain't nobody content. Kids are off killing right and left... there was more respect back then. *Madonna mia*, when I watch TV and see what young people are up to these days, it makes me feel sick. They have everything they could want and ain't none of 'em satisfied. It's more than I can bear. I think some of them should be taught a lesson they won't forget, but that would make me just like them! They go to school as an excuse to do nothing because they don't even study. They was born in a time when things is too good, and so they don't know how to appreciate nothin'. For us, the smallest, slightest little thing that come our way was a wondrous surprise. They can't even tie their shoes, that's why they made those strap shoes. They want jobs where they don't do nothin' and make lots of money. The people who want to work, folks with some real brains, go abroad. So more and more, Italy is becomin' a country of vagabonds and idiots.

Now we have all the food we want. We can have meat all the time, but ain't nobody feels like cookin'. What they need is a good wave of hunger; then you'll see 'em getting' back to the stove 'cause they're sure not going to eat the stuff raw! Used to be, either you knew how to make food or you didn't eat. Now it's all too easy to stuff yourself to the gills. They ain't got no idea what it is to eat a chicken you raised yourself, pluck it, and roast it up, and eat it with satisfaction. They buy these sickening embalmed chickens from the supermarket raised on who-knows-what. You bake them and they are still squishy. Nothin' to sink your teeth into but mush. But that is what they's used to. They don't even know that it ain't real food. Some things are better though, like coffee. I only ever had caffè d'orzo until after the war but now I only drink the real stuff, three times a day, every day.

Intermezzo

I Surrogati del caffè - Coffee Surrogates

A fter pasta and pizza, Italy is probably best known for coffee, although not a bean of it is grown on home soil. Its Italian-ness lies exclusively in the toasting, grinding and pressurized processing methods.

The first shipments of coffee beans made the voyage from Yemen to Venice in the 1600s, with the first coffee bars opening in the 1700s. One by one, cafes slowly caught on in the major cosmopolitan hubs of the north. In 1901, the espresso machine was perfected and or-dering *un caffè* took on a definitive meaning. The passion for coffee became so ardent that in spite of the coffee tax being raised ten times between 1915 and 1924, consumption increased twelve times over; the prohibitive price only added to its allure as a status symbol. Social commentators expressed fears that Italians would abandon themselves to hedonistic *sensualismo* instead of using good sense to guide their consumption.

By and large, most Italians were unable to afford coffee regard-less, but in the 30s and 40s when foreign importation of foodstuffs screeched to a near halt, coffee was all but banned, and it became dif-ficult even for the upper classes to obtain it despite their access to the black market. It wasn't until well into the 1950s that the vast majority of Italians born between the wars would get their first taste of real cof-fee. But the coffee habit, the curious practice of drinking some sort of bitter black beverage with, or in many cases *as*, the first meal of the day, was a well-rooted custom throughout Italy by Mussolini's time. Surrogates had arisen from political efforts to avoid tariffs, or enforce insular policies. Federico the Great and Napoleon had both appealed to chemists to come up with a cheap local alternative, in spite of being coffee addicts themselves. The resulting concoctions spread throughout Europe, not because they were good, or even similar to coffee, but because they allowed the populace at large to indulge in a habit that imitated the civility of the upper classes. Therefore, when the coffee eclipse blackened the horizon in the 30s and 40s, it merely spread the well-established use of surrogates across the board.

The queen of coffee surrogates was caffè d'orzo, a toasted barley drink. It excelled as a cheap alternative because at the time, it could be grown just about anywhere. Whole barley grains were placed in a skillet with a metal lid that had a closeable peephole from which you could keep an eye on the browning progress without losing heat. It was also fitted with a crank positioned on the top that allowed you to slowly stir the grains around to keep them in constant motion. Well-toasted barley was a decisive dark brown, but a burnt batch would make for an unpleasantly bitter drink. Thus prepared, the grains were then ground like coffee. Caffè d'orzo is still enjoyed today both at home and in cafes for people who watch their caffeine intake. Some even claim that they like the taste, reminiscent as it is of childhood. Toasted barley for the *moka* coffee-maker can be purchased in packages like ground coffee, or in instant powder form, but no one toasts their own anymore.

Chicory coffee, referred to by Italy's elderly as *caffè d'olanda,* literally "Dutch coffee," was the second most widespread coffee surrogate in the period between 1930 and 1960. It too, was easily accessible, as the plant could be found growing wild along paths and bordering cultivated farmland. The roots were starchy, so as they were toasted, they caramelized, lending a sweetish, nutty taste to the resulting drink. Prepared chicory root was also widely available commercially. As far back as 1846, Germany alone had 3,475 processing plants that exported throughout Europe.

Third in popularity, was the surrogate made with acorns. This substitute was wholly abandoned when coffee became affordable again because acorns as a foodstuff, in general, were associated with desperate poverty. They were a last resort for sustenance among country peasants and were also used as fodder for pigs and chickens, which marked them with an indelible stigma. The taste, even when toasted and boiled into a familiar looking black beverage, is remembered as being terribly bitter. Often this cheaper 'coffee' was mixed with one of the other surrogates to make it more tolerable.

Other grains, seeds, leaves, and legumes, such as rye, oats, horsechestnuts, dandelion, lupine, fava, and letch were toasted, ground and brewed, if not for the taste, at least to remind one of the color of the 'black gold' For the majority who had never experienced the genuine article, this *was* coffee.

Ever the bullhorn of fascist culinary propaganda, *La Cucina Italiana* resoundingly defended the regime's position on coffee:

Coffee is not necessary for our dynamic, active, and lively race who need take no part in stimulants of this kind…the love of the foreign that once dominated the Italian table is finally about to be overturned by our new custom desirous of all things Italian to the bitter end, all in favor of a spiritual and economic autarky… Coffee for us is not a necessity but a gluttonous habit … The worker, who best defines health and strength, consumes a minimum of coffee; he drinks it perhaps when he is ill, but at the height of his industriousness, his only beverage is wine, red like his generous blood, with the distinct scent of his homela … not consuming coffee is Italian, it is fascist, but also because our new work consciousness, like social duty, rejects this continuous ridiculous prop in the workday. For you women, the not-so-small savings from not buying coffee will be a welcome change in your household budget, not to mention the advantages to your family's health … as it is known that coffee brings about a marked depression after the initial boost … so even in this small way, as absolute masters of ourselves, let's refuse foreign coffee and return to our own traditions: wine and fruit. (Della Pura, 1939).

The regime had hoped that consumption habits would shift in accordance with unavailability, a gastronomic "out of sight, out of mind." In spite of the numerous brews and tonics invented to replicate the "black gold," none had the caffeine kick or taste of real coffee. In the end, black, bitter, and watery simply did not cut the mustard, so once coffee was available and affordable for the general public, the Italian "bar" phenomenon exploded in every town along the peninsula. "Bar" in the Italian usage is more synonymous with café than with pub. It comes from the Southern American custom, wherein the public was separated from beverages and servers by a *bar*-rier, that is, the counter. In Italy, there are two brass bars that run the length of the counter, the upper one an elbow-rest and the lower one a footrest. They encourage leaning and reinforce the barrier concept. There are no stools at an Italian bar. Coffee is taken standing up, but then, one need not linger over an espresso.

Surprisingly, in spite of Italy's supposed dominance in the coffee culture sphere, it does not even figure into the 2013 top ten ranking of coffee consuming countries, but this may be due to the fact that coffee here is generally consumed in association with meals: Latte macchiato or cappuccino at breakfast and espresso after lunch and dinner. This 3-cup per day scheme is rigorously upheld by 81% of Italians. Any more than that is considered reckless, unless the extra coffee is consumed strictly for social or business reasons. No self-respecting Italian would dream of drinking a cappuccino or latte after the noon hour. It would be unspeakably uncouth. Intriguingly, there are no Starbucks in Italy. A failed venture here would indeed be ruinous to their reputation.

Franca

Born 1922 - Reggiolo

Franca goes against the stereotypical Mediterranean look. Even at 92, she is tall and sturdy with softly coiffed white hair that was once blonde, and large blazing blue eyes. She lives independently in her own condo in Brescia, although a housekeeper assists her a couple times a week at the insistence of her family. The walls of her apartment are adorned with paintings, many of which she did herself as a young woman, denoting the influence of futurism and propaganda poster art from the 1930s and 40s. I remarked on how well she looked, and she said that really, she wasn't so well just then. Her knee was hurting. Her granddaughter, present at the interview snapped, "Grandma, I certainly hope that when I get to be your age that all I've got to complain about is a bum knee!" Franca's family was a large estate owner with vast landholdings in the northern-central region of Emilia-Romagna, in a word, padroni. Consequently, the story of her youth is one of frivolous ease and a comfortable obliviousness to unpleasantries.

I grew up in the region of Emilia. We have the strongest tradition of food in all of Italy. My father was the overlord of an estate farm, you know, a property owner, a padrone. There was a time when the family held vast amounts of terrain, but alas, when my father became ill and the sharecropping system broke down, we had to spend some rather notable sums for his care. Little by little it chipped away at our fortune until it was reduced to a pittance. But growing up, ah, it was a good life!

There were seven of us at home: five kids and papa and mamma. Oh, dear me, how the years have flown by! We lived in a two-horse town called Reggiolo. Like most other towns, school only went up to the 5th grade, and you were left at that unless your parents paid for you to go to study in another town. I liked school, so I did the 5th grade twice just so I could keep going. It was better than lazing around at home. I didn't repeat because I had flunked, oh, no! That, never! I wanted to do middle school, but my father was always saying that there was no point in going to the expense and worry of sending a girl away to school. "Proper young ladies don't need school," but my teacher had said to father, "At least let her do art school. She is so good, and it would be a waste to let someone who wants to study just sit at home." My father said, "It would have been better if your uncle had been your father. He understands this art nonsense better than I do." That's because my uncle was a great artist.

I was the eldest of five children so after I finished school, I stayed at home to help my mother out with the other children. But in the end, my father did let me go to art school. It was a private school for boys and girls to study art with Maestro Boni. Let me tell you, it was a pretty big deal for the last town on the face of the earth to have such a famous art teacher! Reggiolo was a small town for sure! We didn't have decent schools, but there was this little jewel of an art school in town.

Reggiolo is Emilia, but very close to Lombardy. It was like an overgrown village, but at the same time more evolved than most. I went to art school for two or three years, but all the while I kept up with Fascist Saturday, just like most of the girls I knew. It was a way of getting together, like going to the shopping centers is for girls today. I started in Figlie della Lupa, Daughters of the Wolf, and went on to be a piccola italiana. I so loved being a piccolo italiana and couldn't wait to become a giovane italiana, because their uniform was just darling! Gosh, though, if truth be told, the Fascist Saturday activities didn't really change from one stage to the next. As giovane italiane we kept on marching and exercising in formation just like we did as piccole italiane, but the outfit was really swell! We were all fascists then. Don't let anyone go kidding you about that. We were born into fascism so you didn't even give it a second thought. It was such fun! We had big rallies and competitions. There was an art contest organized by our Fascist Saturday leaders and I went on to win second prize! Me, out of the whole darn province! And just think! I was only fourteen then! Golly!

Am I speaking ok? At 92 I might be going a bit daft! I've got a lady who comes to clean because my son said he doesn't want me to kill myself climbing up on stepladders and things. They don't want me to do myself in over something silly like overzealous cleaning…

I know what they say about fascism these days, but truth be told, for me it was better than the Republic we have now. Back then, you sure didn't hear about the delinquency you hear about now. Geez, killing, killing, left, right, and center. Not that the fascist years were all good times. Heck, no! If you weren't a member of the fascist party, well, you didn't work. If you had a job and didn't sign on, you lost it. It was like the expression goes: "they give you both a carrot and a whipping!" For some people who had a mind of their own, it didn't go so well. Got their chops busted, alright. Goodness, did I tell you I have a cousin who makes costumes for Zefferelli? His name is Maurizio Millenotti. He almost won an Oscar! But he did win a Davide Donatello in Venice. We have a definite artistic bent in my family, you betcha!

Before heading off to school we had caffè latte with buttered toast and jam. There weren't any of these pastries like you have now. We always had real coffee at my house right up until the war. Then, we had surrogate coffee because, by gosh, it was near impossible to find the real stuff even on the black market. Papa would say, "Delia, make me some of that black broth," because we were not too partial to the fake stuff. But if you couldn't get coffee, you could at least pretend, I mean, it let you keep up the appearance. It is like when Italians go abroad today. Just to get a taste of something similar to coffee, they'll even drink that awful stuff that foreigners call coffee at those terrible coffee bars. Really, we didn't see real coffee again until the Americans came through at the end of the war. Our milk was fresh though, from our own cows.

My grandfather was a pig merchant. He did very well for himself in that sector, and he even – now, mind you, I'm talking about *my* grandfather – had a car, way back when I was a young girl! It was a Fiat 508-Ballia. My grandparents didn't live with us, but because we had a big garage, he parked his car in the garage with our car. When I heard grandpa pull up in his auto I would run out and ask him for some money! I was a bit of a pest! I remember at Christmas time every year grandpa and his friends would play cards to win a Christmas turkey, one of the good ones, not like the ones these days. I don't know where the bird came from, because we didn't raise turkeys, but we were well off and could afford to splurge on it, but it wasn't one of those lousy turkeys you find now. I just wanted to point that out.

My grandmother, Lucia, had sixteen children by him. Only eight lived, though. One died from diphtheria, another from typhus, still another from some other fever. I'd say to her, "Grandma, how many Virginias did you have?" and she'd say, "You know, I can't rightly remember." Because every time a child died she kept reusing the same name so she called them all Virginia until it stuck to a live one. For the guys, it was Antonio. So, eventually, I had an uncle named Antonio, and my brother, who was an opera singer, was called Antonio as well. My parents wanted one of their grandsons to be called Antonio, but, oh, well, you know how wives are, my sister-in-law said no dice.

My grandmother was a great cook. Oh, the cakes she made! Enormous cakes with a dozen eggs and a half-kilo of butter! Eh, these days they want to keep us away from butter, glorious butter, saying that it is bad for us! Horsefeathers! Well! Let me tell you, I have one aunt who died in her 80s and all the rest were over 90! And look at me! Raised on butter. You see? There is not a bit of truth to it! Enough of all this talk of butter being bad for you, I say! I got out of the habit of having lots of butter and lard, not that it would matter much now that I've got one foot in the grave, but, oh, the way we cooked then! Ah, no one eats like that anymore. We had cakes all the time; they were so good and rich! Our Emiliana cuisine has a lot of butter, and lard too. When you simmer the fat to render lard, the crunchy solids left over were called *ciccioli* [*scruncions*]. Everyone loved those. You can still find them in some shops today. They are dried and look like chips. You can pop them in your mouth just as they are. *Buoni!*

There was always good food at my grandmother's house! But, I have to tell you something, I do thank God that we never wanted for anything. Even when things were rationed, we could pay the price on the black market to get whatever we needed or wanted. If we wanted cake during the week, we had cake. It wasn't just for Sundays at my house.

When I came home from school, lunch usually started off with some sort of homemade pasta, taglierini or tagliatelli in broth or with tomato sauce, and then there would be a second course of some meat dish like pheasant or guinea hen, roast beef... we always had lots of meat from our tenant farmers. And vegetables, like stewed or grilled peppers, spinach, salads and tomatoes, but no, I guess people really didn't eat so many tomatoes, not like they do now. In the evening we would have something simpler like soup and cheese, minestrone, pasta fagioli, or even just caffè latte if it had been an especially big lunch. And of course, salami and prosciutto. That was always around, you know, my grandfather being in the pig trade and all.

Once our pigs got to be about 200 kilos, our *norcino* came and went to work slaughtering the pig and curing the meats, salami, cotecchino, prosciuttos. When I say "our" norcino, he was like the shoemaker, or the tailor, someone we trusted who came to the house do the work, but he didn't just work for us. I could never look on at those scenes, killing the poor beasts and working them into salamis and sausages! I just didn't have the stomach for it! The norcino made the traditional spiced blood pudding too, but, my goodness; I couldn't stomach that stuff either. But, oh, the *salumi* were great and we ate lots of them! These days they tell pregnant women not to eat salumi, and I say, balls to that! Women can eat whatever they want just like they have always done! None of my kin were born demented in any way. My grandmother was always pregnant and she most certainly went on eating just as much salumi as she wanted. I remember once after I was married and had moved away, and my husband had put me in a house for safekeeping during the war, my cousin came when I was nursing the baby. He was a lieutenant in the army and he brought a salami that my mother had sent with him. What joy to have a salami from home! Everywhere in Italy salami is different and everyone thinks that theirs is best. But ours in Emilia really *is* best, no fooling!

My mother taught me to cook. Not that she sat me down and taught me, I just picked it up when I tagged along in the kitchen. She and our cook made all the pasta at home, tagliatelle, tagliolini, cappelletti, tortelli di zucca… and all of the famous recipes from Bologna, like lasagna. I remember well the wonderful stewed peppers we had. So flavorful! Nowadays peppers are mostly water. If I had to say what tastes I miss from those days, I'd say *all* of them! All of them! The stuff in shops today might be beautiful to look at, but it's tasteless. You might still be able to find a decent tomato, but not in the supermarket. Chicken is tasteless. All meats are tasteless. Pork, beef, what have you. Tasteless. Of all the salumi, the only one that has survived industrialization is prosciutto crudo. You can still find good cheese if you look hard for it, and the same for bread.

We had a beautiful manor home, but it was not modern like houses now. There was an entranceway, a large central room and a large kitchen just off of that. We had a big hearth in the living room but we didn't light the fire very often. We heated the house with terracotta stoves called *stufa becchi*, with the different levels, and for cooking, we used the modern wood-burning stove with an oven on the side and a four-burner stovetop.

I wouldn't exactly call that heating the house, not in the way we can heat the house now. Heating with stoves isn't the same story. We had a well outside the house, but of course, there was also running water in the house, in the kitchen. It wasn't modern, but it was civilized! There were many, many bedrooms upstairs, I can't say just off the top of my head how many. There were washrooms, and a gabinetto where one took care of one's other toilet needs. There wasn't a toilet per se, but there was a hole that you poured a bucket of water down after you had done what needed to be done, but I couldn't call them bathrooms because they weren't like today. My family lived very well because most people didn't have a *gabinetto* right there in the house; most everyone took their business outdoors in some fashion or another. Even ours used to be a pantry that we later made into a *gabinetto*.

I had always had a passion for clothes. I used to make sweaters and clothes at home just for fun. When I was little, my aunt made our clothes. You couldn't buy anything ready-to-wear in town. When my aunts went to Sasso Maggiore, they would buy little outfits for me and my brother Antonio, but mostly for me because I was cuter than him, so it was more fun buying things for me. We also had our own tailor, of course, as families did back then. We didn't have an armoire full of clothes: three or so day dresses for each season, and then, of course, a couple of nice dresses for Sundays. During the war we got down to only one new Sunday dress per season. That was it. Things had gone belly-up, so you made do. Fabric was rationed, so most of what you could get was synthetic, those new cheesy war fabrics. Even in war times though, women still wanted to get decked out and keep up with the latest. Torino was the Italian capital of fashion then. We looked at magazines and the cinema for ideas on what to wear.

My father used to take me to Reggio Emilia to buy shoes. They were straight out of a dream! And the hats! Oh, the ones with the transparent veils sweeping down over the front just like the glitterati in the movies! I was obsessed with hats, and Papa was obsessed with buying them for me! He loved spoiling me! Not long after I was married, I took tailoring lessons to learn to make dress patterns. Really, I taught myself more than anything, because clothes were a great passion for me. I made my granddaughters' wedding dresses myself! I designed the patterns, stitched them and everything!

Ours, was a well-to-do family with large landholdings and share-croppers who worked our land. It worked like this: they would lodge in a house on our land and we would get half their harvest. You see? It was an ideal situation for all involved. I don't really remember how many houses we had or how many families working, but it was sizable. Ah, but I was young then and had my head in the clouds, so I couldn't really say how much land there was. I had my mind more on all the boys buzzing around me! Not boyfriends, but interested callers, let's say! Oh, goodness, I had so many boys stuck on me! Once one of them wrote me, "Baby! I cannot live without hearing your news. I beg you! Write or phone me!" Holy Mackerel! Just think of it! My steady found that note in the pocket of my jacket and demanded to know what was going on! Jeepers!

But, those were the good ol' days of courting. It was done in a gentlemanly way, with style. None of this "*Oh, bella! Ciao!*" stuff! Kids today! Parents kept their children under close watch then. I didn't go out in the evenings for sure! Well, truth be told, maybe it *was* a bit stifling. Today though, there's too much freedom! I was allowed to go out during the day, but if I wasn't back by dusk my father was none too pleased about it! We would meet up with friends in town, in the piazza or on the main street for a walk. I didn't have restrictions during the day, so that's when unmarrieds managed to get in a few furtive smooches! One day my intended and I were coming home, from an outing and we took a wrong turn. My father had said to him, "Remember, you get my daughter back home in the light of day, and no later!" Well, by the time we made it back it was sundown and a good while passed before we were allowed to go out again.

I met the man I would marry through a cousin, the son of one of my mother's sisters. So, this cousin of mine had a friend from Brescia who happened to be in our town, I don't remember what for. One fine day, they came around to our house for a visit, as relatives did back then. Well, after a week, this particular someone wrote to my father and said that he wanted to get to know me better, and would it be possible for him to come for a visit. As one does, before answering, my father then set out to find out what he could about the young man. He was an industrious guy from a well-to-do family, and so my father said, yes, yes, of course, come for a visit. After seven or eight months, a proper amount of time, we were engaged.

During those months, he came by train from Brescia every weekend and lodged in a room at a trattoria. He wrote me love letters and all of the things you are supposed to do. They were exchanged surreptitiously, of course, which made it all the more delicious! *That* is romance! His parents came to meet me, his mother with a big beautiful bouquet of flowers. She was his stepmother though, his father's second wife. She said, "Dario, this one will give you twelve children!" and we all laughed, but in the end, he and I only had one child.

I moved to Brescia then in '43 when we were married because travel was greatly restricted. Bridges were out, there were curfews, and it was just plain dangerous to be out. If I hadn't moved to Brescia I wouldn't have been able to see my husband. We didn't even have a reception or anything afterwards. We were just glad to get the thing over with without bombs or machine guns going off around us. My parents didn't even come, just my cousin Sergio as a witness. It was adios to the good times. Curfew was 8 pm, everyone at home with the lights out.

When I left Reggiolo, the worst hit: there were Black Shirts, and all those resistance brigades, and Mongols, you know, those people with those slanty eyes, soldiers from Mongolia.

Mongolian troupes were recruited by the Germans, despite their close relationship with Russia. Other testimonials by Emiliani record the presence of Mongols, though scholarly historical documentation has little to say on the matter.

My mother said that they stormed into our house and took all the salumi from the room upstairs where they were hung to age. Those Mongols. Then there was the Tote Brigade. My brother was accused of being part a partigiano in the Tote Brigade. It wasn't true. We were loyal fascists, but the fascio took him away anyway. Not just my brother, but my cousin the priest, and my other cousin who became a dentist. As they were being hauled away, their mothers followed behind them crying and pleading their innocence.

They were taken to the fortress – it's a 13th century fortress, eh! – intending to shoot them right there in front of the fortress wall. My mother and my two aunts wailed and wailed, and you know what? They let them go! Then another time, a few fellas and my brother were taken to prison, but my brother managed to get out, because he sang. He sang in that prison with all he had in him, and they were so impressed by his voice that he enchanted them into letting him go. In the 40s, everything turned sour, and there were bad times to come with the fascists. We were scared to death. The Black Shirts were out killing whoever they could for the slightest thing! At the fortress there is a memorial plaque of all for the victims killed in Reggiolo by the fascists. There was one guy, a friend of mine's boyfriend, who was killed right in front of her and then they ripped his eyes right out of their sockets! They had evil in their very blood!

I used to have some photos of Mussolini and his lover Clara Petacci, of when they were killed and hung upside-down like butchered meat in the piazza in Milan. I don't remember who gave them to me, but they spread like wildfire throughout Italy. Her skirt was pinned down. It wouldn't have looked proper to have her underclothes showing. You know, I've looked and wracked my brain, but I've never found those photos. I think my son took them. There is another picture I can't find of a certain suitor of mine. He was quite a looker, that one! I wonder who stole that photo from me. Hmm.

I don't know why my husband wasn't called to serve in the war. Well, in those days, if you knew the right people, had the right connections... And anyway, they said the war wasn't supposed to drag out like it did. They said that maybe, just maybe, it would go on the whole summer. Well. It didn't.

We went to Brescia to live, and well, I didn't much care for their food! Many things are similar, but I remember once they tried to get me to eat horsemeat! Dario had asked the cook to make me a dish with horsemeat, and in those days finding meat was no easy task. Well, she made me a braised dish, like a stew and I could see that they were watching me strangely. "Did you like the meat? Did you like it?" they asked me. They had tried to mask it in a wine sauce with pepper and cinnamon. I said it was good and they laughed and laughed! Well! Ha-ha-ha. That was the first and the last time! I was not about to eat any horse! "Don't make this ever again!" I said. I know it is just an idea, but it is not for me! My son feels the same, but my granddaughters were brought up here and they eat it.

I got pregnant just one month after the wedding. It was during the war and the bombing was pretty constant. There was a machine gunner called Pippo, and people would call out when he was flying over. "Head for cover!" I'll tell you, those were not good times. Word went out to evacuate the city center, and so my husband found me a hideaway in Val Trompia. It was in the middle of the mountains, an unlikely place to bomb. I put a few things in a bag and left. I was about to have my baby then, so it was very confusing. My husband was worried, thinking, "If this one here goes into labor during the bombing, what then!?"

He had been going to Brescia on his bike to work, but the Germans would fire at whoever passed, and I mean with machine guns! So he fixed us up in Villa Caccino, the home of a poor widow with three children who took people in to make a little money. Well, the very next day after I got there I had my baby. That was August of '44. They called the local midwife to help with the delivery.

There was a boy who came to the house where I was staying, and I remember he would hold my baby when he cried. I had one of those unnerving babies that always cried. And one day, on his way to the house, the poor boy was gunned down. It was still morning. There's a stone marker where he died. The partisans hid out in the mountains too, so you couldn't really even say who had killed the boy, them, the fascists, the Germans... We stayed there for eight months with my husband driving the car to Brescia for work every day. He and his brother had a company that made machine parts, and so had to be there every day. The widow was a great help with my baby in those difficult times. I needed some interpreting to understand her dialect, because the people from the mountains spoke very differently from us.

When the war was over, and we moved back to Brescia, I continued cooking the good dishes from my Emilia-Romagna. There is no comparison between our cuisine and theirs! Are you kidding!? My husband loved it. What do they even have to compare with our food!? They have no idea how to cook here! Not an ounce of imagination! Like our traditional Christmas pumpkin ravioli, who could top that?

Tortelli di zucca - Pumpkin ravioli
250g cooking pumpkin
10 amaretto cookies, crushed to a near powder
1 cup freshly grated parmesan cheese
1 tsp grated lemon zest
salt
Fresh pasta:
300g flour
3 large eggs
melted butter

For the pasta:

Make a well with the pasta and crack the eggs into the center. Work the flour into the eggs by pinching it together until you arrive at the outer edges. Knead the dough for 10 minutes. Place it in a plastic container or bag and allow it to rest for 30 minutes.

Heat the oven to 375°F. Cut the pumpkin into large chunks and place on a tray covered with foil. Bake about an hour until tender and starting to brown. Remove and cool. Remove the pumpkin peel. Combine with the other filling ingredients until the consistency is stiff (meaning more or less parmesan).

Roll the dough out until thin. Place a teaspoonful of filling on the dough at regular intervals. Cut round or square shapes and press the dough together trying not to trap air in with the filling. Place the prepared ravioli on flour and repeat process.

When they are all finished, heat a pot of salted water and a large frying pan with a lot of butter. Boil the ravioli until they are just al dente and remove with a slotted spoon, carefully placing them into the pan of melted butter. Pour off just a bit of water from the pasta and continue cooking the ravioli until most of the water has boiled off and they are covered with butter. Don't let them get too dry and do not stir them, just toss them lightly in the pan.

Serve with more grated parmesan and white or black pepper.

Even my in-laws, folks who were rather short on compliments, said that I had "golden hands" in the kitchen. But my husband, rest in peace, did not live long. After only ten years together, he got a terrible ulcer. He went to the hospital to have it operated on, and died the next day.

Things developed very fast after the war. People wanted to get past it and get on with life as soon as possible. One of the first things to spread everywhere was coffee bars with *real* coffee. Restaurants too. I had never been to a restaurant before. I didn't even really know what they were. Sure, there was that trattoria where I said my husband had lodged, but we had certainly never been there. No one ate out. It just wasn't something you did. Even people with money always ate at home. Eating out was for people who were away from home. In the summer, when I was young, we went to the seaside in Riccione, but we rented a holiday-home with a kitchen so even then we ate at home. My mother and a servant prepared the food. We didn't eat fish because unless you lived on the coast, there wasn't any tradition of eating fish. When I think about fish, I think about plugging my nose and having to swallow down cod liver oil when I wasn't well. No, the only fish we had ever had was catfish and eel, and that was rare.

In spite of the thousands of kilometers of coastline, Italian cuisine is not traditionally fish laden, as it was not possible to safely transport or store fresh fish inland due to the absence of adequate refrigeration. Smoked and salted fish, like anchovies, herring, and cod, or baccalà, *were widespread but mostly associated with lower class fare, The story is often told of poor families passing around a single herring or anchovy around the table so that each person could wipe their bread across it to pick up some of the flavor.*

We went to Riccione to take in the salt sea air because it was good for children, not for the seafood. We swam too, but the adults never went into the water. It would have been unthinkable for my mother to put on a swimming costume of any kind.

So, yes, everything flowered after the war. Spice shops, deli-shops, cheese shops. There are so many things we have now that we had never heard of before the war. I had never seen or heard of mozzarella, or pizza. I don't remember the first time I had a pizza, because I am 92, so how could I possibly remember! All I know is that it was much, much after the war. And anyway, pizza came from Naples and we had this idea that Neapolitans were dirty, so it's not like we were tripping over each other to try it.

And like I said, we knew nothing about fish or seafood. Supermarkets offer so much variety these days. There are so many more different, good things to eat than before. Like I said, not genuine, not authentic, but a lot more varied. Like yogurt. We didn't even know what yogurt was, or fruit juice in a carton. You can take it or leave it, but it is here to stay, and there is nothing you can do about it. As the saying goes: *"mangia la minestra o salta dalla finestra"* [*Either eat the soup or jump out of the window*]. Only people who have their own vegetable garden can really eat good food.

There used to be a sense of order during the fascio. It wasn't dangerous to be out after dark. Now you can't set foot outside of the house in the evening because of the delinquency. We've gotten used to seeing women wearing less and less. Relationships between men and women changed quickly too. Probably because before it was too oppressive, you know, the whole thing between men and women. It's true that fewer and fewer women want to cook or know how to cook, but it doesn't matter because more and more men are interested in cooking now. It used to be that a man who took his children out for a walk or did anything at home was made fun of. They'd laugh and say, "Eh! What's this?! Is your wife in charge now? Ha-ha, ho-ho!" Women had to do everything for the home and children. Now men are all chefs and such. I see them on TV! They win all kinds of prizes!

Women work and have their own money now. A woman used to live to make her husband happy. Women used to make fresh pasta every day at home, but now they will do it once or twice a year, if that. I taught my daughter-in-law to cook. She didn't know how to make a thing when she married my son. If you want to learn, you can learn. Some people are better than others, but everyone can learn. After all, Italians have the best food in the world, at least for me that's true. I had always cooked from memory, but my granddaughters have started writing out my recipes. The husband of a friend of mine said, "Franca, if I had married you I would already be dead 'cause you're such a swell cook!"

Maybe it's silly of me, but even now that I am alone, I make myself good meals and set the table properly. It's not easy when you are old, though. You are full of aches and pains; you're ugly to look at, tired, no one wants you, and you know that you're at death's door. Getting old is awful, but you have to put up with it. You don't have to like it, but you do have to accept it. That's why the table needs to be set with care. Eating, of all things, needs to be a pleasure, not a chore.

Intermezzo

Il sacro maiale – The Sacred Pig

R itual slaughter in the Old Testament centers upon the sacrificial lamb, whose frail, wooly innocence lends itself well to personal identification with the cruel blows dealt along life's trajectory, a poignancy that abates once the meat is well roasted with ample rosemary and garlic. The same pathos is more difficult to invoke with swine, although their history as a sacrificial animal is deeply ingrained in mythology that pre-dates the lamb. The word pig itself has roots in the Greek word *thuein,* meaning to offer as sacrifice, and it is believed that the earliest sacrifices, in substitution for humans, were swine. In ancient times, pigs were a symbol of fecundity associated with Demeter, the goddess of the harvest and growth. A lusty Hades had set his sights on her daughter, Persephone, and reached up from the underworld to pluck the flower of his desire, carrying her off into the bowels of darkness. Somewhat clumsily, during the hasty abduction, he also inadvertently grabbed a swineherd and his charges. These events inspired a women-only fertility festival called Thesmorphoros. As part of the proceedings, ritually purified women in white robes confined pigs to a pit where they were left to die. The next year, the women would retrieve the putrefied remains and mix them with wheat grains, which were then symbolically sown in the belief that the consignment of the repossessed rotten flesh to the earth at the start of the winter rainy season would favor the growth of wheat and stimulate fecundity in the devotees.

Fast-forwarding to the modern age, the Italian pig slaughtering season opens canonically on Saint Andrew's feast day (November 30), protector of fish mongers, singers, old maids, nubile women, and significantly, women wanting to get pregnant, a nod to Thesmorphoros. The season ends on Saint Anthony Abbot's feast day (January 17), protector of domestic animals, livestock, farmers, food artisans, fire and shingles (herpes zoster), though the less pious waived the closure of slaughter season until the beginning of Lent. From region to town to the individual butcher, the preparation of salumi, salt-preserved pork products, varied in methods and ingredients. Umbrians, however, feel that they have the better claim to quality, as the very name of the specialist who prepares the meat, norcino, derives from the Umbrian province of Norcia, where they achieved a reputation, dating back to ancient times, of excellence in all things swine. The renown of their surgical precision was such that families whose young sons showed promise as singers would call upon the norcino to carry out the unsavory task of castration: the effeminate castrati were the most admired and highly paid in the opera. A botched home job could have grim repercussions, just as a mismanaged pig slaughter and salumi preparation in the hands of amateurs could bring calamitous consequences to a family.

Proverb: "Those who marry are only happy for a day, but those who slaughter their pig are happy for an entire year."

Most households raised one pig a year, and that pig was coddled like a member of the family. The duality of death and affection made for mixed emotions when slaughter time came around. On the one hand, it was a moment of relief and celebration; like the wheat harvest, it allowed the family to calculate whether their provisions would get them through another year. On the other, it was a solemn moment of loss and reverence for the sanctity of life.

Gratitude for the bounty was expressed through the distribution of blood-based puddings to others in the community. Blood was the first product harvested from the pig, and because it was highly perishable, it needed to be consumed not long after it was collected. To ensure that nothing went to waste, families tried to time their slaughter so that these shared products would not accumulate. Every community had its own traditional method of preparation. For example, a Molisan tradition treated the blood as a fast food, adding it immediately to a skillet with a sautéed mince of onion, celery, carrot, red peppers, garlic, and parsley. This was heated and brought directly to the table to be sopped up with bread. Men and women ate at separate tables. With respect to the rural hierarchy, at the men's table, only when the patriarch raised his glass could the others drink. He could fill the glasses of the others, but no one could fill his. Likewise, no one else could fill the glass of someone who outranked him. Blood products were sometimes the result of mixed species, or rather, as they jokingly say in Tuscany, "'See you in the *burristo!*' said the sheep to the pig," an expression used when saying goodbye. Superstitions surrounding the slaughter abounded and varied according to local customs. Preferred dates for the event were during a waxing not waning moon. Menstruating women were a bad omen, and could not participate in the slaughter. One did not make pasta or bread on that day because it might lead to early spoilage of the meat. Once the pig had been drained of blood, it was shaved all over and the hairs on the end of the tail were thrown onto the roof of the sty as a good portent for next year's pig.

From a more practical viewpoint, some families raised three pigs per year: one for themselves, one for the padrone and one as medical insurance, pay off the doctor. With so much hunger, one might wonder why everyone didn't simply own a sow and raise a herd of pigs. Pigs are hearty eaters and require a third of their weight in food every day. While they are omnivorous and not very fussy, they were happy to forage, (in fact, they have a penchant for truffles, a food that was of little interest to the contadini), but that was not always feasible. The idea of slopping pigs from table scraps was a moot point because if there were any, they were recycled for human consumption. Supplying sufficient food to even one pig required considerable labor and inventiveness, and farmhands were already strapped with work.

The following scenario, one common in the tight-reigned mezzadria context of Tuscany, sheds further light on the constraints of raising pigs: one or some of the sharecropper households on an estate possessed a sow, but the male hog was kept in the custody of the padrone, who hired the stud pig out to the contadino when the sow was predisposed. The overseer kept a close eye on the number of piglets born, and when they were ready for market, a swine merchant came to buy the pick of the litter, profits going to the padrone. The capoccia was left with one or two runts, depending on the number of people in his household. When the pigs were of age, or rather, of weight, the fee owed for the stud service consisted of one hind leg, the coveted prosciutto. The overseer would come round to collect the padrone's due, but the contadino also had the option of purchasing the leg, and thus the transaction would get written up in the infamous accounts ledger.

Pigs were of such importance that in areas like Emilia, home of the world famous Parma ham, they were referred to by the metonymy "the animal," just as cars in Italy are referred to as "the machine." Fat was the most important part of the pig, not only for the satisfying rich taste and calories it lent to foods, but also for its multiple extra-culinary utilities. Therefore, the slaughter date was slated in accordance with the amount of fat the pig had amassed. The prime fat was that covering the kidney area, and was rendered into cooking lard to be used for deep-frying, dessert crusts, and as a general condiment. Olive oil was a cash crop sold to urban markets and used only sparingly if at all at the contadino's table.

Lard was used as a sealant preservative for food as it inhibited oxidation. Prosciuttos were anointed with fat both to keep the outer parts supple and as an effective fly repellent. There was a range of non-culinary uses as well, soap-making being the most common. As a softener and water repellent, the upper portion of a country clog, made with kid or sheepskin nailed to a wooden sole, was greased with pig fat, keeping them more comfortable and dry. It was also used as a lubricant for household objects and tools like handsaws. Simply dab a bit between the saw and the wood, and it's smooth sailing.

With the postwar exodus to the city, the number of pigs kept for family needs decreased significantly. Thus, there was an interim before industrial pig farms were able to meet the high-volume demand of wage earners. In the meantime, however, the "Mediterranean Diet" gurus hit the public sphere with the cholesterol scare, stimulating the launch of the olive oil industry and frightening the public away from the consumption of salumi. The commercial availability of refrigerators increased the consumption of fresh pork, with consumers requesting leaner and leaner cuts. The good name of lard was indelibly sullied and has yet to recover. Recent international valorization of craft salumi, however, has stimulated an increase in the demand for quality artisanal products that could well be described as explosive. Concomitantly, meat and saturated fats are reemerging from decades of medical exile, while the evil dietary eyeball is shifting its gaze towards carbohydrates and sugar as the principal culprits behind our modern ills.

I am indebted to the butchers Lorenzo and Vincenzo Chini of Macelleria Chini in Gaiole, Chianti, for their invaluable contribution to my research of this section. Their forefathers began as swineherds in the hills of Gaiole in the seventeenth century, and today their artisanal salumi are considered among the finest in Italy. Lorenzo has played a pivotal role in the recent reintroduction of the Cinta Senese *breed into the craft salumi market. His singular devotion to his herd and his meticulous dedication to his vocation exemplify the objectives of humane farming practices and the ideals of quality craftsmanship.*

Veronica

Born 1928 – San Martin Pereto

Once our interview is underway, Veronica's daughter, Graziella, appears with a box of cookies, the kind of packaged cookies that are often given as Christmas gifts in Italy – all different shapes, some variegated with chocolate, each one neatly stacked into its separate compartment in a pre-fab plastic tray, and each one as insipid as the last. I am familiar with these bland cookies, but for the sake of courtesy, I take one and eat it. The other three present, Veronica, her husband Giovanbattista and his sister do not partake even when I implore them. They just smile kindly. I am also offered Coca-Cola, from which I am fortunately able to excuse myself, as I cannot have caffeine. When I entreat them again to take a cookie, Veronica says, "We usually only eat things that are made at home. We don't really like boxed food that someone else has made. But please, you go right ahead," she says smiling sweetly, "and have another." A catch-22: If I eat them, I am unmasked as a typical undiscerning American; if I don't I'm rude. I eat the cookies. Giovanbattista then says to his sister, "Keep her company, you have one too." She draws away meekly and says, "No! Not me! I'm not used to those!"

The second time I go to visit them, Graziella has made a simple rustic cake, and they all dig in with gusto. Pleased that I have returned for a second visit, the conversation is quite lively, and at times the volume gets out of hand. Veronica grew up in a very remote area in the hills of Umbria. Agriculturally speaking, they were smallholders, or homesteaders. They owned their own land and were, for the most part, self-sufficient. Although that meant going without what we would now consider some very basic, even fundamental items, theirs was a step up from the lot of the sharecropper or field hand, as they "lived the dream" of owning their own farm.

We lived way the heck out there in the boonies. You know, up there around San Martino. There wasn't even any dirt roads going past our land. We was homesteaders, tucked up there in the middle of nowheres. We saw to everything for ourselves, but that sure don't mean we had everything we needed! But the land was ours, and the house was ours, so in those days, we were sittin' pretty compared to most. It was just me, my father, my brother, and our stepmother; our own mamma died when I was two. Was just us four, takin' care of the whole farmstead. The grandfolks were all long dead. I never know'd them, but they left us the land when they passed.

Not much to say about school. I only did the 2nd grade and a smidgen of the 3rd. Wasn't much of a school anyway, just a room some kind folks let us use in their house. Our teacher was a respectable sort, but her husband was a good-for-nothing bum! Lived off of his wife, that bloodsucker. Naw, I didn't last too long in school. There was work to be done on the farm, and me bein' a girl, well, weren't much sense in it really. Farm people like us didn't have much use for schoolin'. I maybe would have liked doin' more school, but we only had three grades anyways, so weren't no more than that *to* do. Come evening time, the boys could go off after chores and do the fourth grade. Not many of them did it though. When you're workin' on the farm all day, you don't have too much left in you to go openin' books. My husband here, Giambi, he done the fourth grade. He's a sight smarter than me! We didn't do none of that Fascist Saturday business, though. Where did they think we was gonna meet? In the fields? And do what? Run ourselves silly? Sorry, but Saturdays there was work to be done. We learned our three 'R's, a bit about the sacraments, a bit about the fascio and then "Arrivederci!"

Yes, ma'am, there was *plen-ty* to get done on the farm. When school was out we walked home and got straight to it. We had seven acres to tend to. We had wheat and all sorts of vegetable, but not all of our land was farmed. Some of it was woods, an apple orchard, grapevines, and a chestnut grove. In our grandparents' day, chestnuts was just as important as wheat.

While evidence of chestnut consumption dates back 20,000 years, they began to flourish in Italy when the Ancient Romans brought them in from Greece. They rapidly became a mainstay due to their high caloric content and versatility, and even came to be called the "bread of the poor." They could be roasted, boiled, or made into soup, gruel, or bread and were believed to cure myriad ills from headache to gout, in addition to being an aphrodisiac. According to folk wisdom, they played an important role in women's health, protecting against miscarriage, reducing menstrual flow and soothing renal pain during pregnancy. Today, the importance of chestnuts has diminished to the point where they are now mostly an autumnal fireside quaintism. In Morra, where Veronica lives now, they hold a yearly sagra della castagna, *or chestnut festival, in remembrance of its fundamental role in sustaining the populace.*

We raised all the usual sorts of farm animals: rabbits, chickens, sheep, and pigs. Time and again, we got us a goose or a duck. We never had no cow or goat or nothing, so our breakfast was just caffè orzo. I mean to say, weren't no milk in it. Anyway, with no roads up to our place, wasn't no way they were gonna be luggin' your milk all the way out there. People with a milkin' cow, well now, they was a class above us!

When we went into town we would trade some of our vegetables for cheese. You could keep eatin' that even after it had gone hard, and when there weren't nothing left but the crusts, we threw them into the evening soup. So for breakfast, it was bread and cheese or bread and prosciutto. You know what I'm saying? I'm saying it was bread and somethin'. In the winter, sometimes we had polenta. We always had white bread on our table, the *good* bread, none of that coarse, gritty bread. It was good white Tuscan bread with no salt.

The main characteristic that differentiates Tuscan bread from other va-rieties is that it is made without salt. Its origin dates back to a conflict between Pisa and Florence, around the year 1100, when salt imports were blocked. Instead of disarming, they proudly made do without salt. Another version has it that salt taxes in the Middle Ages were so oner-ous that humble Florentines, as a sign of virtue, united in preparing their bread without salt. Regardless, the distinctly pronounced flavors of Tosco-umbro *cuisine marry well with their salt-free bread, reason enough to continue the tradition, which has long been a source of local pride.*

We grew our own wheat, and so high summertime, we threshed it with the oxen and the thresher that got passed around house to house. Folks came round to give you a hand. We filled sacks with the hulled grain, and then hitched up the mule to haul it off to the nearby mill to grind it.

Just about every day at lunch, we had flour and water tagliatelle At Christmas and Easter, same thing, but it was egg noodles. For holi-days sometimes we'd have a sweet like a *crostata* or *cavallucci*, and in the evening, folks would come by and we'd roast chestnuts. But really, weren't nothin' more than good cheer that made Christmas different from other days, not the food. At Easter there was a bit more feastin'. It bein' the end of lent and all, we was hankerin' for something to eat! We had ourselves a chicken and a rabbit and maybe some sausage and cheese too!

Supper was near always tagliolini or quadruccini. Yep, the same pasta as lunchtime just cut up different and ate in broth. Most folks round here had pasta in broth in the evening because it's easy to digest for a good night's sleep. Let me tell you our usual evening broth. You took your lardo and minced it up good, then chop up a potato, some celery, herbs and onion. Toss all that into your cauldron hangin' over the fire and let it go till it gets real good and brown, and then you add a spoonful of conserva to bring out the taste. Put in as much water as you need to get your brood fed, let her boil, and there you go! That soup is still one of my husband's favorites. He wolfs it down like noth-in' doin'. He sure loves his food! Eats everything in sight. These days we don't use lardo though. We use oil because they tell us pig fat is bad for you. Back then, folks who didn't make their own olive oil didn't hardly know what it was. Everybody used lard. You had take care 'bout buying olive oil 'cause weren't no tellin' what was in it. Some people got real sick from olive oil that weren't right. Anyway, we always used lard in my family.

In the 16th century, Bartolomeo Scappi, chef to the pope and one of the first to chronicle Italian cuisine, outlined the use of fats thus: fatback, lardo, and lard were for everyday, butter was for lean days (the Sabbath days – Friday and Saturday), while olive and almond oil were for Lent and other days with religious dietary restrictions. Pellegrino Artusi, writing three centuries later, felt that every region should keep to whichever fat was most available in their area, as the local flavor of dishes were based on those fats. But one's pocketbook played a decisive factor in fat choice. Butter tended to be for the upper classes and the northern regions. It was considered the more nutritive choice for children and the sickly; lard was used ubiquitously amongst the lower classes, hence by most people, while olive oil, where available, was a secondary option and used only in those dishes and regions where it had an established tradition.

We still do like in the old days. Pasta at lunchtime and a soup in the evening, just like we always done. But now, if we want, we can have other things too. Before, it was *that* or *nothin'*. Before, you had to try to stretch everything to the limit. Now, if we want, we can make any sort of sauce for the pasta, or we can eat pizza and focaccia, whatever and whenever we want. Sometimes we even try to make recipes from other regions like *riso alla milanese*. You know, sort of creative like.

In our day, there was plenty of folks was down and out. So much suffering. So much hunger. Workin' the farm was a hard life. Now, with all them machines and what have you, a man can get more work done in a single hour than he could back then in a whole day working with three healthy brothers! Once my brother up and gone off to war, we couldn't hardly keep up, so we got a sow and sold piglets, and sold a bit of wine to make ends meet. We went mushrooming too, otherwise weren't no way to make it through the year.

We never had much though; I never had no more than a couple dresses at a time. My father's everyday clothes, well by golly, today you wouldn't even use them as rags to clean the floors! A man come by who made our shoes, clogs really. The bottom part was made of wood, and after a time that wore out, so the shoemaker fella would take off the top part, if it was still good, and would fit it onto a new wood sole. The top part was made of shoe, I mean, you know, leather.

Even when my husband came courting, all's we had was them clod-hoppers. It's not like I ran in and put on my Sunday best just 'cause he came to call! Everyone dressed like that, so no one noticed. When we got married, we got us each a proper pair of shoes. Real shoes. During wartime, we mostly went barefoot so's not to wear down the clogs too fast. I met this here fella in 1940. I was 22 and he was 26. He had just got his marchin' orders, and on June 10th the war started up.

Gianbattista (Veronica's husband): My father, rest in peace, had been in the Great War. Got a hunk of his head shot off. He lived to see another day, sure, but he died young, poor man. I was called to service March 12, 1940, and they shipped me off to Sardinia for a good long spell. Was six years before I managed to get my discharge. I got malaria while I was there. Oh! Worse thing you can get! Army sent a telegram to my father to come collect me 'cause it didn't seem like I was long for this world. I pulled through though, but as soon as I was able, they shipped me back to Sardinia.

That's when I got to see Mussolini, when he came to inspect the troops. He was always out inspectin' troops. Untirable that man was! We put on a spectacle for him of marchin' and parades. When he walked by us, he came within two meters of me. I swear it! I was here, you see, and he was *there*, right *there*! He walked up onto the podium, all puffed up, chest held high. He was fierce with that jutting jaw, but by gosh, he sure was a squat thing. He was with his brother, who, poor thing, died pretty soon after. When he was finished givin' his speech, darn long speech it was, he called for a meetin' with all of the officers. We regulars thought we were doomed. We thought sure they were plannin' to ship us off to somewheres worse than where we were at. But instead, by God, you know what he did?! He done left each and everyone of us five liras each! Five liras each! And there were plenty of us! And he left us five lire! [*enough to buy nearly three kilos of bread at the time*]. Young people today go round saying Mussolini was a dictator, but for me, times were better then than now! Not for food, of course, not for that, but for the government, hands down! He never took no money for his own personal gain, not like politicians today, all lining their pockets. He didn't buy nothing for himself with government money. We would still have Corsica if Mussolini been around then, instead of losing it to France!

Mussolini's obsession was with power, be it physical, political, or sexual, and he did indeed eschew money, even refusing his pay as Prime Minister. His weakness, however, was personal vanity, which made him vulnerable to the ploys of compliment and the barbs of criticism. His appetite for public adoration made him impulsive in his governance opting for flash over substance.

I'd do in every last one of them in the government today! It's all just jabbering! You'll see. Soon as Letta [*the prime minister at the time of this interview*] has stuffed his wallet, he'll be hightailing it outta there too! I'll tell you a story. I worked three years in the mess hall. So, one day a German officer asks if we have gone to get the provisions. He was a doctor and, well, he got one look at the meat and had it burned 'cause it had all gone bad. Hadn't been for him, we woulda eaten that and got sick, or worse! You see, the Germans are precise, precise about everything. It is the Italians I don't trust. When the Germans stole grapes out of someone's field, they left money pinned to a grape leaf. You didn't see Italians doing that!

Veronica's sister in-law: When I married in '37, Mussolini give me 500 lire and this certificate. [*She had brought down the framed commemorative certificate that hangs to this day on her bedroom wall to show me. With time it has become blackened, cracked, and brittle under its glass casing*]. On March 21, 1937 I married and I got this gift from Mussolini hisself. He done good by us. He give me 500 lire. And he give money too if a girl got with child and was left to raise the baby alone.

Marriage incentives, aimed at increasing the population, came in three standard increments: 1,000 liras for white-collar employees who married before age 30, 700 liras for blue-collar workers who married before age 26, and 500 liras for country folks. Marriage loans were also available, and with the birth of a second son, the amount owed was cut by 30%. Likewise a tax was levied on unmarried men and increase until they were 60 years of age. Income tax for unmarried men and childless couples was also higher.

Veronica: Well, we didn't never get no money gift. Us peasant folks always said what's food for three can make food for six, and the more hands workin' in the field the better, so the Duce's gifts didn't make much difference to us folks about having babies or no. I, for one, ain't got nothin' good to say about Mussolini.

Giovanbattista: He gave me five liras when he came to Sardinia! And anyway, we married in '46 and they weren't givin' money out for weddings anymore. Problem is our own caved in too soon. They didn't stand by Mussolini like they should have. Funny thing is, when the Americans came in '43 and docked in Sicily, they already were callin' the officers by name - Captain This, Major That – 'cause we had already sold our own down the river. Mussolini didn't have a chance! He ran a tight ship, kept a stranglehold over his commanders, so they sold out for greener pastures!

Veronica: The only good talkin' I want to do is about now. Before it was all war, war, war and poverty. Now we live like signori, and I am not gonna go talking bad about it. For chrissake! We didn't even have underwear before, and here you're carrying on about your five lousy liras! They said the war wouldn't last long and it did. But even after a war is over, even after a war is over, it's never *really* over, because there's all the dead to remember. What's gonna happen when we old folks aren't here anymore to remember them? Forgettin' the dead has consequences. We went to war. We wanted to win it, but heck, we lost. Losin's always the worse end of the stick. Meantime, we was hand to mouth and still, whatever you could spare was s'posed to go towards the war effort. Here they were, sending our food, *our food*, off to the Germans! That was the time we called the *fame nero*, black hunger. We didn't have much, but at my house, at least we wasn't starving. Some folks was near to starvin'. We was dirt poor, and I mean *dirt*, but still we had white bread on the table and potatoes under the ground. Trouble was, while we was makin' enough to eat every day, we never had no ready money, no cash in hand.

And then there was taxes to be paid too. When you killed your pig, the state wanted some money for your trouble. The taxman come round and weighed out a prosciutto and give you a figure about the weight of the animal because you paid according to weight. So, you know what we did? Whoever had the smallest pig that year, well, we passed around that prosciutto from farm to farm when the taxman come. He knew what we was on about, but there was always somethin' passed his way to keep him hushed up.

Once in a while a man passed through and took our rabbit pelts and eggs to sell in the market, but if we needed even the smallest things like some thread, there just weren't no money for extras like that. We didn't have *things,* you know what I'm sayin'? There was a fella would come round our parts sellin' wares from what he picked up goin' house to house of rich people. What I mean is, he would go to the rich folks and buy their cast offs cheap, and he would resell to folks like us that couldn't afford to buy nothin' new. Today everybody's got everything. We had food to get by, but we was out there working the land with shovels and hoes, shovels and hoes. We had oxen and ploughs, so it wasn't all by hand, but we made just enough for ourselves and a little extra to trade. We even lived in the house with the farm animals. They was on the ground floor, and we bedded down on the floor above them. The floor was wooden planks that were put down with space between 'em so that the heat from the animals warmed us at least a bit. Nobody gave a thought about the smell. There was a big central hearth where we cooked, and local families shared a big stone oven outdoors where we made bread. In the winter there wasn't a heck of a lot to eat, always the same stuff day in and day out, but what really got you was them biting cold nights in the hills. We didn't have no heat and winters was hard.

Vegetables was kept going year round, so there was always something from the season. In the winter, there was cabbage, potatoes, dried beans and turnip greens; the turnip part was fed to the pigs. So long as you got potatoes and beans, you're going to be all right. In the winter, we slaughtered a pig like most folks did. That maybe sounds like a lot, but I am telling you, it was not a good life like folks think about the country now.

There was no protection for old people because there weren't no pensions. If you needed the doctor you could give him food in exchange, and the really poor folks had a poverty card, so's they could get the town doctor for free. But medicine wasn't free. If you needed medicine then you had to make a trade, and sometimes you couldn't manage it even then. And if you owned a piece of land like us, if you was a homesteader, you didn't have no rights to the doctor. But let me say, about the doctor, we just didn't call for him. If you was sick, well, you was sick. The old folks, when their time come, well you might call the doctor then, but usually they didn't want him. They's afraid his curing would make it worse.

Women had their babies with the other women folk. Who ever saw a doctor? I had four babies at home with my mother-in-law and the midwife. It hurt like hell, but all of them come out like they was s'posed to. Lots of gals didn't make it through, though. There wasn't nothin' for the pain, or bleedin', just hot water! I never seen a doctor. Country women were always working, and so the babies come out easier, but I am telling you, it was a hard, hard, hard life. And the sad part is, now that things is good we are too old. Things was never good when we was young. But a woman used to sitting around at home is going to have a tough time birthin'. For my first baby, I walked three or four kilometers while I was in labor to get home. When I got home, I was hungry so I ate something and then I said, "All right then, I am going to bed to have this baby." It was after the war and my husband had a motorbike, so he went and fetched the woman. There wasn't roads all the way there, so he had to walk some of it. I went upstairs to tidy up a bit, with the midwife coming and all. Wouldn't right be bringing a child in to the world with clutter. Midwife come, I got in bed, and the baby was born then and there.

Gianbattista: At a certain point in the war, I have to admit, things gone all wrong, and we troops in Sardinia were trapped on the island. They had clean gone and forgot about us. For three years, I was stranded there, and my folks didn't know if I was dead or alive. No provisions were coming in, and people started dying of starvation. And I mean dying for real. There were no boats to get away on neither. If any boats came around, we all wanted to get on board, begging them not to leave us there to die. No boats meant no letters, nothing. They just up and forgot about us. At one point we were down to 100 grams of bread a day and half a sardine. If you tried to steal fruit from the natives, they'd shoot at you. I been workin' in the military kitchen for three years, and it hadn't been no feast even before supplies were cut off. We had rice with tomato sauce and fatback every day. Pasta on Sundays.

Military tomato sauce: (serves 100 men)
1.5 kilos pork fatback
2 kilos onion, chopped
1.5 kilos tomato paste
10g pepper
1 kilo parmesan

Pound the fatback and the onion together and put in a large skillet. Fry, stirring frequently so that it cooks evenly. Let the onions start to brown. Dilute the tomato paste in 4 liters of water and add to the pan. Let boil 20 minutes and it is ready to be put on the pasta. To dress it up a bit more, you could add garlic or rosemary, or the pepper could be increased up to 15 grams.

A note on tomato paste from the Military cookbook*: "Tomato paste has little nutritive value and should be used in moderation. It gives color and flavor to dishes. Too much of it can be noxious to the organism especially in hot weather. If sometimes the color of the pasta does not seem red enough – it might still be good, and if the sauce has been prepared correctly it may even be tastier that way."*

A note on pasta from the Military cookbook*: "The soldier's ration of pasta . . . has been rigorously analyzed by chemists for the genuineness of the components, above all to assure the proper quantity of gluten, which as everyone knows is the nutritive part of flour, in fact it is even referred to as 'vegetable meat' . . . The correct proportioning has been established at 10%, that is, 10 liters of water for every kilo of pasta. [Place the pasta in a pan of boiling water] and leave it cook for 18-20 minutes*

> *. . . after taking it from the flame, it is best to add a ladle of cold water to stop the cooking and let it rest a moment before draining it: with this simple operation you can avoid a great deal of that dreadful sticking on the bottom of the pan (especially if it has been slightly overcooked), which would make it seem like goose fodder. Set aside the water from the pasta to make the evening soup. This will make it denser and more nutritious."*

The evening mess for dinner was broth and half ration of cheese. Sometimes, if there was only half ration of soup then we would cut up pieces of boiled meat scraps and the men were at least allowed a bit of meat, though it wasn't much more than one bite for each. The trumpeter announced meals with this tune... *'La zuppa è cotta, la zuppa è cotta da-da-da-da-da'*. At first, in the morning, there was coffee, *real* coffee every day, with milk. But weren't too long before we went to surrogate coffee and canned milk, and then it was watered down canned milk and then no milk at all. I'm not sure what the surrogate coffee was made of. It was a black powder. So basically, breakfast come down to a cup of black water. The officers, well, they had different food. We regulars might as well have been prisoners.

Veronica: On the home front, the Germans were pushing through, but we were more afraid of the fascists than of them! Even the Italian soldiers had it in for the Black Shirt officers. Here they was livin' high off the hog, while our boys were out there marchin' and maneuverin'. Our soldiers didn't have nothin' to eat while the fascist squads were stuffing themselves. I'd say in our area, we were about half and half fascists and communists. In my family, we were all communists. There were times you would hear a woman frettin', *"Oh, Dio!* My husband didn't come home last night!" The fascists would take and beat people they met on the street for nothin', nothin'! 'specially if it got to curfew time. My father said that they went after the communists and made them drink poison. They was really the worst! Ignoramuses! And you can be sure there was always plenty of wine to go round to make matters worse.

> *The "poison" in this case refers to the castor oil torture used widely by the Black Shirts as a means of teaching malcontents a lesson. It was*

force fed to subjects while they had their trousers bound to them. The castor oil stimulated the bowels to violently evacuate, and the victims defecated on themselves. In such a state of humiliation, they were then sent on their way and thus subjected to public shame.

I don't really get out to the supermarket anymore, but let me say this, there is no telling what they're passing off as food these days. I don't trust it. I do like pizza though. I can't really remember the first time I had it, but it must have been forty years ago. It was like a foreign food to us, because it came from Naples. After the war, the Neapolitans came up our way. So, it's been here, yes, about forty years. They used to call out to us in town, "Hey get your fresh pizza here!" I really liked it and ate as many pieces as I wanted 'cause by then I had some cash in my pocket. Those people from Naples they didn't have much else, just pizza, and roast chickens. I'd never buy a pizza at the grocery store. I like the pizza my daughter makes at home, or the ones from a pizzeria. And I'd never buy anything frozen. Just gelato.

The worst supermarket food for me is broth in a box, or them ready-made sauces. Today, young wives buy everything already made. Salad and everything. How can you save the good things when young people's so lazy? And women don't teach their daughters cookin', so the daughters just do whatever's easy.

Graziella: [age 57, Veronica and Giovanbattista's daughter] Women don't want to take the time to cook, so they just pick it up already made, and when they go to a restaurant, it all seems good to them just because they don't know how to cook. We are losing our traditions fast. Making good food takes time and dedication. For example, if you buy a chicken and pluck it yourself, there's a world of difference between that and the ones you buy at the supermarket. Store bought ones seem like they are made of wax! It's like they are embalmed. They aren't good, but then who really wants to pluck a chicken? Today they kill them with electricity, and it is another procedure altogether. Those are some sad looking chickens. When I get chickens, I get seven or eight at a time. I kill them, soak them, and pluck them like it's supposed to be done, and then I freeze them. One by one, as I need them, I take one out and roast it in the wood-burning oven.

Veronica: The one good thing about not havin' nothing is that we was all content. No television, no nothing. We'd meet up with neighbors, danced, sang, played games, told stories, and go to church functions. The countryside seems abandoned now, but there used to be lots of us. When I got married and had my babies, there was near fourteen of us in the house! There was life back then. We didn't have nothin', but we all got together for a good time. Now it's everybody for himself. Even the work that there was to do, collecting the chestnuts, threshing the wheat, someone always come round to give a hand without ever having to ask. Now you don't get nothin' if you don't pay for it. That's how the couples met each other. The folks would say, "Ah you've got to meet Veronica! She's beautiful, hard worker, good at collecting chestnuts! Come to the function tonight and you'll see! Walk her home!" That sort of thing.

Food needs to be good to keep the youngsters at home. Parents need to keep a close watch over them. They can't just eat and run. Parents gotta know where the kids are at all times. In our time, girls got married, and the things that happen today didn't happen then – this one goin' with that one, havin' children from different fathers. What good can come out of that? Nothin'. Now I am not saying a woman should stick with a bad man, but if they have words with each other a few times they can't go runnin' off to the lawyer. Young people have no patience. They get sore at the least little thing. Particularly women gotta be more tolerant. The kids pay too high a price. Women know more than men; they know how to run a household, and that there's no small task. If women would just see that they are in command... that's why they need to be more tolerant. Violence no, that never, and if things aren't good, then separate, but don't go getting mixed up with someone else and complicatin' everything.

Fascist penal code 559 stated that a wife caught in a one-off adulterous ménage could be sentenced up to one year in prison, and her accomplice the same. If it had been a love relationship, her sentence doubled if the husband saw fit to press charges. For an unfaithful husband to face the double sentence, he had to be caught in flagrant with his lover under the conjugal roof or maintain her as a mistress at another address. In either case, both he and the "concubine" would be subject to two years in prison if the wife chose to press charges. In a post-war reevaluation of the law, it was decided that the wife's infidelity did indeed deserve this stricter punishment, because as wife and mother she was duty-bound by her role as protector of the family unit. Therefore, her absolute fidelity was a moral imperative to society at large. A man's dalliances, on the other hand, were deemed significantly less consequential to the family's overall well being. In 1968, the government finally conceded to overturning that portion of the law punishing a woman's casual affair. Feminists were incensed over the paltry concession, and in 1969, law 559 was scrapped in its entirety as being unconstitutional. Just as a coincidental note of interest, the advertising slogan "You've come a long way, baby," was launched in 1968.

We kept living that life until my daughter married and we came to live here with her and her husband. We left the house to our nephews. They had five boys in their family. They fixed the house up, and still work the land, but now they have machines and tractors. I wouldn't want my children to have to farm for a living. You can't live that kind of life anymore because there is no sense of community and there's too many laws. Everyone moved out of the country, and went to work in factories, but now the factories are all closing. What can you do?

Intermezzo

La battaglia del grano - The Battle for Wheat

When Mussolini launched his massive propaganda campaign, The Battle for Wheat, on June 14, 1925, it set political analysts abroad abuzz with suspicions that this might only be the tip of the iceberg of a more grandiose imperialistic plan. Quite astute. In this initial phase, Mussolini's goal was to release Italy from the supposed stranglehold dependence on foreign grain imports by increasing national production exponentially. Self-sufficiency would create a gastronomic fortress around the nation, intended to buttress it against the slings and arrows of outrageous fortune, as they forged ahead with their ultimate goal: restoring the glory of Rome. The carefully chosen word "battle", as opposed to "campaign," "movement," or "drive" was intended to unify the Italian people in a common crusade, just as pinpointing "wheat" as the crop of choice would stir them at a core emotional level. Bread was religion, family, home, health, and hearth – and now it would also signify Patria. In the hungry years following WWI, protesters would carry posters decrying "Work and Bread", the most basic of necessities. Winning The Battle for Wheat meant that they might finally get their due.

In the hope that it would lead the populace back to rural values and away from the morally corrosive effects of urbanization, the Church praised the Battle for Wheat. A healthy outdoor life would purify and elevate the soul, and a morally upright nation could only bide well for the fatherland. Initially, there might be sacrifices, but adversity would bolster character, motivate fortitude and foresightedness.

However, the entire undertaking lacked just that: foresightedness. This political venture, like many, sounded good, was easy to set in motion, but impossible to achieve.

From the very beginning, the scheme was illogical. The import price of wheat was on a decisively downward trend, and remained significantly lower than national prices throughout the 1930s. Importing wheat at the going market rate would have advantaged consumers, and allowed arable land in Italy to be used for a variety of crops as well as pasturelands. Wheat did not fair well in all soils and climates; therefore the change from traditional crops to wheat occasionally met with disaster. The Battle for Wheat might as well have been called "Wheat or Meat;" there simply wasn't sufficient farmland to sustain both. But wheat won out, and the so-called "noble proteins" became even more scarce and costly, as did vegetables. The Battle also greatly distorted the balance cereal varieties while the mono-focus on limited strains of resistant high-yield wheat wreaked havoc on biodiversity, resulting in the disappearance of local varieties.

Prizes were given out for high yields, but profits did not trickle down to the landless workers. On the contrary, the 30s saw a drop in farmhand wages. A family of five consumed an average of twenty-nine dollars a year in bread; agricultural and factory workers respectively earned about $150 and $250 annually. The battle for wheat was especially brutal for those consuming it. It did less to assuage the wages of sin than it did to line the pockets of the large landowners. And as the decade dragged on, calorie consumption diminished. As a French anti-fascist intellectual so perspicaciously pointed out, that in this battle, as in every other battle, it is the contadino who ends up dead in the field.

But the government would not be thwarted, and turned to reclaiming swamplands to extend the acreage to be dedicated to wheat. Mussolini put himself center stage in the Battle, frequently playing an active role (with ample media coverage) in the harvest festivities. He was featured shirtless in numerous magazines, sometimes donning protective eye gear while he toiled like a commoner under the blazing sun. In contrast, his coworkers, who were not playacting, were fully clad and did not wear goggles.

National grain production did increase and imports decreased, but on another fascist battlefield, the potentially disastrous Battle for Births was being waged. In spite of governmental incentives for the fruitful to multiply, annual birth rates actually dropped, although the population itself continued to grow steadily, another stick in the spokes of the Battle. By pulling back on wheat imports, prices rose as more people worked harder for less pay. In the final analysis, the experiment succeeded for a time in feeding the masses with a diet that cost less per calorie but had little regard for the spectrum of nutritional needs. As WWII drew near, the Battle came apart at the seams, as statesmen lost interest in beating a dead horse.

Luigina

Born 1920 – Ovanengo

Luigina lives alone in a three-room ground floor apartment near the historic center of Orzinuovi, a small town in northern Italy where Brescian dialect was spoken as the first language until only a generation ago. Luigina had neither teeth nor dentures and was quite soft-spoken, so although I am familiar with her dialect, understanding her was an undertaking. With the exception of the Italian she had learned in the four years she attended elementary school, she didn't have regular exposure to the language of her country until the late 1970s when she purchased a television. When I went for a return visit, I brought her a small flowering plant. She was so pleased that she made a concerted effort to speak less dialect, and I found myself, ironically, complimenting her on her Italian. Luigina spent her entire youth and adulthood living and working as a field hand in a cascina, an isolated rural complex. She and her entire family resided year round in the cascina housing provided by the padrone. They were paid for their work both in kind and in wages. As was true with sharecroppers, the family existed as a unit; if one of them slipped up, the whole family paid the consequences.

My papa, he was a severe sort of man. The Great War hardened him, and then of course, his life as a bracciante did away with of the rest of his spirit. Before the war he had two children by my mother, a boy and a girl, and then after the war, I came into the world. During the war, my mother was so afraid for Papa, see, he been away for a good long spell, but without knowin' readin' or writin', she set out looking for him at the front, and she found him! He told her, "Silly woman! You go on back home and I'll be there soon as they let me go." He wasn't a man of too many words, but he'd tell us stories 'bout how it was in the war, always lookin' not to get killed, always seeing folks around you getting shot, and none of them havin' enough to eat. They ate whatever they could find in the fields, whatever they could find.

He came back from the war and there wasn't much by way of work, and him with a family to look after... so my folks picked up a situation working as braccianti in Ovanengo, where I was born. He worked for an hourly wage, paid once every two weeks. The northern folks didn't do sharecropping. We just worked and, well, that was all. Just work.

My mamma died when the fourth baby come. The midwife just come to us straight from another birthing and didn't clean the irons too good, those ones for helping the baby out, so mamma died from infection. Papa had to get him a new wife right quick to take care of us, because a man needs a wife for seeing to the house and little ones. He took his sister-in-law for a wife on account of his brother being killed in the war. She needed a husband and he needed a wife, so that's how that worked out. All in all, she give him six more children, but only one son. So there we were. Ten of us livin' in our barrack house.

The barracks was a long string of rooms where all of the families workin' for the padrone lived, but we each had our own separate part. The padrone, he lived up in the big house, just a short ways away from us. For each family there was two rooms, a real big one and a small one. Us girls slept with my parents in the big room, and the boys got the small room all to theirselves. The big room was really the house itself where we had the hearth, made our food, ate, and slept. It kept us from wind and rain, but other than that, it wasn't too much different from sleeping outside. The winters were painful cold 'cause up here in the north we have real winter. Down at the end of the barracks was the barn, and I remember in winter we'd all take our plate and go to the barn to eat to be with the animals 'cause they was warm. I would run there, takin' care though not to lose any food on the way 'cause there wasn't too much to begin with. We had a fireplace, but it had to be put out at night or you could get sick. On the beds there was woolen blankets, but when it is freezing out, they don't do a heck of a lot! The only real warm place was the barn.

Papa let me go to school until the 4th grade. We had a proper schoolhouse, just a ten-minute walk away, boys and girls separate, but our school didn't have the 5th grade, and anyway, I knew that there wasn't going to be no more school for me. I could never go to Fascist Saturday because Papa didn't have money for the uniform, but he let me go watch them do their marching around the village. When I finished school, I was old enough to work on the farm and learn a trade. So I went to the sisters to learn sewing and knitting. All us girls did that. Busy hands was what was important. You didn't want girls getting too many notions in their heads. Papa was very clear about that. Then when I was thirteen I started working the fields too.

After the harvest, the padrone would give each family a sack of wheat and a sack of corn for polenta. All of us families was allowed to keep chickens and rabbits, so on Sunday we butchered one of them. But you can understand that, well – what I'm saying is that with ten of us to feed, three of them males, there wasn't much meat leftover for us girls. We braised it in the cauldron or roasted it in the bread oven. There was one oven on the farm that we all used. We took the innards, cleaned them up good, chopped them into bits and stewed them with tomato paste. That would make us a sauce to eat on another day with polenta. Those farm animals at the end of the barracks didn't belong to us folks. There was a man who looked after them, but they weren't for us to eat. They were for the padrone.

We had the ration card for buying food in town, cheese, rice, sometimes pasta. We made our own bread though, didn't use the ration card for it. With what the padrone give us for the harvest, and the little bit of wages coming in from the boys and Papa, we made do, but we had to forage for herbs, mushrooms, snails, and frogs to round it all out.

How to prepare snails

Bring a pot of water to the boil. Toss in your snails. If you listen closely they will cry out as they are put in the water. If the smell is not to your liking you can add a fresh bay leaf. Boil for one hour. Pour cold water over them to cool them to the touch. Prepare a dish of coarse corn meal and a small pan of vinegar. Using a small fork or a toothpick, pull the snail out of its shell. You want to keep the muscly foot and toss out the intestine. Boil the feet in vinegar 5 minutes. Remove them and rub them with the corn meal to remove any residual slime. If they are really big you might want to cut off the mouth. Rinse. They are now ready to be made into a sauce.

There was too many mouths to feed in our house, so breakfast was watered-down milk and caffè di olanda. It isn't around anymore, so it probably wasn't very good, but when you are hungry you don't notice so much how things taste. If that is what there was, you ate it. We weren't fussy. We were lucky to have bread in the morning 'cause bein' in the heart of polenta country like we was, lots of folks had polenta for breakfast, lunch, and dinner. Part of the bracciante pay on our farm was wheat. We threshed the grains ourselves and hauled the sacks off to the local mill to be ground.

Lunchtime, though, was almost always polenta. Most days we'd have half an egg per person, greens that we foraged, cabbage, and polenta. School children and the men out in the field came home for the midday and evening meals. The family ate together with the pot of polenta in the middle of the room. We had bowls, forks and spoons, but no knives. The food was well cooked, so we didn't need them. There was no wine, just well water. Dinner was a bit leaner, a brothy soup made with leftover scraps or whatever could be found. No one cooked "dishes", like recipes. You just made your food. I don't know how to explain it. Recipes were for holidays, feast days. The other days, we were just glad not to be hungry.

The patron saint of our village was Saint George. That is a day when we made a recipe. Every year in spring, at the *Festa di San Giorgio,* we made a sort of beef ravioli, here in the north they're called *casoncelli.* We ate the casoncelli in beef broth, and for us it was a down right feast. As part of the festivities, the womenfolk would set about making flour and water pasta noodles that you hung and left out to dry. More work for women even on feast days! But with summer coming on, we had to finish off what was left of the old wheat before the new wheat came in. That was it really. There wasn't no sweets or special cakes for our saint day. Women was the first ones to wake in the morning to get the fire going and breakfast ready. Then they saw to the housework and set to fixing the midday meal. In high season, they were in the fields alongside the men, and home again to make supper and see to the children. They was the last to go to bed, straightening up and putting out the fire. Feast days and holidays was anything but a day of rest, with all that food to make and clean up after!

There was a special cake my stepmother would make every now and then called the *sbrisolona*. It is a hard crumbly cake you make with corn flour and almonds, but it has sugar, butter, and lard too, so it cost a bit of money. Our way of making it was the same as it's been for 400 years. We mixed all the ingredients and put them in a copper cake pan. You set that on a mound of hot embers in the fireplace. Surround the pan with more embers and let it cook for about an hour until it is hard and crisp.

Sbrisolona – Crumble cake of Mantua
200g white flour
200g sifted corn flour
200g chopped almonds
200g sugar
100g lard
100g butter
2 egg yolks
grated lemon zest

Mix the flours, almonds, sugar, yolks, and lemon zest. Add the fats without letting them melt too much. Quickly mix together without making it completely homogeneous. Form a layer in a metal tray about an inch high without pressing it down too much. Bake at 350° until it is golden and dry. Smelling it works well to determine when it is done. Pieces should be broken off rather than sliced.

Our saving grace, like for most families, was raising a pig every year. We used every last bit of that pig, even the bones. If your pig died before slaughter time it was a terrible tragedy for your family. We made everything outta that pig that you could make: salami, prosciutto, head-cheese, cotecchino, sausage, everything. We made the fat into lard and put it into amphora-like clay jars, because all of our cooking was with lard, and butter if you happened onto a bit of luck.

After the war, the number of families that kept a pig for the winter slaughter dropped off considerably following the mass exodus to the cities. With the economic miracle underway, mortality rates from accidents, infectious disease, and illnesses provoked by malnutrition decreased, propelling degenerative diseases into the medical spotlight, with heart disease taking center-stage. Search for a fall guy quickly led to a culprit, and thus began the battle against dietary cholesterol. Lard and butter became public enemies, and everyone was encouraged to switch to olive oil; commercial production accelerated to meet demand. Hospital laboratories enlarged on a grand scale, and in no time, testing your lipid profile became standard practice. The cholesterol message permeated collective thinking so quickly and thoroughly that lard can only be found in small tubs, tucked away on the upper shelf of the refrigerator section of the supermarket, and many would have no idea what it is for. Butter, once the queen of fats hailed for its health-giving qualities, is looked on with disdain and used parsimoniously if at all. The word "buttery," burroso in Italian, is akin to saying "greasy." It does not elicit the same connotation of decadent delectability that it does in many other countries. In Italy, burroso is not a descriptor that sells products or compliments your host's dishes.

Everything was preserved. We didn't roast fresh pork and eat the meat. That would just be a foolish waste. At most, we had fresh sausages, and that's only because we finished them off too quick, 'fore they had time to dry! It wasn't a problem in my family! Only pigs with something wrong got roasted.

The traditional preparation of porchetta *used most frequently today (a whole, gutted, boned pig, seasoned, trussed and baked with the skin intact in an oven) was first recorded by the master-cook Maestro Martino who lived and operated in Rome in the fifteenth century. Porchetta was a central feature at banquets and festivals, particularly in central Italy, but deliciousness cannot be contained, and it spread throughout the country. It was and is a practical, thrifty way to make use of pigs that were not up to standard for* salumi*: old sows, pigs that had been irreparably injured, runts, weak and sickly pigs, and, by the more unscrupulous* porchettaro, *dead pigs. Nothing went to waste. Today, it is a regular item at most weekly open markets, and one will often see the sign posted outside the butcher shop* Oggi porchetta! – *Fresh roasted pork today!*

We cooked up the lungs and liver of the pig in lard and then preserved all that together under lard in a vase. The big hunks of fatback were cut into slabs, seasoned, and salt cured to make lardo. We would leave little scraps of meat on the bones, salt cure them, and then pack them into lard. Then what you'd do is boil them bones with their little meat scraps still stuck to them and make a nice broth. Just throw in some wild greens you found down the road and you got yourself a soup. We salt cured the ears, snout, face, and tongue. Ears gotta be cooked for hours and hours before you can chew them, but sooner or later they got tender enough. Those were the pieces we stewed all together with cabbage, like a poor version of the cassoeula. Folks today don't eat this dish anymore because they think it is too fatty and fattening. Of course, if you go stuffing yourself, like folks do today, anything gonna make you fat. But when you're eatin' tiny portions and trying to make every bite last, you don't get fat. Food then was more about what we *didn't* get to eat then what we ate. We filled up on vegetables and polenta because the other things you could only get a taste of. Certain things, like salami, were rationed out in small portions, more for the boys and men because they needed more meat than girls and women. Salami was a Sunday treat. Anyway, at least we didn't have to share our pig with the padrone. He let us keep the whole thing for ourselves.

The blood cake ritual was real important when you killed your pig. Everybody's got their own tradition, but the way we did it 'round our parts was to cook the blood with salt and cinnamon till it got stiff. When you put thickened blood mass into a mould it turned solid. Then we divvied it with the four other families at our cascina. One by one, when the other four families butchered their pig, they would give us some of their blood cake, so we all had to agree on when to butcher our pigs. There weren't no way to keep it, no refrigerator, so your timing had to be right to get blood cake to everybody without there bein' too much and it goin' off. You never waste nothin' that's food.

There was a good amount of eating on a pig, but anyhow, you couldn't raise more than one because you had to feed the poor beast too, and if you didn't have enough to eat yourself, then how were you going to feed him? They weren't grazing animals. We slopped our family pig with the water left from washing-up after meals mixed with the corn bran that got took off when you make the corn kernels into polenta. Wasn't too much more to spare than that. But if you wanted to fatten your pig, well, you had to find something for him too.

We always had our mind on making everything last long as we could, but still, there was some lean times, times when we come up short. When we had to go without meat for a spell, we ate more eggs. It was 'specially important for our menfolk working the fields to get enough to eat. Each one of 'em would get a whole raw egg in the morning to get through a hard day's work. When times was hard, eggs helped give 'em the strength they need 'cause if they couldn't bring in a wage, that was the end for all of us. Except for the blood-cake, there wasn't no sharing or helping between field hand families. How could you? Nobody had nothing to give out. And, no matter how hard up you might have got, you sure didn't bother to ask the padrone.

Not being property holders, we could see the town doctor for free. We was a big family, so we always had to keep something aside for the doctor, like a ration of rice or sugar, to keep on his good side. Then at Christmas, we give him a chicken or a salami so's to keep favor. He was a civil servant, sure, but dues had to be paid on the side or he might well take his business to another family 'fore coming to see yours, or be hasty in his ministrations. That is how it worked. And he knew well and good who was good for the payment and who could...wait.

The medico condotto *was a civil servant position established in Italy in 1865. They were often young men without clientele looking to gain experience. Services were free for the landless indigent, while those who could afford to pay went to private doctors. He was obliged to be on call 24-hours a day and to live in the town of his jurisdiction. The first woman to get a degree and practice medicine in Italy was Ernestina Paper in 1877.*

To give us a hand earnin' something extra, the padrone set us up with silkworms. He put down the money and then took half of the profits that came in. If it hadna been for that silkworm money, with so many in the family, we'd have all been goin' round in nothin' but rags, so we was right grateful to him.

Silkworm cultivation was one of the ways that women were able to contribute financially to the family income. Silk prices had bottomed out after 1920 due to the competitive Asian market and synthetic imitations, so the profit/labor ratio was low, but in an increasingly insular Italy, internal production was encouraged.

As it was, we wore our clothes until they was so tattered and patched they couldn't be patched no more. We had one everyday dress, one Sunday dress, nightclothes, and a sweater to put over your nightclothes in the winter months. We wore wooden clogs with pieces of metal nailed to the bottom to keep them from wearing down, sort of like on horses. They sure did hurt! And, oh, they made such a clatter! We all clomped everywhere like a herd of cattle. We made ourselves wool socks so they wouldn't hurt so much. There weren't a lot of sheep around then like now, so if you bought wool and made the yarn yourself, it was cheaper than buying socks, and anyway, it wasn't easy to get real wool socks. Didn't leave you much choice but to make them yourselves. Women gathered in the barn after dinner to spin yarn and knit socks between lot of talk and stories and a good bit of gossip too. Nothin' like that anymore though. It kept us going.

In 1941, they blocked all the roads heading in and out of the village and the ones in surrounding villages too, first the Fascists and then the Germans. I remember them German soldiers walking up and down with their rifles. We were all mighty scared of them even though they were supposed to be on our side. If you didn't have permission from an authority, you couldn't get in and you couldn't get out, and they only give permission to the head of the family, so womenfolk stayed put. There was times we needed some supplies from town, and getting out took some doin'. Worse was that most times, when you got to the shops they didn't have what you wanted anyway! The government give us a ration card, but didn't make much sense if you couldn't even get your ration. Then, with folks like us, folks who had nothin', they come 'round and took every little scrap of metal that could be spared. Only it was them decided what we didn't need. They stripped us clean even of the farm tools; didn't have barely enough to carry on with the farm and housework. They had to leave us the cooking pot though!

That was the same year I got with child. You see, the old padrone died, and his son become our new padrone. He was just a year older than me. He was kind and smiled at me. He let me come up and do work sometimes in the big house. He'd say nice things. He said he'd take care of me. Right after I knew I was pregnant, he got called off to war. He promised he would marry me just as soon as he come back.

After a time, I had to tell my father about it, and he was none too happy. Well, no, no…he was furious. He beat me, and I mean he beat me good. I told him that the padrone give me his promise. I said, "When he's back from the war, he says he's going to marry me. He's going to make it all right." But that just made Papa angrier. "He ain't never gonna marry the likes of you! You stupid girl! Now you've disgraced me!" Papa was right. The new padrone, when he come back from the war, didn't want nothin' to do with me or the boy. Said that he didn't love me. Papa knew men. He knew what men were on about. I didn't have the first idea. He went to the padrone, askin' him to make things right, askin' him to take away the shame brought down on his name and on his family. He asked as one man to another man to save the honor of his daughter. But the padrone wasn't having none of it. We were disgraced. We weren't welcome any more and had to look for work on another farm.

Wasn't too long before we found another situation on a nearby farm, and lived pretty much the same life as before. Wheat, field corn. Same old thing, just like before. Papa picked up a little extra cash, though, for looking after our new padrone's horse.

First two years, Papa wouldn't let me out of the house for the shame of it, a girl with a baby and no husband. But in time, he saw that things was just that way and he wasn't going to change it by hiding me and the boy. My stepmother accepted the boy with an open heart, same way as she opened her heart to me when she married Papa. Papa wanted me to leave the boy for adoption, like what usually happened to girls like me. You'd go to the hospital in the big city and come home with no more baby. But I begged my father. I said, "The damage is done; we have been shamed. Now let me at least do right by this baby." I promised I would work for the boy's upkeep. "Well, see to it that you do," he said, "because I ain't having this child be a burden on me." I went to the hospital in Brescia to have the baby because the Duce paid for unmarried girls to have their babies in the hospital. And he gave us wayward girls a thousand liras and a package of things to start off the life of the child. And after that I got a little bit a month from the government. The padrone didn't do near as much. No, wait, I remember, at the start of school, he sent money for the boy to get school clothes and proper shoes, but that was the last we ever heard from him.

Winters I worked in the osteria washing up glasses and dishes. Then come the growing season, I hired out as a field hand. In Vercelli, I worked the rice paddies. Now there's some ugly work. Forty days up to your knees in water every day, weeding, weeding, weeding. You couldn't even feel your feet after a while, they was so soaked through.

The rocky terrain and vast swamplands throughout the peninsula presented a constant challenge to providing food for the population. Therefore, rice cultivation, which needs wetlands, provided a practical solution. Rice farming began in the Lombard plain in the mid-1400s and spread, mostly in the northern provinces. By the 1940s, practices had changed little, with the possible exception of chemical fertilizers, whose hazards were yet unknown. Women made up 90 percent of the workforce in rice paddies and it was one of the few jobs in which they

earned the same wage as male farmhands. Besides the stress that lean-
ing over for hours on end exerts on muscles, joints and bones, workers
suffered from eye infections, digestive problems, and multiple forms of
skin irritation and dermatitis due to the roughness of the plants com-
bined with the constant contact with water. Rice paddies are also noto-
rious breeding-grounds for various parasites and mosquitos.

Interestingly, the most renowned rice varieties used in risottos
throughout Italy and the world are post-WWII hybrids: Carnaroli,
created in 1945, is considered the crowning glory of risotto because it
withstands the longer cooking time required and releases enough starch
to create the desired creaminess, or mantecatura. *The more commonly*
used rice, however, is the comfortingly plump Arborio. It too is a hybrid,
created in 1946, though it requires a bit more knowhow to render the
characteristic creaminess of risotto. Baldo is the most recent hybrid con-
tender in the race for risotto excellence. On a rather disconcerting note,
the laws regulating the labeling and packaging of rice are lax, catering
to manufacturers and marketing. As it stands, consumers cannot be
sure that a box labeled Carnaroli is indeed that, or if it is a masquerad-
ing imposter. Proposals to remedy the situation have been presented to
the government, but as yet, no action has been taken.

Once you finished your rice season, then came wheat, and I worked
that, and then moved on to *scorzanera* [a very bitter, long, white root
similar in appearance to parsnips] season. I met my husband working
the scorzanera season. I was thirty-four and, by then, my son was fourteen. We worked side-by-side in the field for a season. I took a fancy
to him and he to me so, after a year, we got married. We was the same
age, and he still hadn't taken a wife, so that's how it worked out. When
I met him, he'd been keepin' company with a woman for a good long
time, but she was keepin' company with some other fellas too, when it
suited her, so when he met me, he gave up on her.

When we got married, he came to live with Papa and our family.
My stepmother was dead by then, and Papa was getting on in years. He
was a good father to my boy, and never raised a hand against either of
us. The boy's real father had gone and got married at the end of the
war. After five years, she got a terrible illness and was in pain for a good

long while before she died. For me, that was the divine hand of God come down on him to even the score.

We lived in that same place there for thirty years, working the fields. But after the war, things was easier for us, easier for everyone. I started buying bread from a baker and not making it myself. We started eatin' rice, and we even bought store-bought pasta, *pasta compra,* like spaghetti and penne. Polenta stayed the main food for folks around here, though. We started having tomato paste, tomato sauce and even fresh tomatoes. In the 1970s, I got a proper oven with a gas stove and a TV too.

I learned to cook meat like roasts and do those fancy dishes like lasagna. I never read a recipe 'cause I'm not so good at reading. I just learned talking to other women. I taught my daughter to cook too. It was easier for her because she already knew these new foods. There's lots of things in the supermarket that I don't know what they are. Some of them things I see in there, I wouldn't eat, them things that women buy today, breaded meats, broth in a box. I'm not saying that because it isn't traditional food, but because that stuff isn't good food. Even though it is kind of hard to get around with my walker, I still make my own meals. My son pays a woman to come help me dress and bathe, and she cleans the apartment before she goes, but then I clean it again after she leaves, just to be sure.

I know a lot of women don't want to cook or learn how even. Oh, well. They'll just have to depend on things that the supermarket cooks for them. There's not much point in worrying about traditions and food because *whatever* they make *is* Italian cooking, because *they* are Italian. They'll have to work it out for themselves. It is up to them to say what Italian food is. If families want to sit down at the table and eat ready-meals because no one wants to bother, that's just too bad for them, but I am not going to worry about it. They don't know what is in that food. They don't know who made it or if their hands was clean. I don't know how they can eat food that they didn't make themselves, but it doesn't seem to bother them. Oh, well. So be it. I tried pizza for the first time only a few years ago, just a plain cheese pizza. It was really good. I just hope the people who made it washed their hands.

I've been here too long, lived too long. I wake up in the morning and I can hardly believe that I have to live another day. It isn't the age so much as my health. If you get to be this old, it is better if you don't have so much pain. On the days that I feel better, or if someone comes to visit me, I am happy to live another day, but I spend most of my days, day and night, alone and lonely. I think a lot about the old days. The work was hard, terrible hard. But it was a happier time, because we were all in it together. We were hungry, but we sang. We sang all the time. At home, working the fields, husking the corn, and when the families got together during the hot summer nights down by the river. Folks don't gather together like before, young and old. No one was left out then. I wish I could afford a live-in caretaker just to have some company around. Now I am afraid to go out, and my son said I can't answer the door if I don't know who's there. Italy is all turned upside-down now. It's dangerous. Singing made it all better, but nobody's singing anymore.

Intermezzo

Focolare e casa – Hearth and home

Vesta, the Roman goddess of hearth, home, and family. She is the channel between the earthly life and the divine. Fire, in its opposing forces, is both lust and purity, comfort and rage. It can be used to create or to destroy, to warm or to burn. The priestesses of Vesta, six Vestal Virgins charged with keeping the eternal hearth fire dedicated to their goddess lit, were bound to an oath of chastity for thirty years. If they went astray, the punishment was live burial, which allowed them back into the good graces of the earth. Their sacred fire was vested with the power of protecting Rome. Anyone in need of fire for the home could appeal to the virgins for a starter. This made them, in essence, the housekeepers of all of Rome. Should the flames go out, the consequences could be cataclysmic. But, as history would have it, not only did the fire go out, it was put out in 391CE when the Christian Roman Emperor Theodosius disbanded the order and prohibited all public pagan rites. In so doing he also banned the Greek Olympics, which would not be resuscitated until 1896.

The hearth was the center of family life, so much so that in the Middle Ages, a nuclear family unit was referred to as a *fuoco*, or fire. The number of troops a lord had to make available for war was calculated in terms of the number of home fires on his land. A family tax, called the *focatico*, grew out of the duty that a vassal family owed to its sovereign protector. The tax underwent revision during the fascist regime, but would remain on the books until 1974.

The hearth of a country home was not a mere fireplace, but a vast open space of stone or brick, with a cauldron that hung by a chain over the fire; it was the hub and heart of domesticity. There was an altar-like stone at the center back where the umbilical cords of the male sons were cast as a symbol of ancestral ties to house and family; women would leave home once they were married, while the men remained under the family wing to carry on the work. After Vespers, the family took their place at the table for dinner in accordance with their position of importance. The capoccia and the massaia were at the head of the table, followed by the eldest son and his wife, and so forth. Only the capoccia could make observations about the food. Everyone else ate in silence. Households were usually numerous, and commotion was not tolerated. After the meal, the women tidied up, while the men discussed the next day's workload. As the evening wore on, everyone gathered round the hearth to talk and tell stories. Before retiring, the embers were covered over with ashes to make lighting the fire easier the next day. During the day, the hearth was the center of women's activities: preparing dough, cooking, nursing, knitting, sewing, washing dishes, doing laundry. It was where young women received their suitors, under strict parental supervision. The prohibition of even holding hands stirred the fires of longing, making the promised one all the more desirable.

Even urban kitchens were often fitted out with a hearth or at least a simple fireplace for heating and cooking. Others used the *cucina economica*, or thrify cooker, a wood burning oven that made more efficient use of fuel, although it did not inspire social gatherings around which to while away the evenings. Gas stoves also began to hit their stride in the 1920s. They required access to a company that distributed tanks of methane gas for home use, as city gas lines would be a long time in coming. Stoves that burned coal, or its derivative, coke, were another labor saving option, again, requiring home delivery. The move away from traditional hearth cooking was not about better results, but about diminishing fatigue, watchfulness, expense, and clean-up. Newer methods made it easier for inexperienced cooks to produce acceptable results with less know-how, which appealed to the modern mentality. This 1930s ad had just such a woman in mind:

SAVE *TIME MONEY LABOR* using GAS as your only fuel.
Gas stoves, water heaters, radiators and lights.
Coal – excellent for stoves, and industrial ovens.
Home delivery GAS & COKE Associates – Milano

Webs of electrical lines were being strung throughout the country during the Ventennio. In most homes, this meant the luxury of a light bulb, and indeed, to this day, electricity is referred to simply as "the light." However, by 1940, there were as many as 120,000 electric ovens. Other appliances did not fare so well. In the same year Italy counted 148 washing machines and 268 refrigerators. Although laundry was immensely fatiguing and time consuming, women who are old enough to remember recall the fresh smell of the clothes and sheets, and the brightness of the whites as things that were irrevocably lost with the advent of the washer. Refrigerators too were regarded with a bit of suspicion at first. People were uneasy about eating something that had been stored inside an electrical appliance, in the same way that some people today disparage food cooked in a microwave oven. In the verbose advertising language of the 1940s, General Electric tries to win consumers over:

> The General Electric Refrigerator: The first and only refrigerator built in steel. The entire mechanism is hermetically sealed thereby eliminating any chance of malfunctioning. More than 350,000 of them have been sold worldwide, and up to now not a single customer has paid one cent for repairs. We have the right model for every family.

In spite of the wondrous possibilities modern appliances offered to those with ready cash, the upper classes found themselves in an unprecedented quandary. Newlywed brides were evermore ill prepared for the rigors of managing a household, and the impertinence of domestic staff had reached an all time high. The bewildered readership of *La Cucina Italiana* wrote to the columnists imploring them for solutions. The topic was duly addressed in a 1936 issue:

133

The problem with maids – that was almost non-existent 50 years ago – ... is the lifestyle of well to do girls today, who know nothing about cleaning, cooking, and keeping house when they take a husband. ... It used to be that all girls, even ones with a good dowry, did housework, and mothers saw to it that their daughters knew about all aspects of housekeeping (except for washing dishes, naturally!) so that they would become proper ladies of the house. ... Certainly, they weren't perfect, but they were able to evaluate the work of the servants, to take command, not ask the impossible of the staff, but only as much as they could and should do.

Therefore, it is weak mothers who are at fault. When daughters think it is their right to laze about until 10 o'clock, spend the morning at the hairdresser and the manicurist, the afternoon playing parlor games, visiting friends or going to the cinema, when they insist on having a big breakfast, an elegant tea, a lavish lunch and expect to find the house in order without having contributed in the least... mothers today say nothing and think...They'll learn once they have a husband.

It's not true! Taking charge of a household is a difficult science that requires intelligent foresight, love of orderliness, and practice! ...

And the maids? They too have undergone an evolution. They used to enter into service willingly, as children, already accustomed to the idea of servitude and just happy to find some bread and a roof over their heads. ... They were able to go to mass during the week and to Vespers on Sunday. Now they are gluttons for freedom, fun, adventure and the cinema. Serving seems like some sort of injustice and it weighs on them, ... so they do as little as possible, and as soon as they are left alone in the house without anyone to keep an eye on them, they go straight to the signora's make-up or the telephone; they read novels, flirt with the butler, the waiter, the chauffer, the bread delivery boy. ... They dream – not of finding a nice factory worker – but a wealthy man with a car. ... [They are] envious of the lady of the house for the nice clothes and underclothes she has, and the elegant lifestyle she lives... ... the cinema teaches many things...things that are best ignored, ... and that's how they learn to steal from the shopping money, and to make not-so-innocent dates with the first passerby. ... And so we get insolent servants, thieves, liars, ingrates, and spoiled brats, who must be dismissed without being left even one more day to materially or morally dirty the house. We ladies, as a matter of dignity, should in no case tolerate the nasty looks, the impoliteness, or the talking back of lowborn, ill-mannered maids. As a question of Christian charity, let's send them back to their parents or to a youth center. ... Even more so in wartime and under sanctions, ... we need to constantly supervise the kitchen because maids are the sworn enemies of thrift, particularly if the employer is footing the bill. So let's go into the kitchen and supervise, supervise, supervise!" (Morozzo della Rocca, 1936).

Alberta

Born 1929 – Lake Trasimeno

For a town-dweller, Alberta lived a modest but comfortable life, though the comforts amounted mostly to a bit more food, electric lights, and an in-house toilet. Their standard of living was largely due to her father's position, which allowed him to develop a network of favors. These tacit agreements of indebtedness and payback play a significant role in Italian society, particularly in a small town where everyone makes it their business to know everyone else's business. Favors and favoritism is prefigured in the Latin expression do ut des, *literally, "I'll do so that you do," figuratively, "I'll scratch your back, you scratch mine." While Alberta's parents were by no means cosmopolitan, they were forward thinking enough to encourage her to go to school, and did not expressly channel her into the marriage track. Being a modern woman in a traditional world is costly, but the extra perks that her father picked up here and there made it possible for her to conceive of a world that included a modicum of leisure. Fascist propaganda promoted a patriarchal family structure that included a strong female with traditional values. But the age of the great matriarchs was already fraying at the edges by Alberta's generation. Too much access to novels and cinema?*

When the fascists first came to power, Papa was working in the print business, and people in that line of work tended to be socialists, so I think he leaned a bit to the left, and that didn't go down so well with the fascists. He was a very intelligent man. He had finished middle school, which was quite a lot in his day. He even went to Aviation school at Lake Trasimeno, which is where he met Mamma. After I was born, he got a job with the local excise office as a *daziere*, a tax officer for food, but it didn't last too long because it was a state job, and he didn't have much of a mind to becoming a member of the Fascist party, so they fired him. He held out for a while, working menial jobs here and there, dragging the family from town to town whenever some scrap of work came up. The children kept coming though; there were six of us kids in all, five girls and one boy, and it wasn't such an easy haul. They had to do something to lighten the load, so one of my sisters, the first born, was handed over to the care of a childless old maid aunt in another town. Wasn't so far if you think about it in today's terms, just an hour or so's drive from us, but back then, getting around was really difficult, and we sure didn't have a car, so we hardly ever saw her after that. By the time I started school we were living in Santa Maria degli Angeli, in Assisi and Papa was working in a pasta shop. Santa Maria degli Angeli always had a brisk flow of people in and out, because it was a pilgrimage site and tourists came from all over Italy.

> *Our Lady of the Angels, from which the city of Los Angeles takes its name, began as the founding church of the Franciscans. The tiny church Porzuncola, situated inside the Basilica Santa Maria degli Angeli, was given to St. Francis in 1208. As legend has it, it was originally constructed in the 4th century, and housed relics from the grave of the Virgin Mary. St. Francis is said to have rebuilt the poorly reduced edifice with his own hands.*

The Festival of Forgiveness on August 2nd was one of the most important holy days for the Franciscans. I remember in particular the people from the Ciociaria, southwest of Rome. The name, you know, comes from the kind of pointed sandals they wore! They did a pilgrimage all the way to Santa Maria in their traditional costumes, and stayed in the churchyard, sleeping on the ground outside. Then, for the last tract of the procession up to the church, they walked on their knees. They stayed for a few days and always brought their wonderful food with them, spicy salami, and their local black bread because, one, they were very poor people, and two, there weren't restaurants or anything like that. They were very generous and shared their food with us, so I always looked forward to their coming.

The Festival was a day to ask our Lord for his forgiveness for all of the sins committed during the year, you know, wipe the slate clean. It was a day to be humble and recognize your limits, so it was a day that you showed you were willing to get down on your knees and beg for forgiveness. Then for a fee, you could ask the priest to say a prayer for your dead relatives too, I guess to be sure they were getting on well in the afterlife. Today you can go to any Franciscan church on August 2 to celebrate the Festival of Forgiveness. Just that now people go in their cars. No one crawls.

I went to a very large elementary school. There were five grades and one teacher for each grade. Boys and girls were separated until the 5th grade because a lot of children stopped going to school after the 4th grade. Parents took their children out of school because they thought it was more useful for them to learn a trade or go to work, and generally people thought that four years was enough time to learn what you needed to get along in life. So, until the fourth grade, I had the same teacher every year, and then in the 5th, we had a different teacher. I liked school and I liked my teacher, but some teachers were rather strict. As a punishment in my sister's class they had to hold their arms out like Christ and kneel down on dried chickpeas. That was mostly a Friday punishment, because Friday was the day of penitence; our Lord died on a Friday so the punishment was more severe then. Otherwise, during the week, it was the usual rapping your knuckles with a stick or standing facing the corner. It was worse for the boys with male teachers.

We went to school Monday to Friday and then went to Fascist Saturday. Most days were fascist days though! At school and in church they were always going on about the fascio! The only difference was that Saturdays were rigorously organized. We worked very hard every week at our exercise routines because one week we'd have a rally, then the next week Secretary So-and-So was coming, then a competition, and in 1936 we prepared for a visit from Mussolini himself! I was a piccola italiana then. That whole year as we filed into the classroom, the teacher would ask us each morning for money, you know, to fund the program festivities. Some children's parents did hourly work, some had monthly incomes, so they had to ask every day if anyone had brought money. They had to buy flowers, decorations, set up a podium and all that. It was all really thrilling for us because we got to dress up in our fascist uniform, the black or blue pleated skirt and little white tennis shoes and short white socks. It made us feel like we were part of something important.

When Mussolini came we had to stand for three or four hours under the sun while he gave his speech. He talked and talked, on and on. It was really hot and I fainted a couple times. The teachers dragged me out of the group formation, and when I felt better I was propped up in line again. Then we did the exercise routine for him that we had been rehearsing for months. It was all just so exciting for us children. The atmosphere was like a holiday because there wasn't any other sort of fun for children. Fascism allowed fun into children's lives, but an orderly sort of fun. When it was good weather, they even held Sunday mass on the field, and everyone came in their fascist uniform: the piccole italiane, the giovane italiane, and the boys in the Balilla. The whole family came, but we stayed in our separate groups.

Finally, in 1936, with a family of seven at home to support, and times getting harder and harder, and my mother... well, let's just say she was none too happy... Papa gave in and became a party member. He got his job back as a taxman, and things settled down more normal for us, and we moved to Todi. What he did as the food taxman was make the rounds to the various homesteads and farmsteads in the area to collect the tax for whatever they were up to that was taxable, I mean with food. For example, everyone who slaughtered a pig, and around our parts that meant everyone who had a space to put up a pigsty, well, Papa went round and weighed the products, so as the state could take its cut. People being people, folks were clever, and would find a way to cheat by borrowing other people's salami's and prosciuttos that had turned out small. Those would get passed around from farm to farm. Papa was on to their game and would say, "Eh, that pig seemed bigger to me when I saw it around Christmas time!" All the large animals that were killed were taxed, and it was Papa's job to see to it that people were doing their part for the state. Course, tax collectors have always been an unpopular lot, and the daziere working the food sector were probably the most hated of all of them because here you were talking about people's food, their life. Pigs were your life insurance. So, you see, in the end, this meant that there was a good deal of greasing the wheels and turning a blind eye, do you get my meaning? What I mean is, our family had a steady supply of provisions, folks gave us this and that on the side throughout the year, from fresh and preserved meats, to eggs, flour, bread, cheese, and wine. Ready cash was difficult for most people to come by and this system worked out for everyone. Papa himself wasn't exactly pulling in a high wage, so the mutual hand washing kept our large family fed, and that kept Mamma calm. It worked like this, you see; for example, our house was right next to a church. There was a convent of cloistered nuns at this church, and when they had their pigs slaughtered in the winter, they called my father, as they were bound to do by law. But let's say that they killed three pigs. He'd go and write that there was only one, and then the kind sisters would remember us later with, maybe, some tagliatelle for us as their part of the deal. Papa wasn't the one who actually collected the tax money. They would go to the office with the tax slip that he filled out for them to pay, so there was no direct exchange of money that way, but the favor was remembered, if you know what I mean. You have to realize that feeding a family like ours would have taken half of Papa's earnings. Those extras here and there allowed us to spend our money on other things we needed and let all of us to go to school past the 4th grade, which most children couldn't do.

Tax reform on foodstuffs was introduced in 1868, after the Unification of Italy in 1861. Taxes were levied on grains, wine, and butchered animals. Often, the taxes openly favored the wealthy. One of the more absurd food taxes was the "minimum sale" tax wherein, for example, no tax was applied to a sale of twenty-five liters of wine, but it would have been if the purchase had been limited to a single bottle.

We were home by lunchtime everyday after school. At my house we all ate together unless my father was working in the outer lying areas of his district. He'd putter out to the countryside on his old motorbike, doot-doot-doot-doot. It was really embarrassing when he came puttering and sputtering back into town on that contraption while everyone was out for the evening stroll, doot-doot-doot-doot. Anyway, lunch was the main meal of the day, and we had tagliatelle with tomato garlic sauce and pecorino *romano* (parmesan cost too much) every day. Every day, every day. Now and then, just every so often, we had beans and sausage in tomato sauce instead of pasta. We didn't have a first and second course like everyone does now except on Sundays. It was just pasta, every day, with fruit at the end of the meal. Homemade pasta was our mainstay. Papa often got flour from farmers as a gift, so we had flour and water tagliatelle; if we were lucky and happened to get an egg we had egg noodles. If a peasant farmer gave us some eggs, Mamma might make us a zabaglione to go with our bread and milk in the morning, but the first priority when we were able to get eggs was tagliatelle. If we didn't have pasta, something was not right.

Mamma would sometimes buy a kilo of spaghetti from the grocer. It was sold in bulk not in packages like now. Shops had big drawers along the walls, full of pasta. But it was rare that we ate spaghetti. It wasn't as satisfying, and really, it was mostly for convenience because all you had to do was boil it. Not many people ate store bought pasta in our area. Spaghetti didn't really take hold until much later. We hardly ever had rice, but when we did it was either just white with lardo or tomato sauce, none of these risottos you have today, at least not at our house. In the evening we'd have prosciutto, maybe some cheese or potato frittata. We ate a lot of potatoes. And then there were all the things that Papa got as extras from his job. Or we'd have bread and anchovies. Mamma would make them in a parsley pesto sauce with garlic. Or smoked herring; Papa loved herring. In the summer we ate panzanella, a salad made with leftover bread; we kids loved that. We weren't in the habit of having soup in the evening like a lot of families.

No, we were pasta and bread people. If Papa had been away at lunch he would say, "I didn't have any pasta today!" and Mamma would make him a small dish at dinnertime.

We had a lot of milk too. Always for breakfast, and then sometimes it was our dinner too if there wasn't much to put on the table. That milk was different. The cream was very thick and would rise to the top, and Mamma would make butter with it. She was a tiny woman, but she'd shake that cream in a jar until the butter stuck to the glass. Milk today is nothing like that fresh milk that we had delivered straight from the countryside every morning. They came in on a wagon from the country and delivered right to your doorstep. They were there on the dot every morning year round with large metal containers. Mamma would get three liters of milk every day. We didn't need to have a refrigerator because we'd finish that amount, no problem. Sometimes we would walk down the road and get it milked, then and there from the cow.

And there was always wine on the table because the farmers gave us plenty of wine. When we were younger Mamma mixed ours with water, but anyway, that wine wasn't as strong as it is today. People didn't give a thought to wine being bad for children. As an afternoon snack we had bread soaked in wine with a little sugar sprinkled on top. In our area it was not hard to come by olive oil, but people preferred to cook with lardo. It had a richer, fuller taste. We didn't know what cholesterol was, and anyway, I don't have high cholesterol even now. Mamma would pulverize the lardo with the back of a cleaver; everything was done by hand, of course, I guess you'd use a food processor now. Lardo was the base of the tomato sauce, and really, the base of most of her cooking.

We knew we were a fortunate family because you just had to walk out the door to see the rampant poverty all around us. Town families had a harder time of it than people in the country. Papa had his income, and then a good part of our food was gifted to us, so we didn't keep a garden, but if you lived in town and you didn't have a vegetable garden somewhere, or you didn't keep animals in the house or somewhere nearby, then most of your income was spent just on feeding your family, and you just weren't going to make it. My two older sisters went to work in the pasta factory in town when they were old enough, and so then there was more food and extra money coming in. Of course, women's work was paid less than men's back then, but it was at least something at a time when people were hard pressed to put food on the table. You took what you could get.

With the exception of jobs that were an extension of traditional roles, "female employment" was an oxymoron according to the political and religious values of the Ventennio. The fascist Civil Code placed almost unlimited authority in the hands of the husband, while the 1930 papal encyclical Casti Connubii, *a copy of which was given to each newlywed couple, reiterated the God-given superiority of the husband and the consequent subordinate role of the wife. This ideological indoctrination from both heaven and earth may have softened the blow when payday arrived, and "her" salary was less than half the amount of "his." Morals and mores aside, the irony is that, while blatant exploitation reinforced the will of State and Church by discouraging women from seeking employment (and thereby independence), their willingness to accept pitiful wages made them an indispensible asset in the workplace.*

We didn't have domestic help because there were five females in the house. We all cleaned the house, top to bottom every Sunday, but Mamma did most of it really. There was a tap in the basement of the house and a large tub where she did the laundry. Her laundry smelled so wonderfully fresh. Later, when there were washing machines, Mamma didn't want one. She just couldn't believe that things would come out as clean. My brother, being a boy, only had to clean his own room. He had one room, and the four of us girls were in another room. We had a living room with a rattan divan, two chairs and a table. There was a water closet with a toilet and sink, right there in the house, which was pretty rare in those days. The kitchen was the main room of the house and it was very large. We cooked on a wood-burning stove and in an open fireplace, and it was the warmest room too, because there wasn't any kind of heating in the rest of the house, and Todi, being a hilltop town, was quite cold in the winter. We had lights and running water in the kitchen too. At night, Mamma would put hot coals in a pan that was placed in a special frame called a "priest," a wooden contraption that you put in the bed to warm it up between the sheets. Then when we went to bed it was removed. I wouldn't be able to stand living out the winter that way now – now I have an electric blanket and central heating – but it seemed normal then. You don't notice things so much when you don't have a choice. We lived pretty comfortably compared to a lot of other people in town. I remember some of my friends had terrible chilblains, awful sores on their hands from the cold that split open.

It is a bit difficult to live in Todi because the streets are steep and the winters are hard, but it's a lovely town and we liked it. Papa had to walk out to the farms in the winter because of the snow; that was high season for him because that's when the swine were slaughtered. I continued school in Todi and did all three years of middle school. Not many girls did middle school, but my mother thought that was a right amount of schooling for girls of our social class. After middle school, I was sent to learn how to sew, like most girls. Only my brother went on to high school and then university.

A lot of the teaching at school was about fascism, to shape how we were supposed to live a life for the better of the state, so, of course, the day started off with the Roman salute, and we learned patriotic poems and songs and things. But we always knew at my house that our father had been forced to be a party member so we didn't get an earful of it at home too like some kids did. Of course, as children, we were not thinking, "Oh, God, the dictatorship!" but just the same, we could feel that something was amiss. But our papa was a good, gentle man. He wasn't the type with a bone to pick. He didn't exactly jump on the fascist bandwagon, but if it meant getting the family fed, that was enough to convince him. If you had notions of your own that went against the flow, you just kept quiet. No one said what they really thought because you never knew who would turn you in, and spies were everywhere. You could only trust your own family and sometimes not even them. Around our parts they didn't hesitate to give you the caster oil treatment.

No one in our town was beaten, like you'd hear of in other places, but they set you straight in other ways. There was a fascist squad in Todi and everyone lived in fear of them. When Mussolini was finally killed, relief washed over us, and it was like a big party, a great cause for celebration. It was finally over. The squadristi disappeared overnight and never came back because the people of Todi would have had their hide. That might seem sort of hypocritical though because compared to lots of other people at the time, you could even say that we were a prosperous family. Those were good years for us. While things were getting difficult for most everyone, our situation got easier, *particularly* during the war years when my sisters went to work in the local pasta factory called Cappelletti.

They supplied pasta to the Italian army, so it was stable work. They had a very wide distribution from north to south. During the war, Todi was declared a military zone, and a barracks was built for the German soldiers who occupied our town in '44-'45. The pasta factory supplied them too, and then when the English arrived and Italy changed sides, the pasta factory furnished them with pasta too, and so in the end, Cappelletti turned a good profit from the war. The owner was very rich and he was generous with his workers, so with my sisters working there during the war, we often had dried pasta, which was kind of a luxury item then, like most store bought things. It changed the way we had always eaten. If the owner managed to get a large shipment of sugar, as a gift or something, he shared it with the employees. That was like someone giving you gold. Later the Allies bombed the factory because they were supplying the Axis armies.

On the whole we tolerated the Germans, but there were a lot of black soldiers in the German Army occupying Italy who had different ideas about wartime rights.

> *They may have been from the Free Arabian Legion – a Nazi military unit of Middle Eastern and North African volunteers. Strange bedfellows indeed. The problem of violence against women was sufficiently widespread as to merit a public poster depicting a white woman being molested by a dark skinned soldier, with the writing: "Defend her! She could be your mother, your wife, your sister, your daughter."*

At the end of my street, there was a military hospital and they were relieved of duty at 6 pm. That's when the drinking began. I tell you, there was a terrible scourge, a massacre of rape, robbery and destruction took place throughout the countryside around Todi. After that, we insisted that the German army ensure our safety. They came by in a van and accompanied my sisters to work. Really, they did it with everyone; lots of people got escorted to work. They wanted the town to keep running normally, keep tensions down.

Once, at our house, there were some German soldiers who knocked on the door saying that they were looking for wine and women. There were all of us girls in the house so Papa didn't let them in, but he gave them some wine, and sent them on their way. The next day, he went to the German commando and said, "Look, there's been some disturbance." They stationed a German sentinel out on our street to keep watch. In general, though, it wasn't that dangerous in town. We just tried to stay out of the Germans' way. I never heard of anyone being molested in town. It was mostly in the outlying areas, in the country, near the Tiber. The punishment for overstepping your bounds was that you got sent to the front, so that helped keep the soldiers in order pretty much. Anyway, they weren't much different from the Italian soldiers. If you think about it, they were all just kids, out getting drunk, acting bigger than their britches. You even had to be protected from your own. In fact, they're the very ones who cued the Germans in on where to find girls in town. Only the English and the Americans were more gentlemanly. They brought us back to life after such a steady stream of angst.

During the war, there were a lot of things that weren't readily available, like meat; in fact, we rarely had fresh meat. If you have a nice hearty plate of pasta, you can get by without much meat. On Sundays, though, the big occasion was my mother's roast chicken. There was something about the way she seasoned it that I've never had since. My sisters and I watched Mamma when she cooked, but we never did any of the cooking ourselves, Papa didn't want us to because he liked the way Mamma cooked, and he didn't want to have to eat anything else. She was really good. We had more meat after the war because they set up a *mattatoio* in town. It was the place where you brought your sheep, bovine, pigs, and lambs to be slaughtered. It was like a sort of garage, and Papa oversaw the procedure. He checked the health of the animal and gave them a stamp of approval, and so…we always got our cut, a piece of meat for some sort of... exchange. It didn't happen during the war because the Germans commanded in our town.

Mamma also made something like a pizza, but not the pizza you get in the pizzeria. I was already married before I ever had a real pizza. We had a ration card during the war, but even so, without the side benefits of Papa's job, it would have been difficult. Most town people bought their bread with the ration card, but...well, there was a grocer there who... supplied us with bread, you know, in a hidden way. The lady would say to Mamma, "Send over one of your children. I've set aside an extra loaf for you." I was often sent around to the back door to get the bread, and I knew full well that I had to be secretive about it. That bread isn't like bread today that gets hard and stale right away. It lasted a good long time, and in those days bread was a big part of what we ate.

Shopkeepers allowed you a line of credit that had to be paid at the end of the month. As a state worker, Papa was paid once a month, so we ran up a line of credit. Other people who didn't have a regular income found themselves in trouble because they bought on credit, but then they couldn't pay for it and got cut off. You heard about that all the time. But there were some things that no one could have unless you were out and out wealthy, like coffee. I never had coffee until after the war, but my mother had tasted it, and she really liked it. There were a lot of substitutes around, but no coffee. To perk up our caffè d'orzo, we would put anise seeds in. That way it went down better because it tasted like it had *mistrà* in it [*a drink like ouzo or sambuca that is dry, not sweet*].

When my sister married in 1948 wedding receptions were done at home; the people in my father's district brought us almost everything for the wedding feast: one brought a whole lamb, another the tagliatelle; the nuns brought us the dry cakes that they were known for, and yet another brought us the wine and Umbrian vin santo. And so we had this great fete, all with food that had been given to Papa because people remember when you've done them a favor.

My father died in 1953, when I was 24 years old. I followed the example of my older sister, who had gone to Rome to work in a nursery school that trained young women to be nursery school teachers.

It was all free, the studies and lodging at the school. But in exchange, we worked, of course, and we were only allowed out two hours per week. Otherwise we stayed in the institution.

A brochure for the school from 1941 reads: "[W]hose purpose is to give women the necessary practical and theoretical training to prepare them for either women's occupations or home economics. The school provides the skills to carry out these exclusively female activities, and aims to prepare women for their household and familial duties.

The three areas of study are:

a) *family and motherhood*
b) *home economics*
c) *women's occupations*

Particular importance is paid to nutrition. Foods are analyzed for their composition and physiological value, for which choice and consumption is regulated and measured in relation to rational economic and health criteria... whose end is always aimed at a progressive moral, physical, and economic betterment of the family.

Women finally have a school that allows them to competently fulfill their role and to carry out the tasks that are part of their natural tendencies. As such, the students become intelligent Ladies of the House, able to utilize their artistic and practical knowledge to reveal their delightfully feminine personality."

Their studies also included general culture: Italian history, a foreign language, pedagogy, design, mathematics, and natural sciences (L'Istituto di Magistero Femminile, 1940).

It was a home for orphans, and after the war there were plenty of orphaned children. It was also a sort of boarding school for the children of actors and actresses because in Rome the cinema industry was booming, and they needed to have their children looked after while they were on the set. It was also a daycare center for regular working people. There was a separate ward for unwed mothers, but that was off-limits to us trainees. They were kept like they were in prison. It was all very hush-hush. When their babies were born, we cared for them, but we were not allowed direct contact with the mothers ever because they were "sinners." When it was time for them to nurse, the director herself brought the babies one by one to the mothers. Keeping clear of the maternity ward was a strict rule, but we saw the young mothers through the window walking in the garden sometimes. A lot of women in those days had abortions done at home, both married and unwed, but it was dangerous business, and, of course, considered a terrible sin; you didn't dare speak of it.

When I finished the course, I again followed my sister's footsteps, and moved north to Genoa. A signora who was expecting a baby came to the school and specifically requested an Umbrian girl. She had this idea that Umbrian girls were calmer or something, and better with children. One day at Christmas time, I took my leave of absence and I went back to Todi to see my widowed mother. It had snowed so much, so heavily that you couldn't even walk. I hated to think of Mamma all alone in that apartment. All of my sisters were married, and she had no one, so when I went back to Genoa I told the woman that I had to move back home to take care of my mother.

I was out of work for a year, but while I was working in Genoa, I had sent all of my earnings to my mother, because the host family had taken care of all my expenses, they even bought my clothes. I didn't want for anything. My padrone was a ship builder, and they had a beautiful home. My sister also worked for a ship builder and lived in a villa. She too had sent all of her earnings home to Mamma. Our combined incomes supported her and my brother while he went to medical school. When he went to work at the hospital in Todi, he asked the director of the hospital to help me find a job, and I got short-listed at the *Opera nazionale della maternità e infanzia*, The National Agency for Maternal and Infant Welfare. This was an institution set up during the Ventennio, one of the good things that resulted from the regime.

Eventually, I got a job close to home in Perugia, where I stayed until I retired. Every job I ever had was taking care of infants, so even though I never had any children of my own, I certainly took care of a lot of them! In Perugia, I got an apartment with my cousin. In 1967, I met Giorgio, my husband. He was a friend of my cousin's boyfriend.

I met him right there in my apartment. Unfortunately, the boyfriend didn't drive and so he kept Giorgio as a sidekick. Sure, he had a car, but I wasn't interested in him or his car. He was so much younger than me, fourteen years my junior! All the men I met seemed to be younger than me, and I really couldn't bear it. Giorgio badgered me for six months to marry him. We hardly knew each other, but he really wouldn't leave well enough alone. One day, at a work meeting, I asked my coworkers what they thought. I hadn't given him an answer yet. We sat eating our tea and cookies as we did every Thursday, and they said, "Listen, if it goes on for a year, you'll have had a good year. If it lasts a week, you'll have had a good week. Give it a go." It's been 47 years now. I am still evaluating. I don't know if I like him or not. He certainly isn't the sweet man I thought I had married. I sometimes ask him why he put in such an effort to get married. "Shut up!" is his answer. See what I mean?

The first time I ever ate in a trattoria was at one of my sisters' weddings. People normally had the wedding reception at home, and a big family dinner, but we didn't want Mamma to have to cook so we ate out. The food at a trattoria was the same that we had at home anyway: tagliatelle, roast chicken, sausage, sort of similar to what they have today. I like eating out at restaurants now because I like to try new things. I don't want to have tagliatelle and roast chicken. I really like to go to the local snail festival, but that's also because a friend of mine cleans the snails and I know it is done well. I wouldn't go if it weren't for her, you know, if it was someone else cleaning the snails. Anytime I ask Giorgio if we can go out to eat, he whines, "Why do we have to go out? There's no reason to eat out."

I've never used a written recipe. I learned most of what I know by watching Mamma. She would explain to us what was what. But in Genoa they had a family cook, and in all of the schools I worked in there was always a cafeteria for the workers and the children, and the food was actually very good. So I never did any cooking myself. I didn't really start cooking until I got married. But oh, how my husband fussed about my way of cooking because he wanted everything exactly like his mother made it. His mother would make meat rolls in tomato sauce and then pour the sauce over the pasta for the first course. I made meat sauces too, but he had it in his head that hers was second to none, and he would have no other. One day his mother told me that she would make me a pot of sauce and that I could use that for the pasta throughout the week. "Eh, no!" I said, "Sorry, but I am having none of this! He'll get used to *my* cooking, little by little!" When we got home, I was furious! I said to my husband, "Listen, you! I am not going to make pasta for you any more here at home. That's it. I'm done! Eat it out when you're at work 'cause you're not going to find it on the table at home." A month went by with no pasta. Things were tense, but neither of us would budge. One day, I came home at lunchtime and I was really hungry. I got out a pan and put in some canned tomatoes with butter, the way my sister's mother-in-law in Sassomaggiore made it, *Emiliano* style. Then I made some spaghetti. Just then my husband came in, "Mamma mia, what a heavenly smell! Oh, sure! You make pasta for yourself on the sly but not for me!" So, I made him a plate of spaghetti with my sauce, and from that day forward he ate the pasta that I made without a fuss.

In those days we had all been brought up on what was called *sugo finto*, fake sauce, pulverized lardo and tomato with garlic. Now when I make sauce, I use olive oil. We don't have cholesterol problems, but they tell us we are supposed to eat this way now. Lardo and butter are delicious. If I find an excellent piece of lardo, I mince it and use that to make the sauce instead of oil, and my husband loves it. You almost never see those TV cooks using lardo, it's always olive oil. Butter is also just plain good. You have to eat things that are good too, not just what doctors tell you. We had goose breast the other night prepared by my butcher; he seasoned it with wild fennel, rosemary and sage, covered with minced lardo and wrapped in prosciutto. Well, I just can't begin to tell you… We all used to fry in lard too. But food has changed now because women don't want to spend so much time in the kitchen. Things have to be fast and easy. Everyone's afraid they are going to have to wash a dish! I've tried to get my niece to learn to cook but she couldn't care less. Whatever gets food on a plate fast, she'll do it. If there is any time or fuss involved, then forget it. Her solution is to pour cream all over everything. That's not Italian cooking.

Cream, like butter, was a high status condiment whose use spread after the 1950s. As tastes adjusted to richer foods, even the Italian gelato industry looked to the cream and sugar laden American ice-cream for cues, thereby shifting tastes away from the traditional milk-based product.

Now she is going away to study abroad, and I told her it's time she learned to cook, "Yeah, yeah…" is all she says. She knows how to make tiramisu but not our traditional Perugian desserts from the past:

Maccheroni dolci – Sweet macaroni
500g chopped walnuts
200g fine dry breadcrumbs
2 tbsp cocoa powder
250g sugar
160ml honey
1 tsp grated lemon zest
1 pinch ground nutmeg
½ tsp cinnamon
Alchermis (or red food coloring, although alchermis does add a hint of taste)
750g fresh noodles (eggless) or 800g dried tubular pasta like 'maniche'

Mix the nuts, breadcrumbs, sugar, and cocoa powder in a large mixing bowl. Grate in the lemon zest and nutmeg. Add cinnamon and stir to combine. Heat honey in a double boiler then mix with alchermis to obtain the traditional "sauce" color. Cook the pasta in abundant boiling water until it is relatively soft. This is not an al dente pasta dish. Drain the pasta and pour it into the large bowl with the dry mixture. Toss carefully so as not to damage the pasta. Drizzle the red honey over the top and toss again lightly. It does not have to coat each piece completely. Place either into single serving dishes or onto a plate as if it were savory pasta. Let cool. Best eaten the next day.

My husband and I argue about the kind of pasta you use. His hometown was forty kilometers from mine, and so they had their own way of doing it. He thinks his is better, but he's wrong.

Nothing is genuine anymore in the supermarkets. How could it be? It is all new. I still go to a real butcher though. He's very good, but he's pricy. My husband can't bear the sight of the man because he is so expensive, but the main reason I go to him is because he has a clean business, and then, of course, the meat is very, very good, like old times. I trust him. I always bring meat from his shop for my sisters when I go up north to visit them. Everything cooks up tender and you don't see water pouring out when you cook it. When you lift the lid of the pot you get that indescribable aroma of good meat. That man, the one I am married to, he on the other hand buys me crap meat from the supermarket. I can't eat it. I say, "Listen Giorgio, you buy that stuff, you make it and you eat it." I won't even try it anymore. Then he gets these cheap mozzarellas in plastic packages that are as rubbery as tennis balls. Sure, when you see them in the TV ads they look so soft and succulent. It's all crap.

One thing I really miss, that not even my butcher has, is the *pajata*. It's the intestines of lambs that haven't been weaned. They are tied together at the ends so that the mother's milk stays inside, and then you cook them in a tomato sauce or you grill them. They are nothing less than out of this world. But it's impossible to get them outside of Lazio now. It's a Roman dish really. We didn't waste those bits like they do now. We even ate sheep's head, well, not the eyes, but everything else, nose, ears, everything. But by my husband's time, things had changed and people had already stopped eating those things so much. He wants the muscle, but I like all of the innards, and the gristly bits. I love gnawing on the cartilage of chicken bones and such.

I watch a lot of cooking shows on TV. I see that some people are trying to save Italian food traditions. They go into the small villages where they do demonstrations of old-style cooking. But once you start talking about "saving" something, that means it is already pretty much gone.

Intermezzo

La scuola – School

Forty years after Unification, Italy was still struggling to provide a universal minimum education for all citizens. Poor families were reluctant to give up able, albeit young, hands and, although the cost was low, the price of books and writing materials was not insignificant to families grappling with simply getting enough to eat each day. Lack of consensus as to the importance of education, especially for girls, did little to encourage reform. At the turn of the century, 85% of women in Italy were illiterate, but to the popular mind, there was nothing extraordinary in that.

In the first decade of the 1900s, distinguished educator Maria Montessori revolutionized teaching methodology through a holistic learner-centered approach that emphasized what would now be called 'life skills' and creativity, without foregoing the importance of reasoning and order. She determined that the four cardinal influences on intellect were nutrition, housing conditions, the father's profession, and use of free time. Slow learners, she observed, were usually those who went without breakfast or subsisted mainly on bread or corn meal. Students who were average and above had at least one balanced meal per day, with the occasional serving of meat.

Spurred on by such findings, in 1911, after an in-depth survey of the deplorable conditions of locally run schools, the state assumed the burden of bankrolling public education, while leaving control in the hands of local authorities. Political luminaries, such as economist Quintino Sella, emphasized the importance of cultural knowledge as a means of insuring the state's economic interests, though Christian doctrine according to Roman Catholicism remained the steadfast core of the curriculum, aimed at producing morally sound, unassumingly knowledgeable individuals. A bit of know-how and a minimum of cognitive acuity were found to be advantageous in preparing the corps of future industrial workers, whose masses maneuvered the machines of the age. Military personnel who had not received an elementary education were provided for under these laws, as well. Nevertheless, in spite of the decisively Christian framework, religious instruction deliberately stopped short of equipping the pupil with sufficient knowledge to take a stand on spiritual issues.

With Mussolini's ascension to power in 1922, school reform was foremost among his schemes to resuscitate the former glory of Rome. He called it "The most fascist of all reforms," though the absence of previous fascist reforms to compare it with made the superlative a moot point. Philosopher Giovanni Gentile was called upon to head the reform committee, and within a year he had laid out the structure regulating schools that largely holds sway to the present day. The 1923 reforms gave Montessori and her methods the fascist stamp of approval. Her metaphysically inclined viewpoint that the teacher is not an information dispenser, that children need to be coaxed into learning through interactive stimuli, and that notions mean nothing if not assimilated into a perspective of purposeful living, gelled well with Gentile's own philosophy of education. What it did not gel well with was reality.

The earliest recorded lauding of corporal punishment is from Proverbs:

> He that spareth the rod hateth his son: but he that loveth him correcteth him betimes. Withhold not correction from a child: for if thou strike him with the rod, he shall not die. Thou shalt beat him with the rod, and deliver his soul from hell.

And for many educators, this was, as it were, gospel. Indeed, a child's ability to learn without the looming threat of physical abuse was a topic of heated debate. To put an end to the dispute, corporal punishment was formally banned in Italian schools in 1928, though actual application continued until well after WWII. In most cases, however, public shaming and humiliation, or directives of self-inflicted pain took the place of actually striking a child.

From a practical standpoint, the Gentile reforms made attendance obligatory for both boys and girls from all walks of life until the age of fourteen, and children were to be rigorously separated according to gender. This meant five years of elementary school, begun at age six, and three years of middle school. Elementary school was conceived of in two phases: Grades 1-3 focused on the main principles from the Gospels, stories from the Old Testament and the Lord's Prayer, after which came reading, writing, basic math, and translation from the local dialect into Italian. The fourth and fifth grades included history of religion, focused particularly on local saints, the Ten Commandments, parables, and knowledge of the Sacraments. History and geography focused mainly on Italy. They learned about the constitution, government, some natural science, Italian, and arithmetic. Needlework was compulsory for girls. The three years of middle school were mainly aimed at setting the child up with the rudiments of a vocation from which s/he could either continue on to the corresponding high school or legally discontinue, having fulfilled her/his obligation to the state. Again, reality did not coincide with reforms.

The realization of these reforms varied wildly from one locality to the next. Italy, fundamentally a network of small towns, suddenly had to supply every single town in the country with a handful of qualified teachers. In the post WWI economy, this was simply not practicable. What occurred more often than not was that one teacher was sent to teach all five years of primary school to both boys and girls in a single room that was not a school house per se, but a room that was made available by the town, church, or some generous citizen. It was also common for the schools to stop at the 4th grade, after which children were allowed to repeat the last year of school until they were fourteen. That is, if their parents allowed it. Generally, for girls, whether or not there was a 5th grade, four years of school was deemed sufficient. By then, the child was ten years of age and could be put to more useful purposes. There were no repercussions whatsoever from state authorities if a child was removed prematurely from school.

Although middle schools, or *Classi Integrative di Avviamento Professionale,* were supposedly the tail end of required education, they were few and far between. Attendance necessitated commuting, or even moving to another town, and the costs incurred just for the schooling itself were prohibitive. For nearly all girls, middle school was absolutely out of the question. For the fortunate few who could attend, the *Avviamento* was a cut above. Although for all intents and purposes it was a vocational school, the curriculum included Italian language and literature, European history, principles of Italian law, a foreign language, math, physics and biology, economics and bookkeeping, drawing and handwriting.

But there was progress to report: by 1930, illiteracy had dropped to 12%. Only certified teachers who were over eighteen were hired to teach in public schools. No longer were the days of the barber-cum-teacher or the kindly sister who was good with the little ones, but could just barely read herself. The modern teacher had a high school certificate from the Istituto Magistrale Inferiore and Superiore (elementary teacher training school), though it was tainted with a reputation of being for second-rate students who weren't capable of achieving anything better. In a word, it was *standard* for girls, *shameful* for boys.

This new generation of teachers was expected to exemplify fascist ideals, and was obliged to live in the communities where they taught. Predictably, teachers were required to be active party members, and were "encouraged" to become officers in fascist organizations in order to embody the connection between the school and political organizations. In an effort to enhance their low status role, state schoolteachers responded enthusiastically to the party call, rendering schools veritable fascist centers.

As the grumblings of war grew louder, teaching became increasingly fixated on the inculcation of fascist ideals. The regime was tenacious in its drive to create a New Rome by reshaping the consciousness of citizens. By the early 1930s, Montessori and her methods had fallen from favor, and "child-centeredness" had plummeted by the wayside, as the Oath of Allegiance for Teachers attests:

I swear to be faithful to the King and his royal successors; I will observe loyally the Statute and laws of the State; I will fulfill all the duties of my office diligently and zealously in the interest of the common weal and of the administration; I will keep the secrets of my office, and behave even in my private life according to the dignity of my public duties. I swear that I do not and never will belong to any association or party having activities that are not in accord with the duties of my office. I swear that I will fulfill my duties aiming solely at the inseparable happiness of the King and country.

The regime, not content with its single reader outlining the rudiments of fascism for children, took complete control of the publication of all scholastic texts in 1936 so that they would "adhere to the fascist spirit." State directives permeate children's school notebooks. From a composition: "The piccola italiana has many duties: don't let your clothes get dirty, don't leave anything on your plate, when you buy a doll, be sure she isn't a foreigner;" a story problem: "4 communists earn 8 liras per day, because they don't feel like working hard, and 4 fascists earn 15 liras per day. How much more do the fascist earn in 20 days?;" or class dictation: "The small deaf mute Giuliano was first able to hear when the Duce proclaimed the foundation of the Empire, and was able to answer, 'yes' to the Duce's words. Then, slowly, he tried to say 'Du-ce Du-ce,'" (Rossi, Pastacaldi, 1992).

A third grade primer, for example, offers this as an explanation of the war in Africa:

In Africa there was a vast empire with a barbarous population dominated by an incapable and cruel emperor: that empire is Abyssinia. And the Abyssinians dishonored us; they damaged and invaded our colonies and land holdings. This was too much. That is why the Duce decided to go to war. All of Italy is behind Mussolini. Give all of your iron, paper and gold to the Patria. The Queen, as an example to all wives, was the first to offer her wedding ring. (Zanetti, 1940)

In 1938, in accordance with the newly instated Racial Laws, Education Minister Giuseppe Bottai instituted the expulsion of all Jewish children from public schools and libraries. In a circular to town commissioners, he insisted upon widespread distribution of the booklet, "In Defense of the Race," throughout the Italian school system. Bottai's 1939 School Charter stressed military preparedness and implicit obedience to authority; it lengthened school hours to allow adults to work longer, and accentuated anti-feminism. The second "cycle" (4th and 5th grades) of elementary school was used as an expedient for introducing children to the concept of work and was even called Work School. The objective was to stir interest in and love of applying oneself to practical tasks. As Bottai himself conceptualized it, "the intention is to raise consciousness about manual labor as it applies to the state, and to exalt it to its highest moral dignity."

Vera

Born 1930 – Sinalunga

Vera drove up to our arranged meeting place in her FIAT Panda, having just come from the hairdresser's for a dye touch-up and a water-perm. She is the youngest of my interviewees, but well exemplifies the hardships faced by the have-nots of Italy's small towns.

For the duration of our interview, Vera and I made the famous Tuscan crostini neri. *You find them everywhere in central Italy, in every trattoria and supermarket. While they are usually edible, they are a far cry from the ones turned out by a capable Tuscan signora. I felt greatly indebted to her for the recipe because these crostini neri were by far the best I had ever had. For Vera, it was just making food, nothing "culinary" or "gastronomic" about it. She did not see herself as the gatekeeper to anything, though she was keenly aware that once her generation is gone, an era would end and be forgotten.*

I was born in Sinalunga. That would be a small town in Tuscany, in the province of Siena. It's one of those places that tourists find so quaint and idyllic, but as soon as I got a chance I up and left.

I was one of six children. You see, the fascio wanted folks to make lots of babies, lots of little fascists, and so they'd give you some prize money, like a reward or something, for having lots of children. So, even though there wasn't half an anchovy to divvy up in some families, the babies kept coming. You could say it was because we are Catholics, you know, and we are supposed to be making lots of babies, but it's more like this, that there wasn't a whole heck of a lotta entertainment, you know what I'm saying? You follow me here? I mean, there wasn't so terribly much for folks to *do* in the evening, and people couldn't afford hobbies. You getting my meaning? Then there was the curfew and, well, that in itself is sure to put a damper on your good times. No one had a car, and bicycles had really hard wheels, so it wasn't like you were going to go too far, were ya? No. So, that helped keep the babies coming. Capisci?

Men who had ready cash went to an osteria during the day, and well, in the evening too, until they had to be home. Yeah, there was a lotta drinking in Tuscany, and the wine was pretty cheap, so unless you were some really down and out sod, you could hang one on pretty regular. Plus, back then they thought it was healthy, that it gave you energy, you know? But you gotta know that an osteria wasn't like it is today. It was just drink. All these places calling themselves osteria today are really just restaurants. You didn't go to a restaurant unless you were really rich, you know, folks with serious money. And they weren't places for women. The only thing women was allowed to do was stay home and have more babies.

My papa, he was one unlucky fella. He worked at the local brick-yard. Backbreaking work that was. My mother was mostly an invalid, so Babbo's mother took care of runnin' the household matters. We had a three-room rental on the ground floor in the center of town. Them's the sort of houses go for a pretty penny these days to all you foreigners, but back then they were bottom of the barrel. Ground floor was as low as you could go; that's why it didn't cost much. Prostitutes and that sort lived on the ground floor. When you opened the front door, anybody passin' by could get a good eyeful at what was going on inside. That made it tempting for thieves and other violent types. And well, as everyone knew back then, that's the floor where you kept the animals; let's just say it straight out. I'm just telling you like it is. Capisci?

What we had was one large room with a fireplace where we cooked, and two bedrooms with two beds in them, each one. Us four girls and grandma were in one room. I slept in bed with grandma, and the two boys and my parents were in the other room. When the boys got older and could, well, you know what I'm saying, they were starting to pick up on certain things, we moved to a house where they had their own room. In the new place there was a small space underneath where we kept a rabbit pen. Everyone kept rabbits, if they could, for the little bit of meat you could get out of them. Now, let me just say, we are not talking about a big rabbit dinner here. We would kill one a month, but you can imagine how far one scraggy rabbit is gonna get you with nine mouths in the house.

> *While in town and church registers, families were listed as* fuochi, *referring to the family hearth, the individual family members were called* bocche *or "mouths", indicating how many mouths there were to feed in each household.*

There wasn't a whole lotta washing going on like you people do today. Every day was somebody in the family's turn for their scrub down. First, we had to haul the water from the fountain in the center of town, and it weren't none too near, let me tell you! Then you took and heated your water in the cauldron that hung by a chain over the fireplace, so once the water was boiling, we filled the washtub and added cold water. Then, well, obviously you got in the tub. I don't have to tell you about that part. Anyway, you see what I am getting at here? It just wasn't possible for everyone to wash more than once a week. If somebody skipped their turn, like when it was cold out, well then, if you were up to it, you could get in a couple baths a week. We washed our face and hands every day, and left it at that most of the time. Folks didn't get worked up about being dirty or smelly. And I am not talking about only in my family! Everybody was like that! And no one had a toothbrush, neither. Sure, of course, when we got older, and you started taking an interest, if you follow me, you know, I mean, if you started taken an interest in someone special, someone you wanted to get to know, well, then you wanted to have clean breath and keep your teeth looking nice. I got my first toothbrush when I was 17. I was a young lady then! You weren't likely gonna meet too many boys if you run around reeking of onions and garlic!

In an effort to differentiate their eating habits from that of their inferiors, the growing middle classes of the Ventennio, avoided 'foul' smelling, strong tasting foods such as onions, garlic, cabbage, and anchovies that were the typical fare of peasants and the urban poor. Former Prime Minister Berluscone resuscitated the trend in his a campaign against garlic, not allowing any of his staff to consume the malodorous bulb. Today's Italian yuppies, who tend to avoid it for social reasons, have influenced the flavors featured in upscale restaurants, and it is now difficult to find garlic infused dishes, stereotypically considered the hallmark of Italian cooking. Some restaurants purposefully distinguish themselves by not using the "offensive" substance at all. It would indeed appear to be a widespread inclination, as Italy produced 70 tons of garlic in 1970, as opposed to 27 tons in 2012.

Only time people went to the dentist was to have their rotten teeth yanked out. Pulling teeth was all those charlatans were good for because a dentist wasn't anyone really. What I mean is that anybody who wanted to could say they were a dentist. You didn't have to have no special studies or nothing. Everyone lost at least a few teeth. That's just how it was. My old folks would have laughed themselves silly at all of this toiletry stuff; we didn't have any of this! Their heads would be spinning at how fast the world changes today. It was just unthinkable for them. Every year is filled with novelty now. Always something new. Weren't never anything new then. Same old thing, year in, year out. Same stuff. Nothing changing. Then suddenly everything started changing all the time!

Anyhow, in my family, I was the fourth child of us six. I got through with the fourth grade before my parents pulled me out of school. Like near everyone. Girls didn't need more than that. By fourth grade you could read and write, in a way. In poor families with a lot of children Mussolini saw to it that we got free books and notepads. But even with that, in my house, with only my father working and my mother being an invalid most of the time, well, you understand what I'm saying? Folks like us didn't go to school. That's it. People like shopkeepers, they could keep their children on in school, but even then, it was usually only if it was a boy, and only if he was really clever. If their boy was a dunce they wouldna bothered. We didn't think school was for every-body. The law said we were supposed to go, but the *people* didn't believe it yet. It hadn't set in.

In Sinalunga there was lots of children, so girls and boys had sep-arate schools, not just separate classrooms. Each grade had its own teacher, and only women taught the girls. We had pictures of Mussolini and the King of Savoy on the wall, but when we came in, first thing, we said our Hail Mary. If some fascist personality came from out of town to visit our school, we stood at attention, but we didn't have to do the roman salute or say "Long live the king!" like in other schools. We learned about the importance of war and sacrifice. Lots of talk about making sacrifices for the patria. What sacrifices! What did we have left to give?! Already we weren't eating, so what else did they think we were supposed to give up? I'll tell you, as a girl, it scared me! There I was, small and skinny as a rail, and having them preaching at you all the time that you have to try and do without! Without what?! I'm telling you, without food, the children don't grow right. Not in the body and not in the head.

On Sundays and holidays, when he wasn't at the brickyard, my papa would go up in the hills with a cart and cut wood to sell so that we could have a bit more money. Him and my grandmother would sneak out at night to steal stuff to eat, like grapes from other folk's vineyards and fruit and vegetables from other people's gardens. My grandma would keep a close eye on them vegetable gardens, and go clip a few things in the dark of night. Otherwise, I tell you, we wouldna made it. I have no shame whatever in telling you this. That is how it was then. And we wasn't the only ones sneaking around after dark.

In the morning, before we were off to school, we had a cup of black caffè d'orzo with bread to dip in it. We couldn't even afford milk. When I tell these things to my grandchildren, they can't hardly believe me. They can't get their heads around how something like this could be possible, with all the things that they have. Even my own children say, "It just isn't possible that you managed to survive that way." Sometimes we had a bit of onion to flavor our bread or a few beans. But for as bad off as *we* were, there was folks who was worse. The town beggars could go up to the friars on Tuesday and Friday for a handout and get themselves a piece of bread, but I tell you, there was always about forty to fifty people up there with them, what with all them children and teenagers and what have you needing food.

During school months the children were fed at lunchtime by the town council. Some people sent their young'uns to school just to get some food in 'em! At one o'clock, we'd all go to the school cafeteria to eat. Some kids paid a bit money if their parents were working decent jobs, and others ate for free. Lunch was usually just something like bean soup or chickpea soup. Just every so often, we had pasta, rice, or polenta, one time with tomato sauce, another time with oil. When school let out, my grandmother would have a piece of bread ready with a drop of oil or some tomato smeared on it. After we finished our homework, we were off running house to house with our friends. Not for food 'cause didn't no one have any of that. We just ran wild. In the evening, we came home hoping there was something for dinner. It was always pretty skimpy. Nobody dropped dead, but we was always hungry.

Every summer, we went for a month to the fascist summer colony to learn about fascism and play sports. It was a law that children had to go to the colony in the summer. We'd get to have both breakfast and lunch under a big tent, all for free, all paid for by Mussolini. There was milk in the morning, pasta in the afternoon. Things were good then.

Summer colonies for children were camps set up on the seaside and in the mountains. They were a means of offering a summer vacation to underprivileged children in a healthy environment where, of course, they would receive a more concentrated dose of fascist indoctrination. A main attraction was that there were regular, albeit frugal meals. One participant recounted that discipline was so stringent that if you spilled your caffè d'orzo, one of the camp matrons would sponge it up and squeeze it back into your cup.

I started off in Fascist Saturday as a Daughter of the Wolf. When you was born, your parents got a letter of congratulations from the government, and a card asking you to pay for your little one to have party membership. But no one was forced! If you didn't want to pay, you could take the card back to the local authority. Well now, you can imagine how many people did that! And this was right after they stuck you for the *Giorno della fede*. They may as well have just come and took food outta the baby's mouth straight off.

> *The word* fede, *in* Giorno della fede, *has a double meaning: both "wedding ring" and "faith." In order to buffer the nation against the sanctions imposed in 1935 for the invasion of Ethiopia, Mussolini called upon his citizens to donate their gold wedding rings to defend the cause. In return, couples were given a steel substitute to be worn with patriotic pride. The day, December 18, 1935, had religious undertones, as people were requested to give up an object not only of monetary value, but of affective and sacramental significance. As such, it stirred a sense of communion and complicity with the state, in effect symbolically marrying the citizens to the will and whim of Mussolini. The celebration in Rome was presided over by the dizzying power trinity of the Archbishop, various heads of government, and the queen. The Pope, Mussolini, and the King, however, were notably absent. Other gold donations were made that day too, among which was Luigi Pirandello's Nobel Prize for Literature.*

On Fascist Saturday, us girls learned about keeping house, and how to take care of babies the right way. And of course, we did marching and exercise in our uniform. My parents couldn't buy the uniform for me, but Mussolini gave them free to families who were really down and out. The important thing is that we were all the same. Children didn't complain or nothing about going to the exercises because it woulda meant trouble for your folks if you didn't go. Everybody knew that. There was some people made examples of just to make sure we got it straight. My own uncle had an unfortunate dealin' with the fascio. He just come back from the war with a big ol' terrible wound in his belly, and so his doctor told him to have himself a walk after dinner to help him digest. Well, walking at night meant breaking the curfew law, and he got picked up by the Black Shirts. There was some field hands found him a few days later, moaning in a ditch. They took him fast as they could to the local hospital. Those doctors saw right away the fascist signature: the clean whack to the back of the head. He went to his maker, rest in peace, three days later at the age of 28. The town commando came and told my grandparents, they said, "Look here now, if we had known he was your son, we would have gone a bit easier on him." The old folks just stared and took the news in silence. Weren't no telling what would happen if you put up any sort of fuss.

There's this other time some young Italian kids ganged up on a German soldier. Well, as payback, fifteen young fellas were picked up off the streets at random, and were buried alive as a warning. The families of the missing boys went to the *Commandant*, but weren't no way to communicate with 'em; they didn't speak the same language. Not too long after the boys were found and dug up so's their kin could claim 'em and give them a Christian burial. But that was just a thing that happened because all in all, weren't no problems with the Germans. They even brought us a loaf of bread now and again. We was more afraid of the fascists, if anything. Everybody in town was. I kept up going to all the Fascist Saturdays until they stopped during the war.

My father, rest in peace, passed on when I was fifteen. That's when I went to the brickworks and started working as a cleaning girl. What else could a youngster like me do but clean? I used to dream of getting married and moving away from my big family, but after Babbo died, I didn't let myself dream about nothing no more. I only had that job for a year and a half 'cause the workers occupied the factory when they got wind it was gonna close down. They didn't know how they was going to eat. So they made a cooperative of it, but you had to put your money down. Sure, and what money did I have? So I had to move along outta there.

I stayed at home with my grandma, who was getting on by then. Only one in the house working was my brother, who had got hisself a barber-shop business. We done used up all our credit in the shops in town, so wouldn't nobody let us have nothing no more. We'd try to pay some of it off when we could, but we always owed more that we could bring in, so we wasn't welcome. My older sister went to work as a live-in servant for a baker, but women's work paid much less than men's, that is, hardly nothing, but they did pass on a bit of bread to us now and then.

It would be silly to say that I learned to cook from my grandmother because she just made what she could with what there was. There weren't no recipes, or nothing you could call "cooking". Breakfast was caffè d'orzo and a piece of bread. Lunch was another piece of bread. Dinner was bean soup or rice and a piece of bread with oil, or rubbed with a tomato. Beans and chickpeas, chickpeas and beans, and whatever my grandmother could steal. Not me though. I didn't steal. When it was turnip time, they went and got turnips. Maybe you don't get my meaning here. Turnips was considered pig food. Then, once a month, we had a rabbit on Sunday. There was one bite of rabbit for everybody. I don't know if I am explaining myself. Funny thing is, now that I could have rabbit every day of the week, I don't even like it! The other Sundays, my grandma made tagliatelle. She'd buy a couple eggs and a bit of flour and we'd make pasta with *sugo finto*, lardo and tomato sauce. That was high living for us! You may think what we are making here [*the crostini neri*] is the poor folk's food, but this here stuff? This here was from some other people's kitchens, not folks like us:

Crostini Neri: Tuscan canapés
1/2cup olive oil
1 med onion
1 carrot
1 stalk celery
1 bunch parsley
2 cloves garlic
500g finely ground beef
300g ground beef spleen
150g finely chopped capers
100g chopped anchovies
1 tsp grated lemon zest
¼ cup vin santo (or marsala wine)
salt and freshly ground black pepper
day-old Tuscan bread

Heat half of the olive oil in a skillet. Mince the onion, carrot, celery, parsley, and garlic and sauté on med high not stirring too much so that it browns slightly. Cook until

171

softened, about 5 min. Add the ground beef and spleen breaking up the chunks as it cooks. Add the rest of the oil, the capers, anchovies, and lemon zest, and continue frying until the meat is completely cooked. Add about a half-cup of water and keep breaking it up as it cooks, about 5 min. Pepper heavily, or to taste, and check for salt. It should tend towards the salty side. Add the vin santo and cook until it is a spreadable consistency, neither too wet nor crumbly. Slice the bread and spread on top. The stiffness of the bread determines how soon you have to eat it. These can be served warm or at room temperature.

When I was nineteen, I got married. That's when life began for me. He was nineteen too. Worked for the woodsman who supplied wood for the baker's oven. You remember me saying that? Where my sister worked. Well, time passed, as it does, and my husband got in good with the baker and started learning his trade, and that's how we met. More time passed and we took over the bakery ourself, and made quite a living of it. I had more than a toothbrush then! I even had a toilet and a bidet! We were up before dawn to set the dough to rising. We'd sleep a couple hours, and then shape the loaves for the second rise. While we was baking, we had to ready the shop for opening. So again, I didn't have no time for learning to cook. My mother-in-law saw to most of that. Husbands don't like it when they have to stop eating their mother's food anyhow. All women know that. It's why the new wife and the mother-in-law get to fighting like they do. The proverb says: "Tra suocera e nuora, tempest e gragnuola," [*Between mother-in-law and daughter-in-law, storms and hail*]. But I just let her go at it.

If anything, she was the one who taught me to cook because before that, there wasn't enough food around to talk about cooking. She was well regarded in town for her cooking. Come threshing time, she was the one who made the food for the Goose Festival. There was one threshing machine, and all of the neighbors come round together to thresh the wheat. Some would toss the bales; others held the sacks of grain, and others still would guide the mules or oxen because our thresher was powered by beasts. Then, the padroni would come and take away their share. The traditional foods she made was stewed rabbit, or goose soup. Goose is the traditional food for the threshing season.

The wheat harvest was a crucial moment in the agricultural calendar. Reaping and threshing were communal activities, and causes for celebration; as such they were among the few times when the peasants relaxed their strict parsimoniousness at the table. The ritual butchering of the goose evoked the solemnity of a sacrificial rite, tinged with apotropaic practices underscoring the community's gratitude for the generosity of the earth. The full mechanization of reaping, threshing, and milling brought an end to the collective bonding that once characterized harvest time.

In town, here in Lucignano, they still do the Goose Festival, but now it is just a demonstration of how it was done then. The TV people come, and you can see it all on the news.

After that, we had enough wheat for a little while for bread and pasta. During the war, we were all allowed 200 grams of bread a day. Now you tell me, what is a teenager supposed to do with 200 grams of bread? How are you supposed to grow straight and strong on something measly as that? Sure, we all had our card to buy the meat, but they weren't giving it away. Who the heck cares if you have a card says you can buy a chunk of meat if you don't have any money? And then, everybody's out there watchin' everybody else to see what they're putting in their mouth! Well, you slap hunger and envy together and it is not a pretty sight! *Capisci?* We was afraid of the fascists, the Germans and the neighbors in that order!

It was a terrible thing for the whole town when the brickyard finally failed for good. The families came into our shop wanting bread on credit, and didn't have no means of paying it off. That meant that I started getting flour from the mill on credit, and well, you know how that story ends. In disaster.

Then one day, we got wind of a piece of news about a job in Switzerland. There was this wealthy couple with a meat processing empire who was looking for a married couple to come and administrate their household. We only ever run our little bakery in Sinalunga, but they seemed all right with that and sent us a work contract. We signed, packed our bags, and left our children with my mother-in-law. In the end we stayed sixteen years.

They spoke Switzerland language, I mean German, and sent me to evening classes to learn German. My husband wouldn't go, though. He never even bothered trying, said he didn't want to know German. Well, what can I say? He only ever done the 3rd grade of elementary school. Maybe that's why. I wasn't too good at it myself, but I gave it my best shot, and in the end I learned it pretty good! I got my driver's license too, so I could run errands. Those folks were always so kind and generous with us, and they even paid for me to get my teeth fixed! I was scared to death to go to the dentist, on account of my teeth being all full of black holes. But he put me right. The lady of the house, she was an angel and treated me like a sister. When they went on vacation, we went with them. They had a summer home in Milan 'cause the master of the house played polo. More than played! He owned the whole darn polo club there! They liked to go to the gambling houses, and he'd win some and lose some. But more than anything, we ate like we ain't never eaten before. We saw food, and lots of it, food that we never seen, or even heard of, lots of meat of all kinds, grilled steaks, and all that fancy Swiss food, and desserts. It was a dream! We was in heaven. Or at least, I was.

We stayed until 1976, because by then my husband was fed up. He done had enough. He wanted to be near his family, and I'll tell you, in all those years, he never did learn German. I'da stayed forever. I was the governess there. I was somebody. I was important. I managed them others who cleaned, cooked, and ironed. We was given a month's leave every year, and sometimes my husband come back at Christmas too, but for him it wasn't enough, and our children didn't want to move to Switzerland. After sixteen years of service, it broke my heart to leave, and the master and the lady was right upset about our decision.

We moved back to Italy when my daughter got married. The children done growed up without me, and I was sorry about that. But how I missed Switzerland! For a time, I went and stayed a month every year with my Swiss family.

What I can't understand today, is that now that there is all of this food around, and everyone eats as much as they want, nobody wants to cook. My generation is the last generation that knows how to cook traditional Italian food. When we die, everything else's gonna be an industrialized copy of what we do now. But maybe it can't be no other way. My daughters work, so do my granddaughters. You can't all get home *al tocco* (at one o'clock) and make a meal from scratch. The best you can do is open packages. Even salad comes in a bag these days! The whole family comes to my house every Sunday for the midday meal, but no one gives a thought to learning how to make these dishes. I haven't written them down, and so it'll all be lost when I'm gone. You know what they do? They buy a cutlet, already breaded, and flip it over in a pan, or they throw pre-cooked meatballs in the microwave. What is strange is that they love my food, but still they don't seem to mind buying ready-made food. They don't seem to care who made it or how. It is the same with dressmakers and shoemakers. For us, it didn't make no sense buying shoes from somebody who didn't repair them too. Now, everybody buys off the rack, and you toss 'em out when you don't like 'em no more. The same with food. They buy ready-made sauce, even meat that's already been cooked - by somebody they don't know! But anyway, I say, do as you please because it is better than being hungry. Even if all they ever eat is pizza and gelato, well, so be it because it means they have money and they can afford to waste it. We can eat meat whenever we want without even thinking about it. Nobody has to sell eggs or rabbit pelts like the country wives used to do just so's they could buy some salt or rice. We ate more rice than pasta because it was cheaper, and more polenta than rice 'cause that was cheaper still. Today, my family can choose anything they want. Everything is better today. Sure, the things they eat these days aren't good, but women don't want to stay home nowadays keeping house and raising children. And anyway, why should they!? I only had two children because times had changed by then, but if I coulda chosen, I'da only had one.

Intermezzo

Autarchia in cucina – Autarky in the Kitchen

Fascist Italy, strapped by the collective siege organized
by 52 countries, had entrusted you with a delicate
and decisive task: that of making every Italian
family into a fortress to resist the sanctions. With
magnificent discipline, with superb patriotism, you,
oh, women, have carried out this task…. The Patria
pays you the tribute of its gratefulness. Your example
will be inscribed on the pages of Italian history.
— MUSSOLINI, 1936, PIAZZA VENEZIA

The word "autarky" became a household word during the
Ventennio fascista. This yearning for national sovereignty and
self-sufficiency was understandably in the air in Europe, following the unprecedented horrors of WWI. Shadowy tensions lingered,
even as the ink dried on the peace treaties, leaving governments jit-
tery about future alliances. The Battle for Wheat was an initial step in
Mussolini's vision of insulating Italy, but autarky required resources
that were ultimately unattainable from the peninsula proper. The colonization of North Africa shone on the horizon as the beacon of hope
that might eventually fulfill the ambitions of the Patria and restore
national pride, putting Italy back on the map as a world power, a force

with which to be reckoned. Parts of what would become Libya were already under Italian dominion when Mussolini came to power, and in 1935, troops were dispatched to conquer Ethiopia. Heretofore, France and the United Kingdom had turned a blind eye to Italy's ambitions, preferring to keep it as a potential ally while Germany flexed its muscles. However, deliberate peacetime invasion could not be ignored by the newly formed League of Nations, and the motion for sanctions against Italy was passed.

The toothless LN sanctions lasted a little over seven months. In most cases, commercial interests overrode lip service for world peace, and it was business as usual even between supposedly sworn enemies. England and the US, for example, two of the more vocal countries against the Ethiopian invasion, continued importing 85% of Italy's canned tomatoes. Dwindling Italian gold reserves and the Great Depression had squelched Italy's import potential, but the sanctions themselves were anything but punishing. On the contrary, they were exactly the boon the regime needed. Once there was a palpable enemy to point the finger at, the people could be called upon to make sacrifices for the cause. Dearth could be, and would be, blamed on sanctions long after the actual threat had dissipated completely. A nation already stretched to the limits would be stretched beyond them.

Under Mussolini, autarky became synonymous with austerity, as the country cinched its belt yet another notch. Statesmen reminded the masses that food restriction should not pose a problem because Italians had long been accustomed to parsimony, or rather, to doing without. Mussolini (who suffered from chronic gastrointestinal disorders) ate very frugally and presented himself as an example to the masses. The ancient Romans, whose foodways were simple, sparing and wholesome, promoting the flawless, idolized, physical form, were once again exhumed as a model of purity. *La Cucina Italiana* openly declared itself the trumpeter that would lead the march of middle class housewives, wheedling them along with a monotonous barrage of numbing titles touting the darlings of the autarkic kitchen: "How to Cook Fish"; "How to Use Leftover Fish"; "How to Cook Rabbit"; "Notions to Housewives on Chicken Coops"; "Women in the Ranks" (whose accompanying photomontage features a woman feeding a peep of chickens in the foreground with men on the battlefield in the background); "Polenta: a healthy nutritious food"; "Housewives, Make Rice!"; and "How to Use Leftover Bread". The initial titles were geared towards freeing pasturelands for wheat production, while the latter aimed at alleviating the burden on wheat supplies. More generic titles included "How to Cook Under Sanctions"; "Gentility in Wartime"; "The Cooking of Imperial Rome"; "Sanctions and Cooking"; "A Time of Thrift"; and "Anti-Sanctionist Food". Every issue implored: "Italian women! Eat the Italian way!" Recipes in a bellicose vein included Abyssinian Cake (chocolate), flanked by a recipe for White Cake, accompanied by the sideswiping Fried Frogs, and Bread Bullets in Broth.

Meatless days were decreed on Tuesday and Wednesday, in addition to the traditional Friday abstinence. Nutritionists scrambled to defend the reduction in the availability of meat by deducing that it was not a physiological necessity. One expert declared that humans can only digest meat protein halfway, while the rest lingered to poison the body, boldly adding, "Animal protein is the worst kind of protein because it has died twice, once when slaughtered and then on the fire, which destroys the vitamins. Expecting to build a healthy organism with food that has died twice is a grave error." (Ferrari, 1936).

"Less is more" became the battle cry of patriotic Italian housewives, as evidenced in the hyperbolic article "Women of Italy, to the Kitchen!" in which Rina Simonetta admonishes her readers:

Some people may not feel like making any sort of concession; … There are those, for example, who don't think they can live without eating steak every day, or maybe even twice a day; they can't live without having that bloody piece of meat on a plate. But fortunately, in Italy they are few … the majority … are satisfied with a nice plate of pasta or rice, or perhaps bread and a piece of cheese, just like the bricklayers that I see every day on their break … sitting on the ground, enjoying their food, and having the strength after their healthy, but very frugal meal, to work the whole day building and demolishing.

So what then? We have pasta and bread: flour and cornmeal and fruit and vegetables and starches and legumes and citrus and game and fish ... and we have wine, milk, eggs ... What else do we need? a bit of meat...But we do without it willingly. You can bet that your men will value you for your bravura, and they'll have one more reason to appreciate and love you. Just think, women of Italy, that the eyes of the world will be upon you, and that those populations used to eating from morning to night, used to filling themselves up with beer and alcohol, getting drunk and slumping down under the table, eating raw meat and salt fish until the wee hours, they don't even realize that we couldn't care less about it ... because we are a moderate, frugal population who live more by our brains than by our stomachs (1935).

Price controls were instated to quell the public's fears of inflation, but this in turn played havoc with merchants' interests. The solution was to garner their support for the war in Ethiopia by making frugality into a moral imperative. Once shop owners had rallied behind the cause and were willing to sell at rock-bottom prices, the momentum could undulate seamlessly from one war to the next. With the passing of time, austerity became ingrained in the public psyche, an automatic reflex geared toward spending as little as possible, inventing ways to use and reuse even the smallest amounts of food and materials, embracing cheap foods, fabric, and lifestyles as a sign of virtue and patriotism.

The alliance with Hitler and colonial ambitions had a far more detrimental effect on the availability of foodstuffs in Italy than sanctions did. As part of the Pact of Steel, thousands of able-bodied men repatriated to Germany, reducing the workforce at home. The agreement also included shipments of rice, cheese, fruits, and vegetables to Germany with nothing, at least nothing edible, in exchange. By 1943, the Italian ration card counted 990 calories daily, compared to the German allowance of 1,980 calories. Build-up of the military arsenal had precedence over food supplies. The Italian diet was thus defined by what was available, not by what the body required. The colonies also drained Italy of manpower. For their sacrifices to the Patria, colonizers expected imports of the foods to which they were accustomed. The idea had been to set North Africa up as Italy's breadbasket, but there simply weren't enough resources to bring the plan to fruition. A half-baked project, it too drained the fatherland of both manpower and food supplies while offering nothing in return.

Bread accompanied everything. It was dipped in the morning milk; it mopped the plate at lunch, and gave substance to the evening broth. Frugal daily portioning advised 500 grams of bread for active, robust men and between 150-250 grams for women and children. When the 1941 bread ration was set at 200 grams across the board, it sent the population reeling. To restore public calm, Mussolini had to make some adjustments: pregnant women were allowed 100 grams more; underprivileged children on the school lunch program were allotted another 50 grams; and manual laborers' rations were modified in accordance with exertion. Miners, for example, were at the top of the list with a total provision of 500 grams. Domestic workers, it was decided, would have to be provided for by their employers. Indeed, before accepting a job, savvy maids would ask what the family intended to feed them beyond the ration card allowance.

Carla

Born 1927 – Imperia

The city of Imperia is a fascist creation located in the northern most part of Liguria. The year after the fascists took power, it was formed, in October of 1923, by conjoining two small adjacent towns, Oneglia and Porto Maurizio. The artificial fusion did little to change the fierce rivalry between the two areas, though over time their chiding has eroded from evocations of deep-rooted hatred to mere poking fun. The San Mauritani say, for example, that the best thing about Oneglia is the view it offers of San Maurizio, which is indeed a splendor to behold. Carla is a proud resident of Oneglia. She is unusual in that she was an only child of parents who valued education, even for girls, though they had received little of it themselves. She offers a very articulate impression of the fascist era, and a lucid elaboration of the difficult awakening in store for those who had been instilled with an unquestionable enthusiasm for the regime. Her memories of the era are kept sharp because it is the main topic of conversation between her and her 103-year-old aunt. After our interview, Carla's friends Sandro and Laura Antonucci treated us to a fine home cooked meal of local Ligurian specialties.

My grandparents were all Liguri DOC [*a gastronomic term for certified local products*]. My father worked down at the docks unloading merchant ships, and he was a fisherman on the side to make ends meet. My grandfather and uncle did the same work, and all of them had a side job; my grandfather made shoes and my uncle whitewashed houses. My mother was a fishwife and had an early morning stand in the market selling my father's catch. Afterwards, she went to work at the Agnesi pasta factory, but when she got pregnant with me she got sacked, as always happened. You worked as long as you could, but then when you got too close to your time, they fired you.

The baby was me. I am an only child. After I was on my way in the world, my mother got a job in a box factory; I mean a factory that made boxes for packaging. She had to give me away to another family for a year because her milk didn't come. I was very small and frail so I had to stay away for quite a while until I was strong enough to go home. Meanwhile, my maternal grandmother had died from a complication in the birth of her third child, an infection, those things happened quite often, and my paternal grandmother died from the Spanish flu in 1918.

The so-called Spanish Flu was a virus brought by the U.S. military to France during WWI. Consider that 10 million people died in WWI, mostly military, while 50 million died of the Spanish Flu; in Italy the death toll is estimated between 400,000-650,000.

My father had to nurse both of his parents through it, but only his father survived. I started school when I was five because the new fascist law said that if during the school year you turned six, you could start school at five. I did elementary school, middle school, and then two years of bookkeeping school. It was rare for girls to finish so much school, but both of my parent - and I mean in *their* day - had finished elementary school, so they thought education was fundamental, even for girls. Most of the girls I knew only finished the third grade. For my family, culture and education were more important than bread. Plus, I really wanted to study, so they did everything they could to make that possible. It was very important to my father. He himself had done a middle school equivalency test. Not for any gain other than his own satisfaction. He was proud to see me studying and achieving.

The house I was born in was bombed during the war and isn't standing anymore, but until 1936, we lived in Via Dejuener. There was a big central room, a kitchen, or rather a kitchen corridor with the usual hearth and cauldron, and a bedroom. We also had a sort of bathroom. You stepped up a couple steps where there was a sort of hole and you squatted. When you had done, you poured water down it, and that swilled off into a cesspool that had to be emptied every now and then. Some houses that were near the prison had plumbing because they could hook into the same sewage system that emptied out into the sea. That wasn't a very nice aspect of it, but people didn't think about those things then. The sea seemed, well, it seemed so... large.

My father was always out first thing in the morning, and my mother had to be at the box factory at 8:00. If I was well enough, my mother would take me to my step-grandmother, who I always thought of as my grandma. She had a permanent stand at the open market and she looked after me. But I was a sickly child, so usually my great aunt came to the house to take care of me. By the time I started school, I was sturdy enough to walk there on my own. Breakfast was milk and an artificial coffee we made with orzo and chicory. We had that because that is what there was, but I recall I didn't care for it too much. If I wanted something else, my aunt would say, "I've got a real treat for you!" She would dampen some bread with water and sprinkle a bit of sugar on top. You didn't get sugar too often, so it really did seem like something special. Our local bread then was coarse, whole wheat bread. Later it was hard to find even that, and most people ate sorghum bread. But because I was a frail child, my family would try, whenever they could, to get me a white bread roll on the black market because that was considered healthier. I was sort of the darling of the whole family. They loved to spoil me.

Anyway, we went to school from 8:00 to noon. Then home for lunch and back to school from 2:00-4:00. You know, I still have all my schoolbooks with the fascist teachings, "The Italian people are hardy workers, but even a strong people needs someone capable of taking the lead." And, well, seeing the mess that we have made of the world today, maybe they didn't have it all wrong! "Without a strong figure at the helm, the Italian population is worthless." Everything was directed towards teaching us to love the Patria and be obedient. They wanted us to feel proud of being Italian. And that we were! Even us girls, who knew nothing about the realities of war or defending the country, were swept up in a tide of emotion. I remember how I was always gripped by this awful feeling when we wrote compositions in class because the teacher would ask us to write on the top of our paper whether or not our parents were fascist party members. No one in my family was, and it was gravely humiliating for me. I was so ashamed. That's why my father had to work at the dock, in spite of his education. Him, my uncle and my grandfather had all refused to be members and that means you did the lowliest jobs.

Before fascism, my grandfather held a job at the ironworks factory. It was round about that time that the unions started stirring.

The Metal Worker's Federation formed in 1901. They fought for a 48-hour workweek, and achieved their goal with the signing of a national agreement in 1919.

Of course, it was difficult for workers to organize then. This was before Mussolini became fascist and was still socialist. Mussolini had come right here, to Oneglia, as a teacher, an assistant teacher really, at a boarding school. He was someone who looked after the boys after school, or helped with homework. A nobody really! He didn't even really have a position as a teacher.

Mussolini's mother was a teacher and felt that education would be the only way for her son to arise from the obscurity of their social status. He received his teaching certificate in 1901. He tried to escape the draft by falsifying his passport and immigrating to Switzerland, but he was caught at the border and sent back. An article was written about this political gesture in which, for the first time, he was referred to as the "Duce," and it was very much to his liking. He fulfilled his military obligation with honors, after which he accepted the teaching position in Oneglia. Here he headed a socialist newsletter, and began acting upon his political directives of the moment, thus beginning his climb to power.

People remember seeing him out walking with the students down by the docks. He was from Emilia but somehow he got a post up here. Anyway, my grandfather was a man who spoke well and carried himself with authority, more than the others, and so he headed up the reform group. The men wanted to reduce their hours because, at the time, they were working long, backbreaking hours and had no rights. So, he and a couple others went to the bosses; meantime the workers occupied the factory. They got the reduction of hours, all right, but after the strike, when work resumed, my grandfather and the others who had negotiated the compromise got fired. The unions didn't have much power then, so he had no defense. He went to work down at the dock because it was lowly work, and when you're at the bottom of the barrel, no one bothers with you. Plus, no one would touch him after that, I mean, no one would dare hire him; the same for my father and uncle. It was like a disease. But they were tough, industrious men, who were not afraid of a little hard work.

I couldn't understand these things at the time, so I would beg my father, "Papa, please, why don't you join the party?! I hate writing that you are not a party member!" But he never did. All of us at school believed fascism was for the good of everyone. It was all we knew and we heard it every day. We were figlie della lupa and piccolo italiane! We wore our fascist uniforms with pride, the little black skirt and mantle, and we loved marching on Fascist Saturday. My teacher, who was fascist, of course, would pin a pink bow to my white school smock because I took great pains never to get dirty, and she said I was an example of tidiness for the others, a good fascist. I loved order, and fascism was all about order. I reveled in precision to the point of mania. Fascism told you how to behave, how to dress, how to work; and I wanted to do all of it exactly as they told me. But my father had seen how his mother suffered after my grandfather had lost his job. She was a seamstress and had a regular clientele, but after he got turned out, they were both shunned, and people stopped giving her work, or at most, they would sneak by after dark for fittings because they couldn't dare be seen associating with her in the light of day. They fell on hard times for a while, but were staunchly against having any political associations.

They were people of principle who wouldn't even get a card on the pretext of getting better employment. In our area you would hear every now and then of people who got pretty roughed up by the squadristi, or were given the castor oil treatment, but my father kept his nose to the grindstone, and was left alone pretty much. Every so often, someone would come by to remind him who was in charge, but nothing more than that. Everybody knew that if you tried to organize any sort of protest or assembly, you were shipped straight off to isolation in the far south. It wasn't prison, but you were not allowed to move out of the town they put you in. Generally, they were placed in a house where they had to report in every evening. My father held his tongue about the propaganda they were teaching us at school, though. He understood that it was beyond his control, and that it was better for me to conform.

My mother might have had a bit of a fascist bent, except that she had spent some time in prison. The crate factory where she worked had started building beds for the military, and so the workers got it into their heads to ask for a higher ration on the ration card. They thought, "We are basically working for the military, so we should get something more for our efforts." Armed with their righteousness, they marched off to the prefecture to get their due, just a half point more to get a couple more potatoes, maybe some flour, but they were willing to settle for just a couple potatoes. They headed down to the Empire Bridge and found the military waiting for them. Their boss at the factory had tipped off the militia that the workers were on their way, and they were all put in prison. They were left there for about a week, just to teach them a lesson. The ones who had stirred up the revolt were held a bit longer. It wasn't even that they were protesting against fascism or that they were insubordinate, they just wanted a couple more potatoes for the stew pot!

Before the war, when I was still at school, I would come home for lunch to a bowl of minestrone or a dish of pasta with tomato sauce.

Every region has its own version of minestrone, generally distinguished by some signature local ingredient. The classic Ligurian minestrone is made with pesto, the pride of Genoa.

My step-grandmother had a vegetable and fresh pasta stand because my grandfather had a piece of land in the country where he grew vegetables, so we didn't have to buy them, and he had also found a plot of land where he could plant wheat, which is where they got the flour to make the pasta. He'd take it to the local mill to have it ground, but it was nearly whole-wheat flour because you lost too much of the grain if it was polished up too much. Today they make you pay more for whole grain like it's something special, but it used to be the cheap stuff that no one wanted! They also had chickens, so we never wanted for eggs, and rabbits too, and olive oil. Liguria is famous for its oil.

Colonizers from Phocaea, Anatolia, introduced olive cultivation into Italy by way of Sicily. It reached Liguria and nearby Provence between the sixth and seventh century BCE, although Ligurians proudly point out that pollen studies have revealed the existence of wild olive groves in the area at least since the Bronze Age. As with lard, olive oil was put to many uses, above all as a base for medicinal and perfumed unguents. Benedictine monks set large-scale cultivation in motion in the twelfth century, utilizing the Taggia variety, which to this day accounts for 99% of the olive trees in Imperia. Ligurians claim that their olive oil is il migliore in assoluto, *the absolute finest for quality, taste, smell, and color.*

The traditional method of collecting the olives was to lay netting around the tree and let the mature olives fall to the ground; those in reach were picked, and the higher branches were shaken to loosen the others to the ground. The modern method consists of forcibly striking the olives down from their perch with a long stick (contrary to other areas, the olive trees in Imperia are quite tall, which excludes harvesting by hand). Purists claim that this encourages unripe olives into the mix, negatively impacting the quality.

We didn't use lard like other places in Italy. We didn't have the tradition of raising pigs in Liguria, or animals in general. For us it was all olive oil. The land in Liguria is very rocky, and inhospitable for crops. But between my grandmother and grandfather, we were well supplied with food. And, of course, as a costal region, there was always fish, particularly when it was the season for *zerri,* a fish just a bit bigger than a sardine, but with tough scales. My father used to say, "This is a fish that a lot of people don't take to, even though you can do so much with it." When the season was right, and zerri were abundant and cheap, the way most people made them was to lightly coat them, fry them, and put them up in glass jars in vinegar. So, it was a layer of fried zerri, some garlic, then vinegar and so on. The smell of zerri is the smell of the sea. It's not a fishy fish. So, in those moments when you found yourself in a bind about what to put on the table, you just got down your jar of preserved zerri and cut up a tomato, and there you had your second course all ready.

When we got home from school in the afternoon, we had to do our homework. When we were little, it was hours upon hours of *puntini.* Our notebook paper wasn't lined; it was in squares, and we had to draw lines and slashes, backwards and forwards from one point to another point in order to work up to getting each letter perfect, and it wasn't easy! Calligraphy used to be considered very important. But today, they go to school and learn to write words. No one does puntini anymore. In the end though, I don't think it makes much difference. I think good handwriting is a gift. You've either got it or not. At school we had our "good" notebook and our "bad" one. We took dictation in the bad notebook, and once the teacher had approved your work, you had to recopy it into the good notebook in your very best handwriting. I was never any good at it. My handwriting never got any better than it was in 5th grade.

When I was a bookkeeper, there were people who came into town from the countryside to pay taxes who had never held anything in their hand all their lives but a hoe, and my word, some of them had the most elegant signatures! Even though I was a bookkeeper, my husband would rewrite our income tax forms because he was embarrassed to have his name on a form with my handwriting. All records were kept by hand then, so it was important that it be legible. It used to be that commercial ledgers had to be taken to the courthouse to be review and approved, so you couldn't be making scribbly blunders!

Our teachers were severe, and children were well disciplined. I remember noticing how manners started to slip, little by little, after the war. Young people would not give their seats up to the elderly on the bus, for example. During fascism when you got on a bus you looked around before you sat down to see if there was an elderly person or a person in need before you yourself took a seat. If you just plunked yourself down, you stood the chance of having a plainclothes fascist patrolman tap you on the shoulder and say, "Stand up! Name and surname! Now!" It's not that buses were full of Black Shirts. Anyone who was a fervent party member took it upon themselves, whoever or wherever they were, to maintain decency and order. If that were to happen now, oh! Everyone would get thrown in jail! And you couldn't curse in public. It was absolutely forbidden! Now people just let it fly!

What I mean is that we can't say that everything the fascists did was in the wrong. For example, in 1933, Mussolini started social security, and you could say to your employer at the end of the month to withhold two or three percent for your retirement, sick days and all that. My father signed up right away because he saw it as something that was right and sensible. And people chided him, "What? You mean you? You are going to sign up for a fascist initiative?!" But my father was a man who thought in the long term. There wasn't much of a public health program to speak of then, so illness and growing old was a great hardship. It was frightening for a lot of people. But, in a hand to mouth existence like ours, not too many people could understand the importance of setting something aside for the future. My father would say to them, "Well, what about you? All of you party members out there on Saturdays, marching up and down like fools in your uniforms, waving your flags, and carrying your banners, but you can't see past your noses! When you're sick, you can't do anything about it because you don't have money for your medicine! But, sure, go on out there and march! March! Lotta good it'll do you!"

Later, Mussolini made it obligatory for employers to deposit money into the retirement fund for their employees. It was the beginning of national healthcare because, in the end, Mussolini knew that a healthy nation was more productive for the state. It used to be you had to work until you dropped, literally. There was just no end to it; there was no retirement, only dwindling and decay. So, Mussolini created the retirement package together with the pension. The industrialists were outraged because they had to chip in a part, but he convinced them by saying said it would only last until 1939, ten years, because surely, by then, the country would have stabilized enough. Once we had got past a period of crisis, then social security wouldn't be necessary anymore. But when rumblings of war began, that threw everything into a tailspin. By then, the idea of a retirement pension had taken hold, and no one wanted to give it up! At some point during the night, people started to see it as their civil right, and wouldn't give it up!

Mussolini had also set up the first day care centers and the National Bureau of Mothers and Infants, which meant that in the afternoons of our Fascist Saturdays we girls would make clothes for the little foundlings, orphans, and poor children. When we were little, it was all done by hand, but then in high school, we used sewing machines supplied by the party. Sure, it was work, but we enjoyed ourselves. It wasn't forced labor because we were all together. We chatted the time away, and then at the end of the school year, there was an exhibition to show off our work. I entered the little shirts and baby booties that I had made. Mine were embroidered too because in the afternoons, I went to the sisters, who taught me needlework, so I always had something extra on my pieces.

Our teacher was in charge of our Saturday activities, so above all, she had to be a dedicated fascist; otherwise she didn't have a job, especially not in the teaching profession. We got our marching done with straight away in the morning. "Straighten those shoulders! Hold in your stomach! Chest held high! March! March! March!" And we marched like lots of little soldierettes, the tall girls in the front rows and the small ones at the back, that way the more attractive girls made a good first impression. As they say, *Altezza è mezza bellezza* (Tall is halfway to beautiful).

Then, after marching exercises, we did our sewing, but we also had two hours a week of "Pedology," where our teacher and a woman doctor taught us about how babies were born. That was important because all children were born at home then. I still remember today the diagrams showing the ovaries, uterus, and the whole reproductive business. Then they also taught us how to take care of a baby, how to wash it, and how to hold it. When they complain today about sex education in schools, well, really! What is the problem? We studied it even in my day!

The boys were separated from us and had a man doctor who explained to them about the sicknesses that men got, you know, the sexual diseases, and all the things they had to be careful about; but I don't really know what else they talked about because they were private "boy" things. We girls had dolls and had to learn to swaddle them because babies were still bound back then. They thought that it would help children grow with straighter bones; it wasn't meant to constrain them. They thought that if you crossed your legs they would come out curved. I think that practice stopped right after the war. They had figured out by then it was pointless.

> *Binding an infant in swaddling cloth was presumed to correct the effects of rickets, prevalent in Northern Italy, exacerbated by the poor diet of lactating mothers. Historically, swaddling was based on the idea that babies would be calmer if their motor activity was constrained. It was also believed to prevent sudden infant death, though in the end none of these theories stood up to scientific trials.*

On Sunday, I went to Sunday school with the sisters in the afternoon to learn the doctrine of Christ our Lord and practical tasks for girls. After church, we had pasta as the main dish, usually with oil and maybe a bit of garlic, other times with tomato, onion, basil sauce. We had pesto but it wasn't like what people think now. It was a general condiment you kept on the table, not just for pasta, and it was just oil, basil, and garlic – not all of this business with pine nuts and cheese. It was very simple.

> *Despite its national and international fame as a classic condiment with deep historic roots, pesto alla Genovese, in the form known both inside and outside Italy, is a relatively recent concoction. Zealots claim its origins date back to the Ancient Romans, but the first identifiable approximation was documented in the mid 1800s. It was called Minced or Flavored Garlic (Pésto): 1 clove garlic, basil (if none is available use marjoram or parsley), Sardinian cheese, Parmigiano cheese, olive oil, butter. A recent scandal arose in February of 2015, when chef Davide*

Oldani acknowledged the importance of butter in pesto. "Heresy!" cried the Academia Italiana della Cucina. *Oldani defended himself by referring to Ada Boni, one of the most famous culinary authorities of the Ventennio fascista, as his source. The addition of pine nuts and the use of olive oil as the only fat is a modern, post-war variation. An irresistible, yet unreliable, source asserts that Frank Sinatra, of Ligurian descent, was instrumental in the commercial packaging and exportation of pesto that led to its worldwide fame.*

Barilla makes pesto in a jar without garlic now. What on earth is that!? That's not pesto! If you take away the garlic you've ruined it. All over Imperia around noon, you could hear the pounding of the mortar and pestle making pesto with garlic. Everyone made it, but as I said, not for pasta necessarily, but for whatever you wanted, particularly minestrone. I always went easy on the amount of oil, but my husband, with whom I used to bicker a good amount, lived in oil. He'd just pour it on, while I used an eyedropper. But then, he was from the *other* side of Imperia.

So anyway, the second course on special days, and I mean when times were good, was the *milanese* (breaded cutlet). Otherwise, we usually had fish. We also made meatloaf, stretched with lots of filler and vegetables, and we called it "fake roast." Most second courses were served with the bitter root called *scorzanera*, one of the most commonly eaten vegetables in this area. And we often had the *farinata*, a simple oily flat cake made of chickpea flour, salt, and water, very famous in Liguria.

The history of the farinata, if not factual, is at least entertaining. Its origins date back to Ancient Greece and Rome, when soldiers in need of a quick cheap meal would prepare a chickpea batter that they would then bake in the sun on their shields. While the Roman Empire was destined to fall, the farinata lived on to become a medieval favorite, often enjoyed with a side dish of pickled onions and cheese. As legend would have it, this modern version was a chance occurrence; Genoese ships, homeward bound from a battle with Pisa, found themselves in a storm on the high seas. Barrels of oil and chickpea flour were tousled to and

fro, mixing with the salty seawater. But alas, provisions were few, and
food could not be wasted, so the sailors put the dampened, oily, flour
paste in the sun to dry. Voilà. Farinata.

The news of sanctions levied on Italy in '35 hit hard. They told us
about it in school in no uncertain terms, about how the world had
turned against Italy unjustly, and how we were going to have to tighten
our belts against this abuse.

Perhaps the tone was similar to this: "The hateful sanctions machine …
is denying arms, credit, and raw materials to our Italy, who taught the
entire world about civilization … [T]hey are trying to starve us, to suf-
focate us, and all the while they are sending the Ethiopian rulers arms
and assistance of every kind, to those slave drivers, those barbarous and
ferocious raw meat eaters."(Nina, 1935).

We had to join together to waste as little as possible and cut out any
and every luxury. The word "autarky" was bandied about as a source
of national pride. We were going to go it alone, in spite of everyone!
The whole nation felt united and indignant. Everyone looked for
any little patch of land where they could sow wheat, like our Duce
said we should do. We were all in the fields; even the little ones were
out there picking up stray ears of wheat. I know! I was one of them!
Everyone according to her ability, we said! When we started to have
machines that threshed the wheat, well, it was just the most amazing
thing! We watched in awe. Those big machines stripping the hull from
the grain... They changed our lives.

In '38, when Mussolini went in with Hitler, things began to change.
We Italians didn't trust Hitler. We didn't, well, I'll say it straight out: we
didn't like the Germans. No, we didn't like them one bit. Of course,
as Ligurians, we felt closer to French culture than to the Germans.
We share a border with Piedmont, and their culture is strongly influenced by the French. For us, Germans are the descendants of Attila
the Hun. Even so, my husband, who had gone to war in '42 and spent
twenty-six months in Germany, would say, "There are good Germans
and bad Germans, just like anyone else." Everyone said that the war

would only last a few months, if that, but the armistice didn't come until September 8th,1943, and on September 13th my husband was still with the German army. First he was stationed with them in Pola, in Istria. They received orders to sink a ship, and his captain, an Italian captain, told the men not to do it, so they were all taken prisoner.

Mussolini didn't trust Hitler; indeed he sent our gold reserves to America to safeguard them from him [*I was unable to verify this interesting piece of information*]. I have an aunt who is 103. All we talk about is this era. Her lucidity comes and goes, but she has never forgotten the war. My doctor says, when I go for a check up, "I don't know what it is about your family, you don't have cholesterol or triglycerides." I think it is recipes like this that have kept us going:

Minestra di lattuga - Lettuce soup
Small bunch of lettuce leaves (four outer ones)
One egg beaten
1/3 cup flour
grated hard cheese

Chop lettuce leaves into fine strips. Boil 4 cups of water. Add the egg and the lettuce. Boil a couple minutes until the lettuce is soft. Make some fregamai by sprinkling some water onto some flour and rubbing it together to make large crumbs. Sift the crumbs out of the flour and add them to the lettuce and egg broth. Boil another two minutes. Salt and sprinkle with cheese. Serves 4.

In Liguria, we were able to trade our olive oil on the French black market for flour. We didn't have shoes either, so we traded for those too. We all wore a very basic shoe of plain leather with thick leather soles that had metal plates on the bottom. Everyone wore the same shoe; only the size changed! You see we didn't have cows here, so we didn't have leather. We used goats for milk. The French had herds and herds of cows, and so had leather. It was too rocky here, and we didn't have the kind of pastureland that cows needed. In the summer, my grandfather, who knew how to make shoes, made us cloth sandals like the ones they had in his day. In '39, my father had been to the front in our campaign to colonize Albania. When he returned he brought his sailor suit. The fabric is very stiff, and so was good for these sandals. Grandpa sewed a lot of layers for the sole, and used the bitumen tar that the Germans used in construction to waterproof the bottom. Then he said, "You women get some fabric scraps for the tops." And so the whole family had sandals!

In 1941, even shoes were rationed. Adults were allotted 120 points per year: a pair of leather shoes consumed 65 points, whereas shoes made of felt, plastic, wood, and cork didn't require any points. One thought long and hard before purchasing a pair of leather shoes, and wives were expected to consult with their husbands.

In 1940, my parents were finally able to buy a house, down by the port. My father had worked tirelessly to make a life for us because of his choice to keep out of the party. He did not want us to suffer any lack because of his choice. But, when the Germans came in '43, they set land mines out all along the dock and we had to flee to the country to my grandparents. Then the bombing started in earnest.

It was at that point that I started to look around and to change in my mind. The partigiani appeared little by little. They frightened all of us because they disrupted the sense of order. They were an unruly gang as much as anything, just making it up as they went along. So, there we were with the fascio, who had lost control, the Germans, who were trying to take control, the Americans invading, and the Italians rebelling! It was complete and total chaos. War is ugly, but the ugliest war is civil war. I had a school friend whose brother killed their father because the brother was communist and the father was fascist. That happened all the time at the end of the war, and it left us feeling gutted. How can brothers kill brothers for a political ideal? After the armistice, we felt the division; some became red and some became black and the tension grew more suffocating each day. I had a school friend, Mafalda; she was a fascist spy and informed on a friend of ours, someone we had known all our lives. As a result, he was killed. How do you forgive that?

What happens is that you become very cautious, very careful about ever buying into any ideology, any political line. You trust no one. You don't even know how to take your own life into your hands and guide it down the right road because you don't even trust yourself to be able to do that, to be able to distinguish and discern. You're always afraid. You become critical and cynical. You are suspicious of everyone. Since then, we have seen one government after another in Italy. They rise and fall so quickly that we have become the laughing stock of the world. But that is our legacy. There have been powerful people in the government, but that is different from strong leadership. At my age, I have to say that it is better to have a democratic government that can't get the thing right than a dictatorship that asserts itself and whips the country into shape. Our government now is senseless, ridiculous, but even that is better than a dictatorship. You can't force people to behave correctly. You have to teach them to appreciate the choice and consequences of good behavior.

In church they used to tell us, "You've forgotten your veil! Button your top higher! Your skirt is too short!" And so on. But now no one cares. Everyone goes and does whatever they want, and no one says anything. Surely, that is not right. In my day, a woman didn't set foot in church for mass or confession without a veil on her head. Now who wears a veil anymore? Who even remembers *when* we wore them?! In the gospel it says that a woman should not speak in front of a man, and she must not enter the church without a veil. You can't go to church as if you were going to the beach. At least, when you are entering the house of our Lord there has to be a little respect. If you went to see the president of the republic you'd choose your clothes with care. Why isn't it the same in Christ's house?

[*Carla is a* terziaria francescana, *a Franciscan lay nun.*] We make a promise of charity, humility, and obedience, and vow to live according to the gospel every day of our lives. Both my mother and grandmother were terziarie francescane. If the gospel says, "Do this. Don't do that," that is what we do, no questions asked. Simple as that. To become a lay nun you make a request. Then the group decides if you are a good, practicing Catholic. The one fundamental thing that a francescana must learn never to do is *never ever speak badly of the priests*. Never. Priests must always be respected. If they make a mistake, doesn't matter. They must always be respected. You never badmouth a priest, never subject them to criticism. This, never. That is because the priest is the one who gives you the host during communion, and if for nothing else, that is reason enough. He gives you, symbolically, the body of Christ, and he cannot be criticized. If you don't like that priest, you are free to frequent another church, but our vow is that nothing will ever be said against him. This is the will of Saint Francis.

After a person has been accepted, she undergoes a year of preliminary teaching and observation. Then she is officially accepted as a follower, and studies another year about how to fulfill our creed, and she studies the gospel and the New Testament at a deeper level because that is what Christ brought us, not the Old Testament because that has been surpassed. The Lord our God said, "I haven't come to change things. I have come to, to, uh…" Oh, the word is not coming to me. "I've come to interpret, to finish this rule that began in the past, and I've come to, to, uh, give it life. I am the Messiah." That's what he said.

Then, of course, we have to study the life of Saint Francis to understand him better. Then, when the second year is done, you enter into your last year of trial. You study for a final year in more depth with the theology teacher. She explains the gospel, our creed, and the spirituality of Saint Francis, after which you can enter into perpetual study for the rest of your life. Once you have given your promise to follow the gospel for the rest of your life, you don't ever leave the order. I've been in the order for thirty years. My daughter is not interested, even though I named her Francesca! She isn't made that way and she has sons so…

I see young people today who don't have the drive to go on. When the war ended, we had to reconstruct. It united us. But young people today are demoralized. They don't have the wings to fly anymore. All they see is darkness. This is not just an economic crisis; it is a spiritual crisis. They have no ideal, nothing to believe in. Sure, we were fascists, but we had an ideal that we believed in. When I looked for a job I asked what I was required to do and what the hours were. Today, all young people want to know is, "How much are you going to give me?" There is a joke that goes, "A guy gets a job and the first thing he asks is, 'When do I get my vacation time?' 'Right now,' the boss answers! 'Out!'"

Intermezzo

La *"pasta compra"* – The Pasta Industry

There are few things in the world as Italian as
pasta and pizza. Above all, few things like these
that define the Italian identity...and this from the
beginning of the century, when pasta and pizza
had not yet even become national dishes, and
were far from being appreciated in all regions.
— FRANCO LA CECLA, *LA PASTA E LA PIZZA*

During the Ventennio, patriotic Italian food writers like Ada
Boni sounded the rallying call for Italians to take pride in
their own cuisine. As was true for the fashion industry, women
were admonished for slavishly looking to France for the last word in
culinary finesse.

We have got to cook Italian food everywhere in Italy. . . .
Above all, we should not hesitate to write culinary words in
Italian. . . . Our language has a rich vocabulary capable of
expressing the most complicated list of foods without having
to rely on any other language. . . . But all will resolve itself
when . . . we firmly decide to follow and spread only our own

fine cuisine, whose foods have precise names, consecrated by tradition and use (Boni, 1946).

But even as she wrote those words, the terminology for something as quintessentially Italian as pasta had not yet found its land legs.

In the 1891 keystone work *Science in the Kitchen and the Art of Eating Well*, by Pellegrino Artusi (see Intermezzo – Cookbooks), he uses the word "minestra" to indicate all first course dishes, from broth to risotto, to pasta. The word had not yet resolutely assumed the exclusive meaning of "soup" because the starch based first courses had not fully achieved independent standing. Therefore, the distinction was between liquid soups and dry soups, respectively, those eaten with a spoon and those eaten with a fork. Reasoning has it that, regardless of the final result, the main ingredients of dry soups had been *prepared* in water, although in the finishing ministrations, they were *served* without their liquid. A dish of pasta thus prepared was referred to as *pasta asciutta,* dry pasta, as opposed to *pasta in brodo,* pasta served in broth. Soup, the traditional French first course and definitive "supper" dish, would not begin its descent into obscurity from the standard meal structure until after WWII. As it did, the "asciutta" tag became a superfluous appendage. These days, "manly men" turn their noses up at soup due to its association with nursing the sick and the aged. The T-shirt would read: Real men don't eat soup.

"Pasta," in Italian, simply means paste, any paste, be it dough or otherwise, although its main association is with...pasta. Dried pasta is made with durum wheat, while fresh, or rather, homemade pasta, is made with *grano tenero,* or a mixture of soft and hard wheat, often with the addition of egg to increase the protein content, and therefore, the bite. These are the tagliatelle that were ubiquitous in most Italian homes during the Ventennio, whereas dried pasta, also called *pasta compra* or "bought pasta," was neither the preferred pasta, nor the most utilized. Dried pasta is not simply fresh home-style pasta that has been left to dry. Semolina flour, made from durum wheat, renders a distinctly different product, whose processing requires an industrial context equipped with the proper technology, as well as craftsmen experienced in what were called *le arti bianche,* the white arts. One could make tagliatelle at home, but not spaghetti and macaroni.

There is a dizzying corpus of both scholarly and anecdotal research into the hairsplitting historical mutations of pasta minutiae. But perhaps here, a brief schematic perusal of the broad developments of industrial pasta will suffice to shed light on the standing that the pasta industry had achieved by the Ventennio.

1150 – Al-Idrisi, born in present day Morocco, writes of a workshop in Sicily that "mass produces pasta in the for of strings that is transported everywhere ... even by ship"

1546 – The first pasta makers guild is established in Naples, followed shortly thereafter in Liguria. Not being an area that produces durum wheat, Ligurian pastaficci rely on imports, notably the prized Taganrog wheat from Russia. This wheat, above all others, is considered essential to achieving the highest quality dried pasta, for nutrition, taste, and mouth feel. In Naples, King Ferdinand II devises a mechanized method of mixing durum wheat dough that replaces the human foot method. It allows for the use of boiling water and increases output.

1740 – The first prototype pasta factory is authorized in Venice. It is essentially an iron press operated by a team of men.

Around this time, the great pasta industries that continue to dominate the market today begin to make their mark:

Late 1700s – The municipality of Gragnano, Naples, gives Michele Garofalo exclusive rights as a proto-industrial pasta-maker. Garofalo is reportedly the most successful *pastificio* in the 1920s, with an output of 40 tons daily. The Spanish company Ebro Foods is now the dominant shareholder of Garofalo. To keep prices down on this quality pasta, the company does not advertise on television.

1824 – Agnesi in Oneglia, Liguria, is the oldest surviving brand name pasta factory. The family fits out a fleet of sailing ships to travel to the Sea of Azov with the specific aim of importing the coveted Taganrog wheat, considered the finest in the world for dried pasta. By 1917, their pasta-making process is completely automated. After 1970 the company falls on difficult times. It is bought and sold a few times over, and in 2015 it will close definitively.

1827 – Buitoni opens a small shop in Sansepolcro, Tuscany selling pasta. By 1886, Giovanni Buitoni and Brothers is created. The multinational Nestlé now owns Buitoni.

1846 – Rummo opens a mill in Puglia that also makes durum wheat pasta. In 1935, they transfer to Benevento Campagna as a joint-stock company. In 2010, they win a Friend of the Environment award for having reduced C02 emissions by 30%.

1879 – Voiello opens a factory that sells exclusively in the piazzas of Naples until the technological advancements allow them to broaden their marketing horizons. They are supposedly considered superior in taste and quality, and marketed in the north of Italy. In 1973, in desperate need of modernization, Barilla takes over the company, building them a new plant that opens in 1976, respecting the autonomy and traditional processing of the historic pastificio.

1877 – Barilla opens a small bakery, which grows into industrial pasta production in 1911. Today they are the best selling-multinational pasta company in the world.

1882 – The first hydraulically operated press is built, quickly followed in 1884 by a steam-powered press.

1917 – Perforated bronze die-cut disks are invented, allowing for myriad shapes to be expelled continuously and uniformly. These disks leave the pasta with a slightly rough surface that sauces more readily cling to. 1917 also marks the end of importation from Taganrog due to the October Revolution and other internal strife in Russia. In the grip of starvation, all the grains of the coveted grain are reportedly consumed.

Post WWII – The process of kneading, forming, and drying pasta is completely mechanized by Brabanti, the leaders in pasta-making technology.

The principal cultivators supplying durum wheat to pasta factories were in southern Italy, North Africa and Russia, specifically the city of Taganrog whose port had a history of trade with Italy, as they were once a colony of the Maritime Republic of Pisa. Sicily, Naples, and Liguria were key centers of pasta production, as their climates and natural aeration were particularly suited to the crucial moment of drying the pasta: too quick and it became too brittle for transport or disintegrated in the pot; too slow and it risked acidification or molding. Pasta manufacturing underwent a constant, albeit slow evolution, but by the dawn of the Ventennio, all of the cards were in place for the nation to witness the development of a veritable national food. On the heels of WWI, the main focus in Mussolini's Battle for Wheat was to get a higher yield per hectare given the limited arable land in Italy. Imports of Taganrog wheat had long been discontinued. Strains grown in Sicily that were similar to Taganrog were abandoned in favor of Senatore Cappelli, which produces longer ears with more grains per ear that were larger in size but, alas, lacked the depth of flavor of Taganrog. During the ventennio, dried pasta was stretched with grano tenero, which grew more readily, and start-up industries, looking to exploit increased consumption, ignored the measured exsiccation times and aeration requirements. Dried pasta had reportedly hit bottom in terms of taste and quality during the fascist regime. Today, by law, dried pasta must be 100% durum wheat.

The preference for a store-bought item, as opposed to a similar one that is made from scratch, is revealed in writings from the 1800s, which observed that initially, commercial pasta was not associated with the poor, as is commonly thought, but with the middle classes. Therefore, like white bread, it represented something to aspire to. "Anyone who has entered into the shanties of the poor or the humble dwellings of craftsman to observe consumption habits will clearly see that the macaroni that appears six days a week on the middle class table is for the craftsman, but a desire that is fulfilled only on Sundays" (De Renzi, 1863). Buying pasta was a sign of purchasing power, the ability to afford ease and leisure. Traveling salesmen, whose wares included dried pasta, frequented to rural areas where access to shops was limited. There they found a willing clientele in housewives strapped with the endless work of both house and field. For those who had ready cash, dried pasta made putting a decent meal on the table fast and convenient, though crafty vendors notoriously took advantage of unschooled housewives when weighing and pricing the goods.

Not only was dried pasta time saving, but it was also admissible for the religious observance days forbidding the consumption of meat. Home economics expert Lidia Morelli, writing in 1942, (mis)informed her readers that "*maccheroni napoletani*" (dried pasta) was mostly protein, and when prepared with butter and a few gratings of cheese, it represented a nutritionally complete food. She advised that it was even better than the so-called egg noodles sold in shops, whose yellow color was often just food coloring and not actual egg. Taganrog, boasting the highest gluten content of all durum wheat, was at best 17% protein.

Dried pasta was considered hygienic and genuine in an era tainted by unscrupulous food adulteration, and unlike the unprocessed grain from which it was made, dried pasta was not vulnerable to parasites, allowing for long-term storage. Given the lack of refrigeration, these factors were of no small importance, not only to those who lived hand to mouth and were dependent on store bought food, but also to those who could afford to hoard food, given the precariousness of the food supply throughout the Ventennio fascista. Dried pasta was generally sold in bulk, but enterprising pasta makers began packaging their product in an attempt to garner brand name loyalty by capitalizing on prevalent fears of contamination, evident in this catchy ad from 1933:

Pasta PURITAS
Must be appreciated for three important characteristics:
CLEANLINESS – QUALITY – FAIR PRICE
(Not to be confused with any other commercial brand)
Pastificio Moderno Puritas – Pescara

Dried pasta was initially distinguished (oh-so broadly speaking) by the term *maccheroni* – macaroni, for the sake of simplicity. By the time of the 1946 edition of Ada Boni's *Talisman of Happiness* (see

Intermezzo – Cookbooks), it is evident that the dust around culinary terminology for pasta had yet to settle. The section for first courses is not left simply "Minestre," as it is in Artusi's *La Scienza*, but is elaborated into Minestre – Minestroni – Maccheroni – Risotti etc. (though notably, not Pasta); thus, a distinction is made at this point between dishes that are strictly soup and those that are non-liquid starch dishes. However, the word "macaroni" itself appears to be a promiscuous catchall at this juncture. The main ingredient in recipes called "Macaroni with..." run the gamut from spaghetti to vermicelli to fresh tagliatelle with egg to short durum wheat pasta, whose precise shape is never specified, apparently being left to the home cook's discretion. This seemingly haphazard array of usages, however, mirrored the random application of the word throughout Italy, which varied from city to city. For example, the Brescian dialect word *maccarù* means any sort of short dried pasta, while maccheroni, when they speak Italian, only indicates the tubular shape *tortiglioni*. In Tuscany, maccheroni, was used interchangeably with tagliatelle, the fresh homemade pasta. Although the Neapolitans came to be referred to by the derogatory term *mangiamaccheroni* because dried pasta was their main staple, their dialect word *maccaron'* was only used for ziti, or as a pejorative for stupid, as in: *Si' nu maccaron'!* They referred to the other shapes specifically by name, all of them falling under the heading – pasta. And yet, for much of Italy, dried pasta would remain maccheroni napoletani until well into the 1950s.

In spite of gastronomic disputes at home and discrepancies in Ada Boni's own book (in which she both honors and denies pasta's preeminence), she is quick to take foreigners to task:

> Foreigners have no idea about real Italian cuisine and think that our gastronomic patrimony is limited to three or four specialties, all headed up by macaroni. The very same macaroni that they have encountered so erroneously in the grand hotels beyond the Alps, that we Italians would not even want to taste. Besides being served as a side dish to meat and not as a first course, they are prepared in a way that is so completely different from our way as to be unrecognizable. Not to mention the "discovery"

of some American companies that make spaghetti with tomato sauce in a can – food that you wouldn't wish even on your worst enemy! [*She can only be referring to Ettore Boiardi – better known as Chef Boyardee – who began his canned spaghetti business in 1938*]... Hotels abroad...present our pasta overcooked...and dressed in a muddle of different sauces...none of which are Italian . . . and it gets called one of two different things, either *macaroni à la na-politaine* or *nuilles fraiches à l'italiaenne*. (brackets mine).

Why doesn't Boni rail on about Buitoni's innovative contribution to the 1930 Milan Expo, where they presented their patented novelty, called the Spaghetti with Sauce Cooking Box? One box served 3-4 people and contained spaghetti, butter, sauce, cheese and salt. As the advertisement beckons, "You just place the entire box in boiling water for 12 minutes, and ... even the inexperienced cook can easily make Italian style pasta with perfect results. It is particularly useful for excursions, soccer games, and quick meals at home." Cooking Box? There was no point in her bringing it up. It did not catch on and was dropped from the market in the same year, never to be proposed again. Ettore Boiardi, on the other hand, died a rich man at the age of 87 in Parma... Ohio.

But what of Taganrog, the wonder grain that made the world's finest pasta? In 1970, Vincenzo Agnesi wrote of the incomparable taste of golden Taganrog pasta, a taste that was lost during the fascist reign. His article caught the attention of the Latini family, who decided to resuscitate the grain for commercial production. The seeds had been kept from extinction in an Italian germplasm conservation institute, where every year a one meter plot was planted to refresh the seeds. The Latini's took the few seeds, and in 2000, began their cultivation project. Each year there were more seed grains, and each year they were all planted until in 2006, when they had the first harvest bountiful enough to allow them to utilize some of the grain to make the prized pasta. Last year, they produced 7,000 packages of Taganrog spaghetti. It is now available for purchase online in limited quantities under the brand name Pasta ALA.

NORTHERN HEIGHTS

Celestina

Born 1922 – Capovalle

I met with Celestina in her modest home in the small pristine village of Moerna, tucked away in the mountains of northern Lombardy near the Swiss border. At 93, she looks after her own home and extensive vegetable garden, in addition to caring for her retired son. After a lifetime of arduous work living in the mountains, she had developed thick steely arms like the women in Michelangelo paintings, but also frightfully knobby fingers that she says came from years of laboring outdoors in the cold. Celestina was amazingly lucid and talked up a blue streak about any topic I put forth. For our supper, we made her local version of one of the many water and bread based soups common to her generation. For now Moerna is untouched by tourism, although rampant depopulation has left the few remaining inhabitants little choice but to consider publicizing their village as a museum piece, just to keep it going.

I was born in 1922 and raised in Capovalle, a town of about 1,000 people. Wasn't until '48 I got married and moved here to Moerna. My father was a sort of a forest ranger. It was a government job, where he did piecemeal tasks in the woods, like checking for animals grazing there, folks hunting out of season, or hunting animals they wasn't supposed to, poachers and what have you, you know, all those things having to do with the laws about the woods. With them planting all that grain everywhere in those days, wasn't 't all easy to find a place to pasture the animals. Meat was hard to come by, so people being people, and there being mouths to feed at home, well, they did what they could to get around the law, so folks like my father was paid to keep them from doing it.

During the Battle for Wheat, the highest wheat production came from northern regions, coinciding with a significant loss of pasturelands and consequently a significant reduction in sheep and goats. Although raising goats was legal, a prohibitive tax was levied per head. The same tax was later extended to other pasturing animals, even if they grazed on the proprietor's land. Taking animals to graze in the woods was also forbidden, in order to encourage the improvement of woodlands.

My family raised goats and sheep too, but goats are easier to look after than sheep and cows, and they're made better for mountain life. They have their young in the cold season. That way they don't get in the way of summer work.

The lactating period for goats is also longer than for cows; per kilo, they produce twice as much milk as their bovine counterparts. The loss of pastureland for goat herding had a major impact on this important source of milk and protein.

Up round these here parts, there wasn't any of those big landowning padroni. Most folks was like us; we owned and worked our own land for most of the food we ate, and we hired out now and then in order to get cash. My mother was a housewife, a farmwife really, but she hired out as seasonal day labor, a bracciante, and sometimes she picked up some hours here and there as a maid when she could. For the most part, the men had to do scrappy work where they could find it, either as braccianti in other towns, or doing odd jobs for cash. That pretty much left us women home to take care of the farming on our own. Every year we planted wheat, field corn, barley, potatoes, beans, and a few other vegetables. On days when the men couldn't get outside work, they would help on the farm too, but the women bore the brunt of most of it. Problem came when you had your babies. You had to go back home regular for feedings until you could get them weaned.

Brubrusao - Formula for weaning babies
Brown a handful of flour in a pan and add milk and salt or sugar. It should be thin enough to put into a baby's bottle. As a food for children, make it thick enough to be eaten with a spoon. For sick people add a touch of butter.

People was very poor and families was large. Doesn't seem to make much sense, does it? Maybe because our Lord said we had to do that. "Go forth and multiply," he said, and well, there you have it. Lots of folks didn't even have basic necessities, and in those days, basic was more basic than anything people today can even start to imagine. I know I am saying the word basic to you, but I know you can't possibly know what I mean.

Every now and then, Mussolini sent in a shipment of wheat because here in the mountains we didn't produce near enough to go round. A single person can only work so much land in a day, or in a season, before they drop, and the mountains didn't give you a whole lot of good farmland. We worked every last possible square of dirt we could. What you see out here, these grassy meadows, it wasn't like that before. It was all planted, and most it with wheat for the Duce.

Then, when they started in with that rationing business, and we could only buy small amounts of food, well, I tell you, it was a bad situation got worse. And that rationed bread! That was something awful! It was greenish because they tried to stretch it with some kinda vegetable filler. When we complained about the green bread, it went all whitish, and rumor was that they started putting bone meal in the bread made from the bones of dead people, folks who wasn't from round these parts. That made the bread whiter, sure enough, but when we didn't have enough of our own wheat, wasn't no choice but to eat that miserable stuff. We tried to make our own bread last as long as we could, but when it dwindled down to nothing, it was the government bread for the lot of us.

Some folks who managed to hook up with a factory job in town could shell out for food on the black market. Trouble was, factory work didn't leave them time to work the land, so they wasn't growing any of their own food, so there was a kind of slavery in that too. Six of one, half dozen of the other. Sometimes it was worse if you had to buy your food because, even with the ration card, sometimes there just wasn't any food to be had. I mean, let's say you could buy 100 grams of rice for each person in your family; even with ready cash and a card to show what you had coming to you, if there wasn't any rice there in the shop, you didn't eat. None of us went hungry, though. You could always rustle up something to put in your stomach, so long as you didn't get too choosey about it. As they say, *O di paglia o di fieno hai lo stomaco pieno* "Whether with straw or wheat, your stomach will be full". Wasn't too long before my day that folks dropped off from having nothing to eat.

There was seven of us in my family, four children, my parents, and my grandfather. He was like a woman, did women's work, tending the house while my parents was out. He lived to be 91.

We had our own oven in the house, so breakfast was bread, and since we kept goats, there was goat's milk and surrogate coffee with that hunk of bread. What we called coffee was a drink made from vetch beans, sort of like lentils. We toasted them up, ground them and boiled them in the pot to make a black drink. We had another dark drink made from acorns, which was a good tonic. I don't remember exactly what it was supposed to be good for, but anyway, let's just say it did more good than harm. It cleaned your liver or something like that. We would add a drop of wine in it too sometimes if there was any to be had. This not being wine country, that was considered something special.

Then it was off to school. In my school, there was more than a hundred children come from all the little towns around, but there was just two teachers for the lot of us, one for the first and second grade, and the other for the third and fourth. The Duce didn't give us any fifth grade like we were supposed to have. It was a two-room schoolhouse. Boys and girls all sat together on long pew-like benches. The teacher carried a stick to whack the kids who misbehaved. We had to buy our own books, but sometimes patrons would donate pencils or paper.

When we walked into the classroom, we gave the Roman salute to the portrait of the Duce first thing. He was always there in the teaching. We learned songs and memorized poems about the Duce and the King, but I can't remember any of them anymore. Ha! Not after 80 years. We were taught all about the life of the Duce and the history of the party. They told us again and again that Italy was going to be an important empire just like it was in Roman times, and so we all had to work hard, make sacrifices and honor the Duce and the King. Then one day, there would be plenty to eat and warm houses for everybody.

We did our exercises on Fascist Saturday because you had to do everything they commanded you to do in those days. We girls was the piccole italiane. It didn't cross our minds to not follow orders and anyway, we loved the uniform, the little black skirt with pleats and the pretty white blouse. When we got older, about 14, we became giovane italiane and then when we got married, giovane fasciste. We marched every week, "one, two, one two", but we had a good time because it was the only fun we ever really had. Everything else was work. The boys' groups learned to use rifles, and as we got closer to the war, they were out every day shooting at targets.

I say it was fun, but I also have to say that then, we didn't have any choice. We had to participate and become members of the party. Some people were against it at first, and they didn't take part, but it caught up with them, you bet it did. Later on, many of them was shot, you know? They was made examples of. And we all learned real fast that there was no choice, so you didn't ask, you didn't wonder about it, and you didn't complain. You just marched when they said march. Order, they wanted to maintain order. People even wrote fascist slogans on their homes, "Obey in Silence" and things like that. Or here in Moerna you can still see the writing over somebody's door that says, "We dream of a Roman Italy." The anti-fascists had to keep tight-lipped about their views. Every village had somebody who was one of *theirs*, an appointed watchdog for the party, someone who was sent to keep an eye on things. Spies was everywhere, 'specially after the Duce got together with Germany.

I did the four years of elementary school, and then stayed on for another two years. I always did good at school. We was allowed to stay at school until we was fourteen if we wanted to, but that meant repeating the fourth grade every year because they didn't give us a fifth grade teacher like in other places. We did six hours of school a day. Sometimes we went home for lunch, and sometimes they fixed a lunch for us, either a plate of pasta or soup, never polenta, because it's difficult to make polenta in big amounts. They melted lard in milk and water and added the pasta, not fresh pasta but hard pasta, like broken spaghetti or tortiglioni. Whatever we had at school was made with lard as the base because everyone had a pig and it was the cheapest fat there was.

We didn't never use olive oil. You could buy butter, but we didn't unless somebody in the house was sick. It is lighter and easier to digest than lard, and has healthier qualities. Real butter was for the signori, and not many of us regular kind of folks could afford it. Even people who had a cow didn't hardly ever use their own butter because they could sell it and get a little cash. You have to understand that what you could sell, you didn't eat at home. I know that is hard to understand when people were hungry, but that was your cash, your money, and you don't go eatin' your money.

On the days when we came home for lunch from school, it was almost always polenta. Polenta with cheese, polenta with eggs, in the summer, we had it with vegetables like green beans. People who had a pig had salami too, but there was always lots and lots of polenta with goat's milk. In my house, like was usual with lots of folks, we'd put the pot of polenta on the floor and we'd all eat from the pot. It tasted better that way, and you got to pull the crusty bits off of the pot; that was the best part! We usually ate it by hand; one hand held the polenta and the other held a piece of cheese. I'm not saying we didn't have plates, though. Grandpa made us a whole set of wooden plates and spoons; that way we didn't have to buy them. Lots of times we had soup for dinner instead of polenta, with potatoes and beans or squash, if you had some on hand. Just boil it all up and add a dollop of lard. If any was leftover, we'd have it for breakfast too. Another soup we had was Panada that I am making you tonight.

***Panada*: Bread soup** – serves 5
6 tbsp lard or butter
6 slices 3 day old (or older) Italian bread broken into chunks
2 eggs
grated hard cheese
salt and pepper

Bring 2 liters of water to boil with the lard or butter. Add bread chunks and simmer until softened. Beat the eggs and off heat stir them into the pot of hot soup. Add salt and pepper to taste and top with a grated hard cheese.

Sometimes when it was really cold, we would all pick up and go eat in the barn with the livestock where it was warmer. It was right cold in the mountains, and we got chilblains on our feet because our socks weren't heavy enough. We only had a few pair because those were store-bought. Our bedrooms wasn't heated, but we was used to that. If you got sores from the cold, that's just the way it was. Grandpa made all of our wooden-soled shoes, but your feet sure took a beating from them! For Sunday best we had a good pair of shoes, bought special from a real shoemaker. When times got better we had house-slippers made of felt. Ah. The floors in our houses were either stone or brick so the slippers were easier on your bones, and you didn't go clickety-clack everywhere.

I had three everyday dresses that I would change once a week and a Sunday dress that I took off right after Mass, so's not to muss it. My mother had a pedal sewing machine and she would get leftover pieces of fabric from the tailor in town and piece things together for us. She was really good at it. If not for that, we really woulda looked like a gang of ragamuffins! People didn't pass clothes on to anybody else like hand-me-downs because you wore what you had it until it wasn't worth anything anymore to anybody.

As for our women's business, we would cut up swathes of cloth from old clothes or sheets to use for menstrual rags. Were plenty of folks didn't even have underwear, so sometimes women just let it flow. It was a real problem! I'm telling you! Another thing we had was a shirt with long tails that you rolled up between your legs and then you washed it out. Later, we made pads out of cloth that hooked onto a belt. We'd have nine or ten of them that we could change. But before that, it was not so easy. Everybody ruined their clothes, but then we wasn't running around in see-through clothes like women do today! Sheets and mattresses all ruined, too. The mattress didn't matter much because ours were just cornhusks. As times got better, we had feather beds, and then proper wool mattresses. Now they make bedding with everything under the sun, latex, coconut fiber, and what have you. They tilt up this way and that. To hear the commercials, you'd wonder how anybody got any sleep before all these modern mattresses came into being! It's gone from one extreme to the next. But I tell you, you will never be able to conceive of the poverty and hardship that we knew back then.

We cooked everything in the cauldron over the fire in the hearth. Some lucky people had a wood-burning stove, but they was rare. Some people had electricity too, but only for lights. There wasn't anything else to plug in!

Once a week, we washed everything outside, which is why my hands are knotty like this. The cold river water destroyed my hands. In those days we had to make our own soaps and detergents. We would take a dead dog or cat and pulverize it good with a hatchet, put it into a pot with some lye, and everything just melted together nice. Then we added alum and talcum powder. You boiled all of that together, poured it into a tray, let it sit for a day until it hardened, and then you had soap! Really great for laundry. You could use fatback too, but that was food.

But then so were cats, if all be told. They was just like rabbit. Really tasty, in fact. If you saw someone who had a big fat cat, it was because they were going to eat it, not because they was animal lovers. To fix him up right for cooking, you skinned him and put him in the snow overnight to temper down that wild taste. Then you cut him up in chunks, just like you would with a rabbit. You can hardly tell the difference with the skin off. Skewer the pieces on long rods with chunks of potatoes 'tween each one. Throw on some sage and salt, and prop your skewer on the stand in front of the fire. Keep turning it slowly while it cooks over the fire, and baste with melted lard. *Buonissimo!* There is lots of talk about people *havin'* to eating cats during the war, but were plenty of folks ate them 'cause they liked them, and had no scruples about it. I only ate cat when it was an animal that I knew and saw was in decent enough health. You couldn't just go round eating any old cat.

> *From the infamous recipe for roast cat by Ruperto di Nola, chef to Italian nobility in the early 1500s, to Sweeny Todd's Mrs. Lovett "popping pussies into pies," cats have, more often than we like to imagine, ended up on the dinner table, particularly in times of hardship, famine, and war. In Italy, the inhabitants of the northern city of Vicenza cannot live down their past, legendary or not as it may be, as cat-eaters and are still called* mangiagatti. *However, pointing the finger at the Vicentini would be unfair, as the practice was known to exist throughout Italy during the war. In 1943, the Minister of the Interior put an official stop to it by passing an ordinance that prohibited killing cats for food, needed, as they were, to take care of the overpopulation of mice.*

Some people ate dogs too, but I couldn't stomach that. Even so, during the war, meat was meat. Badger, fox, dog. You didn't go round getting too fussy about your victuals. Those were critters we couldn't sell, and you ate what you couldn't sell. Our goats and sheep were cash animals, so we didn't eat them, and it wasn't legal to kill the deer and antelope in the woods. Some people killed them in secret, you know; that couldn't be stopped, but you couldn't let anyone know. We loved woodland birds too. I mean we loved to eat them, but now it's illegal to trap them. There's a famous local specialty here called *lo spiedo,* made with small whole birds that's made the same way as the cat skewer, but now when we make it, you have to use chicken thighs, if you get my meaning.

Around these parts, you had to buy wine if you wanted it because no one around here had vineyards. We'd buy it at Easter and Christmas. That was when wine was real grape wine. Today they put in chemicals and methanol - grapes often don't have much to do with it. You have to ask yourself, how can they possibly produce all of the wine people drink today with *just grapes*?! I mean, there just aren't enough grapes to make all that wine! Sure, there is plenty of wine, but there are more wine drinkers than there is wine, so that's why the law allows them to add all that dangerous crap to it. A few years ago some people died because there was too much methanol in the wine. Sure, sure, it tastes good, but then it kills you. They messed around with the beer too.

Although not normally associated with Italy, Italian beer has had a long and prosperous history. It reached the pinnacle of its popularity in the early 1920s, and had become affordable for the lower classes, only to fall prey to fascist programs. Barley fields once dedicated to the burgeoning industry turned to wheat production for bread and pasta, and the regime imposed the use of 15% rice in the brewing. A hefty tax encouraged by wine lobbyists was the final blow that brought consumption down to a fifth of what it had been when the fascists came to power. Advertisers fought back, plugging it as a tonic for young and old alike with the appealing slogan: Beer drinkers live to be 100!

My mother kept a goose, a turkey and chickens for special occasions. At Christmas time, we slaughtered a chicken to make broth for ravioli, and then, glory be, there was a piece of meat for all of us! My mother always made the Christmas cake panettone because there's no telling what was inside those store-bought ones. Always better to make what you can yourself. At Easter we had goat. On August 10-11, we made a special sweet bread, like a brioche bread, for the day of the Madonna del Rio Secco. I still make that every year, and it's a recipe that dates back to way before my time. We eat the bread and then go pray at the sanctuary. They still celebrate it today.

Blood pudding, *sanguinaccio,* was another important community food. You take a milk pail and collect the blood of a pig as it's being slaughtered. Heat it on the stove, but it has to be stirred constantly otherwise it congeals. Then add breadcrumbs, grated Parmesan, some cinnamon, nutmeg, cloves, pepper, and some cubes of pork fat. You mix it up good and pour it into a form. Then you put it in the oven and bake, stirring every now and then. Our local blood pudding comes out with the consistency of a risotto. Ours is better than the ones done in other towns because we do a second cooking in the oven, and that way it cooks through more. Here in Moerna, they make it like a solid cake that you can slice. That is their tradition. We eat ours reheated with polenta. The tradition was to share it with others because there was lots and lots of blood, and blood products don't keep so good.

I learned to cook from my grandfather. He knew how to cook just as good as a woman. When I was fifteen, I went to work as a live-in domestic servant and I learned to cook as part of my duties. By the time I got married, I'd worked as a domestic servant in seven different households. I didn't work for really rich people who had a whole staff of servants, just folks who could afford to pay for an extra hand around the house. More or less, they the same things we did, only they could afford to dress them up a little more. Forty or fifty years ago, all the different foods that we have now just weren't around, but they could buy extras on the black market, nothing special mind you, but things that you couldn't come by any other way, and I'll tell you, they weren't cheap! Folks like them could afford beef and, of course, that was a first for me. I have to say, though, I never once made a chicken at one of their houses. One thing I learned while I was in service was to make ravioli with pumpkin, an important tradition for the well-heeled families. The families I worked for were kindly, and even allowed me to sit at the table and eat with them.

Fascism paid lip service to the importance of breaking down class barriers. For a brief time, La Cucina Italiana *magazine had a running series, wherein ladies of the house, signore, could send in the photo of a trusted servant, which would be published with a brief caption lauding the loyalty, obedience, and service of the woman featured. Management of domestic help was a frequent and pressing topic of articles in women's magazines for the emergent middle classes unaccustomed to dealing with such matters.*

After those years working as a servant, I went back to my village, where I met my future husband. He travelled every Sunday to my town. I had got a job working as a waitress in an osteria, and he would come in for a drink. They served up a bit of food too, the fast food of yesteryear. Stew, a bowl of soup, a dish of tripe. Nothing fancy. We didn't even have tomatoes here until after 1948. Once they was here, we didn't all take to them right away. Now they's everywhere, and no one thinks about it. We did have tomato paste before, though. You'd go to the shop and they'd spoon it out for you onto a piece of waxed paper. After the war, shops started carrying all kinds of new foods, and it has never stopped since.

Weddings was once home affairs, celebrated with a fine meal. A typical wedding feast was: first course, salami and pickled vegetables, made at home, then a soup of chicken innards, called "dirty soup". Take chicken intestine, liver, heart, kidneys, and all the inner parts and chop them up fine. Boil all that together with the head (you gotta take off the beak and tongue of course). Make a robust broth, strain the bits, and set them aside to eat on some other occasion. Add small soup pasta to the broth and boil. The next course was boiled meats, beef and chicken, followed by some roasted meat and salad, a cheese course, cake, and then fruit.

The order in which food is eaten has been the subject of centuries of philosophical and gastronomic pondering. The position of salad, for instance, was once at the beginning of the meal because of the vinegar or lemon dressing, which stimulated the appetite, but was later relegated to its present position as an accompaniment to the main meat dish, or even after it, due to its relative insignificance. The cheese course is a late addition, as cheese was once considered an ingredient rather than something to be placed on the table in pieces. Attention to the order in which foods were eaten was dictated both by perceptions of what was healthy and by what was pleasurable. The scheme had fossilized by the time the idea of vitamins and nutrients came into the public eye. In a later addition, a nod to middle class home economics logically positioned the less expensive starch course before the meat. The strict order has only begun to blur recently with the furious onslaught of television cooking programs and the unorthodox concoctions they propose.

Today weddings are ridiculous. They bring you a bean in a shell; then after half an hour they come out with a snail and a grape. Then, another half an hour later, you get a thin slice of tomato in some unrecognizable sauce. You sit like that for hours eating nothing. At the end they give you a big ol' piece of cake. I complain, sure, but the only thing I really miss about the past is flavor. We didn't have much, and I sure wouldn't go back, but everything tasted better.

I've traveled a good bit for a woman, given when and where I was born. I've been to Geneva, France, and Rome. The food in other countries always seemed better than our food, but then after a while, things got better here too. In the mountain towns, there was no running water in the house, no toilet, no paved roads. It took a long, long time after the war for us to catch up with other countries. We started eating better too, and had hearty, home cooked meals. Everything was better for a while, but now things seem to be spinning out of control. I don't know what is happening to food. I don't go to the supermarket anymore. One, I am old and don't eat much, and two, I don't like seeing all those things I don't recognize. I don't mind pizza so much. I think the first time I had pizza was, oh, I don't know, maybe in the 80's. Before that? Hmm, no, before, there wasn't any pizza in Italy. Well, I mean, at least not in northern Italy. We never had a car because my husband worked in France, and after we was married, I hardly ever saw him. My son was the first to have a car, so that was when we went out and I had my first pizza.

But I tell you, in spite of working like a mule every day at my age, cleaning, cooking, and keeping my vegetable garden for my retired son and myself, I still manage to have my daughters and grandchildren come twice a week for dinner, and they find a fine a meal on the table. I miss eating with gusto. Could just be that I'm old, and maybe my taster doesn't work like it should. Once I've had a small plate of something, that's it for me. I don't cook too much during the week because I don't eat very much anymore, and my son, well, he has taken to drink, so he doesn't eat. He is fat in that way from alcohol, not from the food at my table. Same with my older son. He lived in Geneva, suffered from depression and died of alcoholism. Neither one ever got married. Men aren't good without women, but if you don't go out looking for a woman, nobody's going to take care of you. You're not going to find the right one. Sure, this one here lived in a small town, but there used to be lots of young women in Moerna, not to mention all the little villages right around here. And that other one? My other son lived in a big city. You want to tell me there wasn't no women in Geneva? There was plenty of women to choose from, but the both of them gave themselves to drink.

I don't like going to the supermarket. I get confused. I have to have a list because I'm overwhelmed by everything. It is too big and I can't find anything. I don't even know what some of the things are. I couldn't never go alone. I'd be lost! How can you choose things from the supermarket when they're all full of preservatives, coloring, and flavorings? Food just doesn't taste the same anymore. It's all flattened out, lifeless, as far as I'm concerned. There's a lot of artificial foods that aren't good and aren't good for you. At my house we mostly eat vegetables with roasts, stews, and sometimes with Simmenthal.

> *Simmenthal is a beef product that originated in Italy in the 1880s. Gino Alfonso Sada began the commercial canning of boiled beef scraps suspended in a beefy-tasting gelatin in 1923. It was widely advertised in women's cookery magazines as early as the 1930s, and became a trusted name brand. Much like the bouillon cube, it was a way to incorporate beef flavor, and in this case even a bit of actual beef, into family meals without the expense of fresh beef from the butcher.*

I don't make polenta very often. With my arthritis, it is too hard because it has to be stirred constantly. Italy is the land of cooks, though! I see on TV those cooks making all those complicated dishes. They don't make any of the things we made, so I can't say if they's any good, and I can't make them myself because they's too difficult, and I don't even recognize the ingredients half the time. Sometimes there's programs about our food from long ago, but even those seem to be done in a different way. I watch the *Prova del cuoco* at noontime. Sometimes they make traditional foods. I like watching cooking shows, and if I was young, I'd try to cook some of the things they make. If I could go back in time, I'd be a cook. Some time back, I started buying recipe books and clipping recipes from the newspapers because I wanted to learn to cook better, to use some of the new foods that's in the shops, but today there is just too much out there and I wouldn't know how to begin.

Intermezzo

Ricette e ricettari – Recipes and Cookbooks

Cookbooks vs. the oral transmission of recipes and urban panache vs. rural practices are a hotplate of controversy. The image of the country farmwife, preparing flavorsome simple meals with love and time-honored expertise is one of most cherished of our modern terroir narratives. In a speech in 2006, Slow Food's Carlo Petrini incites this well-loved imagery: "Italy's gastronomic memory used to have a name: hunger. But even so, that memory was shaped by the wisdom of countless women; within a subsistence economy, these women created food masterpieces that were very simple, but good." Compare this, for argument's sake, to an inquest from the 1880s, reporting on the kitchens of agrarian families who were paid in wages and not in kind: "The results are many, but in general, rather dangerous. . . . The family victuals are consumed much more irregularly, and, in general, prepared very badly. . . . Women . . . are busy all day, and in the kitchen they apply themselves quickly and badly. Thrifty, wise, prudent housewives who know how to best prepare poor food are, unfortunately, very rare" (*Inchiesta agraria* vol. VI, 1881).

Culinary scholar Piero Camporesi maintains that foodways passed on through oral tradition by Italy's poor were based on a limited variety of those foods that were less marketable. The commonality or obviousness of their ministrations precluded the impulse to commit them to writing. Out of sheer necessity, they wouldn't be forgotten.

Food served a precise function, that of feeding the body, for which "recipes," as such, tended towards practical conservatism. Camporesi asserts that once these foodways are lost, as is arguably their ultimate destiny, they cannot be salvaged. In their stead, the nostalgia industry fills the void by reinventing authenticity for mass distribution. From the other side of the tracks, he contends that the written word, the recipe books intended for the urban bourgeois, were a playground for experimentation, exploration, evolution, and revolution. Ironically, however, once these cookbooks become museum pieces, the vibrant innovatory intension of the original fades, and the work morphs into an archival treasure trove, a codex of supposedly time-honored traditions. Antropologist Franco La Cecla argues that conceptually speaking, any cookery book is a mere still life, a disservice to the gastronomic wisdom of a culture. They freeze the innate fluidity of the entire act of cooking, thereby damming the *panta rei*, the eternal flux. La Cecla defends the oral transmission of foodways as the only means capacious and bold enough to bring to bear the direct relationship cooking has to magic and alchemy.

The perspective advanced by food historian Vito Teti proposes that recipes of the oral tradition, or those "stolen with one's eyes," should not be summarily construed as simplistic in comparison to the written recipes of the elite. While his own position is that the foodways of the contadini superseded those of the elite in sophistication, he concedes that individuals who have developed a different gustatory sensitivity, owing to a dissimilar availability of foodstuffs, may be unable to fully appreciate or comprehend the ways and combinations of others. It is the perpetual dilemma of the "emic" vision – originating from the inner circle, vs. the "etic" perspective – observations of those looking into a culture from the outside.

The ephemeral nature of the oral tradition, and the increasingly unbalanced ratio of sorcerers to apprentices, makes the written manual, the cookbook, not only useful, but necessary. A look at the modern age of Italian cookery books must begin with *Science in the Kitchen and the Art of Eating Well* (1891) by the amiable Pellegrino Artusi. This text is considered the first concerted effort to assemble a set of recipes that attempted to both reflect and forge a common gustatory identity that celebrated the newly unified Italy, or at least a unified bourgeois Italy, thereby combatting its reputation as a mere geographic expression. Artusi's collection represents a broad array of dishes originating from many regions, particularly from his place of birth, Romagna, as well as his home, Tuscany. Once his slant had garnered a modicum of success, other authors would follow his lead in showing that Italian cuisine was varied, with a significance all its own that could stand proudly without having to kowtow to French culinary terms or methods.

Artusi was a bon vivant, a gastronomic enthusiast. He had little culinary experience himself, but, as he says, one "needn't have been born with a saucepan on one's head" to make a decent go of it. His intended readership was clearly the middle class housewife, evidenced by the simple fact that he was appealing to literate women, a very small population indeed. His public had to be able to afford leisure items, like cookery books, and have a household budget that allowed for the ingredients in his recipes. But there was also a ceiling to his intended audience: they had to be women who were involved to some degree in preparing home meals. More sophisticated text references were available for professional cooks. The recipes lent themselves to the all-important idea of the *bella figura,* making a good impression. Urbanization was on the rise, and keeping up with the Joneses was just as important for new initiates as it was for established affiliates. Artusi began *Science in the Kitchen* on a whim, but then got caught up in it. It was not an overnight success, but over the years it attracted a sizable following and underwent many printings and revisions.

Publication ceased during WWII until 1961 because, as the publisher explains, the dishes seemed too rich for the pocketbook and frugal mentality of the times. The decision to reprint was based on the idea that, with a little kitchen know-how, the home cook could simply dispense with extraneous ingredients they couldn't afford. The 1961 publication date is significant not only because by then the booming economy allowed families to entertain the idea of entertaining, but also because it coincided with the date that migration within Italy was legalized, although the countryside had been emptying into the city for some time. Enough time had transpired, and enough people had escaped hardship that romanticism about the past could begin.

Bandying the name Artusi about and having *Science in the Kitchen* on the shelf, whether or not it was actually used, became a badge of culture for educated, post-war urbanites. A personal caveat: in my numerous interviews and conversations with women over 85, only two actually owned the cookbook, a couple more had heard tell of it, and none of the rest had any idea of what I was talking about, in spite of the near-sacred authoritative aura it exudes today.

But what accounts for the long backward glance to the days of Artusi when there were many publications in between?

In many ways, the fascist regime had always been of two minds: one yearning to be a contender in the modern world, and the other vehemently clinging to past traditions, particularly those ideals that reinforced a sense of duty and subordination. Cookbooks from the Ventennio embrace both mindsets. With a few exceptions, they tend to be less about cooking than they are about reframing the consumption of food with regard to the new Italian identity, the political climate, class awareness, and modern developments.

The magazine *La Cucina Italiana*, founded in 1929, was conceived as a forward-looking, fascist culinary publication for the middle classes. As stated on the cover, it addressed pressing household concerns on a broad range of domestic topics: home cooking, haute cuisine, entertaining tips, folkloristic cookery, cooking for the sickly, hotel cooking, culinary arts, and recipes. The front-page headline of the March 1930 issue, for example, announces a menu contest for a simple, inexpensive, healthy home cooked meal. Next to that is one of the seemingly inexhaustible favorite topics of the period, social etiquette. How and who to invite to a dinner party, appropriate attire, what to do when the guests arrive, and how to graciously herd them into the dining room. Again, on the front page is an article reminding women that their role as emotional managers of the home begins with a good meal. It is delivered in a reprimanding tone so frequently used by CI columnists of the era: "A man will forgive a woman many things when she knows how to make delicious food, and the woman who knows this should make every effort not to disappoint him, least of all in this. ... And it's not just the rich girls, who have never set foot in the kitchen, and wouldn't even recognize their own cook; middle class and working class girls are just as ignorant about the kitchen" (Bisi, 1930). Even the great Jewish intellectual Margherita Sarfatti's contribution delineates a woman's role according to the fascist model: "The bravura of a woman lies herein: that the housework gets done silently, with a sort of mechanical automatism, like a routine, ... the height of achievement is precisely that of disappearing, of going unnoticed, giving the illusion of nonexistence. We Italian women are usually quite able in this" (1931). As time went on, the magazine's views were increasingly aimed at the upper strata of the middle class and the fascist party line. In 1943, with the fall of fascism, the publication ceased altogether. The last issue features sobering articles as "Cucumbers Cooked Many Ways," "Do it Yourself," and a full page on how to make use of edible discards: peels, pods, cores and skins. In 1952, the magazine was exhumed and completely renovated under Anna Gosetti della Salda.

Ada Boni's asserts her authority on the culinary stage with *Talisman of Happiness* (1925). In spite of her friendship with Escoffier, *Talisman* is a declaration of independence from French cooking. In the first edition, she also lashes out at the Artusian model, regardless of their common conceptual premise of encouraging a national cuisine. Boni's husband wrote the preface to *Talisman* calling Artusi, "The author who managed to sell rags and baubles as rare silks and gold, guru to all the families who don't know how to cook." His preface is substituted in 1934 with Boni's own politically correct (fascist) introduction, which was in turn purged of its fascist allusions in the 1950s to suit the postwar readership. Her cookbook underwent many editions, has been translated into English, and is still in print today.

One of the last ditch attempts to reassert French culinary authority came with Jean Marie Parmentier's *The True Book of Cookery: A complete treatise of high and low cooking compiled from the works of the best Italian and foreign gastronomes* (1932). All of the menu suggestions, in accordance with French dictates, begin with soup, none with rice or pasta. All of the recipe titles and terminology are translated into French. Of the over one hundred first course entries, only five are pasta dishes with generic, non-descript names like *Ravioli all'italiana* or *Maccheroni alla lombarda*. With League of Nations sanctions just around the corner, *The True Book* did not see another printing.

Necessity being the mother of invention, ongoing crises, sanctions, and war sent the upper and middle classes into a publishing flurry of recipe books geared towards fostering solidarity, helping each other grapple with the limited availability and variety of foods, and stoking the fires of patriotism.

Amalia Moretti Foggia Della Rovere, writing under the penname Petronilla, gives her book *Recipes for Difficult Times* (1941) a slice of life framework: ten society ladies gather together every day to sew army uniforms and get to chatting about food. The conversation begins with soup, not in reference to haute cuisine, but as a means of curbing the appetite with cheap water laden foods before digging into the more substantial, more expensive dishes:

Anna:"What are you talking about?"

Giulia: "About soup because soup is the most fundamental dish of our cuisine. All on its own, it fills the stomach and lessens the need for other foods that supply too many calories." Thus, each woman takes her turn to talk up her favorite thrifty soup recipe.

Eugenia: "Like you, I prefer to make risottos with my rice ration, and I don't want to use up a lot of gas boiling vegetables, so I often make SOUP WITH CEREAL FLAKES; you can get oats and barley without the ration card."

The ladies run the gamut of the autarkic shopping list, exploring and lauding the myriad possibilities therein. It is an informative, practical excursion, couched in reassuring, gossipy tones. The recipe names are in capital letters as signposts. Things stray somewhat from the party line on the day they talk about meat. Eugenia starts off with a pork loin braised in milk; if you can't get that, then beef tenderloin will do. Giulia's husband would never allow a pork loin to enter his house, preferring a nice beef braise. Anna's husband, Fosco, is Tuscan, so he has got to have his Florentine steak. Mum's the word about where they are getting all this meat, but everyone makes mention of how little butter their recipe requires.

Collective self-restraint at the table was touted not only as patriotic, but as healthy and morally sound. Mussolini's pronouncement, "Fortunately the Italian people are not yet used to eating too many times a day," is seconded by Lunella de Seta's observation that as Catholics, Italians have been well trained for dietary abstinence. In her preamble to the meat section in *Cooking in Wartime* (1942), De Seta suggests that before readers resort to heroics to get the most out of the puny meat ration, they should, "meditate on the great truth that one can live perfectly well on *just* vegetables, while *just* meat would catapult you towards the cemetery. So what is the big deal about not having much meat?" Unlike some authors of the period, who lose sight of their mission even before they get to the meat section, de Seta holds firm to what is allotted by law, even proposing three recipes made with tinned meat, one of which is the creative canned beef meatloaf: Mash the canned meat, add a handful of bread crumbs, a mashed boiled egg, an egg yolk and whipped egg whites for volume. Mix in two tablespoons of mushrooms fried in butter, pour into a mold and steam.

While it is not possible to do justice to the many distinguished authors and prominent cookbook titles stemming from the perspective of the Ventennio, of note are two Jewish authors, Ines de Benedetti and Fernanda Momigliano. De Benedetti's *Hidden Poetry* (1931) was the first Jewish-Italian cookbook published in Italy. She proposes a joyful return to dietary observances, but one that respects and recognizes regional Jewish-Italian influences. Her compilation exalts the gustatory excellence achievable through the intimate intermingling of various traditions of the Italian diaspora, highlighting the important role women play in maintaining religious customs through food. Fernanda Momigliano, from an upper middle class family of intellectuals, wrote *Living Well in Difficult Times: How Women Face Up to Economic Crisis* (1933). Like Margherita Sarfatti, she extols the power that women have to restore calm and reassurance to a chaotic world through something as simple as a well-set table and a modest, though skillfully prepared meal. In 1936, in response to building tensions and suspicions about the loyalty of the Jewish community, Momigliano wrote *Eating Italian*, which included a small selection of clearly marked Jewish-Italian favorites. The book was a subtle entreaty underscoring the integral role of Italian Jews in Italian culture, evidenced through the indelible mark they had made on the national cuisine. Still, like Sarfatti, Momigliano was forced into hiding with the onslaught of the 1938 Racial Laws.

In 1939, even Artusi's *Science in the Kitchen* fell prey to fascist censorship, and was duly expunged of its laudatory nod to the Jews for their astute recognition of the qualities of fennel and eggplant: "which goes to show that on this question, as on other more important ones, the Jews have always had a better nose than Christians for what is good."

Giuditta

Born 1926 – Persone

My fourth grade teacher's surname was "Collier," but unlike "Miller" or "Baker," I had never paused to consider to what trade Collier might refer. Not until I met Giuditta. The first known use was in the thirteenth century, when it was spelled "colier," derived from the base word col, or rather coal. The Italian suffix "aio" works the same way as the English "er." Thus, a carbonaio *was a person who lived in the woods and made charcoal, as Giuditta's family did until she was well into her adult years. They spent their winters in a small, low ceilinged home tucked into a back corner of the village Persone, where I met with Giuditta for our interview. She was embarrassed to have me hear her unschooled Italian, and so spoke mostly her local dialect, with a distinct tremor in her voice. Towards the end of our interview, she prepared a simple cornmeal cake in her wood-burning oven, a recipe she remembered nostalgically from her past. At a certain point, I noticed she was growing anxious and frequently glancing over at the clock. It was getting to be the rosary hour, and she feared she would miss church if the cake did not bake in time.*

I was born here in town because, me being a winter baby, my folks wasn't not out in the woods when I come into the world. My mother was lucky on that count. All three of her babies come during the winter months, and good thing 'cause weren't no way to call on the midwife in the woods. I couldn't right say what woulda happened if somethin' gone wrong when they was in the woods. It was a good couple day's walk to get back to town.

Before 1950, most everyone was born at home with a midwife. Midwifery had achieved professional status under the fascist regime, and all mid-wives had to be registered. While this helped to remove the stigma of witchcraft previously attached to the occupation, it also subjected them to scrutiny by obstetricians, who systematically sought to diminish their status. Hideous accounts of botched births made for sensational news stories and increased the public's fear of midwifery. The fascists' interest in controlling midwives stemmed, in part, from the fact that they also performed abortions, conflicting with the directive for increasing the population, particularly in rural areas. By conferring professional status on midwives through licensing and allowing them to unionize, they were more visible and accountable for their activities. In this way, the fascists succeeded to a good degree in suppressing their illegal under-takings. In exchange for recognition as skilled practitioners, midwives were expected to proselytize the party line in follow-up visits to young families whose babies they had delivered.

Every single year of my life right up to when I was thirty years old, we lived from March to All Saint's Day (November 1) in a makeshift hovel in the woods. We were colliers. We wintered in town, in the small village of Persone. I am shy 'bout speaking Italian for that very reason, I mean, 'cause I never did school right. I got through the 4th grade but, well, what with trudging off to the woods every March, and not starting back till November, I never done learned Italian proper. Everybody in the village here spoke dialect, still do most of 'em, at least as a second language, but them's mostly the young generation. The really young ones can understand it, but don't speak it. These days you sound like an unschooled hick if you go round speakin' the local talk. No, I can't rightly say that I went to school. Really, was them teachers being kind enough to let me back in the classroom every year because I never did learn too much.

They passed me on every year to the next grade, probably out of feeling sorry for me.

We got our Fascist Saturday uniforms for free from the school. I don't reckon many folks coulda bought 'em straight out, and without the uniform it wouldna been the same show. If they waited for folks like us to buy it, they wasn't likely to have many followers! But we didn't have Fascist Saturday all the time anyway. Didn't matter much to me because come March, me and my folks headed off to the woods.

We packed a cart with our vittles and victuals, and journeyed for a couple days to the spot where we set up a shelter. It was uphill all the way, and so on foot, it was slow going especially with three little ones in tow. Soon as we got there, we built our hut. It was a long rectangle-shape thing made of sticks. There was four walls to protect us from the animals and the elements, but an open doorway. We set up in a different location every year, so we had to build a new shack from scratch every spring. Didn't have no mule to haul our stuff, so it was just the bare essentials to get through to November. You had your two goats for milk to make the morning corn gruel, chickens that give us eggs for the whole of the charcoaling season, and a heap o' dried beans. We brought potatoes too and planted a field of them right off. We didn't have no way of baking, so there was never any bread.

And that was it. We stayed for the next eight months with two other families. They done learned charcoaling as young'uns, just like my papa done.

Charcoaling required precision, knowledge, and immense physical strength for the long hours of heavy labor. Trees were felled, the branches and twigs removed, and the trunks were cut by handsaw into logs, some of which were split. All of the wood was then dragged to a prepared clearing and piled into a pyre 2 to 3 meters high and 6 meters in diameter called a poiàt. *The stack was covered with moss, leaves and mud, which limited oxygen flow, allowing for pyrolysis, the process of removing the water from the wood without actually burning it. A small fire was lit in the center and it was left to burn slowly for eight to ten days. Two pyres were set alight at the same time. In order to maintain a slow steady swelter, the poiàt had to be watched constantly so that either mud or wood chips could be introduced into the open space at the top as needed. Without tireless vigilance, they ran the risk of the wood catching fire and burning into ash, or the fire going out. The end result was blocks of carbon, ready for use in trains, factories and farms, as well as for domestic use. For every quintal (220 lbs.) of charcoal they produced, they earned two lira. It took a little over a day to collect enough wood to produce that much charcoal. With three families working together they usually produced 30 quintals of charcoal every two weeks. Consider that school enrolment cost five lira per child, and a loaf of subsidized bread two lira a kilo.*

Every twelve days or so, the padrone would make the trip up with his wagon to collect the charcoal. The bags of charcoal was weighed out and accounts was kept, but most of the balance was paid at the end of the season. Weren't nothin' to spend it on up there anyways.

The men did most of the heavy lifting, but I think the women folk had the biggest burden to bear. My mamma did her share of collecting, cutting, and piling the wood, but she was the one took care of the family, raising the children, cooking, and cleaning. Some mothers had wee ones that needed lookin' after all the time. It was the women who had to see that the little 'uns was keeping up their religious duties of prayin' and sayin' the rosary. My mamma kept after us 'bout it just like the priest told her to do, and she made sure we knew our bible stories what was supposed to teach us the straight and narrow road of the Lord. In the winter, when we was home, she had us in church every evening for mass so's we'd get enough religion stored up to make up for when we was away.

The woods wasn't no playground for us kids neither. There was work to do for everybody. Seeing as how we had polenta for every meal, we had to forage for food to eat with it. Us kids went looking for wild greens, snails, and mushrooms. Depended on the time of year. We had special traps with red-colored bait for woodland birds that they'd get their spindly legs caught up in. We set up our camp an hour or so away from a river 'cause every so often we had to haul water up. So, you bet that there was plenty to do for everybody!

When it wasn't too cold we washed up in the river. After the padrone headed back with his load of charcoal, we was pretty much blackened and dirty. While we was working, weren't no sense in washin' up. It was a dirty, dirty job. Between loads, mamma would take us to the river and we'd have us a good ol' scrub down, our clothes too and our *pezzi,* [*menstrual rags*]. We each had eight or so each and we made do with that. Wasn't perfect, but we managed not to get too much blood on our clothes. We had to wear heavy wool clothes, even in summer 'cause of the kind of work it was. Phew, and sometimes it got darn hot! We only had one change of clothes, but heck, if you're not going to church, and weren't nobody coming to call, what did it matter?

We was a poor family. Poor. We was the down-and-out kinda poor folks. I can't right put into words the way we lived, so you can never imagine how it was. Not only was we poor, we didn't have no contact with nobody but ourselves for months and months, year after year. Weren't no news of family and friends until November when we returned.

It was up at dawn and then working straight through the morning to lunchtime. Then back to the hut for more polenta and goat's milk. No point in hiding it. That is what we had for every meal. Our polenta was good quality polenta and we ground it ourselves. We had it with beans or potatoes or what we found. Day in, day out. But, we was never sick.

Many, however, did suffer the debilitating effects associated with a monophagous diet of cornmeal. Lacking the know-how of the Native Americans, Europeans who adopted corn as a base staple did not pretreat it in an alkaline solution, which rendered the nutrients more bio-available. When eaten with beans, treated cornmeal provided a more complete protein spectrum. This process, called nixtamalization, also resulted in a flour that could be worked into dough, which was not possible with unprocessed cornmeal.

You people live in another way. You live different from how we lived and you wouldna been able to eat like that without getting sick, so it ain't that I'm sayin' that's the *right* way to eat. In the winter months when we come back to town and met up with other folks, we got all kinds of sickness, but we was never sick in the woods.

When we was back in town, my mamma worked making yarn, and my papa did nothing. Men rested, or drank. Women worked. Men met in the osterias for a drink, and the women met in the barn. There was a single electric light bulb, and they would sew and knit and gossip the time away. Every November at the end of the charcoal season, once we settled up with the padrone, we could pay off the debt we piled up over the winter. But by March, we was up to our necks in debt again. Every year, same thing. It's a wonder shopkeepers kept giving us credit. Even when we was back here in the village we ate more or less the same as in the woods. It was the cheapest food there was. Sometimes we would get some lamb meat, but not often. We had a little garden where we grew wheat, barley, beans, turnips, and potatoes, like everyone round here. We crushed the barley and made gruel. I didn't take such a liking to that. You know, we had polenta every day, and still, I ain't never tired of it. I even made it today! I made pork ribs and polenta today for lunch. Mmm! Buoni! Sometimes mamma would make rice when we was in town, but I didn't care for that too much neither. I loved it when she made tagliatelle, though! We ate it with minced lardo and cheese. Lardo tastes better than butter and we didn't have olive oil then. Everything is better with lardo. I changed to olive oil because they say that we will get high cholesterol. My cholesterol is 180, so maybe I should change back to lardo!

Except at school, you didn't really feel fascism so much in your everyday life. Not this high up in the mountains. The anti-fascists kept quiet for the most part, and I never heard about nothing happening here, nothing violent, like what happened other places. In the woods you heard 'bout folks getting stopped at random and checked to see if they was carrying banned stuff or food. They always took your food away, but you didn't really even know who *they* were. Were they fascists? Germans? The Resistance? Or just hungry folks pretending to be someone and stealing your food?! The only time we ever heard about the Germans was when they was already clearing out. Weren't no reason for them to pass through small outta the way towns like ours.

236

After the war, there wasn't so much call for charcoal no more. So in 1956, I got a chance to take up under the employ of the clergyman and I accepted. He was a young man, three years younger than me. We met while he was out on his rounds carrying out his Easter benediction duties; we got to talking and he said that he was in need of a *perpetua.*

"Perpetua", literally "perpetual," is the word used to denote the personal housekeeper of the parish priest. As a proper name, Perpetua in Christianity dates back to the 22-year-old noblewoman, who in 203 CE was executed for refusing to recant her faith. More recently, in the Italian epic classic Promessi Sposi, The Betrothed (1827), *a book that is obligatory high school reading, the character named Perpetua is the domestic servant of Father Abbondio. She is a typical country-woman in her 40s, outspoken and gossipy, but well grounded in folk wisdom, which allows her to command with a tight rein, taking care, of course, not to overstep that prized feminine virtue of knowing her place. She had never married; firstly, because she had refused suitors, and secondly, because suitors had been few. She is therefore the unofficial companion of the priest.*

This is a classic case of antonomasia, whereby the name of a well-known character becomes a noun. The housekeeper of a local parish priest was from then on out referred to as his perpetua.

Many priests and perpetuas lived as husband and wife, some less surreptitiously than others. As such, the perpetua was closely scrutinized and subjected to harsh criticism, especially if it was evident that she held sway with the priest. Given this tendency, both the church authorities and the local community preferred that the perpetua be a "spinster" over forty, or even better, past menopause. Priests' preferences have not been documented.

He just been ordained two years before and was setting up at the parish house in the next town over. I had experience with domestic work at that point and was unmarried, so I was happy to make the move. I saw to the household business, cleaning, cooking, and tending the garden, the usual potatoes, cabbage, beans, and turnips. In the north it would be a while yet before we saw stuff like eggplant, celery, tomatoes, zucchini, peppers, and other vegetables like that. When we could get some sugar I made him a simple cake that we made up north:

Torta di granturco: Cornmeal cake

½ cup softened lard
2 large eggs
¾ cup sugar
½ cup water
1 cup flour
¾ cup fine yellow cornmeal
2 teaspoons baking powder
½ tsp salt

Preheat oven to 375°F. Brush the bottom and sides of an 8-inch round cake pan with lard or butter; line the bottom of the pan with greased parchment paper. In a large bowl, whisk together eggs, lard, sugar, and water until smooth. Add flour, cornmeal, salt, baking powder, and stir lightly to combine. Pour the batter into the prepared cake pan. Bake until cake begins to pull away from sides of pan, about 25-35 minutes. Cool the cake in the pan 20 minutes. Run a knife around edge of cake to separate it from the edge of the pan. Invert the cake gently onto a plate, and remove the parchment paper. Re-invert the cake onto a rack to cool completely before serving.

Father Natale and I got on good, but for some reason he got transferred in 1964 and we had to part ways.

After that, I got me a post as a domestic servant in a mid-range hotel in Limone. That give me enough experience to get a job in a real nice hotel in the province of Verona. I wasn't crazy about Verona, but I was told there was good money to be made there. Well, I know what hard work is, but I wasn't expecting nothing like this. They worked us so hard I have terrible memories of it. We was up at 6am and worked till midnight everyday, and we was watched every second to make sure we wasn't slackin'. Couldn't even ever sit down. I did everything from cooking to cleaning to stocking to serving. I found this job through a girl I'd known whose family was colliers with us in the woods. I stayed two years, didn't earn but a pittance and quit.

But the food! There was so many foods I ain't never seen or even heard of in all my life! The money was nothing and the work was killing, but the food! Oh! And they gave us plenty to eat. The pastries they had! The filled pasta, roasts, galantines, risottos, every kind of vegetable and everything made right then and there from scratch, so I saw it all. I learned to cook there, in the hotel kitchen, oh, so many beautiful things! It was the first time I ever seen things like ravioli. They made such wonderful sauces, with cream and cheese and meat, so, so good! This was food for rich folks, so they ate in courses, one dish at a time: antipasto, primo, secondo, side dish, dessert, fruit. So much food! Goodness, me! Once regular people started having money, everyone wanted to eat like rich folks, you know, in courses. But I couldn't take the work, and for them, if you didn't like it, good riddance! Plenty of other girls to take your place!

I went to Trento to work as a domestic servant in a boarding school for boys run by Franciscan friars. The school was set up to get the boys into the mind of wanting to be priests. The church got wealthy people to donate money to take poor boys off the street. They thought if the boys got 'em some schooling and they learned 'em about the good Lord... but I guess the friars wasn't so convincing because a few years after I got there they closed down, and I was out of a job. They expected the boys to hear "the calling" just from giving them a home and something to eat. My duties was mostly cleaning, but when necessary, I gave 'em hand in the kitchen too. All in all, there was 200 people, including the staff. It was a big place, with a laundry service and seamstresses and everything. After the slavery of the hotel, I was happy there. We was all left to do our jobs without nobody checking up on us. At the hotel we was reprimanded if we so much as stopped to look at something, or if we talked to each other, but the friars were kind. The boys had hot chocolate and bread for breakfast, which was new and pretty fancy for a school. Lunch was risotto, pasta or canederli (bread dumplings), and for the second course there was always meat, every day except Fridays, in remembrance of Good Friday. They served salt cod in the winter on Friday and trout in the warmer months and then eggs on Wednesdays in remembrance of Ash Wednesday [*the first day of Lent, a day of fasting and repentance*].

Dinner was soup, but by then soup had a fall from grace, and boys in particular wanted pasta, so they had to start offering a choice of pasta or soup. Second course was cheese, tuna, würstel or salami and all kinds of vegetables, potatoes, salad, and a lotta sauerkraut 'cause that is what those folks in Trentino ate, being close to Austria and all. For me, they can keep their sauerkraut. It wasn't like the hotel, but it was good eating. They even had dessert a few times a week. Only time I had sweets growing up was at Christmas. But them boys didn't want to be priests no matter what you fed them.

After fifteen years with the school, I went to work as a cook in a convent of the Order of Friars Minor Capuchin, or the Cappuccini. They's part of the Franciscans and take an oath of poverty. I done fifteen years with them too. Them was good years. Peaceful. I ain't never had a family of my own, and I felt needed and important with the friars. I was afraid to retire because my brother and sister done both passed on, and I had to face being alone. Not working for me meant that I wasn't young anymore and retiring meant facin' that fact every day for the rest of my days. I don't know why I've lived so long or what the secret is, but if I could go back and live my life again as a cook I would gladly do that. What I miss most is having a reason for being on this earth.

Without a doubt, Italian food is better now. Starving ain't a cuisine. Coffee was one of the best things that happened after the war, to me and to everybody. In 1956, when I was thirty, I had real coffee for the first time. I was an immediate addict. I had coffee three times a day. It was the ruin of Italy. Without coffee I am a dead woman. I cannot live without coffee. I am 87, and if I am still here it is because of coffee. There was only caffè d'orzo and vetch coffee when I was young. Stuff's as bitter as poison. Once real coffee got here, I tell you, it was coffee, coffee everywhere. We was all crazed for coffee. I don't think my folks ever had real coffee, neither of 'em. I think before the wars they only had coffee in the big cities like Venice and Milan. I ain't never heard of nobody ever having real coffee before the war. No one ever talked about it so I don't think there was any, and seeing as how we all went crazy for it afterward...

But, today there's too much choice. Too many nonsense products. If women don't feel like cooking anymore, I say fine. They can eat panini. Have a panino and *buon viaggio!* I ain't got nothin' more to say 'bout today's youth. I am a Christian woman, and the good Lord says if you can't say something nice, you have to keep your mouth shut. Plus it is almost the rosary hour.

Intermezzo

Andate e moltiplicatevi – Go Forth and Multiply

We will create the new generations by way of a
project of strict and tenacious selection, and in the
new generations, everyone will have a defined role.
Sometimes I smile at the idea of the generations
as a laboratory in which to create a class of
warriors, always ready to die, a class of inventors
seeking out the secrets behind mysteries, a class
of judges, a class of great captains of industry, of
explorers, of statesmen. And it is through this
methodical selection that we create empires.
— BENITO MUSSOLINI

Between 1876-1910, eleven million Italians emigrated. The United States, in particular, was a safety valve that absorbed the glut of rural poor, whose banks, it was feared, would have otherwise burst unchecked into urban areas. The Italian government encouraged emigration until the 1921 American quota strictures slowed the influx to a trickle. Contrary to his predecessors, who favored the occasional state phlebotomy, Mussolini believed that there was power in numbers, and that emigration had to cease. The rural excess, he reasoned, could be absorbed as cheap labor into developing industries, and the residual agricultural forces would work the land to supply their needs. It was a win-win situation. By increasing the population from the current forty million to sixty million, the nation could resolve its internal strife and achieve its imperialistic goals. Countries that did not become empires, Mussolini menaced, were destined to become colonies.

Thus began the Battle for Births. Both positive and punitive measures were set up to encourage early nuptials and copious offspring. Unmarried men paid a bachelor's tax; homosexuality was outlawed; and fatherhood became a prerequisite for positions of civic leadership. Cash awards and preferential loans were allocated to prolific couples; or rather, the woman had a baby, her husband got a check. Abortion, the main means of birth control, and the proliferation of contraceptive information (let alone devices) carried a prison sentence. Both were classified as crimes against the race. A woman's duty to the state was, in no uncertain terms, that of baby-maker, motherhood being defined firstly, in quantity and secondly, in quality. In effect, the regime simply re-codified centuries old religious canon with earthly punishments and rewards, instead of heavenly ones, the former representing the will of the state, and the latter the will of God. It was a deadlock.

Paradoxically, in spite of the profusion of incentives and penalties, birthrates steadily decreased throughout the duration of the Ventennio along the entire length of the peninsula, including the islands. It was a tendency that that was already ongoing before the Great War. Scientists at the time associated the decline in fruitfulness with an ever more blunted genetic instinct to reproduce, which alas, could be slowed, but not stopped. Placing the blame for declining birthrates on the lack of food and unbalanced nutrition would likewise have been an over simplification, given the upheaval of social reorganization that characterized the early twentieth century. Notions of family planning, socioeconomic awareness, and emancipation were spreading throughout the western world, in addition to a reassessment of religious precepts. Children were seen as individuals, whose nurturing required an investment of time, money, and energy. Parents carefully weighed how much of their resources they were able and willing to dedicate to each child.

There was yet another paradox: the population continued to grow.

To sustain the image of a civilized state, welfare programs for women and children were unquestionably fundamental, and so in keeping with the trend already underway in the other western European nations, Italy instituted the National Agency for Maternal and Infant Welfare (*Opera Nazionale della maternità e infanzia,* ONMI) in 1925. It was the first state agency aimed specifically at assisting underprivileged women and children. The infant mortality and morbidity rates in post WWI were critical. Begging, homelessness, and delinquency were rampant. State intervention was overdue and desperately needed. However, like many of the fascist regime's overly ambitious programs, the broad-spectrum package set out for ONMI was out of proportion in relation to available resources. The tax revenues garnered from deviant bachelors was the agency's main source of funding, a tactic that was twistedly logical and incongruent at the same time. It was not dissimilar to lottery tickets subsidizing gambling rehabilitation.

As with schools, ONMIs ultimate goal in safeguarding and overseeing the development of children was that of molding the cultural and moral foundation of the race in accordance with the needs of the national collective, in so doing, bending their inclinations towards protecting and defending the state. Eugenics was abuzz in Europe, but in Italy, while there were concerns about "contamination" and talk of preserving the race, particularly after the invasion of Ethiopia and the imminent closer ties with Hitler, the fascist take on eugenics focused mainly on increasing numbers.

Experts were stumped by falling birthrates and high infant mortality. In the search for a culprit, women were deemed "scientifically" unsuited to raising children without institutional intervention. Assistance centers called *Casa della madre* were set up as consultancy hubs for mother and child, and were opportunely used to dispense propaganda, reminding women of the glory of subordination. ONMI's overriding attention on the child, as opposed to the mother, diminished her role to a mere means to an end, providing farmhands, factory workers, and "human cannon fodder" (De Grazia,1992). Even her function as domestic manager, instead of being valorized, was perceived as another area to be revamped and updated. Domesticity should be carried out with clinical efficiency and in shadowy silence. Modernity did not empower women. It reinforced feelings of inadequacy and failure in the one realm that had, heretofore, universally been their sphere of dominion. The word for housewife, "massaia," acquired such negative connotations of subordination that it fell completely out of use in the late 1940s, and was taken over by the more convivial *casalinga.*

Illegitimate pregnancy and its by-product of neglected infants and abandoned foundlings accounted for much of Italy's high infant mortality rate. The crackdown on abortion had resulted in a surge of unwanted children. (The only other available means of birth control at the time were condoms. However, given their intended prophylactic use for soldiers, they carried the stigma associated with whores and venereal disease.) Illegitimate or not, these babies added to the head count. ONMI, therefore, provided a government controlled haven for all unwed, widowed or abandoned mothers, all women who lacked the necessary financial resources, all women whose husbands were institutionalized or in prison, and all women who found themselves in any sort of condition that did not allow them to adequately care for themselves or their expected child. There was one condition, however. Only women who agreed to breast-feed were entitled to social services. Women who were unwilling to make this small sacrifice were dismissed as unfit mothers, undeserving of aid. Nursing the infant, it was believed, would forge the mother and child bond, thereby lessening the risk of abandonment.

State orphanages were also set up under ONMI. Again, needy children at risk of abandonment, and all manner of orphaned waifs, beggars, and vagabonds, including neglected and abused children were provided for under the tutelage of the state until the age of eighteen.

In spite of harmonious appearances, tensions with the Church over ONMI did arise. Illegitimate strays were not to be put on equal footing with their legitimate peers, so as not to tarnish the sacredness of the righteous family. Their documents would always bear the shaming stamp of "no one's child." In a strategic power play, Mussolini instituted the Day of the Mother and Child – on Christmas Eve. The purposeful blurring of Catholic symbolism surrounding the Madonna with the fascist agenda was meant to underscore the state imperatives of reproduction, abnegation, purity, and obedience. In a public spectacle, one prolific couple from each of the 92 provinces in Italy, were convocated to Rome to receive a cash gift from Mussolini himself. To achieve his end, Mussolini even paraded out the image of his own "sainted" mother, as well as that of the queen mother Margherita. As the expression goes, *tutto fa brodo*, anything makes broth, or rather, "it's all good."

In 1939, the year before Italy entered into the Second World War, the population stood at nearly 44 million people. By 1946, it had risen to 45.5 million, regardless of casualties and a sharp drop in the birthrate. But to achieve his goal of 60 million inhabitants, Mussolini would have had to wait until 2014. Over the next two decades, a power struggle ensued over the fate of ONMI between those seeking to transform it into a care center addressing the specific health and counseling needs of women and children, and those who felt that its utility had been surpassed by the modern hospital. In 1975, ONMI was officially dismantled and its obstetric and pediatric functions were absorbed into the national healthcare system. That same year, fascist laws pertaining to the family were reviewed and revised, and both contraception use and abortion were legalized.

Ida

Born 1927 – Persone

In the mountains of northern Italy near the Swiss border there is an area called Valvestino. It was part of the Austro-Hungarian Empire until the end of The Great War, when it was relegated to Italy and became part of the region of Trentino. Mussolini decided to make it part of Lombardy during his reign and it remained so until a 2012 referendum mandated its return to Trentino. The insular life of mountain towns offers a relaxed pace, a stunning natural environment, and a close-knit community. But for many, the anxiety of stagnation is unbearable, and the 5-town area is depopulating at an alarming rate as the townspeople are drawn to the bright lights of the big city and the opportunities therein. The hope of the hangers-on is that Trentino will recognize the loss of their pristine heritage and come to their aid. The villagers are resigned to the probability that theirs is a lost cause, and they are simply looking for the slowest, least invasive way to transition from ghost town to tourist attraction. If tourism necessarily means a uniting of greed and bad taste in order to turn a profit, then they'd prefer the ruin be of their own doing rather than see their towns overrun by foreign investors.

Ida is from Persone, one of the five towns tucked into Valvestino. She calls herself a "mountain woman," though in her varied life she lived in the small town, big city and country contexts. I went to the restaurant she bequeathed to her daughter to interview her. She tried to speak Italian, but in the more emotional moments, when speaking from the heart, she reverted to dialect, which allowed her to express herself fully without artificial restraints.

I was born right here, in this here town of Persone. I lived other places 'cause destiny dropped me there; you don't have to do no more that take one look around you to see why I settled back here. I grew up here in town, but the town is so tiny, it wasn't too much different from living in the country. All you gotta do is open the door and you are in the country. We all had our piece of land that we worked, but we wasn't so much town or country folks or any of that business, as we was mountain people. Not a lot has changed here; even the old schoolhouse I went to is still standing. It was sold to a private buyer not too long ago. It's a small town, but there was enough kids here back then that we had a regular schoolhouse and all five grades. But still, there was only one teacher for the lot of us, I'd say about thirty in all. We all sat in rows according to which class you was in. The teacher gave the day's lesson to one row, set us to doing our work, and then moved on to the next row until we was all working quiet like, and then she would begin again to see how we was getting on. That's the way it worked in all of the Valvestino villages. One teacher, one room. five grades.

First thing when we stepped into the classroom we gave the Roman salute to the pictures of the Duce and King Vittorio Emanuele hanging up there on the wall and say, "*Viva il Duce! Viva il Re!*"

The same gesture in the United States, called the Bellamy salute, was once used in schools for the pledge of allegiance, but FDR had it changed to the now familiar hand-over-the-heart gesture to disassociate from the Nazis and fascists. The fascist party attempted to make the salute a compulsory substitution to the handshake greeting, emphasizing that it was "more hygienic, more aesthetic, and faster." But only very zealous fascist adherents conceded to the request.

Next to the pictures of our leaders was Christ on the cross, so after getting the politics out of the way, we all said the Lord's Prayer. That way, we covered all the powers-that-be right off the bat! Ha!

Soon as we could string a sentence together, we had to write compositions about how important the fascio was for us, and how good they was to the people. I remember I wrote one about the day some outsiders came to town for Fascist Saturday and brought us bread and bologna sandwiches. Boy! We sure did remember that day 'cause it weren't too often round here you got to eat real bread or meat!

Lot of folks was wretched with poverty. And what a sorry joke that ration card was! For folks who ain't got no money, it was a useless piece of paper. And no one was givin' out no handouts. Whenever they could, lots of women would come into town asking round for a day's work so's they could make ends meet. When I was a girl, I got a bit of work that way too, just easy jobs like stacking wood 'cause I was just a little thing then. The church wasn't no help whatever. Weren't no better than them big landowners. Sitting pretty with their big plots of land what was given 'em by the church. They sharecropped the land, pullin' in half the take. Sure, pretty good deal for sitting on your haunches doing nothin'. Them other wretches working the land didn't have two coins to rub together.

My papa couldn't find no work, and even though we had our own land, we couldn't get by, so like lots of our menfolk, he went to France to work. He left when my sister was eighteen months and I was just born. My mamma worked the whole farm alone and saw to us girls. She planted all of the usual vegetables, potatoes, field corn, and cannoli beans. When there's beans and potatoes, you got food, and ain't no one gonna drop dead from hunger. We had two cows too, and that was like money in the bank. Folks looked up to you if you had cows. We took the milk to have it made into cheese and sold it. That was how we got our spending money. Every year we got us a piglet and come winter we slaughtered it. You can get a decent amount of salumi and all the rest off just one pig. It was a cycle 'cause the pigs ate the potatoes what didn't come out good, the whey left from making cheese, grass, and the polenta what gone bad. Then, we ate them.

We ate a lot of polenta too. You had everything with polenta. Twice a month, we would kill either a rabbit or a chicken for our Sunday dinner. Rabbits was easy to keep because they just needed grass and they make lots of little ones. Chickens was good twice over, for meat and eggs. We had a plot where we grew our own wheat too. We threshed it ourselves and had it ground, but it wasn't fine white flour. Plenty of other folks went hungry a lot of the time, but we made it all right. If anything, you almost dropped dead from the work you had to do just to keep food on the table! In fact, my mamma died when I was ten years old. Yeah. I think it was the work done killed her. That's when Papa came back from France.

I never seen him but a couple times in my life before that. He married again right quick. My new stepmother and me, well, we didn't get on so good. My sister and me was took out of school. I just finished the 4th grade. We was shipped off to Milan to work as servants in two different families. We lived far away from each other but we met up every Thursday because our padroni had stands in the same market on that day.

I worked for a nice couple from the south whose kids were away in some boarding school. Strange, but in the whole two and a half years I worked for them, I never once seen them kids.

I had a pretty hard time of it with the way those Milan folks talked, but I couldn't hardly make heads or tails of the padrone and padrona! They talked all funny like they do in the south. The padrona was a schoolteacher. The padrone had a clothes stand and I worked for him. Him and me would go every morning to some outdoor marketplace sellin' his wares.

The great Italian fashion gods, in the guise of Valentino, Gucci, and the like, would not come on the scene until well after the war. The savvy pre-war Italian designer took his cues from the Parisian silhouette, considered the ultimate in style and sophistication. However, when the regime set about pursuing all possible means to achieve autarky, the fashion and textiles industries were encouraged to look inward. La Cucina Italiana, ever the faithful mouthpiece for fascist propaganda, railed against women who slavishly followed French fashions.

Donning politically correct synthetic fabrics became yet another way women could do their part for the patria. These included rayon instead of silk, cafioc instead of cotton, salpa instead of leather, and the crowning glory – lanital, a synthetic wool made from milk casein. It was mothproof, but difficult to sew and press. Designers joked that it was like ironing mozzarella. In 1937, when Ida had taken up employment in Milan, a lanital/viscose blend won first prize in a fascist sponsored textile competition in Forlì. From then on, it was declared, all party flags should be made from lanital. Advertisements implored women to wear clothes made from lanital to demonstrate their national loyalty. The fascist stamp of approval removed the "chintzy" stigma attached to cheap synthetic clothing purchased at the outdoor market, freeing the piccolo borghese, *the lower-middle and working classes, to appear patriotic and not merely "off the rack". In so doing, they proudly upheld the slogan: Dio, patria, famiglia!*

I was just ten years old. I didn't know nothin' about keeping a city house, so the padroni taught me how to keep house in a proper way, and how to look after the market stand. I learned to make beds, scrub floors, dust here and there, and how to take care not to break nice things, you know? Then in the market, I had to keep an eye out to make sure people wasn't stealing and tell folks about the clothes and prices. It was a big stand with everything, trousers, underclothes, dresses... The padrone taught me how to use the tram system so's I could get to the different places where I had to be on different days. That was a lot for a little girl who never set foot out of her tiny village! Lot of times I felt lost, scared, and confused, and I missed my mamma. But they was good people even though I couldn't figure out what they was saying half the time.

We finished at the market and was home by 2:00 for lunch. The padrone made our midday meal, because his wife wasn't home during the day. He always made that southern sort of food, like pasta with tomato sauce. They had store bought pasta all the time like spaghetti and penne, stuff I never seen the likes of before. I didn't like it too much neither. When the lady was home, she made pasta, handmade tagliatelle. The worst part was Friday when they made fish!

They liked that awful kind, oh, what's the name of that fish, the one with all them paws? Octopus! Oh, horrible! I couldn't hardly choke it down. But if I didn't like something, it was tough luck 'cause there wasn't gonna be nothing else, so after a while I got used to it. Dinner was always something small, a little broth and maybe some salami or cheese. They wasn't in a bad way for money, and there was always plenty of bread on the table. They let me have as much as I wanted! But I know now that all that bread meant that they was picking it up on the black market. In the morning I had *orzo* and milk with bread and jam before going to work. Jam was just for rich folks so I have to say, they treated me good. They always said whatever was put on the table I could eat too.

I made 47 lire a month, but I never seen none of my own money 'cause come the end of the month, my stepmother's sister collected my pay. The couple saw to me getting proper shoes and clothes, but there wasn't never extras or spending money for me. I just worked. When the lady decided that she didn't want one of her dresses no more, they sent me round to the seamstress and had it cut down to a dress my size.

After two years and seven months my time in Milan was done. In 1940, the padrone signed himself up for the army and got shipped off to Africa. A young man from the fascio was assigned to me to make sure I made it to Salò.

Salò, a small town on Lake Garda, played a significant role in fascist history. In July of 1943, the Allied Forces forced Italy out of North Africa, and then made their way north into Sicily. With the support of the King, Mussolini was ousted through a vote of no confidence, and "secret" negotiations began with the Allies, about which Hitler was fully aware. In a matter of months, Germany retaliated, setting up a puppet government headquartered in Salò called the Italian Social Republic, with a sickly and reluctant Mussolini at its head. This split the peninsula in two, with the Germans ruling the north, the Allies the south, and the Italians questioning where their loyalties lay. After nineteen months, the neo-government was brought down on April 25, 1945, a date celebrated annually as Liberation Day. Mussolini attempted to flee but was captured by partigiani who assassinated him on April 28.

From there, it was a good eight hours' walk back to Persone. Once there, I went back to working the land with my family. When I say work, I mean work. We didn't have any machines or animals to work the land. All the plowing and hoeing was done by hand. No tractor, no mule. The landscape you see today, it wasn't like that before. It was field, pasture, field, pasture. It wasn't covered with trees like it is today. We worked all of the land like Mussolini told us, and we worked hard. When I hear women today who say they don't want to cook, they're tired, they don't like having to make food for the family, well, ma'am, I have to laugh! No one knows today what the word "work" meant for us. It is all too easy today. When the change came after the war, it was too much, too fast, too soon. They say that today there is a crisis on, but folks are still out there with their credit cards, spending and buying. That is not a crisis. Of course, we are all safer and more comfortable now, and that is a good thing. But, all that money is not good for raising a family. Kids today are real strange. Young girls running around half naked. Here, there, and everywhere dressed in whatever you please! There is no modesty! They leave one boyfriend and pick up with someone else as soon as they turn around. The church wouldn't have allowed that in my day! You get richer and in the end you are poorer for it. You see? Sure, good times for everyone! Even the church isn't the same.

But anyway, not long after I got back home, I got a real bad sickness. Peritonitis. It was so bad I had to go to the hospital, but seein' as how my family owned a piece of land, the government didn't cover none of it. I had to pay for it, and I sure as heck didn't have no money! We all had a terrible fear of getting sick and not having the money to pay for it. I found a woman, a benefactress, who put down a deposit for me. I remember that hospital seemed so nice and clean, with all them starched white sheets. In the end I was there forty days, and it cost me 750 lire, a year's pay as a housemaid! I was out working everywhere I could to make up my debt, even as a field hand, wherever I could find a spot open. After two years I paid it off, but then my father came to fetch me. It seems his wife had up and left him and, seeing as it was time to bring in the wheat harvest, he needed me at home. After a month she returned, though, and we started gettin' in each other's hair just like before. One day we went at it like two hell cats, and my father decided he was gonna put a stop to it. He beat me bloody, so with no money, nothing, I left during the night.

Come daytime, I hitched a ride on a bus. The driver saw the sorry state I was in and said he'd let me off just before the ticket checkpoint, which wasn't too far from where my uncle lived. It only took one day 'fore I was set up with a job working for a well-to-do family that had a string of butcher shops. Four days a week I was at the lake just washing clothes. I had to clean all the butchers' bloodstained clothes and towels, the clothes of the couple's eight children, and the grandparents too! Then one day a week I spent cleaning the house from top to bottom and another day I cleaned bovine heads. The meat from them fetched a good price, the face, tongue, brain, and the nerves. Those were all very expensive bits! I'll tell you, it was a daylong procession of heads! Ha!

Braised beef jowl and tendons, are making a comeback in today's Italian trattorias. Brain and tongue, which used to grace wealthier tables, are associated with older tastes and are shunned by the under-50 set. Other parts of the head, like eyes, ears, and snout, were then left for the indigent, but now are not even proposed in conjunction with the fashionable "poor cuisine."

In spite of 'em being rich, they was modest at the table. Rich folks usually ate in courses, but them people put a simple meal on the table, ate it and was done with it. Lots of times, they even had polenta with a sauce or salt cod. If they had pasta, that was the whole meal. I don't remember when in Italy everyone started this habit of first and second course. Maybe it was different for us in the north because we always had polenta. I know in the 50s, when people started going out, restaurants didn't have it, but now they all do, every last one of them.

Anyway, it happened one day that I met a relative of my employer who asked if I wanted to go work at the Lancia factory shop in Bolzano on the Austrian border.

Bolzano had been a longstanding thorn of contention between Italy and the Austro-Hungarian Empire, both sides feeling they had the more substantiated claim. After WWI when accounts were settled, Italy was awarded the coveted region of Alto Adige, and thereby the city of Bolzano, for having sided with the Allies. Under fascism, an intense campaign to denationalize and Italianize all of the newly acquired territories was launched in an effort to suppress every trace of previous cultural dominion. When Mussolini allied with Hitler, the citizens of Bolzano were given an ultimatum to choose Italian or German citizenship, in effect, a threat: either integrate into the Italian culture, or leave. Most favored Germany and the Teutonic culture, but few emigrated. The backlash struck after WWII, when terrorist groups emerged. In spite of intervention by the UN, terrorist activities continued through the 1980s until a compromise was achieved. The recent economic crisis, however, has once again stirred extremist groups to seek regional independence or annexation under Austria.

They had always been kindly to me, so off I went in 1946, right at the end of the war. The shop sold discount stuff to the 700 men and women who worked at the Lancia factory. They lodged in the army barracks the Duce had built - 350 men on the ground floor and 350 women on the upper floor. They was almost all foreigners, most of them from the south of Italy, but there was people of all sorts, including some Italians. Uh, what I mean is there was folks from cities everywhere. [*In northern Italy, it is not uncommon to hear people speak quite freely, even heatedly, of southern Italians as outsiders, and worse.*]

But I wasn't there too long before I went to stay with my sister. She'd done good for herself, married good, to a man that had a big fancy hotel. It was a real upper-class deal. My brother-in-law wasn't a nobody. He done worked as a waiter to Mussolini and the King! He taught me how to do that high-class cooking. Around the *Lago di Garda* area there was plenty of spas and sanatoriums, and so he got a lot of them VIPs at his hotel. Now these here folks, they had their antipasto, first and second course, side dishes, fruit, dessert, cheese plate, and coffee. All well and good for them, but wasn't for me. I never went in for that swanky sort of eatin'.

When I was 21, in 1948 I married a man from my hometown of Persone. His folks had a *dopolavoro* that after the fascist times turned into an osteria.

The Dopolavoro clubs, literally "after work" were established as part of an agreement between the unions and the regime. There were intended as recreational meeting places for men, along the lines of a YMCA, with leisurely but intentionally structured activities like sporting events, lectures, and evening classes. But many of them were de facto fully licensed pubs, where men drank and played cards, making them similar, if not identical, to osterias. The dopolavoro were partially funded by the regime and frequenters paid a yearly membership.

They was for men only, and the joke is, there wasn't no "dopolavoro" for women 'cause women never stopped working! Men would come in on Sundays, drink the day away and play cards. Same thing when it became an osteria. Now you see, the difference between that and a *fiaschetteria* is that osteria could sell *all* kinds of alcohol, tobacco, and salt, all the things taxed by the state, and the *fiaschetteria* could only sell wine. Folks around here didn't grow grapes, so all of the wine was brought in from other places. That meant that men didn't do their drinking at home 'cause they didn't have homegrown. All of 'em was out drinkin' in places like ours.

After 1961, when my father-in-law passed on, I started to serve simple dishes in my osteria. It was still mostly a drinking place, but if the fellas wanted something to eat, I'd whip something up for 'em. I'd tell them what was on hand and they ordered. It was all things with a sauce: a dish of polenta, or spaghetti or gnocchi. Nothing too complicated and no second courses. My cod with chestnuts was a big hit.

Baccalà con le castagne: Salt cod with chestnuts
500g salt cod
fat for pan frying
1 med onion
½ liter whole milk
large handful of breadcrumbs browned in butter
white beans soaked overnight
one cup of dried chestnuts

Soak the fish for two days to desalt, changing the water periodically. Remove skin, chop into pieces, and fry in pounded fatback, lard, or butter. Add onions and sauté. Add milk and simmer for an hour. Add breadcrumbs, beans, and chestnuts and simmer until the chestnuts have disintegrated and the beans are soft, about one hour. Add milk as needed. Serve with polenta.

Time went on and folks started asking for more kinds of things. Osterias everywhere was becomin' just like trattorias, all serving regular home cooked food and wine. After a while, the only thing that was different was the name. The coffee bars started up and men went there if they wanted to sit around and drink. We had to keep up with the times so we started offering first and second courses too 'cause that was the fashion. Italians everywhere wanted to eat that way, like the way rich people ate. So, little by little we got a sort of a menu going and did good business. I retired and left it to my daughter and she runs it now.

> *The habit of eating in courses, or à la française, spread throughout Italian households as soon as the economic miracle of the 1960s took off. Except for the first course, pasta, rice, or soup, dishes are served family style. Restaurants served in a modified à la russe style, wherein menus are divided into courses: antipasto, first course, second course and side dish, dessert, (fruit), and coffee with each dish served individually. Upmarket restaurateurs frown upon customers who only order one course (I discovered this early on when I ordered a first course and nothing else at a restaurant and was told, "Signorina, this is not a spaghetti house!").*

Marisa (Ida's daughter, age 63): I gave it the name *L'Antica Osteria* because there are lots of people out there looking for food that is, you know, "genuine," "authentic," and "traditional", and I cater to what they are looking for [*A quick google of Antica Osteria will produce 920,000 results in the first half second*]. It is an *idea* that we Italians have about rusticity, but one that leaves your palate and stomach satisfied in a modern way. It is not the food of yesteryear. I know that. I tried doing the older local dishes, but this is a business, and I have to keep up with the times. The food here is excellent. It is local, sourced with care, and prepared by hand. But, no, it is not the simple food I was raised on, or that my mother was raised on, or the food her mother prepared for her. There are no generations of grandmothers behind this. Why not? Because *no one really wants that food,* and they sure don't want it when they eat out! They want a menu with antipasto, a hearty first course, and a meaty second course. That is what all Italian restaurants have. Sometimes in the heart of winter, I'll recreate some of the old dishes, which are appreciated by local customers. But that stuff is "novelty" food now. You know, quaint.

Brufadei – Savory pudding:

Sprinkle some milk onto white flour. Make into "rice" by rubbing it between your hands. Bring a pot of half milk and half water to a boil. Sift the rice bits out and throw them in the pot. Stir as it thickens and salt. It should remain lumpy. Spoon into a bowl. Add chopped fontina.

This was a dish that my mother made for us when she was not well enough to made bread. It was good either for breakfast or dinner instead of soup. Standard menus today that you find in a "rustic" eatery are like what people my mother's age ate when it was a holiday, and probably not even that!

I was born in 1950. After school we had to tend the chickens and the rabbits and then get straight to our schoolwork. If my mother saw us in the piazza playing and the animals hadn't been taken care of, she'd come out and drag us back home by the ear because your duties had to be done. After that we played in the piazza, but with stones and things we found lying around. We didn't have toys or bikes. Or we took the goats into the pasture and played while they ate until sundown. Keep in mind that I'm talking about the 60s. We still didn't have anything then, and really, my family was one of the better off families around here.

Ida: We didn't play when I was young. All we did was work.

Marisa: My children, born in the 70s, had toys, lots of them. We took them into the pastures to play, sure, but they didn't have to tend the goats. Everything was different for them. Life in Italy had completely changed in such a short period of time. By the 80s, in an osteria, you had to serve a full meal in courses because people were doing it at home too. *That* was the new Italian way of eating. Everyone wanted to forget the hardship of the war and eat like rich people. It is a big change for us in the north where there is still a strong tradition of polenta. People started to buy bakery bread; we started to have dried pasta instead of fresh tagliatelle because it used to be that fresh was the only pasta we had here. So, once we had dried pasta, we started making sauces and first courses. But before, it just wasn't like that here. We didn't have spaghetti or that kind of pasta until the 70s. It was all new to us.

Ida: All of this "Italian" food is new for us. I only had pizza for the first time 'bout twenty years ago with my grandson. It was pretty darn good, so I learned to make it myself, and I don't mind sayin', my pizza is better. I make the thick crust kind 'cause in the pizzerias it is too thin.

Used to be families was numerous, and it was hard feedin' all of them mouths. They say, "no one died of hunger," but there was lots of children died from diseases and things, 'cause there wasn't enough nutrition. Who cares if you was fillin' your stomach if the food wasn't doin' you no good? Today there is way too much. To right the world again, we'd have to go back about halfway, after the war but before we forgot who we are. I never throw anything away. I tell you I could cry when I see my family today with so much good fortune, and then throwing food away without even looking at it, without a second thought! Simplicity was a good life teacher. Too much food is ready-made. That ain't Italian food. So, in a certain sense, it is already a lost cause.

Marisa: Even most restaurants today make their food with packaged and frozen products like sauces, desserts, even meat. Not many places today cook all their own food like I do. I've got a strong clientele here even though we are in a small, out-of-the-way mountain town. People will come a long way for real home cooking, which says something about how they are eating at home! I learned to cook from my mother. I tried to teach my daughter-in-law, but she couldn't care less. I cook for her children so they get something decent to eat. I tried to teach my son, but he's got other things on his mind, so I know that the restaurant is destined to close if I retire. Everyone goes on about how proud they are of Italian food, but then no one wants to learn how to cook! But not just that, they don't even know how to do their laundry or sew on a button! It is probably the fault of us mothers. We didn't teach them how to live.

Intermezzo

Il mercato nero – The Black Market

> Totalitarianism is chaos kept within the framework
> of an all-powerful state organization which is
> embodied in an all-powerful, irresponsible leader.
> When the leader goes to pieces, as happened to
> Mussolini, and the state organization is wrecked
> by external war, the chaos breaks loose.
> — MAX ASCOLI,
> *ITALY, AN EXPERIMENT IN RECONSTRUCTION*

"Duce, Duce, aren't we a sight? By day without bread, by night without light." This ditty of discontent started circulating around 1940 with the first murmurings of the ration card. The froth of indignation whipped up in the name of autarky had fizzled by then, and the prospect of even more stringent measures did not stir the same communal enthusiasm. But word on the street was that the war would be won in short order. In no time, Italy would be able to return to its former parsimony.

From the onset, the rationing initiative was a calamity on a steady slide into chaos. The already compromised food distribution infrastructure only worsened as the war progressed; key roads, bridges and railways were systematically bombed to impede transport. Bicycles and mules drawing carts became the main means of transporting goods and were seen hauling wares at a snail's pace at all hours. As rationing was only intended to be a temporary measure, it had been administered haphazardly with an erratic regard for daily caloric requirements, to say nothing of nutrition. The Battle for Wheat complicated matters further by significantly reducing the variety and availability of both rationed and non-rationed foodstuffs. The momentum for agricultural productivity dropped off as the anticipation of war heightened. The colonies, the alliance with Germany, and the war removed men from the fields, creating a vacuum of food production that could not be corrected through rationing.

Wartime recipes began to circulate that were peppered with the word "without," as in, salad without oil, jam without sugar, pastry cream without egg, meatballs without meat. The *polpetta*, though traditionally a meat-based ball or patty, was made during wartime with any combination of things one had on hand. So long as the minced ingredients held their shape, and didn't fall apart when fried, it was a polpetta. It was an ingenious, often tasty way, to make use of scraps and discards. Just take bread, an egg, mix it with any mishmash of ground up leftovers, form balls and fry. To top off the meal, one could indulge in a bar of Government Issue chocolate, whose mouthwatering catchphrase was: "Autarkic Chocolate 'Robur' prepared in conformity with the most recent laws."

Bread held top position for many people as the fulcrum of every meal. Most everything else was a *companatico*, an accompaniment to bread. Like soup, bread was stomach filler. In a bit of etiquette that grew out of frugality, it was even considered uncouth to eat certain foods without bread. Bread rationing struck close to basic survival, making it an easy target for unscrupulous practices. The crafty element, geared towards cheating the system, adulterated flour with all manner of whiteners and fillers: clay, chalk, calcium carbonate, and barium sulfate. More commonly, however, good flour was mixed with old or contaminated flour or other vegetable matter.

To avoid falling prey to the wiles of dodgy bakers, it was common practice, in many towns, for women to take their own bread dough to the local baker who baked it for a modicum fee. Once cooked, the "baker's boy" loaded the crusty loaves onto a board and carried them on his head through the town, consigning each to its rightful owner. This assured purity, and to a degree, it freed the family from relying exclusively on the government ration.

Whole wheat had long been the official bread, but even before rationing, it reportedly contained up to thirty percent other cereals and fillers. On this unpleasant topic, patriotic home economist Lidia Morelli advises her readers,

> Don't turn your nose up at bread that is a bit darker, ... Whole wheat bread that also contains bran ... [however] should not be used uninterruptedly as it is not easily digestible ... Out of the necessity of war, we now have to eat pane unico, which is not made entirely with wheat. It is not so bad, and might even be good if the bakers would just leave it to rise a bit longer and cook it more thoroughly. Better to put on a happy face than to complain, so try toasting the slices slightly. That is certainly better than just eating the crust, then crumbling up and wasting the inside part...like so many young ladies that I know do. ... There is no sense in complaining; on the contrary, it is unpatriotic. Trying to increase your provisions through fraud, clandestine markets, and paying exorbitant prices for under-the-table products is enough to mar the conscience of any Italian. There is nothing to do but accept the state of things, as they have been forced upon us against our will (1942).

Morelli perhaps underestimated how many were willing to put up with a marred conscience, as everywhere, shrewd profiteers stood at the ready to make out from the dearth and an ever-increasing clientele. The government resurrected some of the worn-out propaganda from the time of sanctions and feeble scare tactics to warn people away from black marketeers: "THE BLACK THIEF! You all know him! THE BLACK THIEF is defeated when shoppers insist on quality and the right price and weight." Propaganda preyed on shoppers's conscience: "Compare your sacrifice to that of our soldiers at the front!" as well as merchants: "Merchants! Be patient and courteous with your customers. But be inflexible about requests that run counter to the rationing laws." A bewildering number of both local and national laws regarding food and the black market went on the books, but there was a chain of civil disobedience that made the black market, de facto, legal. It became a problem without a solution.

As early as 1939, both sellers and buyers on the black market were subject to two years imprisonment. But it deterred few, as there were large fortunes to be made in the scramble for food. Demand was high and so were profits. Fascists, Germans, partigiani, and the church had all appropriated goods from the country as their due. The black market gave farmers a way to retaliate against the requisitioning of their tools, livestock, and produce. Urban dwellers, however, bitterly resented the stranglehold the country folk had over provisions, seeing them merely as food hoarders taking advantage of a crisis situation.

Bakers continued making the coveted contraband white bread, selling it under the counter at a premium price. Grocers claimed to not have foods in stock, to the dismay of customers armed with their families' ration cards (one for each member according to age and need). Favoritism became more pronounced and quality goods were only brought out for long standing loyal customers. Some shopkeepers reputedly concealed supplies normally for sale in their shop in order to funnel them onto the black market. Grocery stores at the time were not places where the customer browsed and was free to pick and choose items off of a shelf. The storefront consisted of a counter from which the grocer dispensed goods (and favor) upon request, much like a pharmacist. Journalist T. E. Beattie wrote a description of the typical small town grocery during his visit to Italy in 1945, which rekindles the scene:

> Shop interiors are small, crowded, poorly lighted, cold in winter and hot and smelly in summer. Fixtures are few: a stubby counter at the rear; a few wall cabinets and storage drawers; and a chair for the proprietor to sit on during slack hours. In winter a prominent fixture is a hammered brass charcoal brazier to heat the store. Now and then an especially progressive establishment may have a computing scale or a cash register;

more commonly, however, a primitive balance scale and cash drawer suffice. Always there is a wall shrine to the Virgin Mary or to some patron saint.

For people with ready cash, there was little choice but to turn to the black market, as legitimate means did not provide enough food to live on. Unlike the black market for sought-after luxury items that dominated during the push for autarky, the wartime black market was mainly about obtaining the basics, which had, in turn, become luxury items. Illicit goods were not within reach of everyone's budget, however. In Naples, for example, unskilled workers earned between 30-50 lire per day; the fixed price of bread was four lire per kilo, and on the black market it went for 100-150 liras. Much of the business was done at sidewalk pop-up stands, where goods fetched 25-100 percent more than at retail stores.

Particularly high profits were accrued from foreign soldiers. The government virtually pushed them towards the black market with menacing public bulletins like this: "Without a ration card, the sale of rationed goods is forbidden, even for the German military." Vendors found it behooved them to peddle wares at train stations to military personnel, who were tolerated "as a necessary evil and partly as a sucker who – regardless of price and value – will buy if given time" (Beattie, 1945). The blatant disregard for the politics of their clientele was a thorn in the side the politically minded. Military presence also proved to be a boon for their lavish throwaways. A loaf of army bread salvaged from the Allies' garbage bin carried an exorbitant price tag.

For the most part, law enforcement organizations turned a blind eye to the black market. Stopping it was not only futile, but inhumane. Altruism was not the only reason for lax law enforcement. An entire system, from inspectors to police, amassed under-the-table benefits through orchestrated cooperation. The government itself seemed to be in on the racket; the estimates of wheat supplies and the estimated ration allotment left large quantities of wheat unaccounted for.

The profitability and unchecked transactions of the black market made it an attractive prospect for organized crime networks. Far from being just a handful of farmers on a corner selling their wares hush-hush, a complex system developed for the unlawful sale of food items. The situation worsened the farther south one ventured, where abject destitution spawned corruption. Writer and diarist Magda Cecarelli De Grada describes a scene from her sojourn in Sicily:

> Is it surprising if the adults are stunted, with short legs and ra-chitic heads and have poison in their characters? You only need to look at the children. Ragged, with shirts in shreds, bloated stomachs, emaciated shoulders and wrinkled skin. I saw three of them begging: . . . They were three little skeletons, three little old men, but their immense black eyes were filled with so much evil (Ceccarelli De Grada, 1942, in Duggan 2013).

Although meat consumption varied from class to class and region to region, statistics report that the average consumption per capita was nine kilos annually, while in the southern provinces the figure was below one kilo.

Warned of the dire straits they would face, the Allied relief effort spread counter-propaganda of the plentiful food they would bring, in order to set the stage for their arrival in Sicily in 1943. Upon embarking, however, they were taken aback by the gravity of the hunger situation, and found that their calculations fell far below necessity. They were also ill equipped to deal with the deeply entrenched black market system, wherein an estimated 60% of food aid disappeared for resale.

> Allied Military Governments were from the beginning in no condition to face all the problems . . . problems of food, un-employment, black market, rampant inflation, and widespread corruption and thievery. They needed the co-operation of local authorities, but it was hard to rely on them or to trust them (Ascoli, 1944).

To prevent the Allied forces from getting swept up in the rampant corruption, the resale of goods by military personnel became a court martial offense, in spite of which, sacks of provisions were reported to have "fallen off" of military trucks. In 1944, in cases of organized food trafficking by civilians, the Italian court imposed the death penalty, while lesser offenses carried from one to ten years' imprisonment. Rationing finally came to an official end in 1949. The death penalty, which had been reinstated by the fascist regime and Vatican City in 1926, was repealed by the 1948 Italian constitution. The Holy See followed suit in 1967 although it was not officially removed from their constitution until 2001.

DEEP SOUTH

Concetta

Born 1923 – Castronuovo di Sant'Andrea

Basilicata is historically one of the poorest regions of Italy. The people of Basilicata are "Lucani," from the latin lucus, *meaning sacred woods. The lack of work there has meant that the small towns pressed into the steep rocky hills, like Castronuovo, are depopulating at a furious rate, and many homes are for sale at give-away prices. The solemnity of Castronuovo's natural landscape was awe-inspiring and the over-whelming kindness of the inhabitants revived my spirit. In all my years in Italy, I have never been made to feel so thoroughly welcomed as I had there. Southern hospitality is alive and well in Basilicata.*

When I arrived at the destination for my interview, Concetta was carefully coifing the few hairs she had into a neat bun atop her head. Before I could utter my first question, she shouted, "We had an osteria full of drunkards here!" and then looked around searchingly, as if we were in the theater and she had jumped her cue. But in fact, our interview did take place in the front room of her daughter Maria Grazia's house, which was once a small grocery whose back room was an osteria where men gathered in the evenings and weekends to down a few glasses of wine and forget about their worries for a while.

I was named after my two grandmothers, Concetta and Filomena. That's me! Concetta Filomena! I am ninety years old this year, but I feel like I'm fifteen! I eat pasta with or without sauce and I like it spicy! And I like to have me a drop of wine! Ah, yessiree, I do! A drop of wine every now and then keeps the blood flowing in your veins! You've got to have your vegetables too, of course, but no meat or fish for me, please! And I like my chilies! Keep them coming!

> *In spite of the scarcity and cost of meat, the regime did not encourage vegetarianism as part of its autarkic imperative. Declared vegetarians were associated with generalized pacifism, which did not coincide with the regime's imperialistic objectives. The future founder of the Vegetarian Society, Aldo Capitini, who did much to spread Gandhi's credo of non-violence in Italy, was expelled from the university in 1933 for his daily silent demonstrations of vegetarianism in the dining hall and his refusal to join the fascist party. Regardless of his personal position, he felt that vegetarianism only made sense in a context of choice, not of lack. When meat was readily available, however, many people did not indulge simply out of habit, and the political stigma of actually calling oneself a vegetarian remained.*

My mother and grandfather died when they were 99, my great-grandfather at 105. My brother is 93 and still drives, but watch out! Ha! He's a bit of a hazard on the road! Every last one of my people had their wits about them to the end! I went to the countryside to visit a cousin a few years ago when he was 102; he died at 105. He was tickled as he could be to see me, invited me in and made coffee! So! What do you say about that!? Ha!

My father was a shoemaker. He died in 1935. He left us three children war orphans. Ah, yes. He was born in 1893 so he was in the Great War, but the poor man got hit in the shoulder with a hand grenade. It blew a good sized chunk of his shoulder off, but when he died twenty years later, the doctor wrote that it was because of a piece of shrapnel left inside him that never give him a moment's peace. Even after all them years, it was still the war killed him. I don't know, though. Coulda been the doctor was just saying that so's my mamma could keep getting his war money, and us children could get benefits. Weren't no doubt though that he was hurtin' a good amount. He told us that he seen that fella with the grenade take the stopper out and throw it over his way. It was like a snapshot he kept in his mind. Click! Three days later he woke up in a hospital bed. He got a bronze medal for his troubles. I guess that was what a shoulder was worth. Bronze.

Papa had a workshop in town. He was *ciabattino*, a shoemaker. He went house-to-house making shoes for families, you know, like they did back then. He traveled on his mule into the countryside, or sometimes he just walked, and would make the shoes right then and there. The folks he was working for that day would let him bed down in their barn or wherever they found a spot. A family paid a flat rate of, let's say, twelve kilos of wheat, or the like, for a pair of shoes and a year of shoe repair, because the man who made your shoes also fixed them. Well, of course! That just makes sense! Like shoe insurance. But, for the repairs, they had to bring the shoes in to the workshop. They had metal plates on the bottom so they wouldn't wear out. Back then you could always hear folks coming from far away! And, we knew some people's gait, and we'd say, "Oh, that's so-and-so coming!" Ha! When he was away making shoes, he would leave Monday morning and return Saturday evening, trying to get to as many folks in as he could from a certain area. He had three apprentices who helped out too.

My mother was born in 1896. I was eleven when my father died, my brother thirteen, and my sister seven. Things were very hard for us then. Mamma would get up at 4 o'clock in the morning so's she could get some work done in the fields and be back at 7 o'clock to wake us kids up and open the shop. She never stopped. Work, work, work, work, work. That's all she did.

I went to school until my father died. There weren't no real school here, I mean, no schoolhouse. Kindly folks in town would take turns letting us come to their house, one day here, another there. There was five different houses that let us do school and three teachers. first and second grade were together, third and fourth grade, and then fifth separate. I finished the third grade, ha-ha! And then I did the 4th grade three times because, well, I didn't take a liking to school! Ha-ha! How could the teacher pass me when I never did a stitch of work!? Ha! Nope, I never made it to the fifth grade. They didn't want the likes of me no how! My mother was none too happy 'bout it, and she made no bones 'bout lettin' me know! She only finished the 3rd grade herself and wanted better for me. Papa never went to school but he picked up a little of reading and writing on his own. When he died, Mamma quit hounding me about it. She was a good mother and loved us dearly, rest in peace. The teacher felt sorry for us, for our loss, and I remember her crying, begging me to try to do better. She was at her wits end with me, poor soul!

In these parts, when the head of the family dies, you nail a big black cloth bow up over the front door, and the mourning time doesn't stop till that cloth fades to white, till it is all weathered and faded with the sun and rain. You can still see them even today, and here in the south, a widow wears her black mourning clothes for the rest of her life. My mother was always dressed in black and she died in black. She was 39 when she became a widow and she died when she was 99. Always in black, black stockings, black skirt, black blouse, black shoes. Black. My father died on March 14th. There I was, eleven, and dressed in black every day 'cause us kids had to wear black for three years. A year after my father died, I was still dressed in black, and my teacher saw me and tore my black scarf off my head and said, "That's enough!" She was a friend of the family and she couldn't bear to see us that way. Mamma let us stop wearing our black clothes before three years was out, but it went against customs.

I was sort of a dunce, but my brother Francesco liked school and went to do his exam to qualify for middle school when he was still in his mourning blacks. He had a real drive for school. He wasn't gonna be like everybody else around here! He wanted to be a real somebody.

As was true of most small towns, Castronuovo had no middle school, and Concetta's mother could not afford to send her son to study in another town. Commuting was out of the question for Francesco, as it was a three-hour walk just to get to a bus that could take him to a town with a middle school. Although they rarely succeeded, children were allowed to qualify for middle school, get a private tutor for three years, and then take the middle school equivalency exam. Concetta's brother not only qualified, but he organized his own studies in accordance with the school curriculum and taught himself. After finishing middle school, he continued on in the same way for high school. After another five years of self-study, he took the high school exam and received his diploma. All the while, he worked at the local post office getting up at 5:30 a.m. to run the mail to a drop-off point. Once he finished his studies he became a schoolteacher and later the town mayor.

Sacrifices, sacrifices! Ah, but the envy! Envy! Lots of people were envious of him: no father, hard worker, self-taught. He did his exams and finished school, and right out of school, he became a teacher. Others who were better off didn't do near so well. Then when the war came, he didn't go because he was too short! Ha! Lots of folks from here went to war. Lots of folks died.

When we was little, my mother already had the small grocery and osteria. The grocery gave us an extra bit of trade, but the real business was the osteria. Here in this very room where we're sitting was the shop, and that room back there was the place where men went to drink and play cards. When I was about twelve, I started working for my mother in the shop, serving in the osteria. I had to keep an eye out too that nobody pocketed our glasses. It was only a few tables and chairs, nothing more than that. We had wine, vermouth, and liquors – rum, licorice, *strega*, marsala – everything. Lots of drinking, lots of yarns spun, and a few fights, even ones with knives! Once when I was just a signorina, I reached up and grabbed the arm of a man who had a drawn knife and was about to stab somenody! But even though I was a fatherless young woman with nobody there at the end of the day to defend me, the men was always real respectful of me. If somebody used foul words when I was serving, the other fellas would say, "How dare you use that language around young Miss Concetta! Now you make your apologies!" Nobody ever laid a hand on me. That goes for my mother too, who was a young widow. Sometimes things got heated when the men was tipsy, but this was a respectable place. Nobody ever got hurt, just drunk and sometimes, oh my! Sometimes they got stinky drunk!

The police didn't come round poking their nose in because an osteria could stay open even all night, so long as there was customers. Some folks wore out their welcome because we had a fireplace and kept it good and stoked in the winter. There was five other osterias in town, so we had to keep the place warm to bring in trade, or the men would be headin' off to cozier corners. Them other watering holes had to heat their place by bringing in hot coals and puttin' them in a brazier. We was the only ones with a right good fireplace, so we had lots of regulars. In the summer some of 'em wandered off to the other places, but our place was full up in the winter. This might seem like a sleepy town to you now, but there was about 3,000 folks living here back then, and only a little over 1,200 now.

To keep 'em drinking and happy, we made roasted dried fava beans and chickpeas as a snack to go with the wine. And if they stayed, they drank; we saw to that. Some of them drank on credit, and at the end of the month it was always, "Come on, Giuseppe! Time to pay up! Come on you all! Payment's due!" Some did, some didn't. Sometimes there was somebody would come into the shop begging my mother for food on credit. She knew weren't no way they could pay for it later, so she'd ask them to give us a hand in the field in exchange. We didn't have no animals, so everything had to be done by hand. An extra body in the field worked out for us too.

Folks in town tried to help each other out when they could, but it was asking a lot when there was so little to go round. Usually, folks didn't even have enough for themselves. And in the end, it was usually poor folks helping other poor folks. You didn't dare go to the church for help, eh, no siree! They was drinking our blood, they was! Every year we give them priests our "devotional wheat," and it piled up higher and higher! Those gluttons! What they didn't use for themselves, they sold, makin' money off us poor folks, widows and children! They didn't do nothing for the poor! Me and my family wasn't even the worst off and we was always just round the corner from hunger.

Lots of kids didn't have the uniform for Fascist Saturday because they didn't have the money, but we all went. Us kids who had the uniform was real proud because weren't nobody had clothes of their own that nice! My mamma bought me the uniform because I done pestered her for it till she couldn't bear it no more, but my brother and sister didn't have one. Most people around these parts didn't even have underwear, so the uniform seemed like something out of a dream. The teachers would say, "Come, children! Let's all sing, sing, sing! Songs of

Mussolini!" And they told us about all the good things Mussolini was doing for the poor people, and how we should love the Patria more than anything. It was the New Empire, they said, and we was gonna get rich in Africa, and everyone would have all the bread they could possibly eat! At school and on the street we gave each other the Roman salute. If you didn't do it, there was talk. Everyone was always watching. "Something should be done about those child-eating communists!" they used to say. Folks jabbered on and on about the "Patria," but I don't even think we really knew what that meant. Heck, I sure didn't know! Ha!

We didn't have a mayor here; we had a *podestà*, a fascist magistrate. He was a bad, bad man. They was Black Shirts and they put a good fright in us! You know, there's lots of folks round here my age named Benito because you got a compensation from the government if you named your son after the Duce. If you wanted to work, you had to be a party member, no bones 'bout that. You wasn't gonna get no social assistance of any sort if you wasn't a party member. My family really didn't care one way or the other about politics. My brother Francesco was always on a low boil inside against the fascio, and later in life, he became the first communist mayor of our town!

Ernesto Pelo and Angelo Schetino, and some other good-for-nothing fella... eh, I can't remember anymore, they was the fascist heavies. There was plenty of people wanted to punch their lights out, but they had to keep quiet. We was all poor folks here. Most of 'em couldn't read, but worse, the ones who could read didn't! Folks here didn't know nothing about this or that government, and those men in charge, well, they was just as ignorant! They could write their names, but not much else.

Just to tell you how it was, on Fascist Saturday you couldn't work because in the afternoon you had to attend fascist functions, and one Saturday, I saw a poor peasant farmer out hoeing in his field, minding his own business, and them ignoramuses come by and beat him sore for it. Them Black Shirt fellas didn't know nothin' about government; they wasn't politicians or police. They was just pushing and shoving to make sure the folks stayed scared. The fascists didn't want smart people because they had ideas of their own. They wanted tough stupid people to do their dirty work. Shops couldn't be open on the fascist day but they could be open on Sunday, on the Lord's day! Most of the business came through then because the country folks were in town on Sunday for a little church, a bit of trade, and lots of drinking. Let me tell you what life was in a nutshell: lots of poor people and lots of other people taking advantage of poor people, like doctors, overlords, and priests.

There wasn't no health system here, so if you needed the doctor, it was a terrible problem. Things may have been different in the north, but here we didn't have nothing! Doctors knew what you had and would take whatever they could get their hands on. I know someone called the doctor and he said, "There is no point in me curing your son because it will cost more than you have, so you should just let him die." To get the doctor to come for a difficult birthing, you had to sell your mule. The woman upstairs from us died giving birth because the doctor wouldn't come. She didn't have nothing to sell. They took your livestock, your house, your land... whatever you had. Yessiree, them doctors was rich! Yes, indeed! Some people would raise an extra pig each year just in case they needed the doctor! There wasn't no midwives round these parts till later. The older women of the village would come round to lend a hand when it was your time, but if there was something wrong come birthing time, then the baby or the mother or both died. That's how it was. Birth was always in the shadow of death. They went hand in hand. This is how it was until a good piece after the war.

The richest folks were three overlords in town with big manor farms and lots of folks slaving for them. But even they wasn't really rich. They was just the rich of the poor. They ate meat and drank coffee, though, so to us that was rich! And the priests wasn't too bad off neither. And then, you had your contadini, who'd walk three hours into town to sell vegetables from a wagon, and walk another three hours home. They only ever made a few lire. At the end of the day, so's to make what money they could, and not drag them vegetables home again, they'd sell off the lot of whatever was left for a pittance. My mother tried her best to get in on those sales, but lots of folks were up to the same game.

We didn't live here then. This was our shop. We lived just up the road from here. There was a big room with the hearth and two bedrooms. The brick oven was in my bedroom. Everybody had a brick oven in the house because we all made our own bread at home; weren't no bakeries here. There wasn't no running water in the house neither. We kept a 25-liter barrel of water in the house and we drew water out of that whenever we needed it. Then, when it was empty, we went to the pump and got more and carried the barrel back on our head. We didn't bother bathing. Used up too much water. There was a sort of cliff area not far off where folks went to take care of the other business. It was sort of private. We just didn't watch the other people. Skirts was long then, and most people didn't have underwear, so you squatted and did what you had to do. There was a woman in town who never knew underwear, couldn't be bothered. We didn't have no toilet paper neither. I don't really know how we stayed clean. I guess we didn't think about it. Maybe, just maybe, you took a bath once a month. Maybe. I don't remember. Are you recording this?

We didn't have store-bought soap; we made it ourselves: caustic soda, five kilos of lard. Lard was very important. When you split open your pig, the first thing you looked at was how much fat was on it. The meat was a second thought after the fat because we needed that fat to cook, preserve, and clean. The fat got cooked down into lard, and you were left with your solids, called *ciccioli, mmm, buoni!* We had olive oil here, but we was real, real sparing with that. *Poco poco!* There was three butcher shops in town. Once a week they each took their turn butchering an animal. Folks ate so little meat here because no one had any money, and there wasn't no refrigerators, so if they wanted to make a living, the butchers had to take turns. One week this one, another week that one, you know? This one did a goat, that one did a sheep. When the meat was freshly butchered, it hung outside the shop so that everyone could see what was for sale that week. In the warmer months, they covered it with a veil to keep the flies off. That was well before the war even.

Our town had always been a poor town, but near everyone had their own vegetable garden, with potatoes, beans, favas cabbage, peas, and everything, but most of all peppers. We's famous for our dried red peppers.

The Peperone di Senise *bears the highly prized title IGP* - indicazione geografico protetto. *These sweet peppers are a deep red, mid-sized, conical variety. They are strung up by the stem in large bunches like garland and hung out to dry in the summer sun. To prepare them, they are deep-fried until crisp and just browned then added to different dishes.*

We used to make beans and cabbage with crispy fried peppers on the side. The beans was slow cooked in a terracotta pot on the fire and the cabbage was boiled. Then we fried the peppers. The beans and cabbage got mixed together with garlic and a bit of oil, and then we served it with the peppers all around it. There was a lot of stealing going on from other people's vegetable gardens, ha-ha! Everybody knew, but folks sure got steamin' mad when they saw their cabbage gone!

My father was a hard workingman. He built a mill that run with a cistern system, just a simple mill. We let it out to a man and in return he give us a bit of flour from the trade he took in. Plus, we grew our own wheat and he ground that for free [*Basilicata is one of the breadbasket regions of Italy because of its ideal climate that produces high quality durum wheat*]. At my house for breakfast, we had milk from a neighbor woman's goat and a piece of bread. Sometimes, though, breakfast was water and bread, bread and water, when times was bad. It wasn't white bread though. Mamma kept as much of the grain as possible because you got more bread that way. White bread was for signori! As it was, we'd have to buy a bit of wheat to make it through the year.

The wine in the osteria came from our own vineyard. It was pretty big. Come harvest time, my mother hired eight or ten men from town to bring it in and make the wine we used in the osteria. They started work at 6 a.m. and then at 9 o'clock, she brought breakfast to them in the fields, a frittata with onions or something. Each of 'em got one liter of wine for the day, so they usually started out to work after a small glass of wine in the morning. Lunch at noon was *pasta fagioli,* with bread or calzones filled with chicory. Snack time came at around 4 p.m., a frittata or a fried dried pepper with an anchovy inside; then before they went home, they had dinner in the osteria, *cavatelli* or *orecchietti* [*short, typically southern homemade pasta*] with beans or turnip greens and maybe, maybe a piece, a small piece, of salami. It was mostly pasta and beans, beans and pasta, maybe an itty-bitty morsel of meat, but, oh, teeny-tiny! If there was an egg it was like a holiday! Mamma kept a watchful eye on costs. The farmhands didn't make too much money, so food was an important part of the their pay. We always ate a lot of beans and cabbage, pasta and beans, and beans with vegetables, and just beans.

We couldn't have pasta every day 'cause that was a luxury, and in my house we hardly had meat more than twice a year, at Christmas and Easter. A lot of folks kept the cookin' animals in the house, right there in the house in their own living space! Some let them just run free, and others kept them in cages, here and there, under the bed, or in the space for wood under the oven. It was mostly chickens and guinea pigs. We called them "baby rabbits", but they wasn't really rabbits. In my house the little critters was in cages, though. Guinea pig is a specialty of this area. We's famous for our "little rabbit" dishes.

You can get them even if you don't have a trusted butcher because there's always someone in town who raises them. Just the other day, Angelo says to me, "You want to come over and get a few rabbits? I got way too many of them!" I heard that some children these days keep them as pets. How strange! They are tasty so many ways. You can fry them or make a nice fricassee. They're good roasted too. Ain't a whole lot of eatin' on them, but it's a nice tender meat.

Last year the national TV come to do a story on our traditional foods. We set them a nice table with a big platter of guinea pigs. We fixed 'em up whole, braised in a clay pot and then arranged spread-eagle on the platter. When the journalists tried them, one of them said right out loud, "I don't know how many years it is that I have not come across this dish! It is exquisite!" He left a plate piled high like this with their little bones! When we was sayin' our good-byes to the TV crew, we asked him, "When are you going to come back again?" and he said,

"When you make me the guinea pigs again!" They also make a good sauce for pasta.

Coniglietti brasati ripieni: Stuffed braised guinea pig

4 guinea pigs
2 thick slices old bread
2 onions
oil or lard for frying
1 egg
½ cup grated hard cheese
salt and pepper
1 garlic clove
1 small bunch parsley
1 small carrot
white wine

Using a small sharp knife, cut a quick slit in the throat of the guinea pig over a sink or container. Remove the fur without damaging the under skin, which must remain intact. Remove the internal organs, setting aside the liver, heart and lungs. Leave the carcass to soak in water, changing continuously until it is limpid and free of blood. Soak leftover bread in a separate bowl until soft. Squeeze out as much of the water as possible and set aside. Wash the offal and mince finely. Fry in oil or lard with one chopped onion until cooked through. In a bowl, mix bread egg, cheese, offal, salt and pepper. Stuff it into the cavity of the guinea pig and sew closed with kitchen string. Prepare a mince of onion, garlic, parsley, and carrot and sauté until soft in a Dutch oven or terracotta pot. Salt the bundles and place in the pot with the sauté with the limbs outstretched. Pour in enough water and white wine (half and half) to just cover. Cover the pot with a fitted lid and braise over a low flame for about an hour and a half until the outer skin and meat are tender. Males will have a tougher skin and may require longer cooking times.

Most everyone had a pigsty, but that was outside. Chickens inside, but pigs outside, thank you very much! Ha! So, at Easter there was a special dessert, a calzone filled with salami, eggs, and cheese from the manor farms.

*Although this is a savory dish, they refer to it as an Easter dessert be-
cause it was eaten at the end of the meal. Given the costly ingredients, it
was kept until the end when everyone had already been sated and could
only eat a small piece.*

We had real coffee in our shop. The beans came in raw and we would
toast them for customers, but we never drank it ourselves because my
mother needed to sell it. We could smell it, but we couldn't drink it!
Really, though, we couldn't eat most of the stuff Mamma kept in the
shop. She'd collect the broken pasta bits, little by little, and when there
were enough she would make us a plate of pasta. I remember one terrible day when she was out, and had left me alone in the shop. For
some time, I done had my eye on the *confetti* [*sugar-coated almonds used
for celebrations like weddings and baptisms*] and left there alone, me and
them, I couldn't resist no more. I ate a handful, that's all! No more! My
mother had one keen eye, though, and noticed that some was missin'.
Oh! Did she give me a talking to! "How do you think we's gonna make
it with you eating up our profits, Missy?! How ever are we gonna make
ends meet!?" I felt guilty for months!

You see, before Papa died, seemed like things they was picking
up, so my parents borrowed money to buy a flat. Then, when he died,
Mamma was left with us three kids to raise and a huge debt on her
hands. And so, from then on, she was out laboring in our fields, taking care of the shop, and serving in the osteria in the evening, so she
didn't need her own children gobbling up the profits while she was
out! She was a worker. Some years, she would say, "Let's raise two pigs
this year. We can sell one in the market (as we always did) and keep
one for ourselves." But that was almost never how it went because
when it came slaughter time, she would say, "Don't look too good for
folks with debts to have meat on the table and a full larder." So she
would sell both pigs. Doctors had meat, not people like us. That debt
tortured her night and day.

Mamma minded the grocery during the day because the men usually only came into drink after work was done. There was coffee, dried
bulk pasta brought in trucks from Salerno, sugar, salted anchovies in

twelve kilo tins, canned sardines, and those sugar-coated almonds I already told you about. The pasta come in fifty-kilo crates, spaghetti, ziti, perciatelli, bucatine. There was six groceries in town. Most everybody made everything themselves, so groceries only had the things people didn't already make at home. Everyone made conserva so we didn't keep it in the shop until later when things got better and folks had the spending money to buy things instead of making them. But before that, everyone made what they could at home. Everyone, everything! *Tutti, tutto!* So, a grocery round these parts was only a side business.

When I met my husband... I don't remember exactly when that was... Anyway, he was 1'90", *un bel giovane!* Don't know what on earth he saw in little me! He was a Specialized Mechanic, repaired olive oil presses. He come here from another town to do a job for his aunt, who had married here in Castronuovo. One day, I saw these two figures on the road and I called out saying, "Hey wait up and we can walk back to town together!" And that is how I met him. He was supposed to be leaving the next day, but he said to his aunt, "You know, I think maybe I'll stay on a bit longer 'cause I met this girl and I want to get to know her." I had some other fellas interested too. I was even engaged for four years and then out of a blue sky he just up and went, ain't never come back.

When someone is interested, they test the ground by asking around town about "that girl" to see if she might be the right one. So, the whole town knows about it before the girl herself does! When it come time to leave, his aunt said, "Go back home to Bari and you give it a good thinking over." While he was away, he wrote a letter to his aunt about me, but the letter ended up in my cousin's hands and they took the letter to my uncle. My uncle asked if I was interested. Well, his prospects was next to nothing, but he was such a strapping young man, so I said, "Yes, Yes! I'm interested!" He came back and we went to the town hall to sign a civil act.

The civil act was a promissory note, which officially engaged a couple to marry, although it was not legally binding. It gave a relationship public legitimacy. By the 50's, it had fallen out of use. It was also not unheard of for a couple to get married in the town hall with one of the

*spouses absent. Someone else would stand in for the absent member,
and the ceremony took place just the same.*

We was engaged for a long time because there wasn't much work for
him here, and he was a bit, well, let's say he wasn't a tranquil sort. He
couldn't set up shop here because he didn't have no money. But, that
gave me time to work on my *corredo* [*trousseau or hope chest*]. I made everything myself, the sheets all with crocheted borders. I still do stitch-
ery and I don't even need glasses. It is good for me because I have
to count and think about every stitch. My mother taught me, like all
mothers did. We did our needlework even when we was in the wagon
going out to work in the fields. When no one was in the shop, I worked
on my corredo. That's what girls did. We was never idle. It keeps my
brain in shape. I never go walking or any of that business. This old bag
of bones is what it is, but my noggin still works. That's what gives me
the will to go on.

Me and my husband married in '54, but he left for Switzerland soon
after, where it was easier for him to get work. Lots of folks from here
had to leave because there was no work. My sister and her husband
took off for Argentina, where there was a community of Lucani. They
set up a tailoring business, but they wasn't too happy. They moved to
New York some years later and stayed there till they died. My husband
died abroad too, when my daughter was eleven years old, the same age
as me when my father died. He died on our wedding anniversary, April
28. He'd write us from Switzerland and come home for Christmas and
the month of August. He smoked a good bit and had something with
his thyroid, so between some of this and some of that, he wasn't long
for this world. Like my mother, I ran the grocery and the osteria, so I
got by. There was more products in the grocery by that time, canned
milk, flour, and more pasta shapes than before. My daughter started to
work with me just like I done with my mother. My husband died in '72
and we dressed in black for a long time, and just like it happened with
me, my daughter's teacher come and give me a talking to for keeping
her in mourning clothes! Ha! All black. She was right because times
had changed. But I keep to my blacks. Just like my mother done.

I went to Switzerland with my brother to make the arrangements for havin' my husband shipped back home. I had them put a glass window on the coffin over his face because when he died there was three other dead Italians coming back to Italy, and I was scared they was going to mix his coffin up with one of them other fellas! I didn't have my wits about me. I was grief stricken. I wanted to ride back with him, but undertaker wouldn't let me. He says to me, "Signora, he's not the first corpse we've shipped and he won't be the last, so don't go telling us how to do our job."

Even here in the south things started to turn around after the war, but for a town of wretches, it didn't take a heck of a lot to make you feel like you was rich. Just a couple things more than we had before, and we thought we was high class! I see young people today, so unhappy. They want so many things. Things! Everybody's wanting to live like they's rich. There's a little song that goes: *Don't let the contadino know | how good cheese is with pears. | But the contadino is no fool; | he knew it before the padrone did.* Now everybody thinks they gotta have pears and cheese every day.

If something happens to somebody in this town, good or bad, we all feel it like a family. If there's somebody ain't opened their door for a day, we know. We do what we can for each other. When we pass on the street we smile and say hello. What does a little kindness cost you? Nothing! We all grow up together and grow old together. That's the kind of town this is.

Intermezzo

La cosiddetta "Dieta Mediterranea" –
The So-called "Mediterranean Diet"

> In Italy, it is easier for people to scarf down
> tons of potential raw sugar, because that is, in
> essence, what foods made with white flour are.
> The common provincial idea, according to which
> Italian-style Mediterranean food is heaven sent,
> gets repeated like a mantra on every morning
> television program, where a flock of followers,
> believers or non, sing the praises of flour [and]
> pasta. … What really scares me is the propagandistic
> aspect of eating Italian style. … Italian nationalism,
> when talking about food, verges on racism.
> — FORMER ITALIAN SENATOR PAOLO GUZZANTI,
> *DOWN WITH THE MEDITERRANEAN DIET*

In 2013, UNESCO formally inscribed the 2010 decision to include the "Mediterranean diet" on the "Representative List of the Intangible Cultural Heritage of Humanity" as follows:

The Mediterranean diet involves a set of skills, knowledge, rituals, symbols and traditions concerning crops, harvesting, fishing, animal husbandry, conservation, processing, cooking, and particularly the sharing and consumption of food. Eating together is the foundation of the cultural identity and continuity of communities throughout the Mediterranean basin. It is a moment of social exchange and communication, an affirmation and renewal of family, group or community identity. The Mediterranean diet emphasizes values of hospitality, neighborliness, intercultural dialogue and creativity, and a way of life guided by respect for diversity. It plays a vital role in cultural spaces, festivals and celebrations, bringing together people of all ages, conditions and social classes. It includes the craftsmanship and production of traditional receptacles for the transport, preservation and consumption of food, including ceramic plates and glasses. Women play an important role in transmitting knowledge of the Mediterranean diet: they safeguard its techniques, respect seasonal rhythms and festive events, and transmit the values of the element to new generations. Markets also play a key role as spaces for cultivating and transmitting the Mediterranean diet during the daily practice of exchange, agreement and mutual respect.

Throughout the world, nations, ethnicities, and communities everywhere strive for and suffer the encroaching estrangement from this utopic description. How is it that this florid pronouncement has become the exclusive prerogative of the countries whose shores are lapped by the seas of the Mediterranean basin? Surely husbandry, agronomic practices, markets, conviviality, and methods of serving and preparing food, so generically defined, are the essential elements defining the way all humans organize their societies and facilitate coexistence. Sociocultural landscapes vary in their details, but this descriptor is a cultural common denominator, not a differentiator. In the final analysis, it says nothing about the particulars that specifically delineate the Mediterranean diet from any other. Advocates might argue that the tenacity of these tenets is stronger in the Mediterranean Basin, but it still begs the question – What is the Mediterranean diet?

The Mediterranean diet underwritten by UNESCO is limited to Italy, Greece, Morocco, and Spain, although in 2013 Cyprus, Croatia, and Portugal (who wanted to be in on the game, although it rejects the name "Mediterranean diet" in favor of the "Atlantic diet," logically, as they are not on the Mediterranean) were tacked onto the list. Albania, France, Montenegro, Slovenia, Bosnia-Herzegovina, Israel, Croatia, Turkey, Lebanon, Syria, Malta, and the rest of North Africa have not been admitted to "Club Med," in spite of their geographic qualifications. The original 2007 proposal advanced by Spain (excluding Morocco at that juncture) had been rejected. Not to be daunted, the Italian Minister of Food and Agriculture assembled an ad hoc task force, headed by an Italian UNESCO delegate, to push the proposal through, which it successfully managed in 2010. The claim was that of resuscitating, protecting, and preserving the pre-WWII nutritional model that had been lost during the economic boom of the 1960s and 70s. Vito Teti describes the reality of the model they were alluding to:

> In the first half of this century, contadini … in the southern regions were essentially eating cornbread, potatoes, tomatoes, peppers, and legumes and dressing them with pig fat. The "Mediterranean trinity" (olive oil, wheat bread and wine) was usually found only on the tables of the wealthy, and in the hopes and dreams of the poor. Pasta was still a luxury item, and fresh fish rarely arrived to non-coastal areas (1998).

Efforts to fix foodways in time deny the spontaneous culinary evolution inherent in any cuisine: "The mythology of the 'Mediterranean diet' puts us at risk of forgetting the history, the stability and the revolutions, the later adaptations, and the constant combinations that the Mediterranean and southern Italy have traversed from the ancient past to today," (Teti, 1998).

Despite restricted membership, any attempt to reduce and encapsulate the vastly different dietary and cultural practices that characterize the favored nations could not but default to universals. The projection of these universal values as the exclusive claim of one's own select group results in "gastrocentric" posturing and cultural navel gazing.

When the news broke in Italy of the UNESCO benediction of the Mediterranean diet, the English language periodical *Italian Journal of Public Heath* applauded it as a long awaited recognition, interpreting it as an award for "best cuisine":

> The term "Mediterranean Diet" was coined, *paradoxically,* by the Americans in the early '60s and today ... the UNESCO declares that this century-long cookery culture, ... represents a *"Cultural Heritage of Humanity"* ... the UNESCO takes sides in defense of genuineness, flavor, food taste, and chiefly health promotion in order to promote healthy eating habits, handing over the legitimized sceptre to 'Our' peculiar food tradition as well as to our benevolent good -nature.
>
> Into this framework, credit is due to the remarks produced through epidemiological research – and an ethnological one at that: ... Ancel Keys, first disclosed the virtues of the "Mediterranean Diet" and hence 'he' perceived and communicated its beneficial and protective effects (Saulle, 2010). [*Translation/English version theirs*]

Perhaps the more apropos question is, "What is the Mediterranean Diet?"

In 1920, heart disease appeared to be an emerging "epidemic," though the concomitant development of diagnostic tools to establish its existence and determine it as the cause of death may account for this perception. Although the claim was unsubstantiated, an increase in dietary fat was said to be the culprit of the epidemic. A plethora of new technology allowing for differentiated study of lipids hit laboratories in the 1950s, and the Cholesterol Age was off and running. Heart disease became the malady du jour of the medical establishment, and the race was on for the fame and authoritative claim that awaited whomsoever could unlock its mysteries.

Ancel Keys, ambitious originator and propagator of the Mediterranean Diet, is presently undergoing a second wind of notoriety, this time as the demonic poster child of low-carbohydrate advocates. Oddly, his early work set out to demonstrate that dietary cholesterol was *not* the offending element of heart disease and that dietary fat intake had little influence on serum cholesterol levels. "When Keys fed men for months at a time on diets either high or low in cholesterol, it made no difference to their cholesterol levels," (Taubes: 2007).

After attending a conference in Rome, he did a theoretical about-face and decided to investigate places where there was a low incidence of cardio-pathologies to observe what they were eating. Or more precisely, he specifically sought out a community with a low incidence of heart disease and a low consumption of meat, which led him to Crete and Nicotera (Calabria) in order to confirm his new position. Other locations, where the results did not square with his reformulated hypothesis, were summarily ignored. Also ignored were the high mortality rates and chronic malnutrition that characterized the "heart-healthy" areas used to support his claim. Keys forged ahead with his field research, forcibly yoking together high-fat diets with heart disease, and writing off anyone with contrasting studies. The evidence was flimsy, his methods questionable, and his findings biased, but nonetheless, he presented his results to the medical community as foregone conclusions. "From the inception of the diet – heart hypothesis in the early 1950s, those who argued that dietary fat caused heart disease accumulated the evidential equivalent of a mythology to support their belief. These myths are still passed on faithfully to the present day," (Taubes, 2007). The circumspect American Heart Association published a lengthy report in 1957 refuting the cholesterol theory and the unscientific methods of its advocates. Only four years later Keys et al. formed a committee and coerced the AHA into issuing a public warning to reduce dietary fat, paving the way for what would later be called the Mediterranean Diet.

Contrary to the overriding emphasis in the UNESCO diet, Key's Diet made no reference to a cultural value system, and indeed, his book, *Eat Well, Stay Well*, is devoid of actual recipes from the local cuisine of the areas upon which he based his theory. Likewise, the menu suggestions do not reflect the seasonal eating habits of any particular region but focus singularly on health rather than taste. The Diet was an artificial construct, derived neither from a naturally occurring phenomenon nor any specific location; therefore, actual study participants verifying the efficacy of the Diet could not have existed at the time he was disseminating nutritional counsel.

In the puzzling introduction to the Italian version of Key's book, Giorgio Bini approaches the Diet from the angle of renunciation, in extreme contrast to the celebratory tone of the UNESCO declaration. He reassures readers:

To the consolation of many, it is indeed an error to think that spaghetti is fattening. Spaghetti is only fattening in conjunction with the quantity of calories that it supplies, because putting on weight is essentially a question of calories, and spaghetti supplies fewer than that of other foods, without sauce, of course. In fact, in Italy, even though the percentage of fat and obese people *is clearly higher than that of the USA* or the United Kingdom, it is also true that the percentage of heart disease is lower." [*As for the recipes in the book,*] Actually, there aren't any awful recipes intended to force people to eat badly. Some of them are just put together better than others (1962). [*Italics mine.*]

Many of the listings in Key's Diet were as foreign to some Italians as they must have been to Americans (St. Hubert Venison Consommé, recipe from the Waldorf-Astoria?). Acquiring even the more recognizable "Mediterranean" foodstuffs had a detrimental effect on the maintenance of regional distinctions and overall quality of Italian food, as culinary scholar Alberto Capatti illustrates:

The prevalence of the American approach, renamed "Mediterranean," created a large market for [olive] oil that extended throughout the regions dominated by butter consumption. The difficulty of supplying the non-coastal areas with fish led to inevitable transports of frozen products from the oceans. The demand for produce meant that the distribution of vegetables would become ever more reliant on processing and packaging, while the intercontinental transport of fruit

would cancel out normal expectations of ripeness and season-
ality (2014).

Even its most staunch Italian proponent, Dr. Anna Ferro-Luzzi, whose
lifework has been to propagate the benefits of the Mediterranean Diet,
concedes that as a scientific term it should not be bandied about until
it is clearly definable. And for now, it is not. The convoluted evolution of the Mediterranean diet has created a vacuum of uncertainty
that hawkeyed peddlers of Med-lore products have eagerly cashed in
on. The nostalgia industry unabashedly assumes many guises, be they
organic, artisanal, or brand name to proselytize its wares, and the pre-
vailing conception amongst consumers is that if it is on the shelves of
the local supermarket, you're good to go. Under "Practical advice for
following the Mediterranean diet," olive oil mogul Fratelli Carli says in
its 100th anniversary cookbook: "All you have to do is use foods that
are naturally available in this geographic area and prepare them in a
simple and tasty way," (2011). The sky's the limit.

The love of Italian food is, as the Italians say, "another pair of
handcuffs," and proponents would do well to steer clear of such mud-
dled ethnocentric/dietetic terminology. In a friendly public debate in
Australia between a French chef and an Italian chef, both of whom
have made their home Down Under, they were challenged to establish
who had the better cuisine. The Frenchman asserted confidently that
French cuisine is the very foundation of all fine western cuisine worthy
of calling itself such. It was they, and no other, who had single-handed-
ly created the concept of fine dining. The Italian chef acknowledged
that there may indeed be some truth in that, but, he added, Italian cuisine is indubitably the most *loved* the world over. The Frenchman had
no rebuttal. Regardless of the mutations, exportations, distortions,
falsifications, and "diets," Italian food is indeed more than a world-
class cuisine; it is arguably the cuisine of the world. It, more than any
other, has been adopted and adapted into homes, hearts, and eateries
throughout the (qualified) world. Italian food is a now a staple with an
international passport, just because it's good.

Former senator and journalist Paolo Guzzanti, quoted at the opening of this intermezzo, was warned that he would surely meet his end

if he dared to denigrate pillars of the Mediterranean diet. "Now they are really going to kill him," said a friend to Guzzanti's wife. "He can't think he can write a book against the Mediterranean diet and get away with it. Tell him to stay on the alert" (2009). But his wife is American, so if push comes to shove, he has a scapegoat.

Rosa

Born 1927 – Giaia, Petralia Soprana, Palermo

As soon as I pulled up the drive, Rosa rushed out to greet me in front of her idyllic Tuscan homestead wearing an apron with "Sicilia" written across on the front. Like many destitute families from the Deep South, she and her husband had taken advantage of the postwar exodus from the country to the city to take up vacant posts as farmhands in the milder clime of central Italy. While many Italians had sought to flee the hardships of country life altogether, others felt they were not cut out for urban life and were content simply to escape the gripping poverty of the southern regions and start anew. After years of hard work, Rosa and her husband had saved enough to buy up one of the many vacant farms in southern Tuscany.

Such was her desire to be agreeable during our interview that she tried to answer my questions in the positive, even if it stood in direct contrast with something she had said before. Fortunately, some of her children were present to keep her on track and would say, "No, Mamma! You know that is not how it was!" Although her first language is the Sicilian dialect, arguably another language in itself, she made a valiant effort to speak Italian, assisted when necessary by her daughter who interpreted for us through the rough spots. Rosa's husband, hard of hearing and a man of very few words, sat quietly in an armchair in the corner of the kitchen, looking my way occasionally with intense, penetrating

eyes. Although he is usually in bed by 6pm, he stayed up until the "wee"
hour of 8, while Rosa taught me to make a Sicilian specialty.

The Madonie Mountains are about 70 km southeast of the city of Palermo. That's where I lived in my little village of Giaia. I guess you couldn't even call it a village, really. There was only about ten or fifteen families. The nearest town that we could go to if we needed something was Petralia Soprano, and that was a good 15 kilometers away. When you got to get from one place to another on a mule, well, goodness me, you didn't just go on a whim. You went because you had dealings. We was in the province of Palermo, but funny thing is, I never in all my days, ever even seen the city itself! It was a good piece away and, anyway, we wasn't folks cut out for the city. As it was, had to go 'bout four kilometers just to get to the church, and our school was a forty-minute walk away. That's sort of why I stopped going. I went through the 3rd grade, and... and I was good at school, I was, but naw, it was too far away. I didn't want to go no more, and my folks wasn't much for me goin' anyway. There wasn't no real schoolhouse, only a little room in a house with benches set around a long table. Used that for a desk. There was one teacher for all of us, but weren't a whole lot of us went to school up there where we lived. We got taught all about Mussolini, and all the good things he was doing for the people. I can still remember some of them songs and verses we learned about him. We had to buy our own books and paper, pen and ink, and that was a sight too much for my father.

He was a farmer, but I mean a real simple kinda farmer. He owned the land; didn't have no padrone over him. We got by mostly selling the wheat we grew, but we had us all sorts of legumes: favas, chickpeas, lentils, white beans, plus tomatoes, yeah, lot of tomatoes, and eggplant, all right their on our land. We grew it all ourselves. In Sicily, there was good durum wheat for bread, so we always had bread on the table. For breakfast, me and my two brothers and two sisters had caffè d'orzo and goat milk with bread from our wheat.

We lived so far out of the way that we didn't live like other folks at the time. What I'm sayin' is, we never had that ration card I heard other people tell about, and we didn't do the Fascist Saturday, not even the boys. We just didn't have it. Do you think they were gonna bother for just a few scrappy kids way up in the mountains? And anyway, there was work to tend to. Chores never ended. I did the women's work in the house with my mother, and come harvest time we was all out in the fields. We made conserva with the tomatoes. For us, it was one of our most important foods. It got you through the whole year, and you didn't have to have a refrigerator or nothing. Now that you can put tomatoes up in jars and cans, people don't make much use of conserva, but before, it was a mainstay.

> *Conserva was made in the south and used throughout Italy as the base for sauces. Two tablespoons sufficed to dress five portions of pasta. Sauce was a mere blush of tomato color and flavor that tinged the pasta, not something that would drip as you lifted a forkful to your mouth. Tomatoes were selected, cleaned, and piled onto a sizeable tray that would be placed into a large heated brick oven overnight. The next day they were worked over a large sieve, like a dresser drawer with a screen bottom. This would separate out the pulp from the seeds and peels. The resulting sauce was left in the hot August sun on wooden boards and bought back into the house every evening until it had dried to a thick, almost sliceable, consistency necessary to inhibit the growth of bacteria and mold. It was then placed in clay pots and covered with oil or lard for storage.*

Conserva was real important 'cause we had tagliatelle with tomato sauce for lunch almost every day. Sometimes we had dried pasta 'cause there was a pasta factory one town over. Worked like this, see, we'd take our flour there, and they would make pasta for us like spaghetti or *mezze maniche*. It was a trade, some of our flour for the pasta-making service. See? We usually had fresh pasta though. When we had the dry pasta, we ate it with cabbage or lentils, that kind of stuff. It was all wheat for us; even our polenta was durum semolina gruel, not cornmeal. Wasn't too much meat to speak of, but we did keep chickens and a goat, so there was usually eggs and milk too. In the evening, Mamma would sometimes make a watery soup with tiny pasta and a hunk of old bread and cheese. Papa would sometimes bring back some cheese when he went to a nearby village.

We kept a couple mules too, for gettin' around and haulin' stuff here and there. You couldn't do without 'em 'cause down south folks didn't live right on the farm, I mean right on their land, the way they do in Tuscany. See, we set up in little hamlet, just a cluster of houses, with all the families packed in close to each other. At most, I reckon we got up to as much as twenty families, but it was usually less. So, you see, every day, you had to get to yer piece of land to work it. You either worked yer own plot, or you was working somebody else's 'cause wasn't everybody owned the land outright; you follow? So, trouble was, the land you worked may not've been so near to… well, it wasn't always so near to where you was livin'. Sometimes, in fact, it was real far away. If you didn't have no mule, and some folks didn't, well then, you was flat out just from walking there, even before you started yer workday. Was some folks had to go even ten kilometers to get to their land. And sometimes you had different pieces of land, one here and one over there, so if you didn't have a mule to carry you and yer tools, eh, *Madonna mia,* it took a toll on you. Weren't no way to come back at lunchtime, so whoever was out there had to bring provisions, so's to get them through to evening. When there was a lot of work to see to, weren't no sense in coming back, and they stayed out in the field for a week at a time. But most times, they was back for supper. In wintertime, when there was less to do, they didn't have to go out in the fields every day. Wasn't easy eking out crops outta that dry rocky land in the mountains. But we got by, selling our wheat and legumes and grapes. We wasn't exactly homesteaders. We farmed for money. We had cash crops.

Everybody's house was pretty much the same. All of 'em was made of stone, and the downstairs part was where you kept yer beasts and yer farm tools. Then, there was stairs goin' up to the part where you set up house. It was one big room, see, and then, another big room. So, yeah, it was two rooms.

In 1934, Mussolini conducted a top-secret survey of the housing conditions of peasants. Presumably fearing bad news, no one was allowed access to the results but him. The survey revealed that only 40 per cent of the peasant homes in Sicily were considered fit for human habitation, and that was according to the standards of the day. Nearly all of the dwellings in Italy that were created out of grottos or mud bricks mixed with leaves were located in the south and on the islands. Overcrowding in homes and beds was commonplace, and distinction between the animal stalls and the human living areas was not always clearly delineated.

There was a little separate space where we cooked because in the summer months wasn't no way you could stand havin' the cooking heat right there where you was livin'. You had what was called yer "steam cooker," but I don't know why. There wasn't no steam. It was a brick thing like a table that you built a fire under. It had two holes in the top, big enough so's you could lower a pot into the hole and it got held in place over the flame. You see?

I ain't sayin' that it was always so terrible hot in the mountains. We was at 1,000 meters, and winters sure got awful cold! The snow got real deep sometimes too, even a couple meters. We got snowed in just like what happened in the mountains anywhere. It snowed, but it wasn't a long winter. Folks heated their house by filling copper braziers with charcoal embers and setting 'em around here and there. The idea was that the charcoal was hot, but it didn't make smoke. Well, I tell you, there was plenty of folks got sick from it. The petroleum lamps made smoke too. Now I keep my brazier on the wall for decoration.

You had to have coats and sweaters for the winter, but they was ready made. Funny thing is, everybody wore the same kind. Wasn't nothin' to choose from. We was all desperate poor, so you can bet no one had a closet full of clothes. If the time came you needed a new dress, you bought the fabric and went to a nearby town to have it made how you wanted. The shoemaker came to the house, though. The man who made your shoes saw to the repairs if they broke or got holes in them. Everyone had shoes made for their own feet. Nothing fancy, but they was good shoes with leather soles.

At my house, my folks slept in the first big room and us kids slept in the other room. We kept an enamel pot under the bed for our toilet use, and we dumped it on the compost pile in the morning. During the day, well, you would just squat outside, you know, in a discreet sort of way, in the garden or behind the fig tree. Everybody in the neighborhood did like that. You just turned your head the other way out of courtesy. There wasn't any sort of sewage system or lights. We didn't have no toothbrushes or nothin', but take a look here; 'cept for these two, these is all my own original teeth! I'd rub 'em with a cloth sometimes, but, gosh, I can't say that I made a habit of it. Not like I do now. I brush my teeth every morning and evening. I'd say it's been about twenty years I been brushin' regular like.

> *Dental hygiene has existed in various forms for nearly 5000 years, although the modern brush with a plastic handle and nylon bristles was not mass marketed until 1938. It had been included as a standard part of a soldier's kit in many countries, and they were instructed to brush daily, though widespread use of the synthetic bristle toothbrush came only after WWII. Throughout history in Italy, desperate prayers had been offered up to the patron saint of dentistry, Saint Apollonia, in hopes of assuaging dental distress. Where prayer did not yield results, the local barber or ironsmith stepped in to oblige. The shadowy reverberation of these barbarous practitioners may account for the fact that, despite the availability of dental care through the national healthcare system, by and large, most Italians prefer to pay out-of-pocket for private dental services.*

There was a dry-goods store in with our group of houses. That's where you bought yer socks, dry biscuits, pencils, and the like. Weren't no other shops, but there was these men who travelled with mules from town to town selling their wares. They packed them poor beasts down with things to sell, or had them hauling carts up and down the mountains. In towns like ours, that was the only way to get stuff you needed. They brought all sorts of things like schoolbooks, underwear, pots and pans. Other mule vendors brought food that we didn't grow ourselves like oranges or squash. They'd walk along chanting things like "Eat squash, they're good!" The mule vendors passed by pretty often, so we could get what we needed.

The tradition of venditori ambulanti, *traveling merchants, dates back to ancient times. Each was specialized in a certain type of merchandise, and they crooned original jingles to hawk their wares. The trade was passed down through the family, and the jingles were often maintained from generation to generation. This sing-song invocation continues today in Sicily, although the merchants now drive miniature trucks and use bullhorns. Curiously, merchants who come from a long lineage of* venditori ambulanti *often retain their family jingle, even if they change the product their forefathers peddled. So, for example, if the family historically sold fish, but the heir decides to deal in fruit, he will still announce his presence with the family's fish jingle. The song is a calling card that carries the genealogical significance of a family crest.*

We didn't have no taverns or places like that for men to go drinking, so what we did for distraction was to go to each other's house and dance. Somebody would play the accordion, and that was how the girls and fellas got to meet. For the dances, you had to reserve a dance with a girl, so you danced in the order you got called on. You couldn't just dance with anybody who suited your fancy. You had to go in order of the askin'. If somebody you didn't take a likin' to asked you to dance, well, weren't no choice. You danced with whoever asked, or you didn't dance at all. You couldna said "no" to one and "yes" to another, but you could say that you didn't feel like dancing no more. But that wouldna been no fun 'cause you wouldna been able to dance with somebody who mighta caught your eye.

On the whole, weren't a whole lotta good times to be had, but we did have a patron saint day. The patron saint of our little hamlet was the Most Holy Trinity. We celebrated it every year, but funny thing is, I can't rightly remember what day it was! I just remember that we ate meat on that day. Sausage and roast castrated lamb.

Lambs are sheep under twelve months of age. When they are castrated, they are called "wethers". Castration reduces male aggression, thereby making the flock more manageable. The pelts of wethers are easier to remove and the taste of the meat is milder. Non-castrated lambs fetch a lower market price, due to the gamey taint. An instrument called a burdizzo clamp is used to bloodlessly crush the blood vessels at the neck of the scrotum, reducing risk of infection. Alternatively, a tight elastic ring is used, and in no time, the testicles will simply drop off thereby becoming the culinary delicacy known as sweetbreads.

We filed into place for the religious procession that took us up the church, where we listened to the holiday mass about the Most Holy Trinity. There was stands set up sellin' local sweets like *torrone*, and in the evening, we had fireworks. Sure was a beautiful holiday. That's one of the *good* memories I have about the past.

The important food we had at Christmas was capon. Like I said, wasn't too much meat to be had outside of holiday times. Meat made it special. We made capon broth and boiled up some pasta compra. At Christmas, we had a special dessert called *cucchie*. These was oval shaped cookies, a sweet shortbread pastry made with lard, flour, sugar, some lemon zest, and eggs, sorta like your *frolla* but no butter. You cut out shapes and filled them with raisins, dried figs, and nuts, like almonds, pine nuts, and pistachios all ground together. Then there was torrone, called the *cubaita*, in Sicily made with pistachios, almonds and honey. We only had sweets at holidays, but we didn't gobble them down. We tried to make them good things last as long as we could. The only other sweets we had during the year was the sugar cookies we made now and then. They was made with lard too. Everything is good with lard, you know! They didn't have no particular name. We just called them *biscotti*.

The biscotti known in the US, the hard twice-cooked cookies (hence bis – *again,* cotti – *cooked), are generally referred to as* cantucci *in Italy. In Italian, the word* biscotti *simply means cookies and ironically isn't used when referring to cantucci type cookies. Biscotti* (the Italian usage), *allude to the rather bland breakfast cookies sold in large bags, which are the standard Italian home breakfast today. These cookies would never be eaten after a meal, as would cantucci.*

Men had 'em for breakfast before setting out to work, and brought some out to the fields for a pick-me-up. You couldn't make 'em during the war because there wasn't no sugar.

That war was so bad, it even reached up into our little part of the world. Even the Germans came in, and we had to clear outta there right quick! I remember them Germans comin' to us and sayin', "Crunch, crunch. Crunch, crunch." They was looking for bread or whatever food they could get, and didn't know how to talk our language. What the heck did they mean comin' round and bothering folks like us? We was just a handful of poor peasants! Weren't a one of us had no time to get all political about it. Gracious me! We had our work to get to! There wasn't even no squadristi in our little area. We didn't bother about them and they couldna give a hoot 'bout us neither. Sure, we knew about Mussolini, but it wasn't none of our concern. Had nothing to do with us. We really couldn't figure what the Germans wanted in our little hamlet in the mountains 'cause wasn't nothing up there that nobody could want! We was afraid, though. We was sure them Germans was up to no good, so we hid out for a while and waited for them to leave. They made off with all the food they could find, but they didn't trouble with the few belongings we had. Why should they? Wasn't nothin' of value. Just a few sticks of furniture. We never heard about them hurting nobody, but then and there, we was scared. They was just passing through, and after a couple weeks we was back home again.

My husband, he been in the war. The men had to go to war. Wasn't no two ways about that. He was stationed in Albania and then in Greece, and that's where the Germans took him prisoner. You see, I guess we was friends with them once, and something happened, so later we became enemies. He was in a concentration camp for six months and took ill; diphtheria it was. I guess they coulda just gone and killed him, but instead they sent him back to Italy. Dumped him off at the border. He stumbled around till a family in the north took him in and saw to fixing him up. He was there for a right long spell 'fore he was up to traveling. Can't really say what happened. Pietro's not a talking sort of man in general, and even less so about them there times. Some folks talk on and on about the war, and you wish they'd just give it a rest, but he kept it all to himself. He weighed 40 kilos (90 lbs.) when he got home. He walked the whole darn way down to the south of Italy and got on a boat to Sicily. He was nineteen when he left for military service and didn't come back until he was twenty-five.

Pietro was born in 1920. He is seven years older than me. I knew there was something up with him when he started buzzin' round our house all the time. He was a handsome young man with a mustache. Before too long, we was engaged, and before the year was out, we was married because we didn't have long engagements around our parts, just enough time to make preparations for the wedding, finish your corredo, and set up the new house. It was the bride's job to make the yarn for the wool blankets and then weave them on the home loom. A local weaver made the fabric for the new linens, and the bride saw to all the embroidery herself. In the corredo, you had your nightshirt for the groom and nightgown for the bride, your underclothes, sheets, pillowcases, bed covers, towels... so, there was lots of work went into it.

The whole lot of us walked in a procession the four kilometers to the church for the wedding mass. Then we walked back to eat. For the dinner, they killed us a lamb and roasted it over a fire. Yer first course was the usual pasta with tomato sauce and cheese, and then you had yer castrated lamb with vegetables. We didn't have no wedding cake like folks do now. We had some sort of sweet, but I don't remember no more what it was. The reception was in my father's house. The house me and my husband got was too small, and the half of us couldna fit in there. An accordion player came to play, and we all danced.

That was 1951, when we got married. We set up house in the same hamlet where the both of us was born. Around our parts, the new couple always went to live on their own, even if it was just a room somewhere else. We didn't have much starting off. My husband's father died when he was a boy and left his few worldly belongings to the church, leaving his wife nothin' but three young'uns to look after. She worked, now and again, as a field hand, but in the end, she wasn't able to make ends meet for the three children, so she gave Pietro to a foster family where he had to work for his upkeep. He was only six years old and they worked him to the bone, kicking him in the ass if he fell behind. When his mother found out how they was using him like an animal, she moved him to another family. He stayed on with that other family till he went into military service. They gave him a small allowance for his work, but he weren't much more than a servant. When he was all growed up, he went to that first family and said, "Try kicking me in the ass now, if you dare!"

When we was married, we worked kinda like sharecroppers. We lived on the land of our padrone and gave half of our crop to him. The padrone lived in the big house, and we stayed in the workers' quarters. You had your animals on the ground floor and your living area up above. There was quite a few of us, families like ours, all living together and working for him. We grew durum wheat and fava beans. The land was so hard and dry you couldn't get much else out of it. The plot we worked was very far from our house in town, and it got to be a terrible hardship once we had little ones. We had to go there by mule over rocky terrain and cross over a river. It was dangerous, really dangerous, and a far way to travel with the babies. Once I was so tired out, I fell off the mule with my son in my arms! While we worked in the fields, we'd set the babies in a basket in the shade nearby. Problem was, if the children needed something, there wasn't no way to get help, so soon as they was old enough we left 'em with my mother, so's they could go to school. But not having no word way out where we was… well, we was always worried 'bout 'em. We never worried for ourselves, though. I think maybe when life's that sad and hard you don't say anything even if you are sick or hurting. What's the use in complaining when nothing can be done? I don't ever remember calling on a doctor.

We had four children when we decided to leave Sicily in 1962. Our oldest was ten years old and the youngest was two. My mother's brother had up and gone to Tuscany just after the war 'cause he had no way to make a living where we lived. He said, "Come to Tuscany! The life is good here!" Well, it didn't take us too long to make up our minds. Soon as we got a chance to make a life somewhere else, we grabbed it. We was sorry to leave the rest of the family behind, but I couldna cared less 'bout Sicily. My husband was attached to it, but I sure wasn't.

In Tuscany, at first, we worked in the same way, as sharecroppers. But that new padrone was a good person. We had to learn to work with the new crops and animals. Everything here was different and new for us. Wasn't always easy for the kids at school because they was Sicilians and we talked different. There was some folks watching us suspicious like, out of the corner of their eye and such, but there was also plenty of kindly folks. When we arrived, it was winter, and we had nothing but our suitcases. But, see, there was somebody who left a bit of wood for us every evening at the back door of our living quarters, without saying a word. Yes, there was some good folks here. After a while they saw that we was a good family, honest, hard workin' people.

Our house seemed so big and had a big fireplace. The children could ride their bikes round the table it was so big! I learned to make some of them Tuscan dishes, but they ate a lot of soups in Tuscany and we weren't so used to that. I put together a bit of our ways and a bit of theirs. Nothing ever went to waste in my house. I didn't start having real coffee till my first son was married, but we did start having meat more often because here they had chickens and rabbits and some beef. Way more than I ever saw down there! I ain't never made anything fancy like tiramisu or lasagna, but I bought the cakes that they had here for Christmas, and we had tortellini in brodo for the first course, just like they do in here in Tuscany. It took me a good long time to learn how to cook their way. I like other Italian foods like ravioli and risotto; it's just that I don't know how to make 'em. In Tuscany, they eat a lot of game, and I don't really like the taste of that. We didn't have no game in Sicily 'cause the land is dry and harsh. The only wild kinds of foods we had was snails. We got used to eating the food here, though. One of the things I miss from Sicily is the devotional dish we made for Santa Lucia on December 13: wheat grains boiled with chickpeas, fava beans, and fennel. All the women pitched in to make it and we would gather together to eat it.

Little by little, my husband got a business started, raisin' cows and sellin' milk. One cow can make 20-25 liters of milk a day, you know? Trucks came by with their steel containers and took the milk to town very early in the morning. We started selling different kinds of cheese too. We always tried to save as much as we could, and so as soon as we was able, we bought us an old house on a big plot of land, and then we started building this farmhouse in 1974. We kept building up our business the whole while. We raised farm animals to sell at the market and sold eggs to a local grocer, so that's where I did a lot of my shopping, but I like the supermarket too. So many beautiful things to choose from! Too many, really! I keep a close eye on my spendin', though. I don't go wasting it on silly whatnots! I don't go to the supermarket anymore because my husband is old and he doesn't want me to leave him alone for too long. We always worked hard and our children ain't never wanted for nothing. I got eight nieces and nephews and they's all good kids. In my day, though, young women and men wasn't hardly allowed to even look at each other. Now young people have all kinds of freedoms! They should be kept closer to home, I say. They go on vacations all on their own, or just take off in their cars whenever and wherever they please. I don't want to go nowheres. I ain't never had a vacation. Doesn't even cross my mind. But really, how can I blame them for wanting to get about their business when my own life gone and changed from night to day in the blink of an eye, from mule vendors to the supermarket?!

Intermezzo

L'effetto pizza – The Pizza Effect

The invention of the pizza has become a matter of fierce local pride, specifically Neapolitan pride. Popular terroir tales would have the volcanic soil, the salt sea air, the composition of the local water, and the precision gestures of kneading the dough and deftly spinning it into thin disks be the defining elements that make the genuine article inextricable from Naples. For the consumer, being able to look on as the *pizzaiolo* carries out the time-honored craft of making a pizza from start to finish, is a fundamental part of the tradition. "The pizzaiolo maintains the air of high priest of the flames, a command that cooks of today have lost. Not only mustn't he be shut away in the kitchen, seeing him should be part of the attraction," (La Cecla, 1998). This ritual performance, carried out in the theater of the pizzeria, is said to be the saving grace that keeps the pizza from descending into the lowly ranks of fast food. But the irony is, that is where it all started.

In the 18th century, pizza as a foodstuff found fertile ground in Naples, due not only to the geographical climate, which favored the choice and quality of the ingredients of the basic pizza, but also to the sociocultural climate:

> Half the population of Naples did not have a stable source of income [and] was forced to take whatever work or odd job

was available, ... The marvelous setting ... juxtaposed with the daily struggle for survival under difficult conditions made the Neapolitan a cunning dreamer, romantic but pragmatic, kind and violent, but enormously creative. Imagination and creativity were lavished on the invention of new trades. One stood out for being so widespread: that of the pizzaiolo and the pizzeria (Mattozzi, translation Nowak, 2015).

Pizza provided a trade for industrious souls who were at loose ends, and a cheap way for the masses of Neapolitan poor to eat on the go. Many lacked the means necessary for cooking and depended on street food; hence, pizza offered a welcomed opportunity for cheap, cooked food. While street food today has become chic and adheres to a modicum of hygienic standards, the fare offered in the 1800s was a catch-as-catch-can affair. Pizza was a lesser evil in comparison to alternatives like cabbage stalk fritters, boiled chestnuts, or snails in broth. The pizzaiolo walked the streets, selling his wares, or set up a table on the street to hawk to passersby. Prices were rock bottom, so the savvy pizzaiolo had to choose a strategic spot where he could turn a brisk business.

But pizza was not everyone's cup of tea, partly owing to the negative connotations spawned from its miserable environs. In the nineteenth century, Naples was the most populated city in Italy. Overcrowding, poverty, and the cyclical diseases that ran rife through the city as a consequence were not prejudicial slurs, but facts of daily life. Upon arrival in his new kingdom in 1808, Joachim Murat, Napoleon Bonaparte's brother-in-law, describes his impressions of Naples:

> The homes of the lowly are low ceilinged, cramped cubicles ... almost all of them kept with little regard for cleanliness and decency, as they make their home with chickens and other animals. There isn't a stretch of road that is not smelly, filth ridden, and poorly paved. Pigsties are both near and inside homes, not to mention the stagnant water and poorly buried animal carcasses.

Travelers to Naples left rather explicit accounts of their distasteful encounter with pizza, graphically describing it as a "most nauseating cake … a piece of bread that had been taken reeking out of the sewer," and (from the author of Pinocchio) as having "the appearance of a hodgepodge of filth that matches the griminess of the vendor."

The reputation of Naples was such that, in spite of the pizza's association with thrift, it remained largely unknown, disregarded, or considered outright unappetizing throughout the fascist era. It was seen as a regional specialty at a time when Italians were wary of crossing unfamiliar culinary boarders into the territory of "others." The few references to pizza in cookbooks and magazines underscored its origin by referring to it invariably as *pizza napolitana*. Ada Boni includes a recipe for Neapolitan pizza (anchovies, mozzarella) at the tail end of the pasta section in her 1946 edition of *The Talisman of Happiness*, clearly speaking to a public that was unaccustomed to it, suggesting in the endnote the novel notion that different toppings could be put on a pizza in place of the anchovies. Everything else that she calls "pizza" is in the pastry section under Easter cakes, and range from sweet yeast cakes (*Pizza di Civitavecchia*) to savory cheese breads (*Pizza col formaggio delle Marche*), all of which are nestled between the recipe for Nougat Cake and Super Cheap Cake (no eggs). The more familiar use of the word, during the Ventennio, was in reference to these cakes and breads. Octogenarians and nonagenarians still call them pizza. How is it then that the "pizza of ill repute" emerged from its murky, quasi-obscurity to splash onto the stage of international stardom?

Anthropologist Agehananda Bharati coined the term "pizza effect," using pizza as the quintessential example to describe an occurrence in which an insignificant cultural phenomenon is exported to another country, and then, following its great success abroad, is revalued in the mother country, where it takes off as an original, longstanding tradition.

Pizza arrived in the United States with the turn of the century exodus. Lombardi's pizzeria became the epicenter of New York's Little Italy, although others had successfully set up pizza joints around the same time. In the United States, where it was untainted by an association with the Neapolitan poor, pizza thrived as a simple ethnic Italian food. "Everyone from opera singers to street urchins gathered at Lombardi's and thus the legend of the pizzeria as a great social equalizer was born" (Helstowsky, 2008). Dipping into the food cultures of others is often tinged with xenophobic trepidation, but neither the flavors nor the appearance of pizza posed a challenge to the average American tolerance for foreignness. It remained within the confines of what La Cecla calls "the borders of reality beyond which curiosity turns to disgust" (1998). American soldiers, who most likely had had no contact with pizza prior to WWII, were reportedly won over during their tour of duty in Naples, and supposedly brought back stories of their culinary experience, which would help ease pizza out of ethnic enclaves and into the mainstream.

The pizza effect, when examined through the example par excellence, has, over time, become a complex, multi-layered Ping-Pong game. American tourists, who later traveled to Italy, expected to find the prototypical Italian food "pizza" a ubiquitous presence on menus. Italian proprietors sought to cater to their customers' expectations, thus encouraging culinary tourism. Post war migration from the southern regions to the industrialized north favored the spread of regional foodways, and in no time, pizzaioli found a wide open market to practice their craft throughout Italy. As time went on, and the Italian economy improved, a society that had always been frugal and tense about spending could finally begin to lay back and spend money on food just for the fun of it. As a quick, cheap option, pizza was particularly appealing to the younger generation of Italians, just as it was to youth abroad. With a little pocket money, you could grab a quick snack with friends. Rest and relaxation as a status symbol made the seaside holiday a mandatory part of one's yearly calendar and budget. This conspicuous consumption of leisure went hand in hand with what was quickly becoming the common denominator of recreational foods, the pizza. It was fast, fun, filling, affordable and delicious, appealing to children and adults alike. And most importantly, you didn't have to make it yourself.

It wasn't long before it became clear that the pizza business was a gold mine. Little by little, other regions began to explore the possibilities inherent in the round, white flour canvas and developed their own "regional" varieties to satisfy the new demand of both travelers and locals who were hungry for more. This led to what scholar Jørn Borup called the "inverted pizza-effect," when the cultural phenomenon is not only revived in the original country, but undergoes further alterations to adhere to or indulge the new expectations of "tradition." To add a further twist, gastronomic pilgrims would then travel to the land of origin to witness the confirmation of their projections:

> Although pizza has some old Italian antecedents, American pizza as we know it was largely a product of Italian-American cooking. However, pizza-loving American tourists, going to Italy in the millions, sought out authentic Italian pizza. Italians, responding to this demand, developed pizzerias to meet American expectations. Delighted with their discovery of "authentic" Italian pizza, Americans subsequently developed chains of "authentic" Italian brick-oven pizzerias. Hence, Americans met their own reflection in the other and were delighted (Jenkins, 2002).

[*An important caveat: in Italy, pizzaria pizzas do not come in sizes, pre-sliced to be shared. They are one size and each customer is served a whole, unsliced pizza. Furthermore, there is not a list of toppings that one mixes and matches. Every pizza is named – the margherita, the quattro stagioni etc., – and has a fixed combination of toppings*]. As "genuine" and "authentic" are made to order terms, all manner of crusts and toppings began to appear in Italy. Each region transformed pizza into their own local specialty: pizzas with peas and a fried egg in Turin, the gorgonzola topped pizza in Milan, or the popular french fry pizza, which originated beachside, but has now entered into the standard canon. The audacious freedom with which other localities, regions, and countries were appropriating the pizza and recreating it in their own image began to alarm the Neapolitans, who then set out to protect their local heritage. Posthaste, they responded to the crisis by founding the *Associazione Verace Pizza Napoletana* in 1984, so that the Neapolitan model might be established as the ultimate measure of quality, diminishing all other pizzas to the status of mere imitations of, or deviations from the one True Pizza.

Finally, in 1997, pizza napoletana received the honorable quality assurance distinction DOC, certifying it as a local product. But some pizzas in Naples are more equal than others. As of July 2015, Neapolitan pizzeria *Eccellenze Campagne* has announced it will be making crusts exclusively with seawater. The innovator, Maestro pizzaiolo Guglielmo Vuolo, says that seawater "allows one to fully taste the authentic flavors of the ingredients." The water is a microbiologically purified product and contains an impressive 92 elements from the periodic table. The owner of the pizzeria supports the initiative, saying he is "convinced that food excellence must always be valued for its solid, irrevocable ties to the territory" (Metropolis Web, 2015). So what if the seawater processing plant is 230 km east of Naples, on the opposite side of the boot? If you have traveled from afar to sample the True Pizza, distance becomes relative.

The approach to pizza making throughout the world has forked in two directions. Traditionalists make every attempt to adhere to the minutiae of the True Pizza, which appeals to customers whose cultural capital allows them to insist on San Marzano tomatoes and request *mozzarella di buffala*. Evolutionists forge upwards and onwards, boldly going where no man (or woman) has gone before with theme creations like Thai Breaker, by Top That!, made with Thai peanut sauce, whole milk mozzarella, marinated chicken, roasted garlic, caramelized onions, chopped scallions, julienne carrots, sharp cheddar and roasted peanuts; and Jamaican Jerk, by Uncle Maddio's Pizza Joint, featuring tomato-basil sauce, mozzarella, grilled jerk chicken, red onions, green peppers, pineapples and cilantro. Pizza sales in the US amassed $37,375,108,000 in 2013, so on the pizza front – it's all good.

For Italians, the knee-jerk association of Italy with pasta and pizza is met with ambivalence. On the one hand they are proud of the internationalization of dishes that pay tribute to their cuisine. Not a single Italian today doubts for a second the preeminence of Italian cuisine on the gastronomic world stage. At the same time, they harbor resentment at being identified with something so simple and reductive as pasta and pizza when Italy is chockfull of so many other wonders and glories. Similarly, Americans cannot live down their identification abroad with the hamburger and Coca-Cola. Many people in the states and abroad boycott burgers and colas for political and/or health reasons. The same cannot be said of Italians with regard to pasta and pizza, which are revered as both healthy and convivial.

In the spring of 2015, McDonalds launched a television commercial in Italy depicting a child snubbing pizza in favor of a Happy Meal. Naples was enraged. Its reaction was swift and sure. A counter ad, set in Naples, was issued, in which a child is dragged to a McDonalds; the tot looks leery-eyed at customers passing with their gray burgers on plastic trays, and says to his father in a delightful Neapolitan accent, "Papa! What is this crap?! I want pizza!!!" McDonalds chose to promote their own product by attacking one of the icons of Italian culinary culture. The hamburger vs. pizza was not an all-in-fun publicity jab. McDonalds is not that naïve. It was a direct in-your-face challenge, an ethnocentric assertion of superiority. What McDonalds didn't see coming was the backlash. The power of pizza and the pride of Neapolitans are forces to be reckoned with.

Barbara

Born 1922 - Benevento

Walking up to Barbara's house in the country, I found her sitting in an armchair outside her front door, intent on doing her needlework. In spite of her 92 years, she does the intricate work without the aid of glasses. Many of her family members had come to hear her talk to me about "the old days" in the countryside of Benevento, in the southwestern region of Campania. Most of them were raised in Tuscany and knew little about their southern origins because Barbara's family, like Rosa's, had moved north in the 1960s in hopes of a better life, taking advantage of the abundant, cheap Tuscan farmland, resisting the allure of city life. After our interview, Barbara demonstrated how to make cavatelli, a short flour and water pasta shape. Her powerful hands kneaded the dough with awe-inspiring speed and accuracy. After rolling out the dough and cutting it into chunks, the cavatelli forms shot out of her nimble fingers as if they had been fired from a machine gun. Barbara's nieces joined in to see who could top her speed and accuracy. No one could.

So? What is it you wanna know? I got plenty to say.

I was born and reared in the south. The countryside, just outside Benevento. Deep south. We was a homesteading family. Owned our own land. Yes, we did. We was a self-runnin' farm, meanin' we done everything by ourselves, for ourselves. Didn't have us no big ol' piece of land, but I tell ya, there was plenty of other folks was trying to get along, homesteading by theirselves with some bitty scrap of land you couldn't even grow a darn weed on. So, I'd say we was gettin' along jus' fine, even though at the end of the day, it didn't amount to a hill of beans. There was eight of us at home, six kids and Mamma and Papa, me being the youngest. The oldest was born in 1906, and I'm from '22, so I never did meet my grandfolks or none of them older kin.

I went to school through the third grade. Yeah, so what? I didn't much care for't. Thank merciful God, my folks didn't make me suffer through no more than the third grade. With the work there was to get done on the farm... well, weren't no point fillin' your head if you couldn't fill your stomach! That's what I say. There was lots of us little 'uns, I think about twenty-five in all, but our school weren't nothin' more than a room in a building that we all packed into together. We all... now, here I'm meaning all us who had our own land... we all had to bring a piece of wood every mornin' durin' the winter months, so's to heat the place. We had to lug our books and our inkwell to and from school, case someone set their mind to swipin' 'em from ya. *Capito?* But sure wasn't like now where kids is loaded down like mules with a backpack full of books. Alls we had was a couple books and our writin' stuff. Weren't no need for no more learnin' than that back then. If somebody was itchin' to read them a book, there was plenty of time for that when you was lookin' after the sheep or the goats. That's the way it was. If you didn't feel like goin' to school no more, well, you just plain didn't go. So, when I was ten I made my escape! Ha!

A'fore leavin' for school, we had milk for breakfast 'cause we had milkin' cows. Then we ate bread and whatever was in season. Weren't never no coffee in our house till a good spell after the war. Didn't even know what the stuff was. We made our coffee with chickpeas. You browned 'em, ground 'em, and boiled 'em. Yeah, well, honey, ya wouldn't catch *me* drinkin' that sludge, not even back then! We drank a lotta milk, and in the summer, we'd get the milkin' done early and take it down to the river to keep it cool. That way we had good cold milk. We'd toss a hunk of bread in and eat it that way. At our house, we always had a little something to go with the bread too, but there was lots of folks had a hard time even scraping a bit of bread together.

Once, after my sister had a baby, her milk didn't come. We asked the doctor if we could give cow's milk to a bitty creature like that. So, this doctor fella says, "If the cow was not sick, you could boil up some lettuce in water and use that water to cut the milk." Weren't so strong that way for a wee little thing. So my papa, rest in peace, had the vet come give the cow a good once over. He picked one cow and said, "Always gotta be this here cow," and the milk had to be mixed straight away with the boiled lettuce water. Weren't no need to boil the milk so long as it was straight outta the cow and still warm. So, now y'all know what ya gotta do if ya got a little one needin' milk. Humph.

Some of our animals was cash animals, you know, for market, like sheep. That's how we got money for buying the things we needed for the house. Eh! Weren't never enough, though! This here one's a needin' shoes, and that there one's gotta have medicine. Then there was land taxes and such to pay. Our Duce wasn't much likin' the folks that done for theirselves, so he made up taxes special for us. Anyway, Papa kept us the sheep's innards, and sold off the meat parts to the rich folks, but didn't matter to me one way or the other. Never could stand the stench of lamb. The organs was worse of all. Still turns my stomach.

We raised an extra pig or two for the market. One for us, for salamis and cured meats. Most folks back then raised a slaughtering pig. At home, everything got divvied up. Ya got your portion of prosciutto, or your slice of salami. Ya couldn't just go putting your mitts on whatever piece struck your particular fancy, even when we was growed up. There was rules to be followed. And my mamma would say, "Eat your bread! Eat your bread!" Was bad manners to eat a piece of salami or prosciutto without bread. And you didn't dare waste a single crumb, not like kids today who just leave bread there, right there! Half-eaten, like the stuff was growin' on trees! We worked hard on the farm, and we had *real* wheat bread. Even through the war. And we didn't never have to eat none of them there breads made outta god-knows-what. All them things they used to slip in to make something that seemed like bread, but wasn't. We had our own wood burnin' brick oven on our land and 'bout once a week we made bread, 'cause it didn't go all hard on ya like bread does now. Weren't no rule about when we made bread. That depended on how much pasta we ate 'cause were bad manners eatin' pasta with bread. We was civilized folks!

Italians ascribe to the guidelines of etiquette laid out in Galateo: The Rules of Right Behavior, *by Giovanni della Casa (1503-1556), and many freely quote his teachings when passing judgment on others or deciding themselves how to act. Galateo forbids mopping one's plate with bread in order to finish off the last residue of the delectable sauces. The exception would be in informal situations, but even then, one should employ a fork. Mopping up is peasant-like, or for those who clearly don't know where their next meal is coming from. Although Galateo does not pass judgment on eating bread with the starch based first course, in most areas in Italy, it is considered the height of bad manners for the aforementioned reason. Stuffing yourself with bread and pasta at the same time is a sure sign of ill breeding. Bread should accompany a companatico, meats, vegetables or cheese, not another carbohydrate. Nibbling on bread before the first course arrives is also considered uncouth, but on that particular count, the stomach, more often than not, overrules decorum.*

We planted all kinds of things on our farm 'cause, like I said, we was homesteaders, and that meant ya had to do it all yerself. Potatoes, white beans, chickpeas, maize, wheat, cabbage, greens, and the vegetables we love in the south, zucchini, eggplant, and peppers. We done all of it with just a hoe and a trowel. We ploughed, planted and picked, all by hand, no machines. It was all by the sweat of our brow. Our skin and the earth. We had a couple field beasts, but we threshed that wheat by hand, sloughing the hulls off the grain, lettin' the wind carry 'em away. Our place was tucked up in the mountains, so it was plenty windy. Other people, they had to haul theirs off to where it was windy to get the work done. Not many folks around these days remember, like I do, when the wheat was threshed by hand.

I didn't go to school too long, but in my town the children all did Fascist Saturday once a month. Mussolini was our leader and he wanted order. We felt like somethin' special and important in our uniform, the black skirt and them pretty white tennis shoes. We met on all them special calendar days too, like the national holidays for '15-'18, ones we used to have that we don't have no more, like May 24th and November 4th. But I have to say, I don't rightly remember what they was for anymore.

WWI is commonly referred to by the generation who remembers it simply as '15-18'. May 24, 1915 commemorated Italy's declaration of war on the Austro-Hungarian Empire, and November 4, 1918 was Armistice Day.

There was always some professor or some somebody come to explain all of them things about the day we was celebratin', and then… oh, then, they went on and on about respectin' the fascio, what fascism was all about, and all that, you know? We didn't do all that marching and gymnastics business until we was fourteen, when we was giovane fasciste. Me, well, I pretty much quit all of it at that point. Wasn't too well organized for us girls anyway. Everything was always for the boys. Boys had to go, even if they didn't go to school 'cause it was fixin' 'em up to go to war. Then when they was eighteen, they had to take a test, real serious like. My brothers kept on with it. Weren't no choice. It was orders, the law, jus' like any military service. There was plenty of talk around town 'bout boys picked up by the fascists, and well, let's say, I guess you could say, they was beaten for not participatin', but weren't no one I knew myself personally. Weren't no one from my own family, but sure, there was talk in town about it.

Sunday and Thursday was special days. Sunday, bein' the day of our Lord, and Thursday, it bein' the day before Lenten Friday. On those days we had a plate of homemade pasta like cavatelli or tagliatelle with tomato sauce made with oil or lardo, but always tomato. We made tomato conserva and used that to make sauce except in summer when we could make fresh tomato sauce. We used the conserva for sauce the whole winter until the next year. If you didn't have no tomatoes, you'd buy the conserva. Everybody used it. I don't know what the store-bought one was like 'cause we never bought it. I guess it was like ours, though.

We had a different idea altogether from you all 'bout keepin' clean. Weren't nobody had a proper washroom that we knew of. Maybe some town folks, but I didn't know them kinds of people. Washin' every day jus' wasn't something we did. At most, ya maybe splashed on some water in the morning. Come to think, I remember my father every morning – my folks died when we were already living up here in Tuscany – liked to splash water on his face first thing, to start the day off right. The women would take a tub into the barn, where we kept the animals, because it was warmer there, and haul in a couple buckets of boilin' water. Two of us at a time would have a good wash down usin' that same water. In the winter, we washed 'bout twice a month, but in summer, we could go down and have a wash in the pond we kept for waterin' the crops, or we'd go to the river with towel, and wash there.

We made our own soap with lard and prosciutto bones. With the ration card, we'd get us our oil and make soap with that, but lard was better. Lard was better for everything! We cleaned our teeth with sage, ain't none of us had a toothbrush. There weren't none to be had! I still got all my own teeth. Not too long ago, I was in the hospital for an operation, and the nurse says to me, she says, "Signora, remember to take out your teeth and put them in the cup before the operation." I was scared outta my wits! I thought they wanted to pull my teeth out! Then, I got my nerve up to ask the doctor, and he said they thought I wore false teeth! "No sir, doctor!" I said, "These is mine, every last one of 'em!"

We hardly never had nothin' sweet would make your teeth sick, and anyway, during the war you could only get that black sugar, you know, that sugar that ain't white. It was sticky-like, not nice and dry, but still, it was sweet. Poor folks, who hardly had nothin' to eat, would sprinkle a little of that on a piece of bread, and for them, it was a dessert. We made a sweet called *zeppole* at Christmas, and the *pastiera* at Easter. We made whole wheat honey cookies too. They was hard and dry and would keep for a good long while, so we'd make us a big batch of them. If you heated 'em up they got softer again.

We didn't make too many cakes, but we did bake a kind of stuffed pizza every so often. We put tomato sauce, oil and cheese on it, but it wasn't mozzarella like you's thinking. Weren't nobody heard of that around our parts at that point. We made our own cheese. We'd trade our cheese to get honey. Something I really miss is the *casatiello*, like a big ol' ring loaf of bread filled with layers of salami and cheese, all rolled up in dough. On top you put boiled eggs, whole ones still in the shell, sort of like a decoration, but you ate it too! It was a Carnival food. I ain't had that for ten years.

Casatiello: Easter Loaf
Dough:
600g bread flour
300 ml water
50g pork lard
2 yeast cubes

Filling
175 g softened pork lard
100 g grated sharp sheep's milk cheese (pecorino) or Parmesan
200 g diced salami and/or scrunchions
150 g provolone, medium sharp, diced
1 tbsp salt
Lots of fresh ground pepper
4 – 6 medium eggs for decoration

For the dough, mix the flour, lard and yeast with room temperature water until the dough is soft and elastic. Let rise in an oiled container until it has more than doubled, 2-3 hours.

Remove the dough and form into a rectangle. Spread ¼ of the lard onto the rectangle. Add grated cheese and pepper and fold over like a book letting the dough rest 5 minutes between each folding. You can use a rolling pin, but delicately, Do not overwork the dough.

Cut off a piece of the dough and set aside to make the crosses that will hold the whole eggs in place. For the last fold, add the salami and the diced provolone and roll it up carefully.

Grease a large Bundt pan with lard and arrange the dough log into a ring sticking the two ends together. Leave it to rise 3 hours covered with a damp tea towel. The time for it to double will depend on how warm your kitchen is and the kind of yeast you've used. Carefully wash the eggs in their shells. Place them on their sides with the small end pointing towards the hole in the pan. With the extra dough, cut strips and form crosses to place over each egg so they look strapped in place. Brush the dough with a beaten egg yolk. Heat the oven to 350° F/180° C, but place the loaf in the oven when it has heated halfway in order to have a slow cook.

Bake for about an hour. Remove from oven and allow to cool 10 minutes before removing it from the pan. Cool completely before slicing. Lasts 3-4 days.

And I loved the cornmeal torte that we cooked in the fireplace. We would grind the cornmeal and then sift it. The finer part we used and the coarse bits went to feed the animals 'cause them poor beasts had to eat something too. After ya had your fire going a good while, ya cleared a space in the hearth for puttin' down your cabbage leaves. You made a thick batter with your cornmeal flour, water, and salt, turned it out onto the leaves, and you sprinkled it with a smidgen of oil or lard to make it tastier. You covered the lot with a flat pan full of red-hot embers and left it there. On top, you'd get a crispy crust, and then on the bottom, you took off the cabbage leaves and you was ready to eat. I tried making it here but nothin' doing 'cause the cornmeal in these here parts ain't no good.

We had a lot of vegetables, cooked a lot of ways, usually tossed around in a pan with lard. It was tastier that way, but they're sayin' lard's bad for you now, so we use oil. During harvest times when we was all just too darn busy we'd buy pasta in a store 'stead of making it. If you had to make the dough when you was tuckered out, well, it took too long, so we just ate bought pasta. But wasn't like now, weren't no nice clean packages. It used to be sold in bulk. You didn't know where it had been, who mighta had their hands on it. The shopkeepers kept it in drawers, and took it out... with their hands, and wrapped it in paper, and you didn't know if it was clean or nothin'. Store bought pasta was just to save time. We'd make our own tomato sauce, but buy the pasta. You know, everyone used to always eat fresh pasta, and then once in a while bought pasta, now it is the opposite. What I'm sayin' is, it wasn't somethin' you ate because it was good. It was something you ate 'cause it was easy. We had our own corn, so we'd have polenta sometimes, but that went for feeding the beasts too. At my house we had enough food, more than lots of other folks, but wasn't hardly no meat. Lookin' back, I'd say we coulda done with more meat. We had the one pig, that had to last us out the year, and then we had some other meat about once, maybe twice a month, a chicken or a rabbit, every other Sunday.

We didn't have no lights or electricity. We used petroleum lamps, or lamps with *olio buono* [*good oil, i.e. olive oil*]. Rich folks had lights. One thing I'm sorry 'bout having left behind is our lamps. I wish I had kept one, just to remember; they was beautiful. Weren't big or nothin', just bitty things like this, but the light was warm. We made a wick, put the oil in, and they didn't smoke or nothin'. [*In spite of Barbara's general no-nonsense tone, she became uncharacteristically misty when talking about these lamps.*] We had them in our small apartment in town, what we used for getting to church on Sunday morning. See, some of the country folks who lived close enough to the church could go to mass during the week, but for folks like us, who lived way out there in the hills, it was a long trek just getting there on Sunday, so we'd sleep in town Saturday night, so's to be ready for church the next morning. Most of the homesteaders like us had a town flat. The poor field hands didn't have nothin' to speak of, town or country. They sure was a sorry lot, they was.

When they could, women would head up to their place in town for birthin' their babies, so that the midwife could be called on the spot when the time came. Nobody went to the hospital for that. The town doctor saw to the better part of your ailments; then if you was in a really bad way, there was a hospital in the city, but it was pretty darn far. Our place in town wasn't nothing to live in, just someplace to lay your head for the night. At our house in the country, part of it was a barn with animals on the ground floor, and bales of hay in the loft above. Then we lived in the other half of the house on the ground floor.

You're American, right? You know, my father went to America after he married my mother. Mamma stayed at home with her folks. She didn't know no readin' or writin', but her brother-in-law, my uncle Giuseppe, could scribble a few words for her. She'd say, "If there is room for me, please let me come too!" She waited and waited for his answer, and when he wrote back all's he said was, "Don't worry. I'll be back soon." There was a frightful poverty after '15-'18. He done lost two brothers in the war, but when my grandfolks died, there was still seven of them who had to divvy up a small plot of land between 'em. Weren't no work for Papa here, and so he went there to try to scrape together some money. When he come back, he was in a right way to buy himself a piece of land, whereon he built a straw hut and started his life. He put a cornhusk mattress in there and slept on the floor, so he wouldn't have to come and go into town day in, day out. After that, he built a rock shelter with stones stacked one on top of the other. Then, little by little, he built the house we lived in. In those days you could do whatever you pleased on your land; you didn't need no permits or to follow no regulations. We stayed on till 1951. Then, our whole family packed it in and moved north. It was just too much of a burden to manage the farmstead anymore, a few acres here, a few acres over there, more someplace else. We wasn't a family no more 'cause, with some working here, and others there, weren't no way for the family to be together. In the south, we couldn't find one large piece of land, so we decided to sell up and move. We dragged around from one region to the next, and finally set up in Tuscany.

I lived with my folks till I was 29. Not long after the move north, I got married. I met my husband, oh, well… I can't rightly recall, how was it? See, there was this character they called "Beefsteak", oh, who was he? What's his real name? Francesco. That's it! Was him introduced me to my husband. We met, and after five months, the deal was done.

At age 28 an unmarried woman passed from the label "nubile" to that of "old maid." A dowry, in accordance with one's means, and a trousseau were essential for a good match. Girls worked maniacally through their youth to finish their bridal linens, and such was the desperation to marry, that women in their late 20s would even take out newspaper ads, specifically stating the dowry figure that they would bring to the union. Women were warned, however, that while fussing over one's appearance might attract a potential husband, statistics showed that too much primping was directly related to infertility. The first beauty contest in Italy (1939) was judged on the best smile, not the nicest body, and was sponsored by a brand of toothpaste. The grand prize was 5,000 lire and a full trousseau of linens.

My father never took a likin' to none of the suitors what come to call, see? There was one I really had an eye for, but Papa said, "Well, girl, you go right on ahead and do what you please, but don't be comin' back into my house callin' yourself my daughter if you do!" It was a fella lived near us. I was 21 and he was 22. I liked that boy. One morning, he come to pay a visit to Papa to do some inquirin' about me, but Papa wouldn't have none of him on account of his hearin' that he, the boy, had to be woke up every morning, that he didn't just wake up and git to work of his own accord, and you see, that did not sit right with Papa. Girls obeyed their fathers back then, and so, well, I didn't marry him.

Weren't no real way to meet fellas. If a girl on the street caught his eye, the fella would ask around about her and make a meeting happen. They'd start to follow ya from afar, then they'd get closer, then maybe they'd stop ya for a chat. But when it came to talkin' marriage, the boy, or his parents, asked for your hand proper like from your father. That's how things used to be. The right way was for the boy's parents to go to the girl's parents to fix the match, and then arrangements was made. My husband, before he was my husband, he says to me, "Well, now, it's been a while we known each other, so we can get married." And that there was the askin'. You see, he weren't no young man. He was a widow and had a child. He was a sharecropper, see, and his padrone says to him, "Listen, man, you gotta either get you a hired hand here or get a wife if you want to carry on workin' this farm because if you ain't bringing in a decent crop for us here, you best be on your way." So, he set about looking for wife, and I was still on the market. It wasn't exactly love, you know, but there must have been somethin' there 'cause otherwise you don't just go getting married, do ya?

If I was young again, I'd move back to the south. We didn't have nothin', no lights, no running water, but things was better back then because we had Mussolini. Now everybody's out killin' everybody else. Kids killin' grandparents, husbands killin' wives, killin', killin', killin'. There was consequences for your actions when I was young. Ain't nobody had a doubt about right and wrong. Not everybody had a soft spot for Mussolini, but them folks who had somethin' to say about him to the contrary was taken care of straight away. Well, I say, they done right. Cleared any doubts right outta their heads. We had the death penalty then and used it! The Duce even had his own son-in-law killed!"

Count Gian Galeazzo Ciano married Mussolini's daughter in 1930, and became Press and Propaganda Minister in 1935. In 1936 he became Foreign Minister, but although he slavishly admired Mussolini, he was consistently against Italy's involvement in WWII. Ciano was eventually shot in the back by a firing squad while tied to a chair for having been among those who voted to oust Mussolini in 1943. The overwhelming majority voted for an overthrow, and Mussolini was momentarily removed from office, but upon his return to power, examples had to be made to keep face. Hitler insisted upon it.

My brother in Foiano says, "We need one Mussolini in every city. Then you can bet things will be ship shape!" He knowed how to command. If it wasn't for that good-for-nothin' Ciano, we'd still have our Libya! We had a paradise there, with beautiful homes, fine estates. We could have all lived the good life 'cept that he gone and messed it up for us. That peace lovin' fool, 'stead of sending cannons full of bombs he sent cannons loaded with flour!

The Italian conquest of Libya had begun in 1912; expansion and reinforcement of power continued steadily throughout the 1930s. It was to be the new America for Italian emigrants. Natives were subjected to the standard practices of ethnic cleansing, forced labor, imposed religion, and concentration camps, all the while Mussolini referred to them generously as "Muslim Italians." At the same time, however, great improvements were made in the infrastructure of the colonized areas, and the economy boomed. The colonization of Libya was hampered by armed conflict after Italy entered into war with England, and in 1943, the Allies forced the Axis powers to retreat definitively after a series of defeats. In 1970, Gaddafi struck the final blow, ordering the expulsion of all Italians.

My husband was a big fascist supporter. One day, when he was a young fella, he went into a field to steal a pumpkin for the seeds, and the farmer caught him red-handed. Well, that there farmer takes him by the ear and says, "Here, boy, I'll learn you a thing or two about what happens to thieves!" And he took and cut part of his ear off. Later, my husband, rest in peace, became a fascist patrolman. So one day, he's out doing his rounds and he beats on the roof of the car and asks the driver if it's bullet proof. That it was, so he tells the driver where to go; he gets out of the car and goes to the house and starts thrashin' the man who was out in the field. "What the hell you beating on me for?" he says. "Look at this ear! You remember this ear?! Now, you're gonna pay!" That guy got his comeuppance!

I think, though, that everybody agreed it was wrong for Mussolini to go in with Hitler. Something never did sit right with that. But when the Duce met his end, it was like with Berlusconi today: yer always gonna have some folks for and others against, and both of 'em through to the bone. During the war, we was bombed without mercy, only Rome was saved because of the Pope bein' there and all. Even country houses was bombed. Bombin' everywhere. That was all the fault of the Americans, that's right. Now every April 25 [*Liberation Day*], we's supposed to be thankin' God for the Americans what "liberated" us? Bah, I say! Mussolini helped this country. He made us roads, he give us schools. If it wasn't for him, I wouldn't know no readin' and writin' 'cause girls wasn't s'posed to go to school; he made schools for everyone. Back then, folks said wasn't no need for girls to go to school, but Mussolini said we was all to be comrades. So where's the wrong in that?!

They went and killed him, and then those democratic people come in and ate up every last thing in sight! Where did the money go?! Where's our pensions! Who stole all the money?! All right, all right, so you say there was a lot of poverty even before, and that people didn't have nothin' to eat. I say that a lot of them people are like folks today, whining that there isn't any work, but heaps of 'em's good-for-nothin' lazy bums! Mussolini made highways, and everywhere the fascists passed, there was work for loads of folks. I say that if people just put their minds to it, there would be less poverty. How you s'posed to make money if you don't move your ass? Now everyone wants to study, study, study, and no one wants to get out and *work the land*. There is work to be had there in the fields, so how can we say there ain't no jobs? Everything good comes from the countryside. That's where we need to go to turn this nation around.

One good change is that women can be more on their own. Before we had to obey: our father, our husband, the Duce, always some man in charge barking orders. Now *I* decide for *myself* where and when I come and go. Ain't nobody tellin' me what to do. Before, weren't no escape. How was you gonna get your daily bread? If you didn't act right or went against the family, it was over for you, dearie, done. Now, everything is different. Back then, family meant that someone was always lookin' out for you if you needed help, but the price was obedience. Now, you don't know who's watchin' your back. Lots of folks losing their houses today, and their jobs, but the families, they's turnin' away, 'stead of stickin' by 'em. Ain't no more pitchin' in and helpin' each other. Grandmothers used to be matriarchs, had an important role in the family. Now they's just old bats.

My mamma taught me to cook, and this used to be important. She would let all us girls in the house take turns, so that we would learn. And on the farm, we all worked hard together, baling hay, planting, harvesting beans, chickpeas, field corn, we all did everything, and there was lots to do, but was the women done all the housework too. Everything is ready-made now, but before, we had to make all of the things for the house, the sheets, towels, soap, everything. There was a tailor who made our clothes, not that we had many. Our tailor was a shoemaker too, and made all our shoes. We didn't have them wooden shoes like some poorer families. We had proper shoes that didn't hurt our feet. The soles was sort of thin, though. You could feel the rocks under your feet.

Our tailor, one day, says to my father, "You got good hardworking daughters in your house, why don't you buy them a sewing machine so you don't have to call on me no more? The family's only gonna get bigger." In those days a sewing machine cost as much as two new cows, so it was a pretty hefty price for us. But he bought one, one of them ones with the pedal. My oldest sister learned first from the tailor, and the rest of us picked it up from her. My mother, rest in peace, teached us to do embroidery and needlework. All girls had to learn that 'cause we made our own trousseau. Were some girls whose folks just couldn't afford it; others didn't have no talent for it, but most of us learned. When you got married, the needlework of your trousseau was showed off in a parade through the streets for two or three days before the wedding day.

The relatives walked from the bride's house to the groom's house, where she went to live. The sheets for the wedding night were draped over a board that was carried on someone's head, displaying the most beautiful parts of the needlework. The whole town would gather in the street to comment. In Barbara's town the man was responsible for making or buying a bed and mattress, and the woman brought a hope chest with towels, sheets, pillow slips, a shirt for the husband, underwear, brassieres, a nightgown, and a nightshirt, all made and embroidered by the bride herself. Barbara still has many items from her trousseau, and they are indeed exquisitely crafted.

In the better families that wasn't down and out, we made the woolen blanket too. I still got mine. Many of us made the fabric itself for the top sheet with thread that we done spun ourselves. My cousin had a loom and made the fabric for my top sheet out of the thread I spun. There was a saying, "*arte del telaio, sedie di notaio*", to say that people who wove fabric was as rich as notaries. For the other things, we bought the fabric.

The trousseau was a tradition from southern Italy, and was not customary in the north. After the war, it disappeared, even in the south.

With the advent of industrialization, household linens were widely available in stores, and the tradition quickly died out.

Was the man had to pay for the wedding dress, for the bride's and his own suit, and she paid for or made his shirt and a nice handkerchief for his coat pocket. In secret, we girls used to set aside any extra money we might get so's to buy acetylene for the lamp, like the miners had. That way we could stay up late and do our sewing after the old folks gone to bed. We'd stay up all quiet like and sew till about midnight. Couldn't stay up too much later on account of the workdays bein' so long. In the winter, there was more time to work on it because the farm work was less, and weren't no need for us girls in the fields.

I really never thought I'd live this long, and here I am, still able to take care of myself. I still cook for myself everyday. I ain't too quick no more, but I get there. I don't use lardo like we used to back then. Didn't used to be bad for you like they say it is now. Ain't no tellin' why. I watched Antonella Clerici on TV today. They's whippin' up all kinds of fancy concoctions these days that I ain't got the first idea what they's s'posed to be. They put all of that creamy stuff everywhere and mix all kinds of nonsense together. I don't like that kind of cooking. I like the old ways. Just give me a plate of plain pasta with a drop of oil and a sprinkle of cheese and leave it at that.

Intermezzo

Curare i malanni – **Curing what ails you**

```
S A T O R
A R E P O
T E N E T
O P E R A
R O T A S
```

The Sator-Rotas Square.
Earliest example: Pompeii, 79 BCE.

These five words can be read vertically and horizontally in either direction to form a Latin palindromic sentence. Although it has no intrinsic meaning, the mesmerizing construction itself seems imbued with mysterious powers, or so it seemed to the ancients who used it as incantation to ward off evil. Belief in its powers continued through to modern times. A practical application was employed by Italian peasantry to protect a person bitten by a rabid dog: Eat a crust of bread with those words written on it for three consecutive days. On Sundays, on an empty stomach, recite the following phrase five times: "For the five wounds that Christ received on the cross." Continue thusly for forty days after which the victim will be in the clear.

Organized healthcare, prior to the Ventennio, consisted mainly of Catholic charity organizations and state run social services for the poor, whose aim was to provide the assistance necessary to maintain a modicum of public order and decorum. Predictably, the fascist hand molded healthcare reform in accordance with the ideology of a totalitarian state, focusing primarily on insuring a productive work force, safeguarding the race, and increasing the population. The well-being of the individual would be a trickle down perk. Their plan was elaborate and looked impressive on paper, but it was one in a long line of overly ambitious programs that overstepped the bounds of economic practicality. The Church resented the regime's attempt to strong-arm it out of one of its traditional roles in public life. Lack of funding proved the undoing of the state, for which it conceded that the Church should continue to provide assistance to the elderly, the disabled, and outcasts.

But while church and state hashed it out in their marble halls, the populace went on much as they had for centuries, relying on folk medicine and healers.

Despite rising literacy rates, the primarily rural society was reluctant to abandon the wisdom of generations of elders, who had honed and crafted folk medicine. God-fearing people, who lived their lives as an integral part of the mysterious ebb and flow of the cycles of nature, looked upon illness and misfortune as an invasive force of evil, one which required an equally potent force to cure, prevent, and alleviate malevolence. The deep-seated belief systems surrounding medical folkways were part of a larger package of identity, along with fables, songs, religion, and foodways. Remedies, spells, and antidotes were handed down from generation to generation within a close-knit social structure, making them all the more resistant to change. While many have become "quaintly backward" over time, others represent the rudiments of medical science and yield the benefits of clinical trials.

Nature was often the instrument through which malice struck. The changing seasons and the weather took the brunt for many ailments. The movement from one season into the next still reigns supreme today as a catchall determinant for day-to-day complaints. Air and particularly gusts of wind were, and are, also commonly faulted for myriad afflictions. A modern residual of this is the firm belief that air conditioning is harmful. Cooling the environment in the summer is seen as unnatural (whereas heating it is not), though many find welcome relief from Italian heat waves in air-conditioned supermarkets.

While many ancient and medieval beliefs waned and disappeared over the centuries, certain shadowy remnants persisted. In particular, forces of the sun, moon, and stars to intervene, as they would, for both good and evil were a universal. And while the medical canon that had proposed the "humours" (blood, phlegm, black and yellow bile) and temperaments as fundamental causes of disease had long been obsolete in science, it lingered on in folk medicine. The belief that imaginary creatures inhabited a host's body where they wreaked havoc also survived into the modern age. The most frightening of these entities was cancer. Cancer victims were advised to eat as much meat as they could to satisfy the beast's voracious appetite, thus saving the flesh of the infirm host. The uterus itself was, according to legend, a capricious seven-headed creature, which pushed women into fits of hysteria. Women's moods were seen as a dangerous force; ungoverned, they were a hazard for both the woman herself and those who might cross her path. Similarly, pent up passions and grave disappointment (or rather "stress") were the cause of a long list of ills and pains, the classic example being tuberculosis. As early as the sixteeth century, Girolamo Fracastoro had hypothesized that "consumption" was caused by viral contagion. Thus, it stands as one of many examples of how reigning currents of belief, deeply ingrained in the communal psyche, persisted even in the light of scientific evidence.

Satan, angered saints, witches, and the evil eye were undisputed causes of illness. Spastic back pain is still called *colpo della strega*, (literally "strike of the witch"), owing to its wicked pain, rather than to any credence in the forces of evil. That said, however, the Curia of Milan has recently expanded its exorcism telephone hotline in order to keep up with the overwhelming demand. In a conversation with an Italian friend, I suggested that perhaps what were needed were more qualified psychologists. She confidently assured me that, even over the phone, the priests were quite capable of distinguishing between those who were clearly in need of psychological assistance from those who were actually possessed by Satan, and that the former would be directed to get proper care.

When home diagnosis and remedies did not suffice, a figure referred to as a *medicone* (literally "big doctor") was called upon. The medicone was a man or woman versed in the local folk medicine who had received the teachings as well as the "gift" of healing. S/he was a fusion of herbalist, psychologist, alchemist, clairvoyant, dietician, and faith healer, who dabbled in potions, amulets, ointments, cookery, and rituals, throwing in a few Hail Marys and Our Fathers for good measure. The Church resented the laity's mixing of magic and religious rite in their healing practices, and requested that they steer clear of matters regarding the soul. Ironically, they saw no conflict in their own mixed role as curators of the soul dispensing healthcare. The state had long outlawed folk practitioners in 1888, clearly stating: "No one can practice the profession of doctor, surgeon, veterinarian, pharmacist, dentist, phlebotomist, or midwife without a degree or certification from an authorized university, institute or school" (Article 23). The medicone should not be summarily written off as a medicine man, a quack, or a charlatan of the ilk who knowingly sold bottled "tonics" of ink-colored urine or sacred splinters from the True Cross. Mediconi truly believed that they were possessed of healing powers and knowledge of the ages, and with every success, so did their clientele. Unlike medical doctors, they asked for little in return for their services, which stood them in good stead in the community.

Demand for the medicone's services was not restricted to rural areas. They were a regular fixture in cities and towns, as well, wherever there was suffering and fear. Patients would often combine both traditional and modern medical approaches. When the town doctor made his exit after a house call, the medicone was called upon for a second opinion, particularly if the physician had used complicated medical terminology, prescribed an unfamiliar pharmaceutical regimen, or had scolded the patient for some "ignorant" practice that s/he swore by.

The medicone are a dying breed. A handful does still exist, but they are reluctant to speak about their craft. There is a secretive aura about the knowledge they hold, owing in part to the historical perse-cution of witches and warlocks, and unremitting attempts by medical authorities to squelch and discredit every aspect of their practices. And with no one to pass the scepter to, the figure of the medicone will soon disappear into the shadows of time.

Food has always been part and parcel to convalescence. The earli-est known cookbooks were, in essence, medical guides proposing the right combination of food or herbs to cure what ails you, a trend we have never tired of. Even through the 1940s, convalescent care was a regular feature of cookbooks and food writing. Culinary-based conva-lescent advice during the Ventennio kept a close eye on politics – the Battle for Wheat, autarky, and rationing strongly influenced its coun-sel. Grapes, for example, kept Italians "buying Italian" and valorizing simple local foods. *Ampeloterapia*, the grape cure (not to be confused with pelotherapy, which employs mud) was among the most common-ly used fruit cures, so much so that Vanna Piccini, in her homemaker's book *Golden Treasure Chest*, almost skips over it saying, "The curative tradition of grapes is so well-established, owing to their tonic and re-storative effects, that there is almost no point in delving into the topic" (1943).

Ampelotherapy was widely prescribed by Italian physicians as a therapy for anything from gastritis to gout to obesity to diabetes to fatigue. Although evidence of its existence surfaced in the late 1800s, nostalgia posited the practice in ancient times when our ancestors cut grapes by the bunch directly from the vine while the morning dew still clung to the fruit. Moderns could achieve similar results by rinsing them before consuming them, although the walk out into the vineyard in the early morning hours was a side benefit of the cure. Dosage: two bunches, preferably of white grapes, per day, one for breakfast on an empty stomach and a second larger one at 5 o'clock, as the enzymes are more active at those hours. Leave the peel on, as that is the part that absorbs most of the sun's energy.

While the grape cure is dismissed today as medical quackery, proanthocynids and resveratrol, found respectively in the seeds and peel, are currently being studied in relation to cancer prevention and anti-aging. The cure is still practiced in wellness centers throughout

Europe as a therapy for high blood pressure, menopause, varicose veins, dermatitis, urinary problems, heart disease, sexual and mental disorders... a veritable panacea.

Ampelotherapy is also recommended as a must for arthritis sufferers in the article "Diet for Arthritics," in *La Cucina Italiana*. They were warned, however, to strictly avoid the new fermented food item "yogourth." Food recommendations for arthritics conveniently read like an autarkic shopping list: rice, dark bread, pasta, white fish, chicken or rabbit (once a week only), eggs, citrus fruits, and low sugar jam.

In 1934, *La Cucina Italiana* had begun running regular medical advice columns with a nod toward the fascist platform. After the Ethiopian invasion, sights turned towards maintaining good health within the confines of sanction rationing. An exemplary recipe suggestion is this whipped egg soup (a precursor to foam?) for diabetics:

Minestra Albumetti – Egg white drop soup

*Beat any leftover egg whites you might have to stiff peaks. Portion out grated cheese, pepper and salt. [Fold in.] Drop spoonfuls of the batter into hot oil and fry. These can be made a day ahead. They are fluffier if eaten fresh. When ready to serve, drop them into hot broth to reheat, or pour hot broth on top after having sprinkled them with cheese (*La Cucina Italiana*, Jan, 1936).*

Saccharin had been commercially available as an artificial sweetener for diabetics since the late 1800s, having been accidentally discovered by the chemist Constantin Falberg while trying to develop coal tar by-products. The sugar shortages of WWI brought it to the attention of the public as a sugar substitute. In Italy, however, it was sold exclusively in pharmacies for diabetics, and only with a doctor's prescription. Real sugar became increasingly more scarce and costly, as the Ventennio traversed one crisis after another. During the autarky alarm of the mid 1930s, sugar producers protected their interests by taking out regular half page magazine ads, sweet-talking the public into keeping up with their daily requirement:

SUGAR

Sugar is a fundamental part of the diet. It is a highly nutritive substance. That means that it is not a mere condiment, but a food in its own right, enhancing the nutritive power of anything it is added to, especially jams, fruit in sugar syrup, cakes, etc. Sugar intake must be kept constant in your diet. It is essential for proper nutrition, acting to revitalize and harmonize the body (Advertisement, *La Cucina Italiana*).

To eat or not to eat meat was answered with a resounding "no" once sanctions had tipped the political scale. The article "Meat or Vegetable Protein?" puts the question to the test by positioning government-issue brown bread and dried biscuits (crackers, cookies, hardtack) against animal flesh, the former winning hands down. This bit of dietary health advice was served up with a side of fascist propaganda:

It is a fact that 40g of dried biscuits provide the same amount of energy as 100g of meat. ... keeping in mind that [the flour in] each and every biscuit comes exclusively from our farms, and that industrial production [of dried biscuits] in Italy has reached a truly admirable level of perfection. One used to talk about English biscuits as being unsurpassable. Well, you should know that before the sanctions, our rusks and wafers were shipped to India, Australia, Egypt, and even to the United Kingdom, where we are convinced that production will pick up, by and by, in the future, once this has blown over. In the meantime, let's start using them more here at home showing that we value this healthy, inexpensive food, produced on our own soil, and elaborated by our own machines (Saldini di Rovetino, 1936).

In the days before Ancel Keys had unlocked the secrets to the heart-healthy Mediterranean Diet, other dietary hypotheses circulated around heart disease. Arteriosclerosis was understood as a calcification of the arteries caused by toxins, excess minerals, and high blood volume. Meat and fish high in omega-3 were targeted as the leading culprits, not for their fat content, but for the toxins that foods high in nitrogen and purines purportedly created in the body. The principle aim of the heart healthy diet, therefore, was to eliminate poisons. To this end, meats, eggs, and some fish were prohibited along with foods high in calcium and minerals. Liquids were to be consumed sparingly as they increased the volume of blood, raising blood pressure, which in turn aggravated the arteries.

Sobriety and parsimony were key, which meant eliminating vices like smoking, drinking to excess, "sexual pleasures," and hearty caloric meals. Repasts were to be small, frequent, and well chewed. Excessive or prolonged physical or intellectual activities were to be avoided. Certain condiments were prohibited, in particular nutmeg, pepper, mustard, vinegar, and acidic foods in general. Blacklisted vegetables included those of the cabbage family, mushrooms and truffles. Asparagus, spinach, cucumbers, green beans, celery, and beets could be consumed, but in moderation. Potatoes were as yet disputed as a yea or nay item. Calming and digestive herbal teas were recommended after meals. The following is a heart healthy recipe from the article "Arteriosclerosis and Dietary Rules":

Polpettone Vegitariano - Veggi Loaf

Boil, peel, and mash some potatoes. Mix with an egg, a handful of groviera cheese, and a knob of butter. Salt. Form into a loaf and roll it in breadcrumbs. Place it in an oblong baking dish, dot with butter, and bake for half an hour. Prepare a Sicilian sauce: take a half kilo of tomatoes, one onion, and one stalk of celery and make it into a sauce; otherwise dilute half a cup of Cirio super tomato sauce in one cup of hot vegetable broth. Brown a knob of butter in 4 tablespoons of oil. Add one spoonful of both minced onion and parsley, a half-cup of both chopped celeriac and matchstick carrots. Stir with a wooden spoon. When they start to fry, add the tomato sauce, plus water or hot broth. Simmer for an hour, after which add cheese. When ready to serve, pour the sauce over the loaf (Piscel, 1936).

Both low-carb advocates and low-fat devotees would find common ground in their disapproval of this recipe. Perhaps with a bit of nutmeg and pepper in the potato loaf, and a handful of sautéed mushrooms in the sauce, it might yet stand a chance with home cooked meal enthusiasts.

FAR REACHES

Ada

Born 1921 – La Spezia

The Kingdom of Italy succeeded in defeating the Ottoman Empire for dominion over parts of North Africa in 1912. Decades of violent tensions with the natives ensued; hence, maintaining a foothold in the area required a sizable military presence. During the fascist reign, imperialistic objectives to expand and develop the colony catapulted military families like Ada's into a life of privilege and luxury. In 1934, the colony was officially named Libya, the name used by the Greeks in reference to North Africa (with the exception of Egypt), and in 1939, citizenship was bestowed upon select natives, particularly those who enlisted in the Italian Army, an odd turn of events given the newly instituted Racial Laws of 1938. Ada spent her teenage years in Tripoli, and recalls them with bittersweet adulation. She considers Libya her true home and deeply regrets the loss of Italian Libya. While we talked, we looked through her pile of old black and white photographs. She sighed nostalgically, now and again, recollecting the golden years of her youth.

My father was from the region of Liguria, and I was born in La Spezia, but my mother was from Taranto, Deep South. Her father, my grandfather, was an officer in the naval marines. She was one of six children, and as happened in military families, all of them were born in a different city, from all over Italy. Whatever port they found themselves in, my grandmother had an offspring! So one was born in Rome, one in Naples, and even one in Pola, in Istria. That was my Aunt Ada, the one I was named after. My grandfather's surname was Mirabella, a southern name, but I couldn't really tell you where they were from originally. They were military, and the military don't have a home. They went where they were told to go. My paternal grandparents were from Genoa and La Spezia. I only lived in La Spezia for two years; then we moved to Rome, and then Naples, and so on and so forth because my father, too, was in the military. You get the picture? He was a captain in the Air Force. Every two or three years they transferred us somewhere else. He was born sometime around the 1890s, but how can I possibly remember the details of his life, when I have enough to do just holding onto my own memories! He was too young to participate in the First World War, but by the end of it, he had already enrolled in the naval marines. Later, Mussolini wanted to develop the Italian Air Force, so Father switched over to that. It was more prestigious, and he liked planes. Generale Valle and De Pinedo helped push him up though the ranks.

So, I skipped around from school to school because we were always on the move. When we were in Pisa, my brothers and sister and I all got kicked out of school because my brother, Mario, had typhoid fever, and so they wouldn't let any of us back in school for the rest of the year. I had two older brothers and a younger sister. When we moved back to La Spezia, I finished elementary school. Even though Father was in the military, he never made me do Fascist Saturday because I didn't feel like going. I went to piano lessons instead. I did five years of piano, but I never got very good at it. After two years of middle school, in 1935 when I was 14, we moved to Africa. I picked up with school and the piano in Tripoli, right off the bat. My piano teacher in Tripoli wrote the famous song *Tripoli, bel suol d'amor*, do you know it? It goes like this: Hmmm hmm hmmm...

The song "A Tripoli" was written in 1911, but was assimilated into the Fascist musical canon. A giornalist wrote the lyrics and Colombino Arona (b. 1885), presumably Ada's piano teacher, wrote the music. It is a typical military propaganda song lauding the defeat of the Turks,

idealizing the glorious sound of roaring cannons and blaring trum-
pets, with the King of Italy's tricolored flag waving all the while. In the
same year, a parody version of the song came out warning soldiers to
stay away from Tripoli and decrying the hideous bloodshed.

I loved the life in Tripoli, my Tripoli. It was an absolute heaven on earth. Oh, but we lived the good life there! Tennis, horseback riding, music lessons, theater and parties. Being the family of an officer stationed abroad came with many perks, a beautiful home, a houseful of servants, and a car with a driver. My father and brothers had attendants called *ascari,* natives enrolled in the colonial army. They were personal manservants who were in the military, but their assignment was to look after the officers. Their duties were to clean the officers' rooms, take care of their clothes, shine shoes, and that sort of thing. Some of our household servants were Jewish because in Tripoli, there were a lot of Jews. [*In 1939 in Tripoli there were 47,442 Italians, 47,123 Arabs, and 18,467 Jews.*] All of them were natives of Libya, but they all spoke Italian; everyone there spoke Italian. We had a housekeeper, laundress, gardener, and kitchen help, who took care of everything we needed.

We often had guests, and so, the kitchen was always abuzz with activity. My mother supervised the preparation of every meal because she trusted no one in the kitchen. For example, the hired help would wash and trim the vegetables, but my mother did a last rinse just to make sure they were cleaned properly. She was very demanding. As the daughter of a military official, Mother had travelled all over Italy, so she knew a lot of different dishes and had picked up different ways of cooking, from north to south. She was an excellent cook herself, anyway. But the food in our house was strictly Italian, no mixing with *their* food. Couscous and company was *not* for us! And none of those spices! No, no, no! We did eat the local dates, though. Whenever I had a craving, I'd have the servant climb the tree, "Could you go up and get me some dates, Ali?" And he'd shimmy right up there with that strap they used – di-di, di-di, di-di – to gather some dates for me. It is one thing to eat them fresh from the tree, and quite another to eat them dried, like the ones here in Italy, which are crap.

Every two years, officers were allowed one month of leave. We'd travel a bit around North Africa, Malta, Sicily, and then work our way back to Liguria to see family. We were never in any great rush to get back to Italy. I loved Italy, but our life in Africa was better by far. Italian Africa, that is. Sure, I learned a few words of Arabic while I was there, but for me it really was an Italian community; it wasn't like living in a foreign country, and it wasn't like living in Italy. It was something in between.

There was an upper crust of Arab families too, rich, high-society families. There were a few Arabs who went to the same school as my brothers. They were Italian speaking Arabs because, of course, school was taught in Italian. They weren't part of the military society like we were, just wealthy Arabs. I continued my schooling there as well, even though I wasn't really very interested in it. There weren't any Arab girls in my school, though. We didn't get too much fascist teaching in our school lessons, but we did have to do the calisthenics that young people had to do in Italy for Fascist Saturday.

Before leaving for school, we had *caffè latte* and cookies or bread and jam. We had always had *real* coffee. Before the bombing started, there were avenues full of beautiful Italian food shops with everything we could possibly want. At my house, Mother had the help make fresh pasta because we always had enough flour. There was a medical doctor at the base who had a massive vegetable garden that he had planted at the airport. He had everything but the kitchen sink in that garden! He really loved my mom's Genoese minestrone, so he'd come over and say, "*Donna* Giulia!" that's the title they used down there,

"Don" and "Donna" are archaic honorific titles once used in the patri-cian classes and high clergy. As a term of respect, it later worked its way into the organized crime hierarchy. Today, "Don" remains in use in Italy only as a title for priests.

Donna Giulia! Will you make some minestrone? I'll bring you all the vegetables!" And he'd come with a huge sack of vegetables from his garden! After 1940, though, times got pretty rough, and lots of things were hard to come by. Even getting something as simple as dried, store-bought pasta wasn't easy. Problem was, we lived close to the coast, and our homes and shops were bombed from the sea by naval war ships. That really took a toll on our way of life. Those were truly some terrible times. I have a photo somewhere in here of a hole in the wall of our house that was made when a navy cannonball shot straight through three rooms of the house. It came out the other side, and then exploded in the garden. It came into my bedroom, felled the wall between my brothers' bedrooms, and then shot right out of the house. Another time, Father was sitting at his desk and General Bonicelli came and said, "Come on! We've got to get out! They are bombing hard!" Father said, "Wait, I've got to finish something!" "No! No! Move! Now!" So he got up and went for cover. As he crouched down next to the General, a bomb flew through the house, and a huge hunk of shrapnel landed right on the chair where my father had been sitting. The General took the plate of shrapnel and had it mounted on a piece of wood. They cut a hole in the center, put in a clock, and the general surprised my father with it as a gift! Well, laughing matters aside, that is when we decided to move to another villa in Via Canova. This one was closer to Italo Balbo's house. He was Govenor of Libya. We were often invited to his house for dinners, parties, and tea.

At the age of 25, Italo Balbo became one of the four principle-founding members of Fascism. He was called "Ras," an Ethiopian title like "Duke," adopted by the Fascist hierarchy for those in positions of power; hence, he was a "Duce" in his own right. Though he had almost no aviation experience, he became Minister of the Air Force in 1929. In 1933, he tested his wings in a transatlantic flight from Rome to Chicago, for which Franklin D. Roosevelt awarded him the Distinguished Flying Cross, and he was featured on the cover of Time *magazine. The Italian-American community turned out in droves to cheer on their compatriot hero. Addressing a crowd in New York he said, "Be proud you are Italian. Mussolini has brought an end to the era of humiliation." Upon his return to Italy, he was showered with honors, including being named Governor of Libya and Commander-in-Chief of Italian North Africa, which, in essence, exiled him from Italy, perceived, as he was, to be a growing threat to Mussolini's centralized power. Following*

347

years of mass deportation, concentration camps, and ethnic cleansing, Balbo's approach was to integrate the native Libyans and the Italians. But his fall from grace came in 1939, when he publicly criticized Mussolini's coalition with Hitler, advocating an alliance with Britain. No other high-ranking military official dared support him, though Galeazzo Ciano, Mussolini's foreign minister, privately shared Balbo's misgivings. In June of 1940, Balbo's plane was mistakenly shot down in Tobruk by an Italian gunner. This, naturally, stirred gossip of an assassination plot carried out on Mussolini's orders. Though it was never proven, the day after Balbo's death, the Duce was reportedly unmoved and said, "He's the only man who would have been capable of killing me."

My father knew him very well because all of the officers met up frequently. Balbo's flight engineer, Captain Gino Cappannini, lived on the ground floor of our villa, and the three of them sometimes went hunting together in the plane, gazelle hunting in particular. They would split up the gazelle among them, so we had braised gazelle pretty often. Let me tell you, gazelle meat is really something special.

Stufato di gazzella – Braised Gazelle
1.5 kilos gazelle meat, preferably in one chunk
5 cloves garlic
6 whole cloves, minced
one bunch herbs (bay leaf, thyme, parsley)
1 onion, chopped
50 g lardo, minced
50 g pancetta, chopped
5 liters red wine
400 g tomato paste
1 tsp cinnamon
salt and pepper to taste

Place the meat in a terrine with the cloves and herbs and pour in enough wine to cover. Leave to soak for 24 hours. Remove from liquid, dry, and bind the meat tightly with kitchen string. Sauté the garlic, onion, lardo, and pancetta in a Dutch oven, or large heavy pot, until the fats have been released and the onion is soft. Remove the sauté and brown the meat well in the fat on all sides. Put the sauté, cloves, cinnamon, a fresh bunch of herbs, tomato paste, salt, and pepper in the pot and pour on enough fresh wine to cover. Cover the pot with a heavy lid and simmer for 1 ½ hours to 2 hours, turning occasionally.

Balbo loved throwing sumptuous parties. His wife, Donna Manucci, often called on us. She and Mother were great friends. We called her Donna Manù. [*Balbo was wealthy in his own right and his wife's generous dowry allowed them to live in high style.*] The military families were a very close-knit group. We met up all the time for tea, and we'd go for outings along the seaboard and long drives. Or we would get together to knit and gab a bit. It was a good, good life. Not a care in the world. When the King and Mussolini came to Libya, we were invited to the grand receptions at Balbo's house.

Mussolini went to Libya in 1937 for an outlandish propaganda staging in which he had himself declared "Protector of Islam," during which he was presented with a symbolic sword. Balbo hosted a lavish lunch for Mussolini, with each dish named so as to have a patriotic ring, though the upper class nod to French cuisine is unmistakable, and autarkic frugality had clearly been left by the wayside. The menu is as follows (the intended humor will be lost in translation):
Malossol Caviar
Fois Gras
Imperial reduction (soup)
Our own Seas Bass with mayonnaise
Capon from Monza with indigenous artichokes and Tripoli peas
Black-faced Bombs (a dessert)
Assorted pastries
Fruit, coffee
Italian still and sparkling wines.
[Ada was in attendance and would have been all of sixteen at the time.]

They came on separate occasions, mind you. They couldn't stand being in each other's presence. The parades were fabulous, with the *Méhariste*, the indigenous cavalry mounted on camels, under the command of one of the *Calvi di Balbolo*, a branch of the royal family, in this case the king's nephew. It was all so dreamy. Our Duce! Oh, my! Such a handsome man. He wasn't nearly as short as people said he was! He was even a bit taller than me. What a talker! Goodness, but he went on and on! The next day, after a fantastic party, he was given the Sword of Islam, and we had front row seats! Can you imagine! It was fabulous, and he cut quite a figure on horseback. Later the king came. He was accompanied by his daughter. I tell you, she and Donna Minù couldn't bear each other! They managed to say *buon giorno* and *buona sera,* but then they had to be kept separate. The princess and I went horseback riding together, but I was a disaster on a horse! We had some laughs, though, watching each other try to manage a horse.

My brother-in-law, who had caught sight of my sister in Tripoli when she was fourteen years old, and had fallen straight in love, was a Méhariste officer. He was an excellent horseman, and looked like a prince when he rode. He was captured and taken prisoner when he was on duty in the desert. They shipped him off to a prison in Arizona because the law stated that you had to be taken to a prison with the same characteristics of the place you were caught. So, he was in the desert, and they sent him to Arizona! Oh, how he'd wail on saying, "I was a prisoner of war!" and we'd say, "Oh, yeah, sure... *in America!*" When he was in prison, he and the other Italians staged a protest saying that they wanted Italian food. "Ok, ok, tomorrow, tomorrow," the officer said every day. After a week they saw a train pull in with a wagon with *Pastificio Rosa* written on the side. Straight from New York City! They could hardly believe their eyes! Eh, sure, he was a prisoner with wagonloads of pasta and other goodies being shipped to him straight from Little Italy. Good Lord above! He was even paid for his time there, but in lira, not in dollars, so by the time he got back to Italy, the lire had bottomed out so much that he didn't get much more than a cup of coffee out of his check! Inflation ate the rest of it!

At Christmastime, all of the military families invited a few of the unmarried officers to their holiday dinner. Libya was full of young people, young Italians, and we had traditional Christmas foods. We even made *cappelletti in brodo*. Absolutely everything was ordered from Italy, capons, beef, and all of the traditional desserts, mostly from Southern Italy. All of the families then made things according to their own traditions, so the Neapolitans had their own food, and so on. In Libya, the prejudices and hatreds between north and south that people had in Italy, we didn't have. We all liked to think of ourselves as Libyan Italians. It united us.

We even imported our clothes from Italy. For our wardrobe, my family referred to the grand fashion house Palagi in Turin. Turin was the center of Italian fashion at the time.

> *Autarky seeped into every aspect of consumer life. In 1935, with the advent of the Ethiopian invasion, the National Bureau of Fashion was established. Those working in the fashion and clothing industry had to register with the office to obtain a costly certificate of guarantee attesting that at least 25 percent of their total output was Made in Italy. Like so many initiatives for the betterment of the Patria, this was an absurdly unmanageable proposal. The elite fashion houses later rebelled when they saw that their creations were awarded certification alongside cheap off-the-rack wear. "The dress and hat of the grand Houses are given the same certification as the little caps and mundane outfits of the everyday factories, leaving the grand dame, in the name of the Patria, to dress up in the same thing her cook would wear. This is a sacrifice one cannot ask of a signora" (Lombardi, 1936 in Gnoli, 2005).*

They kept our measurements and sent us catalogues so we could pick from the latest styles. So, for example, on important occasions, like when the Duce or the king came, and we all had to be dressed in accordance with the will of God, we set about choosing our dresses with exquisite care. The King did not approve of women dressed in flashy colors or in black. I remember for the Duce's visit, I wore the most dreamy pink dress with beautiful flowers hand-painted along the hemline. Oh! I'll never forget that dress! We had so many beautiful clothes, hats, shoes, bags… Just stunning! And everything was tailored for us personally. There was no ready-to-wear. Nothing off-the-rack for us!

We ordered everything directly from Palagi. If things didn't fit quite right, they were sent back to be touched up until they were perfect. And we had to be dressed properly for church. They were rather strict about that. Once I went to church without a head covering and, oh! The priest didn't let me hear the end of it! I ran out of there like a shot from a pistol! Women had to have either a kerchief, or a veil, or a hat on their head, because Saint Paul said that women had to have their heads covered in church and be silent.

I remember when Balbo died, we cried and cried. We were all very close. He had given me a puppy one year as a gift. Balbo and his group of officials, and a couple of his wife's cousins, had lifted off in their plane. They had to go to Tirene, in Chad, I don't know what for. What happened was that the English shot them down, and all of them died, end of story. [*The reader might note the discrepancy in her story.*] Ah, look! Here's a picture of General Graziani when he came to dinner.

Rodolfo Graziani brought the Libyan resistance to its knees through systematic ethnic cleansing and concentration camps, where most internees died of starvation, heat prostration, or disease. He governed Libya until 1934, when Balbo took charge. Graziani was then assigned the task of invading Ethiopia, famously saying, "The Duce will have Ethiopia with or without the Ethiopians!" After Balbo's death, Graziani resumed the governorship of Libya until, as the only Marshal who had remained loyal to Mussolini, he was asked to serve as the Minister of Defense for the newly formed Italian Socialist Republic. After the war, he was sentenced to nineteen years in prison for collaboration with the Nazis. He was released after serving only a few months, under the claim that he had just been carrying out orders. The crimes against humanity perpetrated under his watch in Ethiopia never came to trial.

We weathered two years of the war in Libya until all was lost. Those last two years, it felt like we were always running for cover. As people were killed or cleared out, my father collected their things and locked them up for safekeeping. When we moved to the second villa, my father had a bomb shelter built, and all of the generals would come to us to take refuge. They were always underfoot. The night before we left, even they were white as sheets with fear. There was broken glass and china everywhere. Vases, pots, everything was broken and strewn out along the streets. The last time we went to church, there were dead people everywhere along the road, severed arms, legs, heads... I had never seen so much death. I had worked as a volunteer for the Red Cross, and I remember so clearly a boy, a soldier, whose leg they had to remove without anesthetics because we had long run out of medicines. He was very brave throughout the amputation, but in the end, he died of infection.

While I was doing the exam for my teaching certificate, the bombing was just horrendous. At a certain point, the instructor told us to evacuate. As I was running out, I yelled, "Does this mean we get to pass the exam?" "You just worry about saving your hide and forget about the exam!" I never knew if I passed or not. Sometime later, my father looked into it in the archives in Rome, but they said that nothing had ever arrived from Tripoli. Everything had been burned and destroyed, so I guess not. I had never intended to teach anyway. It was just something for young society girls to do.

The Italians all started flooding back into Italy. We left on one of the last possible flights out. There was our plane and another one in front of ours. Our destination was Sfax, on the tip of Tunisia. An English reconnaissance plane started firing at us, and at the plane in front of ours. A friend of my mother's, a major's wife, was in the other plane, with a small child in her arms. My mother had begged her to come with us in our plane, saying there'd be more room for the little one too. But her friend said, "No, I promised the doctor's wife that I'd fly with her." Passing over Sfax, we could see the tops of submarines everywhere, so we cut over towards Naples and then on to the Rome airport in Ciampino. Then, these stupid Italians sent a gunner plane after us! Our pilot said, "No, don't shoot you idiots! We're Italian!" Well, it just so happened that the other plane with the Major's wife and child were hit, and both of them were dead by the time we landed. There were ambulances everywhere when we landed because they feared that we had been hit too. We had an excellent pilot. I cried out to him, "Reali, please get us home!" A few people in our plane were injured and taken away, but thank God, my family was safe and sound.

When we got to Rome and they saw that we were all fine, we were taken to a fancy restaurant in the heart of Rome where they pulled out all the stops. I tell you, they piled the food on us. During the last few months in Libya, we hardly had enough to eat, so we really appreciated the feast they lavished on us.

We were deeply sorry for the loss of Libya. It wasn't like Ethiopia. Libya had been Italian for a long time. It was ours. A cousin of my father's, who we called Uncle Alberto, had a splendid villa there and ended up selling it for two bits to an Arab. He practically gave it away! Balbo had always said that we should never have entered into the war, and that we most certainly shouldn't have allied with Germany. If we had remained neutral, we would have had heaven on earth. Everything was good there and we wanted for nothing. So, in the end, it was the Duce's fault that we lost Libya. Balbo liked the English and thought we should have allied with them because they were good people, more sincere than we were. He didn't think too highly of the French, though.

Once in Italy, we lived in the royal palace in Caserta for a while, that was nice, and then my father was stationed a bit here and there, until we finally ended up in Arezzo. There was quite a bit of war activity in Arezzo then. The Germans were retreating and the Allies were coming through. A piece of the building where we lived was bombed then. We didn't live in the luxury we were accustomed to, but at least we still had servants and attendants. A couple times, we had to move out into the countryside for safety when the bombing was heavy, My sister and I would bike into Arezzo sometimes to meet friends, and we had to dodge the gunfire, but you sort of get used to it after a while. We had seen worse in Africa.

I have to admit that I was not caught up in the politics of the day. Never was. To tell you the truth, I couldn't have cared less. I was in my early twenties then, so what did I care? But all said, my father, coming from a military family as he did, well, they were for the monarchy. They were not fascists; they were the king's men. Whatever the king said, we stood by it. If we had a king now I would be for the king! I don't want to generalize too much, but the military families were monarchists. The only reason we went along with fascism was because the king did. For us, the only thing that really counted was the King and the Kingdom of Italy. When it came to serious talk about politics, the men talked together after dinner and the women went into another room, so I don't really know too much. We were caught up in the whirlwind of the colonial life and we clung to it tightly. It's not like my father went to Tripoli to open a cigarette shop, you know! We were the elite! Ours was an important military family. My main concern was what I was going to wear to tennis or to tea, and when the next party was. I couldn't be bothered with how the war was or wasn't going. And even if I had known, I honestly couldn't have cared less. When the Duce came, the most important thing on my mind was getting the right dress and shoes.

In Arezzo things were not so bad. Everyone seemed to have enough food, no one was going hungry. There was a lot of countryside nearby, and so there was plenty of food. Plus, my father, being in aviation, had a hand in shipments that came in by plane so we were able to get some rare extras without any problem. If you compare it to what we have today, maybe it would seem pretty sparse, but with what people were used to then, we were doing pretty well. We passed our bread ration on to a family friend because we always had enough, and the restaurants we went to had plenty of bread.

I met my husband 19 April 1945, and we married on 3 May of the same year. It was love at first sight. He was an official with the Alpine military. The front had passed through and he was going up with the English army. His father had participated in the March to Rome that entrenched the fascists as the ruling party of Italy. He was a big landowner, had a button factory and a tomato cannery and he had been a prefect for a while. When Mussolini was in his last hours, the military had already allied with the English, and my husband was reassigned to follow them. Actually, he was with a group of Australians. Ours was a small society of military families, so as they passed though Arezzo, we naturally got to know one another. I was not well that day, and was playing cards with my friend, when he walked in. My hair was in a frightful state and he said, "Well, who's this signorina with the uncombed hair?" That evening, we were supposed to go to a certain colonel's house for a party, but the poor fellow had died, and so, they had to call off the party. So we said, "Well? Now what are we going to do? There's no party!" One of the guys in our group said, "Why don't we go up to my villa in the country?" So we all went to his house. Well, now, can you imagine, there I was sitting by the fire, and Carlo said, "Just think, Ada, some day, years from now we will look back fondly on this moment," and I said, "Well, who's to say where *you* are going to be, and where *I* am going to be!" "Oh, no," he said, "We are going to be together!" Eh, he was a clever one with women! After two days he came to get me for the swearing in with the Bishop.

In Italy, even today, a proposed marriage has to be "published," that is, made public, for two weeks, two Sundays, before a couple can be married. Prior engagements have to be investigated; the public must be given an opportunity to oppose the union, and the couple must reflect carefully, thus avoiding shotgun marriages. Today the "publication" is processed through the municipality and is required for both church and civic weddings. Therefore, during an Italian wedding ceremony, no one asks the famous question: If anyone objects, speak now or forever hold your peace!

We asked the Bishop to wave the publication time because Carlo was a soldier and due to ship out. He did as we asked because back then bishops had the power to go above the law, but not anymore. When my father heard what we had done, he was outside of the grace of God! He was at the Military Gentleman's Club. "Papa," I said getting close in, "look, Papa, I am going to get married." "Eh, sure, in a year or so, of course you will." "No, Papa, I am getting married on May 3rd." "What!!!" he said jumping to his feet. "You are out of your mind if you think you are getting married!" "No, Papa, we have to get married now because Carlo has orders to leave. He wants to take me with him, so we've got to do it now and then leave." It took him a while to get that one down, but he knew how I was, and he resigned himself to the idea.

I was married in 1946, but for the first seven years I didn't have any children because my husband didn't want any. He just wanted to have fun. And we did have lots of fun. We traveled all around Italy. For a while we lived in Turin, the fashion capital of Italy. I went to the studio that had made our clothes while we were living in Tripoli and they said, "Oh, you know, we still have all of your measurements on file!" My husband specialized in mountaineering in the military, and so we were always out climbing this or that mountain or skiing. Here's a picture of us mountain climbing. He fitted me out like a mule and took me along everywhere with him.

I didn't know anything about keeping house, but I picked it up slowly, even though up to then, I had never even washed a pan, poor me! My husband was even more inept than me, and I was the woman, so it fell to me to look after the house. He too was from a well-to-do family, so he didn't know how to do anything. His mother, born in 1891, held a university degree in Literature; I think that's all that women could get a degree in then. They weren't exactly cranking out diplomas for women back then! She had studied with Carducci and then Pascoli in Bologna. She was a beautiful woman too, but she was as horrid as she was beautiful, yes, just as awful as she was pretty.

When I got pregnant, Carlo quit the military and got a stable job with Social Security, the duties office. My first son came in 1952, and the second followed in '53. Got it done one after the other. My youngest says I did a better job the second time round. We had returned to live in Arezzo with my parents by that time, and I had my children in Franco Tanganelli's gynecological clinic, where all the society girls went to have their babies. He was the same fellow I mentioned before, the one who had the country villa where Carlo and I fell in love!

My mother came to live with us. She was an incredible cook. She would get up, not too early, around 9:30, after the cleaning woman had arrived and had a chance to straighten up. Mother would close herself in the bathroom and take care of all of her toiletries; then she would lock herself in the kitchen and start cooking. I helped sometimes, but I was better at doing the shopping, and just shopping in general! She came out at lunchtime, but she was always tinkering with something in the kitchen: canning, baking, putting up jams and pickled vegetables. I was never as good as her. My husband used to say, "Ah, Mamma Giulia, what a fabulous cook you are!"

My husband died young on, March 24, 1977, and in 1993 I came to live in Umbertide, in Umbria because my son lived here. I don't know what has happened to Italians these days. They don't know how to bring up their children. How can you let your thirteen or fourteen year-old daughter out in those skimpy clothes at night, walking around the pubs like nobody's business? My father, who never laid a hand on me, would have beaten the daylights out of me if I had dared anything like that! Children aren't taught anymore to be polite, or even civil, not a scrap of manners. There aren't mealtimes anymore, and that is really sad. That ended with the last generation. But what can I say? My time has come and gone. All I have are the memories of my true home in Tripoli.

Intermezzo

Oral History

There seems to be a fear that once the floodgates
of orality are opened, writing (and rationality along
with it) will be swept out as if by a spontaneous
uncontrollable mass of fluid, amorphous material.
— ANTHONY PORTELLI,
"WHAT MAKES ORAL HISTORY DIFFERENT"

While Oral History, its methods, and corpus of research need
no apology, an apologia may answer dangling questions as
to its purpose, rationality, and importance.

Oral history distinguishes itself from the more general Oral
Tradition in that there is a premise, an investigation into a specific
social phenomenon or event whose purpose is to illuminate the past,
while shedding light on the present and future. Our capacity for empa-
thy, our ability to think ourselves into other people's places, allows us
to profit from the narratives of other people's lives without having to
experience those events directly. The act of articulating an experience
out loud allows the narrators themselves to review the event through
verbally organized thought, and with hindsight, come to terms with
what happened. The very knowledge that their story will survive them,

and through time, continue to touch the lives of others, can transform feelings of pain, confusion, and emptiness associated with upheaval and trauma into courage, triumph, and heroism.

As qualitative research, traditional historians have criticized oral history for falling short of established scholarly standards. What makes oral history so unsavory is the factual, quantitative measuring stick used to invalidate it as "quaint" and "anecdotal," read: unreliable, particularly given its indecorous association with spotlighting the unsung and the unschooled – and women. Anthony Portelli euphemistically refers to these subjects as the "non hegemonic strata," those who made history by forming the foundation upon whose backs the movers and shakers built their empires, the very people without whom there would have been nothing to move or to shake.

Oral history does not seek to flush out factual nuggets, but to flesh out a fuller history, emphasizing meaning and perspective over the event itself, highlighting emotions, ideals, struggles, prejudices, loyalties, and secrets. "Oral sources tell us not just what people did, but what they wanted to do, what they believed they were doing, and what they now think they did" (Portelli, 1998). In the absence of diaries, documents, and letters, the oral history interview provides a means of recording accounts that would otherwise have been eclipsed by historical approaches that are reluctant to admit instances of hearsay, inaccuracies, emotionality, and conjecture.

> The historian comes to the interview to learn: to sit at the feet of others, who because they come from a different social class, or are less educated, or older, know more about something. The reconstruction of history becomes … a collaborative practice, in which non-professionals must play a critical part. By giving a central place … to people of all kinds, history gains immensely" (Thompson, 2000).

Objective and subjective sources of historical evidence are often perceived as being mutually exclusive, opposing sides of a coin. A more accommodating standpoint would recognize that the two faces compliment each other, allowing us to make both heads and tails of an event. However entrenched a work of historical literature may be in verifiable fact, demographics, wages, dates, details of battles, etc., it is, regardless, the product of a human mind and, as such, not immune to contamination by personal perspectives and underlying agendas. By the same token, orally transmitted historical accounts, non-linear and memory-based, cannot be discounted as devoid of fact, insofar as they are not, and are not intended to be, fictional yarns, but collaborative efforts working toward the selfsame purposeful objective of social cognizance. In this light, subjective and objective are not value assessments, but perspectives. They do, however, beg an examination of the concept of truth.

The continuum of Truthfulness is bookended by Fallacy and Truth. As interdependent social beings, we require truthfulness, but are skeptical of the existence of truth, given the fallibility of the human mind, projections of cultural perspective, and the inevitability of experiential filters. Oral histories offer a window onto truthfulness, regardless of their grounding in indisputable fact. Wherever they may fall on the continuum of truthfulness, the value of oral accounts lies in the tellers' sincerity, in the belief that they are telling the truth and nothing but, in the hope that their experience might be respected and understood, and contribute to our ever-evolving sense of social purpose and self-awareness. For the purposes of oral history, what subjects *believe happened* is as valid as what did happen because the former expresses how they lived those events and determines how that memory was carried on through time. Events and conditions perceived at the time as perfectly normal, even laudable, may later have become a basis for intense shaming, and/or identity annihilation for reasons not always fully understood by the interviewee, as was the case with the fall of fascism. Therefore, while the individual's aim is always truthfulness, her personal truth may be tinged by fear, embarrassment, or confusion, resulting in concealed details or distorted disclosures.

A compendium of oral history narratives that provides a broad sampling of perspectives corrects inevitable discrepancies and distortions of memory by offering the reader a selection of viewpoints, each cross-referencing the other, building up to the creation of a single mosaic composed of multifarious realities. In the final analysis, their purpose is not to dispense Truth per se, but to add to the overall historical discourse and stimulate the spirit of inquiry.

Maria

Born 1924 – Montona, province of Pola, Istria

In recognition of their support of the Allies during WWI, a large tract of the former Austro-Hungarian territory was apportioned to the Kingdom of Italy, including Istria, the largest peninsula in the Adriatic. Istria has long standing Italic ties dating back to Roman times, although it does not share a land border with Italy. Today, it is mostly part of Croatia. Regaining these territories, thought of as Italian, was the main motivation behind Italy's involvement in WWI, touted as the "Fourth War of Independence." However, Istria was lost once again, towards the end of WWII, in the wake of the Yugoslavian revolt. Maria and her family were among the thousands Italian Istrians who managed to escape to Italy in the mass exodus. I visited her in her home in Sansepolcro, Tuscany, where her family had settled. It was February and the heat was unusually high in her condominium apartment. She told me that she always kept it that warm as it reminded her of the mild climate of her beloved Istria, whose loss she mourns daily. 22,000 Italian Istrians still reside there, while 200,000 settled in the diaspora.

I was born in Istria when our land, praise God, was still Italian. In April, I will be 90 years old. I've lived in Italy proper for many years now but I've never felt at home here. I even taught at a local school for twelve years, but if you asked me if I had made a friend here, a real friend, I'd have to say no. My husband was from here, though, and he was goodness itself. He was one of those creations that we find so rarely in life, someone who is gifted to us, and then, torn away from us all too soon. My mother was from Sansepolcro, but she moved to Istria when she was just out of school to take up a teaching post, but for her, Istria was her true home. Most of my family lived and died here after the war. I had an aunt who lived to be 101 years of age, and was as lucid as you see me today. She died saying her rosary. Ah, what a beautiful way to die. But up to the day she died, she said, "Could you have found a place that was further away than this?! Why, oh, why did we have to come to Sansepolcro?" But I am starting at the end, and we should start at the beginning of the story.

My father began his career as an elementary school teacher, but was soon promoted to the post of Secretary to the Director of Elementary Schools. My mother was also an elementary school teacher. She met my father when she moved to Istria to work, and they married soon after, when she was nineteen. Our home was in Montona, but the whole family moved to Pisino when my brother and I went to high school because my father didn't want to send us away to boarding school. There wasn't a high school nearby, so if we were to continue our education, and our parents didn't want to send us away, the whole family had to move. That is how families used to be. The school was only twenty kilometers away, but we didn't have a car, so getting there and back would have been a terrible burden. My grandfather implored my father again and again, "Gilo, get a car. Buy yourself a car!" And Papa would answer every time, "I can't because I am certain that at the first turning in the road I'll go straight on." Not many people had cars then, but families who could afford one, and praise the Lord, ours was one of those, all had cars. So we wintered in Pisino and in the summer, we spent three months in Montona near Grandpa, and another month at the seaside in Italy.

After we had finished high school, we returned to our Montona home until '45 when the war was over. When I say *our* home, I mean the house that I was born in, the house where I have all of the sweet memories of my childhood. It was a small town of 1,200 souls. We had a completely different way of understanding the world, and of behaving with each other, that is in no way similar to the way young people are today. I don't know how to explain it to you, except to say that even the way we *thought* was so different from the way people think today. My childhood was a serene one, even during the war. School was the central part of our lives. Our elementary school wasn't a makeshift one like many back then. We had five teachers, one for every grade, and a classroom for every grade as well. Our school was in a beautiful building. Sadly, it was the first one in town that was bombed.

We lived on Via Andrea Antico, named after an Istrian who was the first printer to publish sacred music in Rome in 1516. We could have had a much larger house on an elegant tree-lined avenue because my grandfather had offered to buy a handsome villa for my mother when she was a young bride. But she was a bit fearful because she was a foreigner, being Tuscan, you know, and my father was one of those men, who no sooner had he finished his dinner then he was off to the gentleman's club. She was afraid of being alone in such a big isolated house. She preferred a modest home in town to a lavish villa in the country. So we lived in a 4-story townhouse that was more centrally located. It was between two houses owned by people who made their living selling craft products from the countryside, but their social class made no difference to us. People tended not to put on airs about their status or flaunt their wealth.

But my family did enjoy comforts that not everyone could afford. Not that there were so many luxurious commodities to be had! I am talking about things like a portable bidet or the hipbath that the servants filled with buckets of hot water hauled up from the kitchen. As soon as we cut our first tooth, we got toothbrushes, and those were a bit of a novelty! Papa was very strict about health and personal hygiene. Oh, goodness gracious, was he ever! My brother and I had to get up at 7 a.m. to do the fascist party's early morning exercise program broadcast on the radio. At a certain point, the program also integrated hand weights, and so my father bought us weights as well. My mother protested, "Girls shouldn't do weights! Her arms will look like a man's!" And indeed, after a time I developed big biceps, and the kids at school made fun of me. For the dance of my first year in high school, I had to have a dress made with sleeves that came down to my elbows to cover the muscles. It wasn't the fashion, but sculpted arms were considered very unbecoming on a young lady, and they had to be hidden.

Papa wasn't that way just with us. He insisted there be a strong emphasis on health and hygiene, precision, and order in the school curriculum. That militant bent came from his mother. She was from Turin in Piedmont. She was Quintino Sella's cousin [*finance minister, infamous architect of the crippling austerity measures after the Unification of Italy*]. She required that her own son use the formal address form with her, respecting the old-style decorum of the upper-classes, whereas my grandfather was a pure Istrian, and Papa was allowed to use the informal with him.

> *Until the fourteenth century "voi" was used to address someone formally, like the French "vous." By the sixteenth and seventeenth centuries, "lei" which is literally "she," had entered into common usage and predominated. Some contemporary men of letters complained about the absurdity of speaking to someone directly and referring to them as "she," while others thought it would me more useful to distinguish royalty from commoners. One century later, efforts were made to suppress "lei" due to its erroneously supposed foreign influences. Regardless, it continued to be used interchangeably alongside "voi" until 1938, when Mussolini officially outlawed "lei" as part of a general program of linguistic purification. After the fall of fascism, "voi" dropped out of use almost entirely. Today, it is only used in a few small towns and is considered backwards by the overwhelming majority, who use "lei."*

Once Papa dared to speak to his mother with the informal and she retorted, "You save that sort of talk for your friends, young man, because I am having none of it! Not now, not ever!" My other grandparents were from Sansepolcro, Tuscany. I saw them one month a year, when we went to the seaside in Italy.

In the evenings, when my father was out, we would listen to the radio, or my mother would play the piano. Like most everyone, we went to bed early. The gentleman's club my father belonged to was a genteel association, which also promoted cultural events. My father played the violin and viola in some of their concerts, with my mother accompanying on the piano now and again. The concerts were a real treat because, except for the radio, there wasn't any other musical entertainment, and not many people could afford one of those. In 1929, they brought the electric lines into local homes, and my father was the first one in town to buy a radio. [*A radio cost two months' pay of an average white-collar employee.*]

I remember there was a sort of speaker we attached to the wall and a big box, and when there were international soccer games, Papa would put the speaker in the window because across from our house there was a church with an area in front where you could sit, so men would gather round to listen to the game. There was a beautiful horse-chestnut tree at that church. This one tree produced two different colored flowers: red and white, and with the green of the leaves it was symbolically the tricolore [*the Italian flag*]. Papa always saw that tree as a sign of respect. When the Austrians lost dominion over the territory, they could have chopped it down out of spite for the Italians, but they didn't. He used to say, "One must always remember one's debt to the civility of others. The Austrians are a serious, civil people. When the Italians assumed control, they bowed out gracefully." He wanted to point out that takeovers can be civil affairs. People already residing in a place should be welcomed into the new order and not oppressed by it.

Fascist Italianization of Croat and Slovenian culture in Istria was already a foregone conclusion by the time Maria was growing up. The use of languages other than Italian had been eradicated from legal spheres; in 1923, schools were by decree exclusively in Italian; sporting, cultural and social associations other than Italian ones were suppressed, as was any form of Slav banking or economic institution. The final blow was the "restoration" of names and surnames to their "original" Italian. A leaflet in circulation warned that anyone caught speaking or even singing on the street, or carrying out business in shops in a Slavic language would be dealt with accordingly: "We fascist officials will use persuasive methods to ensure that the present order is respected."

To my mind, Istria was Italy. Even the peasants who lived in the countryside of Montona spoke Italian. They were Italians and didn't know a single word in Slavic. More precisely, what we spoke was Venetian dialect. From what I had always heard tell from my father, the transfer of power to Italy went smoothly, without resentment. Papa always spoke of the Austrians as an advanced people, but it was *Mussolini* who had built our aqueduct because where we were, there was no water. From 1930 on, there was water for everyone. Before, if you didn't have a well, you had to pay a courier, and I am talking about having water hauled uphill by pack mules, not trucks. A funny thing is that, in order to keep the water from spilling out of the buckets during the arduous climb, they put in a bundle of the herb butcher's broom, and for some reason, that kept the water in.

When the aqueduct arrived, well, as you can imagine, it seemed like a dream come true. Clearly, when you receive such benefits, you are going to speak well about the system that made that possible, and if you receive nothing, you are going to speak badly about it. That's just human nature. I had never heard in my community or in my house, any talk that ran contrary to fascist initiatives. My grandfather was a lively talker and had a shop in the center of town, a veritable hub for town chitchat. He sold newspapers in his shop, and so everyone would talk about the latest of whatever was happening, but no one was ever against the fascists. Everyone was a card-carrying party member. Of course, then, you had to be if you wanted to work. Granted, some may have carried it "under their shoe," as the saying goes because they weren't in agreement, but I don't remember any talk of anyone being put in prison because they were anti-fascists.

There was a line of demarcation that signposted the confines of Venetian influence. If you went just twenty kilometers toward Pisino, you'd find that there was not a single citizen who didn't also know Slavic. They spoke Venetian dialect but with a Slavic influence. We all spoke dialect to each other, among classmates or at home, unless there was an Italian present who didn't speak our dialect. And of course, in school, it was strictly standard Italian with our teachers. I don't remember noticing anyone at school who spoke any differently, I mean with Slavic as their first language. What I am saying is, we were *Italians*. Istria was *Italian*, and because of the geographical separation, we felt all the more patriotic towards the mother country. Whenever there was a national holiday or celebration, we eagerly donned our fascist uniforms and gathered in the square or church, even though, of course, attendance was obligatory. But it didn't matter because we *wanted* to go. We all participated in Fascist Saturday every week and did gymnastics performances at the end of the school year. By the time the war came I had been promoted to giovane fascista, but at that point, we didn't meet regularly anymore; resources were needed elsewhere.

Our food was influenced mostly by Venetian cuisine, which is famous everywhere. If anything, the difference in Istria was that our food had a distinct Austrian touch, particularly the desserts. One of our favorite local desserts was called *fritole:*

Fritole Istriane – Istrian croquettes
300g semolina
½ liter water
pinch of salt
100g sugar
2 bars chopped chocolate
150g raisins
150g candied orange peel
100g pine nuts
lemon zest
aquavit
lard
sugar

Boil the water and add the semolina, making a thick polenta. Cool slightly and stir in the rest of the ingredients except the aquavit. Mix well and add in enough aquavit to render the batter soft enough to form balls. Drop spoonfuls into hot lard and fry until crispy. Remove, cool, and coat well with sugar.

In the morning, my parents always had coffee, but it was made from raw coffee beans that had to be toasted at home on the stovetop. We children were given *caffè d'orzo* and milk every morning, and like everyone, we had bread and butter with jam. My grandfather had large landholdings and sharecroppers who lived on the land, so we never had to use the ration card. In Istria, the sharecroppers kept a part for themselves, gave a part to us, and then owed a part to the state as well, so we never wanted for anything. We even had olive oil because Grandpa had an olive grove, but we also used lard because half of any animal that was butchered was given to us as our due.

When my brother Gigi and I came home from school and my parents from work, the table was already set and the serving woman brought out the food. Lunch was still the main meal of the day then. The fare was very traditional. We ate more rice than pasta because rice paddies are abundant in northern Italy. Rice and chicken liver soup was a standard first course. You just cooked up chopped livers and spooned it into rice soup. Or we often had a dish called *risi e bisi*, basically rice and peas; or we had rice with eel or mussels. This was followed by a meat course, a couple of side dishes and then fruit. We always had plenty to eat at our house. And because my father liked fish, we bought fish from the fishwives every Friday. Poor things, they came in on the bus with their crates of fish and then walked from the bus stop to the market area with the crates on their heads. My father waited for Fridays like one waiting for the hand of Our Savior to come down from the heavens because for him, it was fish, fish, fish. He wanted to have three different kinds in a single meal. We had to buy a slab of ice so it would keep for a few days. I don't know where the ice came from, though. Perhaps when you live in a world that is so serene, questions like that never come to mind. We didn't think about *not* having things, or where the things we did have came from.

As I said, the meal ended with fruit, either something in season from our own land, or we would buy whatever local fruit was available. We always had several courses, and I thank God that I never had to experience hunger while I was growing up. Dinner almost always started with a cup of meat broth because my grandfather, like many of his generation, was a great believer that broth in the evening was an elixir. One thing we never had in the evening was pasta. It was too heavy. Then we had a meat dish with two or three side dishes, and then fruit. Like lunch but a bit lighter.

There was a wonderful butcher shop in front of our house, and they had everything you could wish for, beef, goat, lamb, and hens.

They remained in business throughout the war, as well, but the amount you could buy was limited because you had to buy meat with the ration card; otherwise, there was the black market. But there were a lot of favors my family exchanged with the country people, so when they came to town, they didn't come empty handed. It was like during the Great War, when letters would arrive from the front. The country people couldn't read, so schooled people like my grandfather would read their letters to them and write back for them, and so, you see, homage was paid in foodstuffs. Our cook used to say, "There was always so much to eat here you'd have never known a war was on!" Our social system ran smoothly along those same lines until 1943, when the Germans occupied Istria.

Wartime was in the air, and you could sense that a change was coming. Suddenly, one person came up missing, then another. My father had been called into service in 1940, and in 1941, he was hospitalized with asthmatic bronchitis and got discharged. I had a flash, an epiphany that I had to do something. It was then that I asked my father if I could get my teaching certificate to become a teacher. He looked at me long and hard and said, "Forget it." "Why, Papa?" "I am just telling you – forget it." A few days pass and I asked again. "Do you want me to write it on the wall so that you remember?" he said, "Forget it!" I continued asking. After a while, all I had to say was, "Papa?" and he would say, "No." Then after three months, he finally broke. "I beg you, don't ask me anymore. Just do as you please!" I finished my third year of high school in June of '43 and I did a month of intensive private study to prepare for the teaching qualification exam in July. Anyone could do the teaching exam. You didn't have to go to the Magistrale teaching school, all you had to do was study for the exam, and if you passed, you could become a teacher. So, I did and I passed. Papa said, "Hang your certificate on the wall because that is where it is going to stay." Just to let me know that I would never be a teacher. I think he feared that, like my mother, I would be transferred somewhere far away from my family if I were to apply for a position.

When the Germans came in '43, the coexistence was quite civil, although soon after, as history would have it, they became the enemy. Mussolini's government had collapsed, and there was a terrible period of utter confusion when the Slavs attempted their takeover. Of course, there was a difference between the German *army* and the SS, who were a force of evil. The occupying troops were mostly Austrians, with whom we already had a shared history, and not really Germans. There was a great civility about them, and they didn't just overrun places shooting blindly. They were respectful and kept to their assigned duties. We were expecting an attack from the Americans, and the German army was there to help the Italians defend their land holdings. They had their own barracks and didn't disturb anyone's home. We kept on with our lives as far as possible. It was the Slavs that we feared most.

For two years, the presence of the Germans in Istria held the Slavs at bay. The Germans treated the Slavic partisan groups to an exemplary demonstration of power to alert them early on as to who was in charge, but their organization, whose objective was to form a federation, was well underway, so they simply retreated underground and lay in wait until the time was ripe for them to strike.

The day after the Germans received their orders to evacuate, they packed into their trucks and retreated. Not a day had passed before the Slav partisans made their move. They came out of hiding and straight into town. In accordance with their plan, there were certain families who had been earmarked to be sent to prison or thrown into the foibas, particularly if they had been directly involved with the fascist party or had any political involvement, which my family fortunately hadn't. My father had always taken pains to respect the opinions of others and exercise moderation in expressing his own views. Thousands of Istrians were summarily dispensed of in this way because the transition of power had to take place immediately.

Foibas are naturally occurring underground sinkholes that can extend to 200m deep, sometimes with tunnels that branch far into the bowels of the earth. Being thrown into a foiba, like being pushed off a building, meant certain death. One notable example of the numerous foibas in Istria is the Monrupino Foiba. It has a 10x15 meter opening, and is 175 meters (53 stories) deep, with an inclined ridge 10 meters long and 2 meters wide at the 60-meter mark, which would be difficult to avoid striking on the way down; the base was 7 square meters of rock and mud. The victims' hands were tied behind their backs with wire as they were marched to their deaths. Those who were not killed outright beforehand, were thrust into the pit alive, either by the perpetrators, or as a further measure of torture, by their companions, who were forced to shove them in. The Monrupino Foiba alone became the tomb of an es-timated 2,000 victims, though the bodies were never recuperated due to technical difficulties. A massive tombstone was created in 1959 to cover the opening of the pit and dignify the tragedy. The identification of the bodies from other foibas was onerous and incomplete due to the mass exodus of Italian Istrians, the concomitant take-over by the Yugoslav powers, as well as the subsequent lack of attention the Italian govern-ment afforded the massacre after the war.

We locked ourselves in the house, wary even of our friends. A Slav par-tisan came to tell us that we should get together a warm wrap for my brother Gigi because they were taking him away, and she thought he'd need a sweater. A sweater! My mother and I looked at her dumbfound-ed. "He's been taken prisoner," she said. He had been out on the street talking with a few friends, and they were suddenly lined up and filed off to prison. We ran to look for him, but by then they were far away, climbing up the mountain in a line. I spewed out all of the hate I had been choking back, and my mother quickly covered my mouth fearing I'd make things worse. My father wasn't well, so we told him that Gigi had been taken away on precautionary measures. The next morning, one of the friends who had been with Gigi that night was shot, and the other escaped, but only long enough to shout, "Long live Italian Istria!" before they shot him in the back. Every evening, I pretended to take Gigi his dinner so that Papa wouldn't be suspicious. By then, the town was under complete Slavic control. In an effort to humiliate girls from good families, the Slavs put us to doing menial jobs for them. My job was washing dishes in their mess hall. But not being used to it, I think I dropped and broke more plates than I actually cleaned.

One month passed, then another with no news. By then, Papa had found out the truth. Then one day, a family friend from Trieste came carrying a note from Gigi hidden in the band of his hat. "I am in Grobnico in a concentration camp. Please, save me! I can't take it much longer!" I decided to act and went to the highest Slav official I could find to get a document requesting his release. They wrote it, but laughed in my face, which only made me more determined. I took a train to the Prisoners of War Office. The captain there said that it was not in his power to undertake a search and release, but he too wrote a letter to assist me. This took me to another official, who sent me to another, and yet another. I went from town to town on foot under the beating rays of the summer sun. In one town alone, I went to seven different offices until I exploded and shouted, "Do you people even know where your heads are?!" Finally, this official took pity on me and said in a low voice, "Go to Voloska. You'll find what you're looking for there." After walking for hours I arrived at the office in Voloska and the official said that I needed yet another letter declaring my brother's innocence from the such-and-such office in the town I had just left. I stood in the middle of the road to stop an oncoming truck, which nearly ran me over, but I had to get back immediately to the town whence I had come.

The official who had been kind to me was not authorized to write a letter of innocence, but he told me where I needed to go, and he wrote a note in Slavic on the back of his card. Once I had arrived in the town where my dear brother was said to be, and showed my pile of attestations to the official, he told me that that group of prisoners had been moved to another town. I was on the verge of giving up or having a breakdown. I don't know what possessed me, but I showed the picture of Gigi that I had brought with me to the first soldier I found on the street. He started laughing and said, "Sure, I know him! He was worse off than any of the others! No, shoes, trousers in shreds, and hardly anything left of his shirt." He said they had been taken to Karlovaz, 200 kilometers away. I managed to hitch a ride on the back of a truck atop some of sacks of rice.

Once we arrived in Karlovaz, I was once again sent from office to office. Nothing. No one would help. On the street, desperate, some unknown force again led me to tell my story to a man who was standing nearby and ask if he knew who could help. Amazingly, he spoke my language and told me the name of the local official I needed to talk to. I went immediately to this Captain Sablic, who informed me that the prisoners had been moved. I was unable to contain myself and burst out crying. With a hysterical young woman on his hands, he made some phone calls and discovered where Gigi was, and said that I would find my brother waiting for me in Sisak. Sisak was 300 kilometers away from Karlovaz. Captain Sablic assured me that as soon as there was a mission heading that way, I could travel with it, and in the meantime he found me a place to stay and I was allowed to eat at the army mess hall.

After a few days, I was on my way, this time in a car with an officer. This official smoked a lot and kept offering me cigarettes. I was afraid to refuse, and so we both smoked continuously until we arrived. I thought I was going to be sick. Once in Sisak I was accompanied to yet another officer. He looked over my papers and I was overwhelmed by a feeling of dread that he was going to tell me that the prisoners had been moved. "Come with me," he said. We got into a car and went to a work site where there, in front of my eyes, was my brother. He collapsed into my arms crying, "Maria! Take me home. Get me out of here! I beg you!" It was a miracle. He was little more than a skeleton covered with skin. He had a gash on his forehead that was still bleeding and his bony hands were covered with scabs and blisters. I could see his stick-like legs through his tattered trousers. The release went smoothly, and I discovered that Captain Sablic had sent a telegram before my arrival saying, "Free prisoner Giovanelli."

After nursing my brother back to health for a few days, we took the train to Trieste, where we stayed with some of my father's cousins. When I was in Trieste, I wrote a long letter to my parents. I don't know how many pages I filled about the odyssey I had undertaken to find my brother. My mother said that as she read it aloud to Papa, stopping every now and then to dry her eyes. She saw that he was discreetly drying his eyes too. I found that letter many years later and I recopied it in pen because I had written it in pencil. Then, when Mamma died, I put the original letter in the coffin with her, so that she'd always have it.

Our serving woman, who had been with us for ten to fifteen years or so, had accompanied my brother and me to the border because, being from the upper countryside, she spoke a few words of Slavic. We stayed in Trieste, but my parents were unable to get permission to leave right away. When at last their papers came through, they packed a couple bags, closed the door of the house with all of our belongings inside, and gave the key to the authorities, never to return. My father, who was ill, was permitted to travel by car to Trieste. For a time, we managed to find lodgings of our own there, just a room with a kitchen, while my father was put in the hospital.

We descended the Italian peninsula to my mother's hometown of Sansepolcro, in Tuscany, where we rented another room. I slept between my parents on the bed, and my brother slept on a cot. The kitchen was downstairs from our room. It was an open hearth with a pot hanging from a chain, and Mamma didn't have the first idea how to cook that way. She had learned to cook a bit by watching our cook, but we had had a wood-burning stove. Soon after our arrival, our landlady's husband left her and said that he wouldn't come back until she had kicked my father out of the house. Papa suffered from asthmatic bronchitis and the landlady's husband thought for certain it was tuberculosis. Having nowhere else to go, and fearing we'd be put out on the street, we took Papa to the hospital. He died soon after, at age 52, in 1948.

We stayed on another year renting that room. Mamma got a job right away teaching, and not long after that, I too got a teaching post not too far away, so in the end, my teaching certificate was put to use. The pay was so little, though, that I spent most of it getting to and from work. Mamma had been wise when she packed her suitcase in Istria, and so, assisted by the Good Lord, she had had the foresight to stow forty-two Austrian gold coins in the lining of her bag. At the end of the month, if we couldn't make ends meet, we would sell one of them off. Each one was equivalent to about half of a monthly stipend. In the end, we sold all but three of them. My plan had always been to go on to university to become a pediatrician, but that was just one of many dreams that would go unfulfilled.

My brother had applied for a managerial position at the Buitoni factory, but they wouldn't hire him because we were from Istria. No one wanted to touch the Istrians because we were known to have been staunch supporters of the Duce. Our patriotism had been our identity, and we clung to it because that was our protection, our connection to Italy. You see, the communist sympathizers did not have to escape Istria. They were free to stay, so the mainland Italians saw anyone from Istria who had escaped as being a threat.

For eight years, Gigi applied and was refused, the irony of course being that the Buitoni were openly fascist when Mussolini was in power. A table-turning purification was happening all over Italy to remove anyone who had been an outspoken fascist from their jobs, both the powerful and the humble. If anyone continued as a fascist sympathizer, they were out. So it comes as no surprise that the hiring committee at Buitoni was all communist.

Gigi finally got the mayor of Trieste to write a letter on his behalf vouching for his trustworthiness, and that worked. After he had retired, Marco Buitoni himself acknowledged that they had erred in a speech at a company dinner with all the big wigs. My brother said it made him blush right down to his little toe.

I returned many years after the war, to Istria, to see my house. Actually, I think the first time I went was on my honeymoon because I wanted my husband to see the house where I was born. I stood outside and looked at it. I was happy to see that whoever had moved in had taken very good care of it, even though it had been painted ever so garishly. As I stood there in the street looking at the house, a man came out, a young high school teacher, and he said, "I can see by the way you are looking at the house that this used to be your house. Come in and let me show you the changes I have made to it because, of course, over time, things do change." Indeed, I hardly recognized it anymore, but it was all done up very well. He said to me, "If you would like to come sometimes during the summer and spend a few days here, this was once your house and it will, for those days, once again be your house." I at least had the peace of mind to know that our home was in good hands, but the rest of the neighborhood had changed. I didn't see a single person that I knew. It was all Slavs now. The shutters were all closed, and the other homes hadn't been kept up so well. I did return to Istria a few more times, but I always felt ill at ease because it had been so neglected. It made me feel as if I myself had been abandoned and neglected.

Epilogue

A conversation with Dario Cecchini

The Chianti valley is truly one of the treasures of Italy, a cradle of history, fertile land, breathtaking landscapes and unrivaled art. It is here too that Dario Cecchini, known as the "Mad Butcher of Panzano," has his butcher shop, Antica Macelleria Cecchini. *Anthony Bourdain hails him as "the most famous and respected butcher in Italy, and maybe in the world. Dario is not just a butcher; he is something else entirely. He's a repository of knowledge for all things Tuscan, be it foodways, historical canon, literature, or poetry." Naturally, my curiosity was piqued to see how this revered culinary oracle envisioned the evolution of Italian food and the present state of gastronomic affairs, and so, I embarked upon what would be my last journey for this book. At risk of marring his gruff reputation, I found Dario to be truly a prince among men, not a grizzly but a teddy bear, albeit a sizeable, outspoken one, with a fabulously thick* chiantigiano *accent.*

Butchers are the most important link in the food chain because they are the link between life and death. They are the connection between respect and responsibility, knowledge and conscience. In this area, butchers ran a good business. I know because my family have been in the butchering trade for 250 years, right here in Panzano. We were chockfull of noble families, the Ruccellai, the

Strozzi, the Guicciardini, the Orsini... and that brought constant trade to local butchers. The good cuts of meat were sent to Florence and the lesser cuts were for townspeople and contadini. People ate the whole animal back then. Nothing was wasted. During the Ventennio, my family was the only family in town that didn't have party membership. But just the same, when the war was on, the partigiani came for their meat at 6 a.m. – gratis – and the fascio came for theirs at 8 – gratis. Everyone knew their hour, and that's how it worked. No conflicts. The Cecchini family never had to deal in the black market because there were enough people around who could afford meat.

The contadini had to trade for meat, of course, but it was still like that when I was young. It remained a trading society between contadini and craftsmen for a while, even after the war. Sharecroppers never had any ready money because it was a system of abuse. They were taken on specifically because they were illiterate. The first thing they asked a capoccia before they took him on was if he could read and write, that way he'd never know if the accounts were straightforward. The nobility lived off the backs of those poor people, and if one family of sharecroppers didn't suit you, there were plenty more in line who would take their place. Here, there were a whole lot of loafers sporting noble titles, who lived off that system. The butchers mainly dealt with the city, but you were responsible for the needs of everyone in your community.

It's a small town, but it supported four butchers. Used to be that butchers dealt mainly in beef. Fowl was another occupation, and pork and salumi, yet another. Meat was kept on ice back then, no refrigeration, but there was a good turnover, so waste wasn't a problem. Sure, you can't compare it to other places, like Basilicata. That's like comparing New York and Morocco. Our land yielded better also because of the old Etruscan systems of farming that they used. The country poor were never as bad off as the city poor, not in Tuscany. But hunger was a relative concept. If you had one herring, that single herring was enough for your whole family. I've always followed these stories because the way I see it, a butcher needs to feed the community, and there has to be something for everyone. So let me say this, when they bartered for a herring because, as I said, they didn't have any ready cash, it cost one rabbit and one chicken. Ok? One rabbit and one chicken for one herring. Now, if you are going to buy one herring so that you can wipe your bread across it for the flavor, it begs the question – why not just eat the rabbit and the chicken? You'll at least have something to bite into. It is about concepts, about values. Like the old contadini, who fed truffles to the pigs. Truffles only became prized because the noble families wanted them. Then we reevaluated them. People make a big deal out of truffles, caviar, and champagne, but I don't like any of them, personally. Unfortunately, I have to eat them every now and then because people think that they are giving me some sort of treat. Same with fois gras and lobster. Please! I'd rather have tripe, if it is all the same to you. You know what they call lobster in Maine? Cockroaches. They are like vultures that swim. Anyway...

My idea about the past is this: it is all about fatigue and freeing yourself from fatigue. It's like this: Making bread is extremely tiring. You had to take your bags of grain to be milled, haul them back, gather wood for the fire, build the fire; you even had to have built your own oven and keep it in working order. You had to have your *pasta madre* and keep that going day in, day out. Kneading, rising, baking. You see? Tradition comes out of culture, out of *wanting* traditions. This was not tradition. It was fatigue. Traditions come when you can choose to do something and enjoy doing it, not when you *have* to do it to live, and you break your back over it. As soon as the contadino could afford to buy the bread that *someone else* had made, well, that was living! He had found paradise. The industry that was born out of that didn't need an ethic. Their products didn't even have to be very good. They just had to make you feel like you could afford the things that people who didn't work had. The food industry wanted to make money off of that. So, to get you to buy that stuff, they sell themselves as your family, you mom, your dad, and all of your close relatives. Or worse, as local craftsmen. It's big business.

The exodus from the country to the city was not just about escaping fatigue, but also about social respect. A person who was a contadino was on the lowest rung of the social ladder. The peasant family itself was organized with such rigidity and severity that it was a form of cruelty. There were often up to twenty members in a sharecropper house, and so they were like a small business. It was a survival structure, not a family. The capoccia was not so much the father or head of the family, but a sort of enemy. He was the go-between for the property owner and the family. So just imagine, mature males in the family who had to grovel to the capoccia any time they wanted money for a pack of cigarettes, or anything... Why would you keep on doing that once there were other possibilities? Women too had to ask permission for everything, even for a spool of thread. Only the capoccia handled the money. The landowner counted on this family structure so that the family members didn't voice their opinions. You cannot call that tradition. So the main reasons that people wanted to get out of the country were because of the severity of the capoccia, and also because they wanted to have *their own money* to do what they chose. Having money also meant you could have a social life. The city life, even as a factory worker, represented independence, living your own life, having your own money. We all love freedom.

A factory worker was one rung up. A factory job meant you changed class. Expectations in Italy were so low that working the assembly line seemed like the middle class. It was like those old American films where the little husband returns from his little office job with his little briefcase. Factory work allowed you to pay your rent, give your family a decent life, and to have that little car. FIAT, one of the great Italian disasters, opened factories and needed workers, and people poured in from the countryside. I remember when I was young and the countryside emptied out. Farms were abandoned everywhere. All of my school friends disappeared. We didn't see them again until they could come back with a new car. They would come back, even if it was just a FIAT 500, and drive through the main piazza on Sunday for all to see, so that they could say, "We've made it." It is the same story as immigration in America at the beginning of the 19th century, just that this was closer.

People are attracted to what they think represents "the good life." Once people could start to afford filet mignon, everyone wanted filet and tastes turned away from offal. I was brought up eating intestines, blood, tripe, eyes, whatever it was that we couldn't sell. My grandmother always made me cabbage and intestines. I didn't have my first steak until I was eighteen. Ah, I couldn't wait. I smelled the aroma rising off the grill as it cooked. The first couple bites were fabulous, but then I said, hey, is that all there is to a steak? I see the Americans who come here, who are so starry-eyed about the idea of the noble families and royalty. That's what I am talking about. We all bring our cultural baggage to the table.

When you had the power to buy instead of making or growing it yourself, it was a luxury, whatever it was. Look again at bread. Buying white bread meant you had moved up in the world. But now that organic, whole grain bread with seeds and sprouted whatever is no longer associated with poverty, well now, *that* is the healthy choice of the wealthy consumer. But if you took all those organic people and preachers of the natural world and you put them in the field to do some real work, they'd be out there with their iPhones and their Coca-Cola. Maybe not literally, but the point is, even if they weren't, *they could be if they want to.* That's why I say, the value of store-bought food rested precisely on the fact that it was store-bought, and you ate whatever it was they were serving up. It wasn't about having food; the contadini had enough to eat. It was about getting money and being able to waste it. That was an important status symbol.

Tradition is about recovering the past, but you can only have that when you have come to terms with that past, come clean with it. But while you are doing it, while you are living it, it is not tradition. It's only later that we pick and choose what we want our traditions to be, how we want to remember them and what we want to forget. That way, the past all seems so wonderful in comparison to the present, and it gives people something to yearn for. Working yourself to the bone to get food on the table and a shirt on your back was not a tradition, not while you were in the throes of it. People just wanted to get through another day, another season.

How does the craftsman fit in to this picture today? Let's take the butcher as an example. Butchers in supermarkets are not butchers; they are people who cut meat and put it into polystyrene boxes. All you have to do is take a course to work in the meat department of a supermarket. Real butchers are people who know the animals, know how they live, how they are killed. I get my pigs from Spain from a family that I know and trust because there isn't anyone in Italy who keeps them how I want them to be kept. If the animals are not treated well, the meat is not good. "Zero kilometers" makes no sense in that scheme. You need to know your meat. Selection is at the heart of being a good butcher. Selecting, cutting, aging, and advising people about cooking it. It is not just a question of morality and respect, but of quality. I want my animals to be treated optimally because otherwise, the meat is not going to be wholesome and good. Only three percent of meat in America is labeled prime because the other animals are not kept well. It may work well for the meat industry, but we are not talking about quality products. I have another project in Panzano, fifty chianinas, but I don't display the certification because the meat in my shop is *my meat*. It is chosen by me. I am the common denominator of what goes into my shop. I was asked once what was the best ingredient for a good steak and my answer was, "The butcher."

I believe that those of us working in the craft food sector, the artisans, are the key to balancing the negative effects of what is happening on today's food market. If the community holds their artisans in esteem because they have earned it though quality craftsmanship and dedication, those people will expect and choose quality. They will want to find it in their local area and not have to drive half an hour for a decent loaf of bread. Granted, the prices have to be reasonable, but if the system works, and craft food makers are an integral part of the community, then that is possible.

That is the difference between my point of view and Artusi's. He was only interested in bringing the middle and upper classes together through food so that they would be more accepting of a unified Italy. He tried to unify regional foods into "Italian foods," – which anyway, were the foods of the upper classes – in order to unite Italians. In so doing, he contributed to one of the greatest disservices to regional cuisines by flattening and homogenizing them. In the same way, the Italian state, in order to enter into the EEC, took food artisans to slaughter. The price of becoming Europeans was destroying craftspeople and nullifying food, so that it would conform to someone else's model. But we artisans are a resistant lot. We make our own paradise here on earth. We don't need Jesus's paradise, and we most certainly don't need the EEC's either. And we also don't need their hell because we are perfectly capable of making that for ourselves too! Thanks very much, but I've got it covered!

But you see, there is an important point I am trying to get around to here. If there are things that people don't want to do at home in the family anymore, which is perfectly valid these days, and there is someone who will do it for you, *do it well*, and in a way that is cost effective, then that is the direction we should go. But what is happening, in actuality, is that people have been beguiled into settling for low quality. Industry forges ahead and tries to pass things off as traditional when they aren't, and they pull it off because it is so easy to take people for a ride. You are assuming that people are somehow interested in cultural evolution, but people are essentially lazy. That's why it works in industry's favor.

At the other end is Slow Food. It is a religion, evangelizing foods for a market. You've got the faith or you don't. Personally, I don't. I want a secular world. I've met many of the people involved in the Slow Food movement, and I don't like their way of thinking, just like they don't like mine. That is not a negative judgment, but neither is it a diplomatic response. Like anyone, I like being with people of my mindset, my creed. Not because I want to be separatist or racist, but because it makes me feel well, at ease. I am an anarchist. I am full of doubts. I follow Ulysses's lead; I want to learn things, but they, like all religious people, think they have already found all the answers. I think Slow Food is one of the biggest scams, with all of its gastronomic defense. It has created a market of stuff that was already there, but has now been saved and put on a pedestal. Saved for what? Saved *for a market*, and not for tradition or the community.

If you are an artisan, you live as an artisan. You cannot go out and try to convert the world. There are already too many religious people out there. They are trying to go back to primeval times. Not even medieval times – to *primeval* times. People want to get back to some kind of food paradise, a Garden of Eden that was here before original sin. But really, there is no explanation because the earth has never been a paradise. Our move forward at this juncture cannot be about having foods "saved" by Slow Food, like some sacred lamb from the hilltops. What we need in order to progress from here is to eat in a more ethical way, to waste less and try to feed better food to more people – to get decent food to those who do not have it. That is a valid goal. But an artisan cannot go out like a food evangelist to convert the world. This world already has too many evangelists. Just focus on your work and do it to the best of your ability. If the public likes it, fine. But just – do your job.

That is the only way we can go on. We need to raise the average mindset about quality food, and this doesn't mean going looking for molecular cuisine. For the love of God! Who in the hell cares about molecular food?! How can we even talk about whether or not food is better or worse in a world hunting for Michelin stars?! Cooking schools today don't teach the future cooks these simple basics, how to know a good oil, good bread, good meat... they teach them how to get Michelin stars. So the public is led to believe that that is what good food is about.

For me, food is our way of celebrating life, and we celebrate it by using nature well. The food industry has no interest in that perspective. They simply want to make money. However it is that you set out to make that money, for them, the end justifies the means. If there is a market for something like Eataly, you are going to have Eataly. If you can sell it and call it Italian food, where's the problem, they say? For me Eataly is a supermarket. I have nothing against supermarkets. I am an artisan and so my place is, of course, with the artisans. Eataly damages artisans, or rather, it puts craftspeople in a situation in which they can no longer be called craftspeople, by the simple fact that an artisan can only produce a limited amount in a localized area. Once the artisan cannot personally oversee the production, the artisan becomes an industry, and is no longer an artisan. An artisan has hands, heart and head. You make your product with your own hands, or oversee it being made by someone who has learned from you. There is a measure and a limit to how much you can produce. Your production can be no larger than what you can personally check and control. It is as simple as that. Industries delegate not only production elements, but the quality control to other people. If I want to remain an artisan, I cannot aspire to become as large as Eataly. The general manager of Whole Foods asked if I would train his butchers, and I said that if I trained his butchers, then I would not be able to keep watch over my shop. It is a question of how I want to live my life. Whole Foods is a supermarket, sure, organic high quality, but it is a supermarket. How do they know what the work conditions are of all those who are out laboring in all the organic fields where their produce comes from? The Whole Foods market is the American version of Eataly.

So what is the difference for me between Eataly and McDonalds? Only the crowds they draw. Eataly pulls in a clientele with more disposable income. But, the structural organization and the idea behind it is the same. What you have here is a man who was originally in the household appliance trade. He sold out and started selling food. Maybe he was born again or something, or maybe he does it for the money. It is not that artisans don't want the glory, that's beside the point – but the first and foremost quality that distinguishes an artisan is values. A *true* artisan wants to be good at what he does. He wants to challenge God. It is the deadly sin of Pride. He says, I don't want *your* Paradise because I am going to make *my own* paradise on earth. I am a craftsman. I have the power in my hands. It is the longing to achieve perfection, so that you can become a master of your craft and teach others. When you have embarked on this path, the most important thing is to become a master. Of course, you don't mind the money, but it is not your goal. That is what it means to follow the spirit of the Renaissance.

The architect Michelucci wrote a beautiful letter after having paid a visit to the cupola of Brunelleschi's cathedral in Florence. It was full of scaffolding because they were doing restoration work. The scaffolds reached into some really out of the way areas, out of the visibility of the human eye, and in those hidden corners, the artisan had carried out the most perfect and elaborate refinishing work because the artisan is not looking to educate the masses, or to explain to people what is and isn't good. The artisan does what he does for himself. He is egotistical, conceited, and all those things the Catholics consider sinful because he, a man, dares to enter into realm of God. That artisan did that refinishing work for himself and for no one else.

When I explain to my apprentices about how to make the best use of an animal from nose to tail, I am only thinking about my role and the respect that is owed to that animal, which means that I need to know my craft. That may have a ripple effect consequence, but that is none of my concern. I can only care about and focus on my work. When I present my menu, I know that I have done my best. If people like it, I am happy, sure, but if they don't, I am still happy – happy for *myself*. I have never written a book on principle, because I don't want to explain anything. I am still in the phase of my life where I have to *do and give and communicate*, but not *explain*. I may even write a book one day, but for now, I have to be a craftsman.

I read a beautiful tract, written about traditions, that said traditions are not about conserving the ashes, but about fueling the flame. This tendency to rework everything into a museum piece is counterproductive. It is food fundamentalism, part of our fear of change. Just look at Savanarola. Lorenzo the Magnificient was pushing to move forward, to progress. Well, there is always going to be a Savanarola on hand who wants to move in the other direction, to throw a stick in the spokes. Fundamentalists say they are out to protect and save this and that, but in the end they forget about human lives, and the reality of how things once were. Tradition has to feed, not obstruct. Cultures have to be like trees, well rooted in the ground. And out of those roots, the traditions, stands the tree itself that draws up that which nurtures and stabilizes. Remember who you are and your values. Remember what and where you've come from, but always strive to make things better, keep reaching upwards.

About the Author

A professor in the modern languages department at the University of Siena in Tuscany, Italy, Karima Moyer-Nocchi has made Italy her home for over twenty-five years. As an enthusiastic food writer and historian, she travels extensively through Italy studying the social, economic, and cultural factors that characterize cuisine in each region of the country. She is a frequent lecturer in Food Studies both in Italy and abroad.

The author presently resides in Città di Castello, Umbria, with her husband.

GLOSSARY

Caffè d'orzo – toasted barley coffee

Companatico – a food that is eaten with bread

Capoccia – patriarch, head of a sharecropper household

Conserva – tomato paste

Contadino/i – peasant, (plural contadini)

Corredo – trousseau, a bride's hope chest

Duce – the nickname for Mussolini

Fascio – the fascist organization as a whole

Lardo – cured fatback, "lard" is rendered pork fat

Massaia – the female head of a sharecropper household

Medicone – folk medicine healer

Minestra – soup

Norcino – the expert craftsman in preparing salumi

Osteria – a tavern where men gathered to drink wine

Padrone – master, boss, large landowner

Pasta compra – store-bought, dried, durum wheat pasta

Pastificio – pasta factory

Pizzaiolo – pizza chef, pizza-maker

Polenta – although the word polenta indicates a gruel or mush made with any grain, it is used here with its more modern association of cornmeal gruel or mush.

Salumi – all of the Italian preserved pork products (salami, prosciutto, lardo, capocollo etc.)

Signore/i/a/ina – Mr., Mrs., Miss; or to indicate a person(s) from the upper classes, grand dame

Squadristi – Voluntary Militia for National Security, also called Blackshirts

Tagliatelle – handmade flour and water noodles, with or without egg

Terroir – The aggregate characteristics of the environment in which a food or wine is produced, including regional and local climate, soil, and topography.

Trattoria – a rustic eatery serving simple fare usually to travellers

Ventennio – the twenty-year reign of fascism (1922-1943)

BIBLIOGRAPHY

Accademia Italiana della Cucina, delegazione di Mantova, *Petronilla: Ricette per tempi difficili*, Massa: Ceccotti, 1997.

Agnesi, V., *E' tempo di pasta*, Rome: Gangemi, 1992.

Artusi, P., *La scienza in cucina e l'arte di mangiar bene*, Alberto Capatti (ed.), Milan: BUR, 2010.

Ascoli, M., "Italy, an Experiment in Reconstruction," *Annals of the American Academy of Political and Social Science*, Vol. 234, Agenda for Peace (July 1944), pp. 36-41.

Avorio, P., *Tre noci*, Città di Castello: Petruzzi, 2011.

Ballarini, G., "Cucina Barbara degli analfabeti fuzionali," *Cività della Tavola*, No. 247, (March 2013), pp. 3-4.

Bartoli, P., "La medicina popolare e la costruzione del sistema sanitario pubblico nello stato unitario italiano," in Seppilli, T., (ed.) *Medicine e Magie*, Bergamo: Electa, 1989.

Beattie T.E., "Comments on Marketing in Southern Italy", *Journal of Marketing*, Vol. 9, No. 3, (Jan.,1945) pp. 269-274.

Bernardini, E., *La provincia di Imperia. La Riviera e il suo entroterra*, Novara: Istituto Geografico De Agostini, 1994.

Berzano, L., Dino, V., Macioti, M. I., Pace E., *Maghi e magie nell'Italia di oggi*, Florence: Angelo Pontecorboli, 1991.

Bisi, C., "Women in the Kitchen," *La Cucina Italiana* No. 3, (March 1930), p. 1.

Boni, A., *Il talisman della felicità*, Milan: Domus, 1946.

Camporesi, P., Introduzione in: Artusi, P. *La scienza in cucina e l'arte di mangiar bene*. Turin: Einaudi, 2001 pp. XV-LXXVIII.

Camporesi, P., *La terra e la luna*, Milan: Garzanti, 1995.

Capatti, A., Montanari M., *La cucina italiana: Storia di una cultura*, Rome-Bari: Gius. Laterza & figli, 2000.

——— *Storia della cucina italiana*, Milan: Guido Tommasi, 2014.

Caracciolo A., *L'inchiesta agraria Jacini*, Turin: Enaudi, 1958.

Casalini Sereni, M., *Il Buglione: ricordi, proverbi, racconti versi e mangiare del focolare toscano*, Florence: Edizioni Polistamoa, 2009.

Clark, M., *Mussolini Profiles in Power*, New York: Routledge, 2014.

Coltro, D., *Dalla magia alla medicina contadina e popolare*, Florence: Sansoni Editore, 1983.

Comando Federale, *Ricette e consigli di economia domestica*, Florence, 1943.

Cosmacini, G., *Storia della medicina e della sanità in Italia*, Rome-Bari: Laterza, 1994.

Corner, P., *Contadini e industrializzazione. Società rurale e impresa in Italia 1840-1940*, Rome-Bari: Laterza, 1993.

Cunsolo, F., *Il libro dei maccheroni: tutto sulla pasta*, Milan: Mondadori, 1979.

Fornari D., *Il Cuciniere Militare. Manuale ad uso dei cucinieri della truppa del R. E. e degli altri corpi armati*. Novara: Cattaneo, 1932.

De Benedetti, I., *Poesia Nascosta – Seicento Ricette di Cucina Ebraica in Italia*, Florence: Casa Editrice Israel, 1931.

De Grazia, Victoria, *How Fascism Ruled Women: Italy, 1922-1945*, Berkeley: University of California Press, 1992.

Della Pura, E., "Vini tipici e frutta incece di caffè," *La Cucina Italiana*, No. 6, (June 1939), p. 164.

De Seta, L. *La cucina del tempo di Guerra*, Milan: Salani, 1942.

De'Medici, L., *The Renaissance of Italian Cooking*, New York: Ballantine, 1989.

De Renzi, E., *Sull'alimentazione del popolo minute in Napoli*, Stamperia della Regia Università, 1863.

Dickie, J., *The Epic History of the Italians and Their Food*, New York: Free Press, 2008.

Di Renzo, E., *Mangiare l'autentico: Cibo e alimentazione tra revivalismi culturali e industria della nostalgia*. Rome: UniversItalia, 2012.

Duggan, C., *Fascist Voices, An Intimate History of Mussolini's Italy*, London: Vintage, 2013.

Feldstein Mark, "Kissing Cousins: Journalism and Oral History," *The Oral History Review*, Vol. 31, No. 1, (Winter – Spring, 2004), pp. 1-22.

Ferrari, A., "Due giorni senza carne," *La cucina Italiana*, No. 3, (March, 1936), p. 4.

Fratelli Carli, *Ricettario del centanario 1911 – 2011*, Fratelli Carli, 2010.

Fusco, R., *Pagine di storia viste dalla parte degli sconfitti ovvero: La pasta, evoluzione di una lotta*, Massalubrense: Il sorriso di Erasmo, 1989.

Gnoli, S., *Un secolo di moda italiana, 1900-2000*, Roma: Meltemi, 2005.

Guzzanti, P., *Abbasso la Dieta Mediterranea – Il primo romanzo dimagrante della letteratura italiana*, Rome: Aliberti, 2009.

Helstosky, C., *Garlic & Oil*, Oxford: Berg, 2004.

———, *Pizza: A Global History*, London: Reaktion, 2008.

Hobsbawm, E., Ranger, T., *The Invention of Tradition*, Cambridge: Cambridge University Press, 1983.

Inchiesta agraria vol. VI, Forli, Ravenna, Ferrara, Bologna, Modena, Reggio Emilia, Parma, 1881

Keys, A. e M., *Mangiar bene e stare bene*, First edition from the second English edition, Padua: Piccin, 1962.

Jenkins, S., "Black Ships, Blavatsky, and the Pizza Effect" in Sogen Hori, V., Hayes, R. P., Shields, J. M., (eds), *Teaching Buddhism in the West*, London: Routeledge, 2002

La Cecla, F., *La pasta e la pizza*, Bologna: Il Mulino, 1998.

Le Specialità della CUCINA ROMANA, Ricette tratte dalla tradizionale cucina casalinga, Edizione "La Grotta del Libro."

Maccarinelli, G., *Voci di Valvestino: Le donne raccontano…* Arco: Grafica 5, 2003.

Macerati, E., Morelli, L., *Casa Nostra: Trattato di economia domestica*, Milano: Società editrice nazionale, 1942.

Mafai, M., *Pane nero, donne e vita quotidiana nella seconda guerra mondiale*, Roma: Ediesse, 2008.

Manzoni, A., *Promessi Sposi*, Firenze: Sansoni, 1960.

Mattozzi, A., *Inventing the Pizza*, Nowak Z., (ed., trans.), London: Bloomsbury, 2015.

Minio-Paluello, L., *Education in Fascist Italy*, London: Oxford University Press, 1946.

Ministro dell'Educazione Nazionale, *L'Istituto di Magistero Femminile*, 1941.

Max Ascoli, "An Experiment in Reconstruction," *Annals of the American Academy of Political and Social Science*, Vol. 234, Agenda for Peace, (July, 1944) pp. 36-41.

Meletti, Vincenzo *Il libro fascista del balilla*, Perugia: G. Guerra, 1934.

Mencarelli, A., *La porchetta dale origini a Costano: Un paese un mestiere*, Foligno: Il Formichiere, 2013.

Mignemi, N., *Nel regno della fame: Il mondo contadino italiano fra gli anni trenta e gli anni cinquanta*, Rome: Aracne, 2010.

Momigliano, F., *Mangiare all'italiana: Molte ricette inedite*, Milan: Hoepli, 1936.

———., *Vivere bene in tempi difficili: Come le donne affrontano le crisi economiche*, Milan: Hoepli, 1933.

Montanari, M., *L'identità italiana in cucina*, Rome-Bari: Gius. Laterza & Figli, 2010.

Montessori, M., *Peace and Education*, fifth edition, Madras: The Theosophical Publishing House, 1971.

Morello, M., *Donna, moglie e madre prolifica: L'ONMI in cinquant'anni di storia italiana*, Soveria Mannelli: Rubbettino, 2010.

Moroni Salvatori, M. P., "Ragguaglio biliografico sui ricettari del prima Novecento," in Capatti, A., De Bernardi, A., Varni, A., (eds) *Storia d'Italia, Alimentazione*, Annali 13, Turin: Einaudi, 1998.

Morozzo della Rocca, E., "Il problema delle domestiche," *La Cucina Italiana*, No. 1, (January 1936), pp. 10-11.

Mosso, A., *La fatica*, Florence: Giunti, 2001.

Nina, "Noi faremo il nostro dovere," *La Cucina Italiana*, No. 11, (November 1935), pp2-3

Obber, C., *Ballila e piccole italiane: la scuola, i sogni, la vita*, Bassano del Grappa: Attiliofraccaro, 2009.

Ottaviani, G., *La Cucina dell'era fascista*, Milan: Todariana, 2005.

Rocchi, P. F., *L'Esodo dei 350 mila Giuliani, Fiumani e Dalmati*, Fourth edition, Roma: Difesa Adriatica, 1988.

Parasecoli, F., *Al Dente: A history of food in Italy*, London: Reaktion, 2014.

Parmentier, J. M., *Il vero libro di cucina*, Milan: A. Barion, 1932.

Piccini, V., *Scrigno d'oro: Consigli – Segreti – Ricette per la donna*, Milan: Artegrafica E. Padoan, 1943.

Pierotti Cei, L., *il caffè: storie e ricette*, Milan: Mursia, 1982.

Pini, G., *Benito Mussolini: la sua vita fino ad oggi da Predappio all'impero*, Bologna: Capelli, 1938.

Polesini, E. Marchesa, *Cosa preparo per i miei opsiti?* Milan: A. Corticelli.

Portelli, A., "What Makes Oral History Different", in Perks, R., Thomson, A., (eds), *The Oral History Reader*, (London: Routledge,1998), pp. 63-74.

Riley, G., *The Oxford Companion to Italian Food*, New York: Oxford University Press 2007.

Rina, S., "Donne d'Italia, in cucina!" *La Cucina Italiana*, No. 12 (December 1936), p. 15.

Rodogno, D., *Fascism's European Empire: Italian Occupation during the Second World War*, Series: New Studies in European History, Cambridge: Cambridge University Press, 2006.

Rosenweig, R., Thelen, D., The Presence of the Past – Popular Uses of History in American Life, New York: Columbia University Press, 1998.

Rossi, B., Pastacaldi, P., *Hitler è buono e vuol bene all'Italia. La storia e il costume nei quaderni dagli anni '30 a oggi*, Milan: Longanesi, 1992.

Saladini di Rovetino, B. "Carne o proteine vegetali?" *La Cucina Italiana*, No. 8, (August 1936), p. 26.

Salvemini, G., "Mussolini's Battle of Wheat", *Political Science Quarterly*, No. XLVI, (1931), pp. 25-40.

Sarfatti M., "La botte piena e la moglie ubriaca", *La Cucina Italiana*, No. 4, (April 1931) p. 1.

Saulle I., La Torre G., "The Mediterranean Diet, recognized by UNESCO as a cultural heritage of humanity", *Italian Journal of Public Health*, Vol. 7, No. 4, (2010), pp. 414-415.

Seppilli, T., (ed.) *Medicine e magie*, Bergamo: Electa, 1989.

Siporin, S., "From Kashrut to Cucina Ebraica: The Recasting of Italian Jewish Foodways" *Journal of American Folklore*, Vol. 107, No. 424, (Spring 1994), pp. 268-281.

Soldati, M., Alla ricerca dei cibi genuini: Viaggio nella Valle del Po, RAI, 1957-58.

Tamburini, M., "Minestre e zuppe," *Civiltà della tavola* No. 247, (March 2013), pp. 18-19.

Teicholz, N., *The Big Fat Surprise: Why Butter, Meat & Cheese Belong in a Healthy Diet*, New York: Simon & Schuster, 2014.

Teti, V., "Le culture alimentari nel Mezzogiorno continentale in età contemporanea", in Capatti, A., De Bernardi, A., Varni, A., (eds) *Storia d'Italia, Alimentazione*, Annali 13, Turin: Einaudi, 1998.

Thompson, P., *The Voice of the Past, Oral History*, Third edition, Oxford: Oxford University Press, 2000.

Torre, Domenico. *Medicina Popolare e Civiltà Contadina: ricettario fomule magiche, soprannaturale, credenze popolari*, Rome: Gangemi, 1994.

Triolo, N., Fascist "Unionization and the Professionalization of Midwives in Italy: A Sicilian Case Study," *Medical Anthropology Quarterly* New Series, Vol. 8, No. 3, (September 1994), pp. 259-281.

Vene, G. F., *Mille lire al mese: vita quotidiana della famiglia nell'Italia fascista*, Milan: Mondadori, 1988.

Willson, P., *Peasant Women and Politics in Fascist Italy: The Massaie Rurali*, London: Routledge, 2002.

Zanetti, A. and M., *Patria*, Roma: Libreria dello Stato, 1940.

Zanetti, Z., *La medicina delle nostre donne*, Foligno: Il Formichiere, 2011.

Electronic sources:

Brownfield, P. E., "The Italian Holocaust: The Story of an Assimilated Jewish Community," The American Council for Judaism, 2003.
http://www.acjna.org/acjna/articles_detail.aspx?id=300

Capasso, A., Pesto con butto o senza= Lo chef Davide Oldani: "Gusto più delicate". Accademia della Cucina: "Ne stravolge il sapore" 22 July 2015, L'Huffington Post.
http://www.huffingtonpost.it/2015/02/13/pesto-con-burro_n_6676054.html

Collins, B. J., Pigs at the Gate: Hittite Pig Sacrifice in its Eastern Mediterranean Context
http://www.academia.edu/183486/Pigs_at_the_Gate_Hittite_Pig_Sacrifice_in_Its_Eastern_Mediterranean_Context

Coppolino, A. S., McDonald's lancia uno spot contro la pizza. I bambini di Napoli rispondono così.
https://www.youtube.com/watch?v=lqpjHJfo48U&list=PLSzf-S7k-prUpSZoaWCYbfsOr5GJBWmPWw

Curtis, D. R., Reconsidering the Mediterranean 'agro-town' model and escaping a vision of an 'unchanging' Italian South, July 2012
http://www.cgeh.nl/sites/default/files/WorkingPapers/CGEH.WP_.No34.DanCurtis.pdf

Gueranger, Abbot, The History of Lent
http://www.ewtn.com/library/LITURGY/HISTLENT.TXT
Hayward T., In Praise of Stock, BBC radio 4, Food Programme Podcast,
March 2012.
http://www.bbc.co.uk/programmes/b01dtgbj
Hynum, R., The 2014 Pizza Power Report, PMQ Pizza Magazine,
December 2013.
http://www.pmq.com/December-2013/Pizza-Power-The-2014-
Pizza-Power-Report/index.php?cparticle=2&siarticle=1#artanc -
Pipino, M. G., Istituzioni e assistenza pubblica in Italia tra fascismo e
repubblica, Gli enti comunali di assistenza – part I, No. 25, January
2010, part II, February 2010.
http://www.instoria.it/home/assistenza_pubblica_italia_I.htm
Ravicini, L., Macellazione maiale penna sant'andrea
https://www.youtube.com/watch?v=dyxc79ORVjQ&oref=https
%3A%2F%2Fwww.youtube.com%2Fwatch%3Fv%3Ddyxc79ORVj
Q&has_verified=1
Chi beve birra campa cent'anni: overo un secolo di birra in Italia
http://www.assobirra.it/press/?p=22
Dario Cecchini No Reservation Toscana Anthony Bourdain
https://www.youtube.com/watch?v=5Bp8bvlWay0
Il maiale, amico dell'uomo
http://russi.racine.ra.it/vitacontadina/maiale.htm
I Miti del Regime, in Eja, eja – Alalà: Il consenso durante il fascismo
http://www.itismarzotto.it/esperienze-eventi/fascismo/imitidel.htm
Italia e il Sud della Russia
http://dante-rostov.ru/index.php?option=com_content&task=
view&id=12&Itemid=84
La carta della scuola
http://www.dirdidatticamelia.it/htm/storiascuo/1920-1940/
Web/carta%20scuola%20.htm
La Scuola Fascista, in in Eja, eja – Alalà: Il consenso durante il fascismo
http://www.itismarzotto.it/esperienze-eventi/fascismo/lascuola.htm
Leggere scrivere e far di conto – Storia della scuola italiana – prima
parte

http://www.lastoriasiamonoi.rai.it/puntate/leggere-scrivere-e-far-di-conto/561/default.aspx

Libia 1911: *Tripoli, bel suol d'amore,* una canzone di propaganda colonial italiana.

http://www.tlaxcala-int.org/article.asp?reference=4200

Mediterranean Diet

http://www.unesco.org/culture/ich/index.php?lg=en&pg=00011&RL=00884

Nasce a Napoli la pizza con acqua di mare. Il maestro Vuolo: «Più leggera, esalta sapore ingredienti» Metropolitan Web

http://www.metropolisweb.it/Notizie/Campania/Cronaca/nasce_napoli_pizza_acqua_mare_maestro_vuolo_piu_leggera_esalta_sapore_ingredienti.aspx

Made in the USA
Middletown, DE
08 December 2020